BOOK of FLIGHT

FROM THE FLYING MACHINES OF LEONARDO DA VINCI
TO THE CONQUEST OF SPACE

R. NICCOLI

FRIEDMAN/FAIRFAX
PUBLISHERS

Contents

Text by
RICCARDO NICCOLI

Editorial project
VALERIA MANFERTO DE FABIANIS
LAURA ACCOMAZZO

Project and graphic design
MARIA CUCCHI

Picture research
CLAUDIA ZANERA

Translation
NEIL FRAZER DAVENPORT
HUGH SWAINSTON

© 2002 White Star S.r.l.
Via C. Sassone, 22/24 - 13100 Vercelli, Italy
www.whitestar.it

All rights reserved. No part of this publication may be reproduced, stored in a retrieval system, or transmitted, in any form or by any means, electronic, mechanical, photocopying, recording, or otherwise, without prior written permission from the publisher.

This edition published by the Michael Friedman Publishing Group, Inc., by arrangement with White Star S.r.l.

ISBN 1-58663-716-9

2002 FRIEDMAN/FAIRFAX

1 3 5 7 9 10 8 6 4 2

For bulk purchases and special sales, please contact:
Michael Friedman Publishing Group, Inc.
Attention: Sales Department
230 Fifth Avenue, Suite 700
New York, NY 10001
212/685-6610 FAX 212/685-3916

Visit our website:
www.metrobooks.com

Printed in Italy by Grafedit
Color separation by Grafotitoli Bassoli, Milan.

1 top The NASA Space Shuttle "Challenger" in orbit with its loading bay open, seen during its STS-7 mission.

1 bottom A reinforced wing designed by Leonardo da Vinci (1452-1519), who made the first technical approach to the problem of human flight.

2-3 One of the RAF's heavily armed Panavia Tornado F.3 fighters in high-speed flight. The Tornado was the first example of large-scale multinational cooperation in European aircraft design and manufacturing.

4-5 The Stealth F-117A fighter-bomber's futuristic form highlighted during a low-altitude turn over White Sands desert region of New Mexico.

5 bottom An impracticable airship design as imagined in the nineteenth century.

6-7 In the early days of flight, getting airborne called for desperate measures. Here a horse and cart help launch a Caudron biplane glider into the air.

8-9 A Space Shuttle launch at NASA's Kennedy Center in Florida.

Preface

One hundred years. So much has happened since that cold winter day on 17 December 1903 when a powered, heavier-than-air airplane demonstrated that controllable human flight was possible. Rather than a timid flight, it was more of a series of long hops, the first 39 yards in length and the longest about 282 yards, but human progress had taken a much greater leap. Probably few watching Orville and Wilbur Wright on the sand dunes of Kitty Hawk in North Carolina could have imagined that, in just a few years, man would have mastered the air and built increasingly manageable, powerful and fast airplanes.

In comparison to the rate of invention in previous epochs, technological progress in the twentieth century was lightning fast, and much of this was due to the efforts and research invested in aeronautics and space. A little more than a decade after the Wright brothers' flight, planes were able to exceed 125 mph and to perform breathtaking acrobatics. In the 1920s, only two decades later, the first commercial transport planes appeared, able to convey passengers long distances in absurdly short times compared to ships or trains. The advent of World War II accelerated development dramatically, producing conventional, propeller-driven planes with twice the power, speed, distance and load capabilities of their predecessors. More importantly, World War II brought about the invention of the jet engine and the first usable helicopters. Only 44 years after the Wright brother's flight of 12 mph, a jet engine broke the sound barrier. A mere 60 years later, man flew in space. The list of achievements could be continued but this would be pointless: the results of one hundred years of flight are before our eyes every day.

Thanks to air travel, we can now reach every corner of the globe in just a few hours at costs affordable for almost everyone. Lives can be saved as a result of rapid search and rescue facilities, the sick and injured can be carried to distant hospitals where the finest care facilities or transplant capabilities are available. Peoples struck by natural disasters or war can be reached and aided, and life-threatening fires can be reached and put out. Goods and materials can be transported just as easily, strengthening the world economy.

Aircraft are vital in making land and sea surveys and in monitoring the environment and pollution. They are important in geography, topography, geology, archaeology and zoology. In the military, aviation has revolutionized the rules of engagement and become the decisive instrument in land battles and war. The recent conflicts in the Gulf, Kosovo, and Afghanistan have shown how air power alone can decide the outcome of an entire regional crisis, thereby shortening hostilities and making them less cruel than in the past. As a result of specialized optical and electronic recognition capabilities, aircraft and satellites have made the world a safer and more peaceful place, rendering the great powers more knowledgeable about one another, able to conceal fewer secrets.

Space travel has opened new horizons for the scientific world and brought benefits even to the man in the street. Shuttle flights and space station programs have increased human scientific knowledge in many fields, while orbiting satellites have spurred enormous advances in telecommunications and navigation.

This book pays tribute to the History of Flight. Its 25 chapters are dedicated to the most famous people, events and epochs. The powered aircraft (planes and helicopters) that have left their mark on this century of flight are briefly examined. Unfortunately, however, experimental aircraft have had to be excluded despite their technological interest: the purpose of the book is to draw attention to those craft that operated on a broad basis in either the civilian or military worlds. The history of flight is immensely wide and deep in scope, and the limitations of a single volume mean that dozens of aircraft that deserve inclusion in both the text and photographs have to be omitted.

Nor should the impulse that has always prompted man to attempt to fly be forgotten. When all is said and done, this book also celebrates the realization of one of man's most ancient and yearned-for dreams: that of overcoming his physical limitations and the constrictions of remaining earthbound, so that he might float in a more spiritual and divine dimension, that of flight.

Chapter 1

The Earliest Endeavors

Man has felt the urge to fly from the earliest of times. As ancient legends recount, even the most powerful of men yearned for the sensation of potency and freedom that they imagined that the ability to launch themselves into the sky would provide. One of these legends, originating in Persia, refers to King Kai Kawus' flight in a chariot drawn by eagles in around 1500 BC. Another, this time from Greece, recounts that Alexander the Great saw the skies from a wickerwork chest lifted by griffins.

Moreover, eagles and hawks, birds of prey that dominate the skies, have always been seen as symbols of power. During antiquity, flight was considered to be the prerogative of the gods. In fact, in the legend of Daedalus and Icarus and their feathers-and-wax wings, Daedalus escaped death only by flying low. Icarus, intoxicated by the thrill of flight, flew ever higher toward the sun, the symbol of divine power, until its heat melted the wax, with his sacrilegious act receiving appropriate punishment. Alongside these imaginative accounts are others, some thousands of years old, that testify to man's practical efforts to conquer the third dimension. It appears that as early as two thousand years before Christ, the Chinese were capable of using kites to lift lookouts into the sky for military purposes. In 852 AD at Cordoba, an Arab savant was killed during an attempt at free flight, while in 1020 an English Benedictine monk named Oliver of Malmesbury threw himself from the top of a tower, wearing a pair of feathered wings; unfortunately he crashed to the ground breaking both legs. The years that followed were punctuated by a series of similar failures. In 1496 it was the turn of Senecio of Nuremberg, in 1503 the mathematician Giovan Battista Danti of Perugia, and in 1628 Paolo Guidotto, also from Perugia. For these and for others like them, the same irresistible temptation led to the same disastrous fate. In the meantime, studies into the phenomenon of flight were increasingly elaborate. The chronicles of 1630 report that a certain Hezarfen Ahmet Celebi succeeded in gliding from the top of the Galata Tower in Istanbul to the far side of the Bosporus, thanks to a pair of rudimentary wings. In 1670, Francesco Lana Terzi, a Jesuit, described a flying machine composed of four copper spheres in which a vacuum was to be created and a sail provided for the directional control of the flight. Early in the eighteenth century, another Jesuit, Laurenào de Gusmão of Brazil, designed a bird-like glider that he used for experiments: he also built

10 Leonardo da Vinci was the first scientist to consider flight from a rational viewpoint. He transferred the workings of his imagination to sketches and drawings that inspired many other thinkers in later centuries. The two small sketches provide examples.

10-11 Surrounded by Leonardo's standard mirror-writing is a sketch showing an experiment to prove the lift of a wing. Finally published in 1797, Leonardo's famous Notebooks were a great revelation.

what may be considered a primitive balloon, which he successfully demonstrated to the King of Portugal in 1709. In 1764 and 1781, the German Bauer and the Frenchman Blanchard designed and tested flying machines. In earlier times it appears that balloons and other lighter-than-air vehicles were also flown in China and Cambodia.

It was not, however, until 1797 that Leonardo da Vinci's codexes were published for the first time, opening an incredible new window onto the science of aeronautics.

11 right Leonardo da Vinci: a self-portrait. The brilliant master, who excelled in the figurative arts, architecture and engineering, was born in Vinci in Tuscany in 1452. He died at Cloux in France in 1519.

The Tuscan genius, who was born in 1452 at Vinci and died at Cloux in the Loire region of France in 1519, was the first person known to have taken a scientific, rational approach to the problem of flight. The codexes contain no less than 150 designs for devices, machines, or parts of machines of various types, including a parachute, the "aerial screw" (the first example of a helicopter) and the propeller. However, even Leonardo long remained anchored to the concept of imitating the flight of birds and designed the so-called ornithopter in which the weight of the pilot was to be supported by the movement of a pair of mechanical wings. The great defect in this concept was that the power required for flight was far greater than that calculated by Leonardo, who was convinced that muscles alone could supply it. Toward the end of his life, however, he recognized these limitations and intuited the need for a means of multiplying power and for a fixed wing, innovations that were to revolutionize his research. While Leonardo did not survive to put these ideas into practice, his studies and drawings reveal the exceptional clarity of his thinking and observations in all fields. Today many consider him to be the spiritual father of manned flight.

12-13 One of Leonardo's many drawings dedicated to flight: a crank-powered wing clearly inspired by the movement of a bird's wing, which it copies both in form and action.

12 bottom In this drawing, Leonardo drew what today we would call the fuselage of a flying machine, complete with cables and tie-rods for the movement of the wings.

14 left A contemporary
engraving of the balloon the
Italian Vincenzo Lunardi
used in the ascent he made on
13 May 1785.

14 right and 15 left These
late C18th drawings show
two anonymous designs: an
aerostatic balloon pulled by
birds, and a sail-powered
balloon. Their ingenuity and
the approximation to known
concepts is evident. The two
balloons were still based on
imagination rather than on
technical studies.

As is frequently the case, the first efficient
solution to the problem of flight came from an
unexpected source and utilized simple, natural
technology, that of the balloon. The intuition
that made this conquest possible came from
two French brothers, Joseph Michel and
Jacques Etienne Montgolfier, proprietors of a
paper-mill near Lyon. Their observations
concerned the lifting force of the hot air

above a fire and how it was capable of lifting
upturned paper bags. They set to work and in
1782 conducted a series of experiments with
large, light envelopes filled with hot air. On 4
June 1783, a large balloon with a diameter of
over 32 feet was constructed and tested at
Versailles with a sheep, a goose and a cockerel
aboard. The attempt was successful and the
passengers returned safely by balloon to the

15 center This print illustrates the flight Jean-Pierre Blanchard and John Jeffries made on 7 January 1785. They crossed the English Channel (from Dover to the forest of Guines, near Andrei) in a historic "first."

15 right The Mongolfier brothers first balloon project, successfully tested at Annonay, on 5 June 1783. The balloon, which had no passengers, rose to just over 6,500 feet.

ground after a flight of almost two miles. The time was now ripe for the first manned flight. The historic event took place in Paris on 21 November 1783. Jean François Pilâtre de Rozier (a physicist) and François d'Arlandes (an army officer) boarded a balloon 72 feet high and 49 feet wide and were lifted into the air to great acclaim at 1.54 in the afternoon: man was flying!

15 bottom Portraits of the Montgolfier brothers from the Bibliothèque Nationale, Paris. Left, Etienne de Montgolfier (1745-1799); right, Joseph de Montgolfier (1740-1810).

The course had now been set and experimentation flourished. The hot air balloon (known as the *montgolfière* in honor of its inventor) was joined on 1 December 1783 by the hydrogen balloon invented by the Frenchman, Jacques César Charles (and consequently named the *charlière*). He lifted off from the Tuileries in Paris and completed a flight of no less than 26.5 miles. Immense curiosity and desire flared up, and flights were made in many countries. In Italy there were those of Andreani and the Gerlis at Milan on 25 February 1784. In London that of Vincenzo Lunardi with a *charlière* hydrogen balloon on 15 September 1784 and at Philadelphia on 9 January 1793, that of the Frenchman Blanchard. On 5 January 1785, a passenger-carrying balloon crossed the English Channel for the first time.

In 1794 the maturity of ballooning technology was demonstrated by its adoption by the French army for artillery range-finding purposes. Its first use occurred during the battle of Fleurus in Belgium on 26 June 1794, when the French defeated the Austrian forces. Five years later, however, Napoleon Bonaparte disbanded the world's first air force, and military use of the balloon was not revived until the second half of the nineteenth century.

16-17 and 17 bottom
Manufacturing a gas-tight
balloon was a delicate and
arduous task. The lower
picture, from 1794, shows
Nicolas Jacques Cont's
cutting technique

(1755-1805) in making a
military balloon. The
cutting was done outdoors,
using primitive methods.
Above: Cont painting
the balloon, an indoors
process.

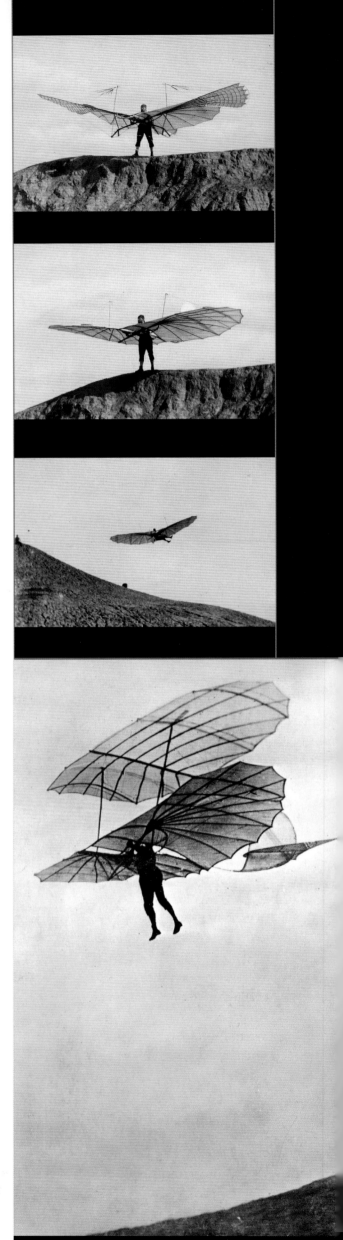

18 top left The steam-powered flying machine of William Henson (1805-1888) was the first heavier-than-air craft. Henson decided to patent his 'steam-powered flying carriage' and founded the world's first air company in 1842. However, the machine never flew.

18 bottom left German engineer Otto Lilienthal (1848-1896) was one of the greatest C19th investigators of human flight, which he enthused about from age 15. This drawing of a glider is from a patent he took out in 1895.

The Englishman Sir George Cayley (1773-1857), who was active in the late eighteenth and early nineteenth centuries, had a great influence on the future development of aviation. As early as 1799 he had put forward the hypothesis that a flying machine could succeed in taking off only if it had separate means of ensuring lift and propulsion. This meant abandoning the idea of the ornithopter and the adoption of the heavier-than-air concept, a remarkable step at that time, given that it was highly unlikely that Cayley had had an opportunity to examine Leonardo's codexes. In 1804, Cayley designed a dirigible powered by a propeller and continued further with his studies into aerodynamics. In 1809, he published his research into manned flight in a paper entitled *On Aerial Navigation*. In this work he codified a number of suppositions regarding the governability of an aircraft in flight and even suggested the use of internal combustion engines for propulsion. He wrote, "The whole problem [of powered flight] is confined within these limits, viz. To make a surface support a given weight by the application of power to the resistance of air." Cayley's extremely advanced ideas were not put into practice immediately, but during the nineteenth century there were numerous other attempts at flight as imaginative as they were ineffective. In 1842 another Englishman, William Samuel Henson, designed and patented an interesting machine, the Aerial Steam Carriage. It never flew, but it was a fixed-wing aircraft designed to be propelled by propellers driven by a 25-hp steam engine. Other machines were designed along similar lines but it became clear that while the concept of powered flight was undoubtedly valid, a means of propulsion more suitable than the steam engine was required along with a truly efficient wing. Until the introduction of the internal combustion engine that would

(No Model.)

O. LILIENTHAL.
FLYING MACHINE.

No. 544,816   Patented Aug. 20, 1895.

2 Sheets—Sheet 1.

Fig I.

Fig II.

Fig III.

Witnesses:

By Attorney: Inventor:
                                Otto Lilienthal

18 right The first three photographs portray Otto Lilienthal in Fliegeberg in August 1894. It is clear that he still believed in gliders that used bird-shaped wings. As shown by the fixed (no longer beating) wing and from the large photograph, the first tail units were appearing. In the last picture, Lilienthal is shown with a two-wing glider in 1896. Lilienthal was killed using one of these, after more than 2,000 flight attempts, in a glide during which his craft overturned at a height of 50 feet.

19 top Lilienthal's 1894 flight attempt.

19 center A two-wing glider built by Otto Lilienthal in 1895. His flight trials of October 1895 at Fliegeberg shows he had abandoned the primitive natural-wing form and moved toward more sophisticated aerodynamic designs, with a tail unit and dual wings.

19 bottom left George Cayley, an Englishman, made this sketch of a glider in 1804. The aircraft became a reality 49 years later when it made a short flight near Scarborough.

19 bottom right The notion of "heavier than air" — an aircraft fitted with means to provide it with lift and power — was George Cayley's.

eventually power a true aircraft, studies continued on the problem of lift.

One of the most celebrated researchers was the German Otto Lilienthal (1848-1896). At the age of fifteen he began to take an interest in flight and together with his brother built a six-and-a-half-foot ornithopter that never actually managed to take off. The determined and technically minded Lilienthal graduated in mechanical engineering and retained a passionate interest in flight, even though his work prevented him from devoting himself to research in the field. Once he had retired he published his studies in 1889 in the book *The Flight of Birds as the Basis for the Art of Flying* ("Der Vogelflug als Grundlage des

Fliegkunst") and dedicated himself to putting his theories into practice. In the absence of an appropriate engine, Lilienthal constructed gliders that made use of the force of gravity and he became the first man in world to launch himself into the air and fly with such devices. In 1892, having abandoned wings based on those of birds, he began to build wings with radial structures and then biplanes that were easier to control. On 9 August 1896, however, one of his gliders overturned almost fifty feet above the ground, and on the following day Lilienthal died of his injuries.

His more than two thousand glider flights were nonetheless a great inspiration for other pioneers such as Rumpler and Octave Chanute (1832-1910). The latter, born in Paris, emigrated to the United States at the age of six with his father, a man of science who had been appointed vice-president of Jefferson College. After qualifying as an engineer, Chanute embarked on what was to be a brilliant railway career, completing great civil engineering projects and earning an enviable reputation. From 1874 he began to take an interest in the problems of flight but had to abandon all serious study because it would have interfered with his professional commitments. He put his projects to one

could not be informed of the danger he faced and saved from his tragic fate. Chanute's glider designs and the publication of his works in America and France in 1897 attracted the attention of the American brothers Orville and Wilbur Wright. Within three years they had established contact with the French engineer in search of greater detail and information. Chanute thus effectively became the Wright brothers' mentor and helped them demonstrate the feasibility of controlled, powered flight in 1903. Octave Chanute lived to celebrate the Wrights' success with them, but in 1910 died in Chicago after an illness.

20 left The Avion III, built by Clément Ader, was a steam-powered, twin-engined craft driven by two large four-blade propellers. Ader was not successful as a constructor but his theories of military aviation were valid, even if appreciated at the time.

20 top right Octave Chanute designed and tested several gliders, like this five-winged craft. Chanute's work inspired the Wright brothers, who turned to him for information that contributed to their own success.

side and only revived them in 1889, when he began to complete his documentation, drawing on the experiments of Lilienthal and others. In 1894 he published the book *Progress in Flying Machines,* in which he reviewed all the experiments conducted to date in the field heavier-than-air craft. He then began to work on his own designs in which the lifting areas of his gliders were automatically balanced to bring the center of pressure onto the same axis as the center of gravity. He also continued Lilienthal's research into gliders and recognized the inherent dangers of his machines. Unfortunately, this recognition came just a week before Lilienthal's fatal accident: he

This review of the most important pioneers could hardly be complete without mention of the Frenchman Clément Ader (1841-1925) and the American Samuel Pierpoint Langley (1834-1906). Ader designed and built two aircraft powered by a steam engine driving a propeller, the Eole and the Avion III, while Langley constructed the Aerodrome, a monoplane with tandem wings powered by a petrol engine that drove two propellers. The Eole attempted take-off in 1890 and the Aerodrome in 1903, but both projects were unsuccessful. They marked the end of the period of improvised attempts and solutions. A new era dawned with the work of the Wright brothers.

20-21 Clément Ader's Avion III, shown here with its wings folded. The plane failed at the demonstration flight before a military commission in October 1897 due to a strong wind. The French Defense Ministry rejected the design.

21 top Clément Ader, shown here with Trajan Vuia, in front of Vuia's monoplane in 1906. After the failures of his projects, Ader destroyed his machines and dedicated himself to his book, Military Aviation, published in 1907.

22-23 Balloons were still
successfully used even at the
start of the C20th. In this
photograph of 15 May
1913, a balloon is being
maneuvered by the
"Eclaireurs de France" at
St.-Cyr France.

22 bottom Two press pictures
showing the world record for
a balloon ascent, achieved by
the Belgian scientist Auguste
Piccard on 27 May 1931.
With his colleague Paul
Kipfer, Piccard reached an
altitude of 51,762 feet after
taking off from Augusta in
Germany, and landing in the
Tyrolean Alps in Austria.
The record caused a large
public stir even though
balloons were by then an
obsolete form of air transport.

23 top right In the early
1900s, balloons were still
highly regarded. Shown are
examples exhibited at the
First International Fair of
Air Navigation, held in the
Grand Palais, Paris, in
September 1909.

23 bottom The starting line
for the Gordon Bennett Cup
of 1907. Six different types
of balloon wait for the off.

LE MAGNIFIQUE EXPLOIT DU PROFESSEUR PICCARD

Chapter 2

The Dirigibles

The first means of aerial transport was the balloon, which since the end of the eighteenth century had been used for both civil and military purposes. The balloon alone was inadequate, being subject more to the whims of the elements, especially the wind, than to the will of its crew. However, after a few decades, progress made in propulsion devices led to the birth of a more complete and versatile aircraft, the dirigible.

The first of these craft was an "airship" powered by a small steam engine. Henri Giffard, the Frenchman who designed and constructed it, flew it for the first time on 24 September 1852. This type of engine proved to be technically unsuitable and, above all, incapable of providing sufficient power for this kind of application, just as it had done with heavier-than-air machines. It was only the advent of the internal combustion engine that allowed successful dirigibles to be developed. The No. 1 of the Brazilian Alberto Santos-Dumont (1873-1932) was the first of these craft. It made its maiden flight in Paris on 28 November 1898. The wealthy Santos-Dumont settled in France and, gripped by a passion for flying, began to construct balloons and dirigibles. He designed no fewer than 18 different examples of the latter before turning his attention to powered airplanes in 1907.

Three major categories of dirigibles were developed. They were the non-rigid type, in which the pressure of the contained gas alone shaped the external envelope; the semi-rigid type, in the pressure of the gas and a longitudinal metal keel maintained the form; and the rigid type, in which a complex metal framework guaranteed external form. This last structure was the only one suitable for large craft.

24-25 top Alberto Santos-Dumont (center) in front of one of his airships. In October 1902, he won the Deutsche de la Meurthe prize for the first aeronaut to complete the St. Cloud – Eiffel Tower – St. Cloud route in less than half an hour.

24 center The first modern airship was built by Alberto Santos-Dumont, who linked a balloon to an internal combustion engine. Shown here is the Santos-Dumont 9, with a large gondola.

24-25 bottom In 1906, Santos-Dumont moved away from constructing airships to concentrate on airplanes. Shown here is the 14bis, an airplane with which he participated in the French Grand Prix of 1906.

key to the eventual success of Zeppelin's designs was the fact that for first time large rigid dirigibles could be constructed. The Count's first airship, the LZ-1 (Luftschiff Zeppelin Eins) was no less than 420 feet long, over 38 feet wide and had a volume of about 400,000 cubic feet. The LZ-1's most serious problem was a lack of power from its two 16-hp Daimler-Benz engines, which provided a top speed of only just over 17 mph. The LZ-1 completed its maiden flight on 2 July 1900, over the Bodensee. Despite the design's evident quality, eight years passed before the German army ordered its first Zeppelins, the LZ-3 and the LZ-5. In 1909, the German navy also ordered its first four dirigibles, to be used for reconnaissance purposes. In that year Zeppelin and Hamburg-Amerika Reederei founded Delag, the first commercial airline equipped with dirigibles. On 28 June 1910, the company inaugurated its service with

The country that did most to develop and perfect the dirigible was Germany, where in 1875 Paul Haenlein built the nation's first powered rigid example. In 1888, Kurt Wolfert built a dirigible equipped with the first Daimler-Benz aircraft engine, a 2-hp unit. The man generally considered to be the father of the dirigible, Count Ferdinand Adolf August Heinrich von Zeppelin, was at this time still a cavalry officer in the German imperial army. Born in Konstanz in 1838, von Zeppelin took part in the American Civil War and made his first balloon flight in America. He fought in the Austro-Prussian War (1866) and the Franco-Prussian War (1870), reaching the

rank of general, but in 1890 abandoned his military career in order to devote himself completely to the development of lighter-than-air vehicles. In 1898 he founded the Zeppelin Company at Friedrichshaven. From the very beginning von Zeppelin tried to interest the German army in his craft but was faced with competition from two other pioneers, Major von Parseval (who proposed a non-rigid dirigible) and Captain Gross, an advocate of a semi-rigid type. These two models were adopted before the Zeppelin airships because the army considered them to be better suited to military operations as they could be easily dismantled and transported. In effect, the

the LZ-7 *Deutschland*, capable of carrying 24 passengers. In Delag's four years in service prior to the outbreak of the Great War, the company carried over 10,000 fare-paying passengers and completed 3,193 hours aloft, covering over 100,000 miles.

When war broke out in August 1914, the German army was equipped with twelve dirigibles while the navy had one. Having received authorization from the Kaiser, in 1915 Zeppelins began to be used to bomb London and other targets in Great Britain. However, as the conflict wore on, anti-aircraft defenses became increasingly effective and Zeppelin losses began to become significant. On 25 September 1916, the German army's dirigible service flew its last mission over London. The German navy instead acquired no fewer than 74 dirigibles during the course of the war and continued to use them until the armistice of 1918.

In the post-war period, Delag resumed operations with two airships, and Count Zeppelin continued to develop ever larger and more capacious rigid dirigibles.

On September 18, 1928, the LZ-127 *Graf Zeppelin,* an immense airship 774 feet long and containing 3,920,000 cubic feet of hydrogen, made its maiden flight. The ship, which was powered by four 550-hp engines, had a top speed of 79.5 mph. The manufacturers intended that this craft should become the principal means of intercontinental transport: it was faster than existing ships and safer than the airplanes of the day, which were handicapped by severely restricted range and could carry only a third of the passengers the *Graf Zeppelin* could. In August 1929, this airship, which could carry up to 39 passengers in luxurious accommodations, inaugurated transatlantic service to North and South America. It also completed a round-the-world trip in 29 days with intermediate stops at New York, Los Angeles and Tokyo only.

28 *Three photographs of the Graf Zeppelin from 1928. Designated the LZ-127, the Graf Zeppelin, the largest airship of the period, was an enormous intercontinental transport dirigible, 774 feet long and containing 3.9 million cubic feet of hydrogen. Above, the control panel, blow, phases of construction building process in the company's largest workshops.*

29 top *The Graf Zeppelin during trials over Lake Constance. It is flanked and escorted by two Swiss army fighter planes.*

29 bottom *Two photographs showing construction of the Hindenburg, the largest dirigible that the Zeppelin company built in Friedrichshafen. Its maiden flight was on 1 May 1936.*

Left, the construction of the large metal rings of the framework; right, the airship is almost complete, it already flies the Third Reich's swastika flag on its tail unit.

30-31 The Hindenburg LZ-129 shown flying over Manhattan in 1936. This dirigible was the pride of Nazi Germany and was fitted out for intercontinental passenger transport. It was 804 feet long and the fuselage enclosed a volume of over 5.5 million cubic feet.

30 bottom left The Hindenburg's radio cabin. Thanks to radio, the Zeppelin could receive meteorological information and stay in touch with radio stations everywhere.

30 bottom right Passenger life on the Hindenburg. It had large inclined windows for observation of the countryside below, and various services and entertainments for the 36 passengers it could carry.

The largest and most famous Zeppelin dirigible was the LZ-129 *Hindenburg,* which was 804 feet long, had a top speed of 84 mph, and a range of about 9,000 miles, while passenger space remained unchanged. The LZ-129 made its maiden flight on 1 May 1936, and completed a further 63 (of which 37 were transatlantic trips) before a tragic accident while docking at Lakehurst, New Jersey, destroyed it completely on 6 May 1937. The *Hindenburg* burst into flames for reasons still unknown, and 12 of the 36 passengers and 22 of the 61 crew members were killed in a catastrophe caught on film by the media cameras. That tragedy was the swan song of the great dirigibles and marked their decline as a means of transport, a function for which even then technical advances in airplane design had made them obsolete. The last Zeppelin was the LZ-130 *Graf Zeppelin II,* which first flew in September 1939. The following year it was broken up along with the LZ-127 on the orders of the Luftwaffe commander, Hermann Goering.

31 *Three pictures of the* Hindenburg *disaster. On 6 May 1937, the LZ-129 mysteriously caught fire as it was docking at Lakehurst, New Jersey. A huge blaze immediately followed, caught by film cameras on the airfield. In the fire, whose causes remain unknown, 12 passengers and 22 of the 61 crew members lost their lives.*

32-33 and 33 top
The Norge expedition was followed throughout the world, even though the airship was beaten by an airplane: Richard Byrd flew over the North Pole in a Fokker two days before the Norge. General Nobile with Governor Cremonesi arriving in Rome on 3 August 1926. The large photograph shows the Norge docking. It was 348 feet long and had an overall volume of 633,000 cubic feet.

32 bottom right 11 May 1926. General Nobile (left) with another member of the Norge gondola crew, shortly before taking off from King's Bay for the historic flight over the North Pole.

32 top, center and bottom left The first polar expedition by dirigible was made in 1926 by Norway. The N-1 airship, designed by Umberto Nobile, was renamed Norge for the occasion. The expedition was led by Norwegian explorer Roald Amundsen, who placed the Norge under Nobile's command. Above, the airship during the expedition; below, photographed at Pulham, Great Britain, Nobile with Crown Prince Olav of Norway, the British Air Minister, Sir Samuel Hoare, and the dirigible's crew.

In the 1920s, however, Italy played a major role among the countries involved in the development of the modern dirigible, as the work of General Umberto Nobile, an Italian Royal Airforce officer, confirms. The Italian army and navy had already been using dirigibles for a number of years when Nobile, born in the province of Avellino in 1885, was assigned in 1915 to the technical office of the Aeronautical Factory at Rome. There he contributed to various airship projects, including the Type O built for the navy and also sold abroad. In 1918 Nobile was promoted to director of the Aeronautical Factory, where he continued with his design work. In collaboration with others he developed the T34, a semi-rigid

dirigible that was to remain the largest ever built in Italy. The *Roma*, as it was named, was 410 feet long, had a volume of 1,2 million cubic feet, and could raise a payload of 18.7 tons.

In 1921 the *Roma* was sold to the United States, where it aroused considerable interest. In 1923 Nobile designed his first airship, the N-1, a semi-rigid dirigible

powered by three engines. It was 351 feet long, with a volume of 579,000 cubic feet. Three years later it was acquired by Norway and renamed *Norge*. Under Nobile's command and with the Norwegian explorer Roald Amundsen aboard, this airship made the first crossing of the polar ice cap, from Spitzbergen to Alaska, actually flying over the North Pole.

Inspired by this feat, Nobile was eager to repeat it in an Italian airship with an Italian crew, introducing the added attraction of a landing at the North Pole. The expedition received little support from the Fascist regime and its preparation was probably not as thorough as it should have been. The N-4 *Italia,* an airship almost identical to the *Norge,* departed from Milan on 15 April 1928. Technical and meteorological problems were encountered, but things seemed to have taken a turn for the better after 11 May, when the *Italia* began a series of explorations of the pack ice. On 23 May, the dirigible set out for the North Pole, reaching its destination at about midnight. Weather conditions were worsening, however, and the landing at the Pole was not attempted. On its return flight the *Italia* encountered strong headwinds and a severe storm. On 25 May, burdened by ice, the dirigible struck the pack ice, and the gondola with its nine occupants was torn from the envelope. This, with the remaining six crew members, regained altitude and disappeared, never to be seen again. Six of the nine survivors, whose only shelter was provided by a small tent (the famous red tent whose color was intended to increase its visibility), held on for about a

month before rescuers arrived. The other three had set out on foot, heading toward Nordaustlandet, and were eventually found, although only two survived. During the search the explorer Amundsen was killed when his seaplane was lost. The enterprise and its disastrous conclusion were followed by a drawn-out dispute, in part because Nobile had been the first to be carried to safety by the rescuing seaplane. In 1929, an embittered Nobile resigned from the Italian Royal Air Force. He moved to Moscow in 1932 and worked on Soviet dirigibles until 1936. Between 1939 and 1943 he taught aeronautical engineering in the United States, and then returned to Italy in the post-war period and was elected as a member of the Constituent Assembly. He died in Rome in 1978.

34 The dirigible Italia, *used on Nobile's second expedition to the North Pole in 1928, is shown docking at Slupsk, Poland, a stop on the way. The* Italia, *designated N-4, was almost identical to the* Norge.

34-35 The Italia shown docking in King's Bay. The airship left from Milan on 15 April 1928 and reached the North Pole on 23 May after several stops and exploratory flights over the ice-pack. Shortly afterwards, the tragedy occurred.

35 center Some members of the Italia's crew during a pause. The expedition had 15 members of which only two, the meteorologist (Finn Malmgren, Swedish) and the physicist (Franz Behounek, Czech), were not Italian.

35 bottom Holding a megaphone, General Umberto Nobile, Italy's greatest expert on dirigibles, directs the Italia during an exercise before departure.

Another country had been conducting interesting experiments with dirigibles, transforming them into flying aircraft carriers. In the early 1930s, the US Navy had two airships, the USS Akron and the USS *Macon*. The latter had a top speed of 84 mph and could carry four Curtiss Sparrowhawk monoplane fighters slung below its belly. The fighters could be launched and recovered in flight. Unfortunately, the Akron crashed into the sea in 1933, as did the *Macon* in February 1935, following a structural failure.

However, the 1930s saw the decline of the dirigibles as airplanes surpassed them in speed, robustness and reliability. The tragedies of the *Italia* and the *Hindenburg* only accelerated the end. During the Second World War, the Goodyear Company constructed a series of semi-rigid dirigibles that proved their worth in anti-submarine reconnaissance work. In the post-war period, the United States and the Soviet Union maintained a number of airships in service with secondary maritime reconnaissance duties. In more recent times the only civil dirigibles were the Goodyear craft used for publicity purposes in the United States and Europe.

The advent of new technologies (such as electronics and composite materials) brought dirigibles back into the limelight in the 1990s. It has become clear that the dirigible is still a valid option for touristic, surveillance and advertising purposes, as well as for camera platforms and for lifting bulky loads. The year 1993 saw the foundation of Zeppelin

Luftschifftechnik GmbH., a company dedicated to the development of semi-rigid airships using non-inflammable helium gas. The new NT series dirigibles have overcome the primary problem of safety during take-off and landing thanks to computer technology and the adoption of three 200-hp piston engines with tri-blade propellers, two swiveling through 90° and

one at the tail that can be used to control yawing. On 18 September 1997, the Zeppelin NT LZ N-07 flew for the first time, and the first production model was completed in 2000. Other companies such as the German Cargolifter, the American ABC and the British ATG are also currently working on the design of new dirigibles.

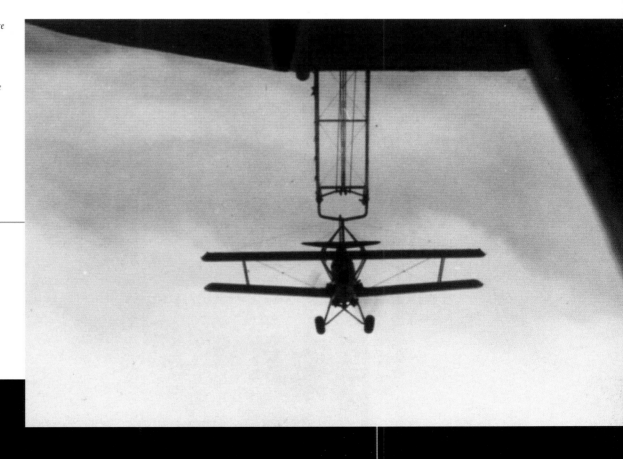

Chapter 3

By the end of the nineteenth century, man's dream of flight had in a certain sense been realized, thanks to balloons and dirigibles. However, this was not the kind of flying that inspired and truly interested aviation pioneers. What they really wanted was to fly controllable aircraft equipped with wings and an engine; to this end, research carried out with gliders proved to be invaluable and finally made it possible to fit them with a power unit suitable for aeronautical purposes. This was the air-cooled internal combustion engine. Its inventor was the German engineer Nicklaus Otto, who in 1877 created a four-stroke thermodynamic cycle, now known as the Otto cycle. Gottlieb Daimler further developed this concept, building the first high-speed (800 rpm) fixed engine in 1883. The internal combustion engine proved to be suitable for automobiles and subsequently for aviation, thanks primarily to progress made in ignition. This advanced first from glow plugs (used until circa 1900), to coil ignition, and then to high-tension electrical ignition using magnetos, which Robert August Bosch introduced in 1902.

The American brothers Wilbur and Orville Wright were the first men to

38-39 The Wright brothers performed many experiments with gliders. In this photograph from 1903, Orville Wright makes a heavy landing while his brother Wilbur runs to his help.

38 bottom Wilbur Wright at the controls of The Flyer, the first heavier-than-air plane to fly successfully with an internal combustion engine. The date: 17 December 1903.

successfully combine a suitable airframe and an internal combustion engine to create a controllable airplane. Wilbur was born in Millville, Indiana in 1867 and Orville in Dayton, Ohio in 1871. Their father, a Protestant pastor, one day gave them a toy helicopter powered by elastic. For the two brothers, then eleven and seven years old, this was a revelation that pushed them toward the worlds of mechanics and flight. After opening a bicycle repair shop, in 1896 the pair became inspired by the work of Otto Lilienthal (he died that year) and attempted to emulate his experiments with gliders.

They considered these to be an intermediate step on the path toward creation of a powered airplane. The brothers began by building a working model, a biplane controlled from the ground via four cables that warped the wings. Then, in 1900, thanks in part to the advice and friendship of Octave Chanute, they began to build and test small gliders. The results were somewhat disappointing, however, and encouraged the Wrights to revise their theories about flight. They built a kind of wind tunnel at their workshop in Dayton, coupling a two-meter long, square-section tube with a fan. Using this rudimentary structure they managed to design and create efficient airfoil shapes and in 1902 they built a glider with satisfactory flight characteristics. Their next step was the design of the first powered airplane.

The first hurdle to be overcome was finding a suitable engine. After fruitless investigation of the automobile industry, the Wrights turned to a mechanic, Charles Taylor, and together with him they designed an in-line four-cylinder internal combustion engine. It produced a maximum power output of 12 hp. Centrally mounted, this engine drove two contra-rotating pusher propellers via a dual chain transmission system. The airframe was a biplane structure with canard-type forward stabilizers, a wingspan of 40 feet, a length of 21 feet, and a lifting area of 510 square feet. The brothers named it the "Flyer."

39 top left and right Two pictures of the Wrights' experiments with gliders. Left, a photo of Wilbur Wright at the controls of the Wright No. 1 in October 1902 during an attempt at Kill Devil Hills, near Kitty Hawk, North Carolina. Right, a flight by Orville Wright on the same site, in a more sophisticated machine.

39 center and bottom Two pictures from the start of the century showing attempts — often naive and approximate — by the first pioneers of motor-powered flight. Center, a twin-engined Pean monoplane. Bottom, a curious seven-winged aircraft with an oval frame. Neither were successful.

The assembly work was completed in December and, impatient to test the airplane despite the cold weather, the Wrights decided to make an initial attempt on 14 December 1903, close to the beaches at Kitty Hawk in North Carolina. This test was unsuccessful: immediately after take-off the Flyer, piloted by Wilbur, and still equipped with skids, stalled and crashed to the ground.

Three days later, on 17 December, events took a different course. Having been repaired, the Flyer was taken back to Kitty Hawk and set up on the launch rails. At the controls this time was Orville. At 10.35 that historic morning, the Flyer took off at a speed of 10 mph, immortalized by a photographer present for the occasion. The airplane flew for just 12 seconds and covered just under 120 feet, but the two brothers completed further flights that day, the longest of which lasted all of 59 seconds.

After this success, the two brothers quietly set to work once again to improve their airplane, trying to maintain a veil of secrecy in order to obtain maximum benefit from their efforts. That first model was followed by the Flyer II, powered by a 15-hp engine and then, in 1915, by the Flyer III, which on 5 October proved capable of flying for over 39 minutes and covering a distance of over 23 miles. However, news of the Wrights' work had spread, in part thanks to the enthusiastic Chanute, and eventually they received a French offer of 500,000 francs to provide a two-hour demonstration flight. The brothers then divided their forces, with Orville conducting a series of demonstrations for the American army and Wilbur travelling to France in June 1908. Following the success of his demonstration flights, Wilbur founded the world's first flying school at Pau, near Bordeaux. The Wrights then continued with their European tour and presented the Flyer, first in Rome in March 1909, and then in Germany. Late in 1909 they founded the Wright Company with associated firms in France, Germany and England, for the production of their flying machine. That same year, the Flyer Model A, the first aircraft of the series, was sold to the American army and thus became the world's first military airplane.

Wilbur died in 1912, a victim of typhoid, and Orville gradually reduced his own activities as an aircraft manufacturer. In 1915 he sold his majority holding in the company in order to devote himself to research. He died at Dayton in 1948.

The story of the Wright brothers' success and photos of their airplane gave renewed impetus to aeronautical experimentation in Europe, and a number of French pioneers, including Ferdinand Ferber, Robert Esnault-Pelterie and Gabriel Voisin, began testing crude copies of the Flyer.

Alberto Santos-Dumont, who was already a pioneer aviator with dirigibles, made the first controlled powered flight in Europe. He built his "14 bis", a bulky canard biplane (an aircraft fitted with lifting surfaces on the nose in front of the main wings) equipped with a 24-hp Levavasseur-Antoinette engine in 1906. On 12 November, after a number of attempts that covered a dozen meters, the Brazilian participated in the Grand Prix de France, organized by the Aéro Club of France, with a prize for the first flight of over 100 meters (327 feet). Santos-Dumont, who had installed a 50-hp engine, covered over 650 feet in 21 seconds, without the aid of any auxiliary launching system. His most famous model was, however, his "19," known as the "Demoiselle," which was fitted with a 20-hp engine. A number of these planes were built and sold. The future French ace Roland Garros was one of those who learnt to fly in this machine.

Louis Blériot was unquestionably one of the leading figures in the pioneering phase of European aviation. Blériot studied engineering and then devoted himself to the construction of headlamps for automobiles, setting up a workshop at Neuilly-sur-Seine. His success in this business provided him with economic security, but in 1900 he began to turn his attention to the world of aviation. All that he initially managed to produce, was an ornithopter with beating wings, which clearly proved to be a total fiasco. Blériot had already abandoned his dreams of flight when he met Gabriel Voisin, a pioneer who had already built a gliding floatplane. Blériot's interest in aviation was rekindled and he decided to found Blériot-Voisin with his new friend in order to build a new floating glider. Results were not all that had been hoped for, and in 1906 the two went their separate ways. Blériot was determined to proceed with his experimentation alone but one of his canard monoplanes crashed in 1907. Perhaps aware of his limitations as a designer, Blériot entrusted the construction of the Blériot VI, a new monoplane with conventional wings and a 25-hp Antoinette engine, to his chief

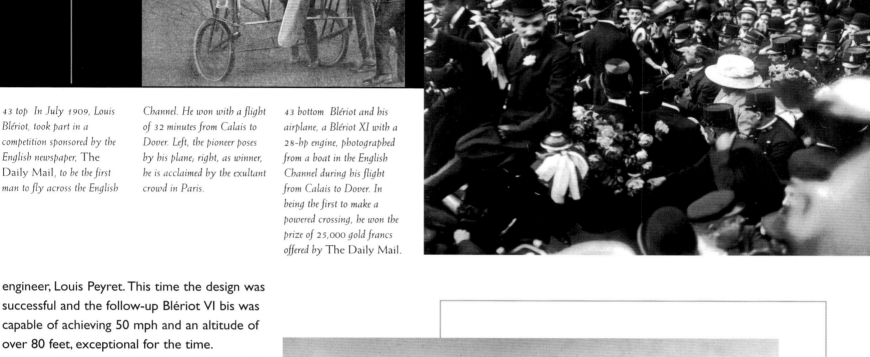

engineer, Louis Peyret. This time the design was successful and the follow-up Blériot VI bis was capable of achieving 50 mph and an altitude of over 80 feet, exceptional for the time. However, the Frenchman's pioneering flights all too frequently ended with crashes, earning him in 1907 the nickname of the "man who always falls." These failures were also exhausting Blériot's financial resources and, drawing on all his painfully acquired experience, he invested his remaining fortune in the last of his creations, the Blériot XI. This sleek monoplane was equipped with a front-mounted 28-hp REP engine with a tractor propeller. It first flew in January 1909. In July, after a number of triumphant appearances at various aeronautical events, Blériot registered for a race sponsored by the British newspaper The Daily Mail, which offered a prize of 25,000 francs to the first pilot to cross the English Channel in an airplane. Louis Blériot lifted off from Calais on 25 July in his Model XI and 32 minutes later reached Dover to general acclaim. This success brought the pioneer aviator glory and the financial rewards he needed to save his business. After yet another flying accident a few months later, Blériot hung up his pilot's goggles to devote himself to his activities as an aircraft manufacturer. By 1913 his company had already sold over 800 civil and military aircraft, a quite remarkable success story for that era. Blériot was also the founder in 1914 of the Société pour l'Aviation et ses Détivés, the famous SPAD which went on to produce thousands of fighter, spotter and training aircraft for the Allied air forces. Blériot's fortunes began to decline in the post-war period. He continued to produce aircraft through to 1930s, when he had to close his factories because of a financial crisis, before his death in 1936.

Other pioneers included the brothers Charles and Gabriel Voisin, who early in the century had built box-section biplanes and gliders equipped with floats. In 1906 the two founded the Frères Voisin company and began constructing two fairly similar types of aircraft with tailplanes and pusher propellers. These machines were failures, however. Greater success came the way of the design built for Henri Farman in 1907. The result was the Voisin-Farman I, equipped with a 50-hp Antoinette engine and structurally similar to the other Voisin planes. Henri Farman, the elder of two brothers famous for their sporting achievements with bicycles and automobiles, was a flying enthusiast. As soon as he had mastered the controls of his new airplane, he decided to participate in the Grand Prix d'Aviation, a trophy instituted in 1904 that was to be awarded to the first aviator to complete a closed-circuit flight of a kilometer (just over half a mile). Despite his lack of aviation experience, Henri made a successful attempt on 13 January 1908 at Issy-les-Moulineaux. Encouraged by this

achievement, the Frenchman decided to tackle the flying business seriously and devoted himself to improving his machine. The Farman Aircraft Company was thus born in a hangar at Issy-les-Moulineaux in 1908. Henri Farman then made the first city-to-city flight: between Mourmelon and Reims, at an average speed of 46.6 mph.

In 1991, in light of this success in developing aircraft, Henri joined forces with his brother Maurice and established a new factory at Billancourt. The firm prospered thanks to the outbreak of the First World War, during which it supplied land- and seaplanes to the French air force and those

of many of the allied countries. Output at the Billancourt factory, which had been extended to a total of over 950,000 square feet, reached the remarkable rate of 300 aircraft per month. Farman managed to adapt to the post-war economy by converting to the production of passenger planes, beginning with the Goliath (1919), and by founding Lignes Farman as a passenger-carrying airline. In 1936 the company was nationalized and the two brothers retired to private life. Henri died in 1958, while Maurice, who had continued to fly light airplanes until the age of 85, died in 1964.

45 top left Henri Farman at the controls of one of his planes.

45 top right A Voisin biplane without canvas lining and fitted with a forward machine-gun, taken during a display in 1910.

45 bottom On 13 January 1908, Henri Farman was the first person to fly a kilometer (1083 yards). Here he is at the finish line.

Another famous French pioneer of the era was Léon Levavasseur. After having worked on a number of experimental projects, he managed to get his first true airplane into the air on 9 October 1908. In February 1909 he introduced an improved design, the Antoinette IV, a monoplane with a large wing area and featuring ailerons, a triangular fuselage with cruciform tailplanes and a front-mounted engine with a tractor propeller. The company produced its own engines which, as noted earlier, were also used by other pioneers. The British pilot Hubert Latham used the Antoinette IV for his attempt to make the first cross-channel flight. In the event, because of an engine failure on 19 July 1909, Louis Blériot preceded him in this endeavor. With the improved 60-hp Antoinette VII, however, Latham collected a number of honors. These

included victory in the altitude competition at the Grande Semaine d'Aviation de la Champagne, held at Reims. There Latham reached just over 500 feet, and won second place in the speed event, recording 42.8 mph. Between 1909 and 1911, the Antoinette monoplanes that Latham and others aviators flew consistently finished in the lead in every aviation competition. In 1912, however, the company ceased production and closed down.

Italy too had its pioneers, among whom Gianni Caproni, the founder of a company that was to achieve international status, was of particular note. Born in Massone d'Arco near Trento in 1886, Caproni attended the Munich polytechnic university and graduated in engineering in 1907. He shortly began to take an interest in aviation, designing and constructing his first airplane, the Ca. 1, a biplane that he completed in 1910 in the face

of considerable economic difficulties. After settling in the moorland area of Malpensa, Caproni began flight-testing his machine: it proved to be unsuccessful. Displaying great determination, the young engineer founded the Caproni-De Agonstini Company at Vizzola Ticino, the result of a partnership with Gherado Baraggiola and the engineer Agostino De Agostini from Bergamo. The first aircraft produced by the new firm was a monoplane, the Cm.1, which successfully flew on 15 June 1911. Together with his aircraft manufacturing business, Caproni also founded a successful flying school at Vizzola. He then suffered a less felicitous period during which he dissolved the partnership with De Agostini, formed another company with Carlo Comitti and then another with Luigi Faccanoni. Caproni's main problems derived from the Italian army's failure to purchase his aircraft and its effective removal of one of his sources of income when it founded its own flying schools. Having sold his factories to the Italian state in 1913, Caproni continued to work on his designs. A large three-engined bomber (which initially re-used the Ca.1 name but changed to Ca. 31 in the post-war period) aroused particular interest. This led to the first military orders from Italy and France. In January 1915, Gianni Caproni founded a new company with factories at Vizzola and Taliedo, near Milan. The firm enjoyed prosperity until

1945. During this period, the company developed 175 aircraft, building many of them in series and exporting them throughout the world. Following the disasters of the Second World War, Gianni Caproni unsuccessfully attempted to convert his factories to produce automobiles. He died in Rome in 1957, but his company was then revitalized, if only briefly, thanks to the acquisition of Avimilano, from which it inherited the successful Calif glider series. The Agusta Group finally absorbed the Caproni firm.

46 Hubert Latham in his Antoinette IV during one of his attempts to win The Daily Mail's prize for being the first to fly across the English Channel. Latham twice finished in the sea.

47 top Hubert Latham's Antoinette IV being prepared for flight in July 1909, before one of his attempts to cross the Channel.

47 center Hubert Latham at the controls of his Antoinette IV. Eventually Latham was beaten by Blériot, but only by two days.

47 bottom The Italian pioneer, Gianni Caproni, shown beside his first aircraft, the Ca.1 biplane, built in 1910 and tested over the Malpensa Marshes, in the province of Varese.

USS Pennsylvania. Curtiss thus began to take an interest in the requirements of the armed forces and above all those of the US Navy, devoting himself to the development of seaplanes. In 1912, the company presented its Model F, featuring a central float. The US Navy ordered 150 of the Model F aircraft. At the outbreak of the Great War in 1914, Curtiss was also working for the US Army, developing a biplane trainer, the soon to be legendary JN or "Jenny," of which over 6,000 were eventually produced and used until the end of the 1920s. After the war, Curtiss concentrated primarily on racing planes, producing excellent designs for a number of years. In the late 1920s, exhausted after giving his all to his work, he retired to Florida, where he died in 1930.

Aeronautical progress was by no means a European prerogative, however. In the United States, the Wright brothers were not the only pioneers working in the field. One of the most talented and best known was undoubtedly Glenn Hammond Curtiss. He was born in Hammondsport, New York, in 1878. His father died when Curtiss was just five years old, and he was obliged to work from adolescence in order to help his family. When Curtiss was twenty, he and his partner Tank Waters established their own cycle repair business. As the company developed and began to build its own bicycles, Curtiss was able to give full rein to his passion for engines, and in 1902 he built his first powered bicycle. This was followed by a number of motorcycling victories and records, and Curtiss received an order for an engine that was to be installed in Thomas Scott Baldwin's dirigible, *California Arrow.* The success of this 5-hp twin-cylinder engine led to the founding of the Curtiss Manufacturing

Company in 1905. That same year Graham Bell, the inventor of the telephone, contacted Curtiss to agree upon terms for the development of a joint aircraft-manufacturing project. Curtiss accepted Bell's offer, although not until 1907, and became the chief designer and engine expert for Bell's AEA company. After the construction of five planes, the last of which proved incapable of take-off, Bell lost interest in aeronautical research and the company closed its doors. Curtiss took over the on-going projects and in June 1909, with Augustus Herring he founded the Herring-Curtiss Company, the United States' first aeronautical manufacturing concern. The new company began to prosper, partly because Curtiss threw himself into new feats of aviation. These led to the winning no less than three *Scientific American* magazine trophies that brought fame and prestige to the company.

Early in 1911, one of Curtiss's pupils and clients, Eugene Fly, made the first deck landing and take-off from a ship, the cruiser

In just ten years from the Wright brothers' first powered hop aerodynamics and aircraft engine design had progressed so much that aircraft could now be controlled easily and even to carry considerable loads, frequently passengers. During the Italian-Turkish war fought in Libya in 1911, the airplane was used as an offensive weapon for the first time, with Italian aviators dropping a number of bombs by hand on enemy troops. The psychological effect was more significant than the physical damage caused, but the new practice showed that the time was now ripe for the airplane to become a protagonist on the world stage. It was, however, no longer audacious sporting feats but rather the First World War that catalyzed aeronautical development.

48 One of the most brilliant American pioneers was Glenn Hammond Curtiss, who began as a bicycle repairman in 1898. Here he is at the command of his biplane, Gold Bug.

48-49 and 49 top Two pictures of the Curtiss biplane, June Bug, piloted by Glenn Curtiss himself. The Herring-Curtiss Company – the first aeronautical company in the US – was founded in June 1909. In the years that followed, the company specialized in hydroplanes and became the supplier to the US Navy in 1912.

Chapter 4

The uncertain, courageous, faltering and fascinating world of aviation had made considerable progress in the ten years following the Wright brothers' first flight. While giant leaps had yet to be made, the airplanes of 1913, no matter how rudimentary, already boasted fundamental features such as internal combustion engines driving propellers, one or more sets of wings providing lift, stabilizers, pilot-actuated moving control surfaces, and a fuselage capable of accommodating the crew. The factor that imposed a revolution in the design and production of airplanes was the demands of a war such as the world had never seen before. With the First World War, in fact, aviation developed at a truly remarkable rate.

Even prior to 1914, powered aircraft had already been used in conflicts such as the Italian-Turkish War of 1911, the Mexican Revolution led by Pancho Villa in 1912 and the Balkan War of 1913. However, these were isolated operations conducted in the main with civil and sporting aircraft perfunctorily adapted for military use. The armed forces themselves had only vague ideas regarding the 0use of aircraft in any sphere other than that of observation and reconnaissance.

A number of farsighted precursors had, it is true, already envisioned the potential of air power. An Italian army officer, Giulio Douhet, laid out very clear ideas on the military use of aircraft: "The sky is about to become a new battlefield, one no less important those of land and sea, he wrote in 1909. In 1911, Bertram Dickson, an English officer, also predicted that aircraft would assume important reconnaissance and combat duties in order to secure control of air space. Other trailblazers included the Frenchman Ferdinand Feber, the American Billy Mitchell and the German Helmuth von Moltke. Rather than receive the attention they deserved, they all came up against the traditionalism of their military superiors and were scorned or even punished. Within a few years, however, history was to prove them right.

50 left The use of aircraft in war demanded the development of counter-measures. Here self-transporting launchers belonging to the French army are used to bring down a Zeppelin airship on 21 February 1916.

50 bottom Anti-aircraft defenses came into being with cannon and machine-guns; the photograph shows some German machine-gunners preparing a placement on the Western Front.

50 right Any kind of defense was used to bring down enemy planes. Shown here is a soldier in the British cavalry firing a portable machine-gun against a German airplane in summer 1916.

51 top In the early months of World War I, the planes in service were still fairly primitive and with little equipment, like this French Morane-Saulnier.

51 center At first fighters did not exist. To bring down enemy planes, various solutions were used, like this French two-seater with a machine-gun raised to avoid firing into the propeller.

51 bottom left Logistical and technical mobility began to assume importance: this truck was fitted out for the unusual task of transporting disassembled airplanes.

51 bottom right This photomontage shows the new war in the skies as it was during World War I.

The Great War of 1914-1918 revolutionized the world of aviation, bringing not only sweeping technological changes, but also operational innovations that led to the development of specialist aircraft such as fighters, bombers, and photo-reconnaissance planes. Entirely new military services, the air forces were created to take advantage of the new technology.

Early in the war, most planes in service had been derived from sporting models and were unarmed. The French, whose army air force was composed of over 30 squadrons, flew diverse types such as the Blériot XI, the Morane-Saulnier H, the Maurice Farman MF.7 and MF.11 and the Caudron G.3. The British Army Air Corps and the Royal Naval Air Service also used these aircraft, together with others built in Britain such as the Sopwith Tabloid, the Bristol Boxkite, the Royal Aircraft Factory BE.2 and the Avro 504. The French and British forces boasted a combined total of around 250 front-line aircraft.

For their part, the Germans also had almost 250 aircraft, mostly Aviatik B.I and B.II and Albatros B.II biplanes and Taube LE-3 monoplanes. No army had made plans for the use of aircraft in offensive roles, and the first such actions took the form of isolated individual initiatives: on 13 August 1914, Lieutenant Franz von Hiddeson hand-dropped two grenades on Paris from his Taube.

52 top With the advent of military aircraft, the first terrible bombing raids began. This is the Belgian village of Poperinge in May 1916.

52-53 The crew of a Russian bomber demonstrate the commonest bombing system of the era: a second crew member lines up the target through the sight and releases the bombs by hand.

53 bottom left Industry had to adapt to the new war requirements in a hurry. Here at the Ansaldo factory, static resistance tests are being carried out on a complete wing structure.

52 bottom Spring 1916: workers in a French munitions factory preparing a stick of plane bombs.

53 bottom right The French inventor, G. Fabre, shows the bomb-launching device that enabled greater precision in aerial bombardment.

From the first weeks of the war there were encounters between enemy aircraft in the skies over the front, but many pilots never even considered the possibility that they might fight against each other. Neither did the respective chains of command; in fact, pilots were frequently prohibited from carrying and using firearms on aircraft for safety reasons. The first air-to-air conflicts were fought with hunting rifles, shotguns and pistols, almost as if they were duels on horseback.

At first, the pilots acted on their own initiative. There were those who decided to try to ram enemy aircraft at the risk of losing their own planes and their own lives. Some dropped hand-grenades or attached hooks to their plane with which they tried to gash their enemies' wings, while others let ropes dangle which they hoped would become tangled up in their counterparts' propellers. However, most authorities were in agreement that only by mounting a fixed or traversing machine-gun could the problem be solved, and thus the era of true aerial combat came into being. The ideal layout for fighter aircraft was a fixed machine-gun mounted in front of the pilot so that he could shoot forward and aim by pointing his airplane at the target. The bullets would, however, have to pass through the disc created by the spinning propeller and they would inevitably, and sooner rather than later, saw through the blades. Morane-Saulnier devised a solution to this problem: apply armor plating to the back of the propeller blades, allowing those bullets striking them to be deflected. Thanks to this idea the Morane-Saulnier L became the first true fighter aircraft, and allowed Roland Garros to become the first pilot to shoot down an enemy aircraft with a machine-gun mounted in the so-called "fighter" position. This plane, designed in 1913, was powered by an 80-hp Gnome rotary engine, had a maximum take-off weight of 1,500 lbs and a top speed of 71.5 mph at sea level. The path had now been traced and future fighters – whether mono-, bi- or triplanes – all to adopt this layout.

55 top right A British poster of 1915 highlights the differences between friendly and enemy airplanes to familiarize the public with aircraft and help them recognize danger.

55 bottom A French engineer installs a reconnaissance camera on a twin-engined Caudron. World War I also led to the development of aerial reconnaissance.

56 left, third picture In 1915 the French Nieuport 11 Bébé fighter appeared, the first of a successful family of planes. It had an 80-hp engine and could reach 97 mph.

56 left, fourth picture World War I obliged the warring parties to produce huge numbers of combat aircraft. Their fragility and vulnerability were one of the reasons for their frequent replacement. Here a French squadron of Nieuports is displayed.

56 bottom right One of the most successful fighter aircraft was the SPAD VII, used by the Italian aviation forces. The photograph shows Major Chiappirone and his airplane at Villaverla airfield in June 1917.

In 1915, the principal aircraft operated by the various forces were the Royal Aircraft Factory FE.2b, the Bristol Scout D, the Fokker E.III, and the Nieuport Bébé. The first true modern fighter, introduced in the summer of 1915, was the Fokker E.III, a monoplane armed with a 7.92-mm Spandau machine-gun and powered by a 100-hp Oberursel rotary engine providing a top speed of 87 mph. The supremacy of the E.III was due above all to the adoption of a revolutionary mechanical device, the synchronizer. Thanks to this mechanism, devised by the aircraft constructor himself, Anthony Fokker, the movement of the propeller governed the firing of the machine-gun, with the firing interrupted as the propeller blades passed in front of the muzzle. Moreover, the E.III was a monoplane, lighter and much more agile than the many heavy biplanes still in service with the Allies. Such was the E.III's superiority during the winter of 1915-1916 that the embattled Allied forces nicknamed it the "Fokker Scourge." Early in 1916, the Royal Flying Corps ordered that each of its spotter plane was to be escorted by three fighters when flying over the enemy lines.

The Allies were not slow to respond to the E.III, the British producing the Royal Aircraft Factory FE.2bn, a two-seat biplane with a pusher propeller that was equipped with two machine-guns and a 160-hp engine that gave it a top speed of 91 mph. The summer of 1915 saw the début of the first of a line of successful fighters, the French Nieuport 11 Bébé, a fast (97 mph), agile biplane propelled by an 80- hp Le Rhône 9C engine and armed with a 7.7-mm machine-

56 left, first picture This French air force Nieuport 17 of 1916 boasts two armaments. The pilot is an American volunteer: non-commissioned officer Lufberry.

56 left, second picture One of the most famous German fighters was the 180-hp, 117- mph Albatross D.V. It was brought into service in summer 1917 and more than 1800 were built.

gun. The aces Guynemer, De Rose and Nungesser inflicted serious losses on the Germans with this machine during the battle of Verdun, fought during February 1916. Shortly afterwards, Nieuport presented the improved version of the Bébé, the Nieuport 17, which was larger, more robust, better armed and much faster than its predecessor. The Nieuport 17 had a 110-hp engine and a top speed of 110 mph at 6,550 feet. It was fitted with twin 7.7-mm machine-guns. This became the favorite plane of many aces, including Guynemer, Nungesser, Fonck, Navarre and the British pilots Ball and Bishop.

By 1916 the war in the air had already changed considerably and the new aircraft that were introduced were ever more sophisticated and deadly. The Germans leapfrogged the Allies once more with the introduction of an aerodynamic new biplane, the Albatros D.I, which reached the front in the autumn and was immediately followed by the D.II. This last model boasted a 160-hp Mercedes D III engine that gave the aircraft a top speed of 108 mph. The armament comprised two machine-guns. Another aircraft with notable specifications was the Hansa-Brandenburg D.I, an Austrian plane equipped with a 160-hp Austro-Daimler engine capable of 116 mph. This fighter, however, proved to be rather unstable, and limited the pilot to a restricted range of vision; it was consequently blighted by a

series of accidents earning it the nickname "coffin" from its pilots. Autumn 1916 also saw the Allies' introduction of an excellent new airplane, the French-built SPAD VIII, probably the best fighter of the first half of the Great War. The aircraft was designed around a V8 engine, the Hispano-Suiza 8 producing 150 hp. This was the engine of the future and was soon to replace obsolete rotary-architecture engines. The fuselage was highly aerodynamic with the engine was enclosed in a metal fairing; the armament comprised a Vickers 7.7-mm machine-gun. The fighter made its first flight in April 1916, and its performance immediately proved to be remarkable: a top speed of almost 122 mph and the ability to climb to 10,000 feet in

just 15 minutes. France immediately ordered 268 of the SPAD VIIIs, with further orders flooding in from the Allied countries. The plane entered service on 2 September 1916, and was warmly welcomed by pilots, including the Italian ace Francesco Baracca who first flew the new plane in March 1917. The SPAD XIII, the upgraded version of the VIII, equipped with two machine-guns, made its maiden flight on 4 April 1917. This version, powered by a 220-hp engine and capable of almost 140 mph, was heavier and less maneuverable and many pilots, including Baracca, preferred the old VIII. The XIII was nonetheless widely adopted by the French, British, American, Belgian and Italian forces and no less than 8,472 of them were built.

57 top A German Aviatik B.I ready for take-off. This 1914 spotter plane had a 100-hp engine and a maximum speed of 62 mph. It had a two-man crew.

57 bottom left An RAF F.E.2b at Ste. Marie-Chappelle in France, 1916-17. This was a two-seater spotter-fighter with a 160-hp engine and a pusher propeller. It entered service in 1915.

57 bottom right A German Fokker E.III monoplane undergoing maintenance in a wood. It was the first airplane fitted with a propeller synchronizer (invented by Anthony Fokker) that allowed bullets to be fired through the revolving propeller blades.

1917 saw the débuts of a number of other excellent and famous airplanes. The included the British Sopwith F.1 Camel and Triplane, the Royal Aircraft Factory S.E.5, and the French Hanriot D.1. The Germans introduced the Fokker Dr.I, Pfalz D.III and Albatros D.II and D.V. Following its successful Pup, Sopwith designed a highly maneuverable new small fighter equipped with two synchronized machine-guns. The Pup downed no fewer than 1,294 enemy aircraft in about one year's fighting. The F.1, known as the Camel because of the humped fairing over its guns, flew for the first time on 22 December 1916, and began to reach the front-line squadrons in May 1917. Powered by a 130-hp Clerget 9B rotary engine, the Camel was capable of 115 mph, but the great torque its engine generated made it demanding to fly. However, the most skilful pilots could exploit this negative characteristic to make the plane even more agile. Almost 5,500

Camels were built between the end of 1916 and 1918.

For a time in 1917, aeronautical technology seemed to be moving in the direction of the triplane layout. In fact, in February of that year, the Sopwith Triplane made its début at the front, a fast maneuverable fighter that proved its worth and, most significantly, threw the Germans into a panic as they hurriedly set about catching up with what they perceived to be a notable technical advance. In reality, despite the Triplane's undoubted qualities, by July 1917 the more traditional but more effective Camel was replacing it; in all, only 144 Triplanes were built. German research had, in the meantime, involved 14 companies. Of the resulting prototypes, a Fokker triplane was judged to be the best. Following flight-testing, it was immediately put into production as the Dr.I and entered service in August 1917. Despite its tricky handling, the plane was immediately popular

with its pilots, thanks to its exceptional maneuverability and climbing speed. Among the aces of particular note who flew it were Werner Voss and Manfred von Richtofen, the famous "Red Baron." The Dr.I remained in production until May 1918, with 318 being built before it made way for the more modern Fokker D.VII.

1917 also saw the début of another famous German fighter, the Albatros D.III/V. (This introduction actually occurred earlier than that of the Dr.I, triplane, and the Albatros D.III/V was built in far greater numbers than the Dr.I.) The D III/V was developed from the D.II. It had sesquiplane wings with V-shaped struts and was equipped with a more powerful engine than its predecessor. This new engine, the in-line 6-cylinder Mercedes D.IIIa, produced 176 hp and provided a top speed of 109 mph. Beginning in January 1917, almost all the fighter squadrons were re-equipped with the D.III/V, which in the hands of aces of the

58-59 The best British fighter of the war was the S.E.5a, which entered service in June 1917. It was fitted with a 200-hp engine that gave it a top speed of 139 mph.

59 right, first photograph The Sopwith Triplane was the British attempt to build a faster, more agile fighter than its predecessors.

59 right, second photograph The Sopwith F1 Camel entered service in May 1917. It had a 130-hp engine and reached 116 mph. The name was given by the hump created by the machine-gun cowling. Over 5500 were built.

59 right, third photograph The Fokker Dr.I, in service from August 1917, was the German response to the Sopwith Triplane. Difficult to handle, it passed into history as the favorite airplane of Manfred von Richthofen, the "Red Baron."

59 bottom Shown during combat, the Fokker D.VII entered service in 1918 and was thought by many to be the best fighter in the war. It touched 119 mph and remained powerful up to 19,500 feet.

D.VII and the Siemens-Schuckert D.II/IV. The Fokker D. VII appeared in April 1918, and was perhaps the best fighter either side produced in the First World War. Early in 1918, the aircraft won a competition held by the War Ministry to find a new fighter; it also won von Richtofen's approval. The D.VII, a biplane of traditional lines, was equipped with a 160-hp Mercedes D.III engine, offering a top speed of 118 mph at 3,280 feet. The War Ministry immediately 400 D, VIIs, and the plane was supplied to the leading fighter squadrons, with von Richtofen's personal group being the first to receive them. The pilots were impressed by the D.VII's qualities, in particular its high climbing speed and high-altitude performance. The model F, powered by a 185-hp BMW IIIa engine that maintained an appreciable power output to an altitude of 19,500 feet, was in production by August 1918. While the Fokker D.VII climbed to 16,500 feet in 38 minutes, the D.VII F took just 14 minutes. About 1,000 were built prior to the armistice.

The Siemens-Schuckert II/IVs were also notable fighters. The D.III model was equipped with a 160-hp engine driving a four-bladed propeller and could attain a top speed of 112 mph.

caliber of von Richtofen, Voss and Udet, helped the Germans regain aerial superiority above the battlefields. This period of German predominance culminated in the month of April, known by the British as "Bloody April" owing to the losses they suffered. In the summer of 1917, the Albatros D.V was introduced. It had a 180-hp engine providing a top speed of 116 mph; it also had stronger wings than its predecessor (which had had an unfortunate habit of losing its lower wings in prolonged dives). More than 1,800 D.Vs were built, and the plane remained in service until 1918.

During the last year of the war, when Germany's defeat became increasingly likely though not yet certain, the nation produced its finest fighter aircraft, the Fokker

By the end of the First World War, the aircraft industry had achieved great technological progress. All fighters were now being fitted with in-line rather than now obsolete rotary engines. Performance levels had increased constantly: the Italian Ansaldo A.1 Balilla boasted a 220-hp engine and a top speed of almost 137 mph, while the British Martinside F.4 Buzzard, powered by a 300-hp Hispano-Suiza 8F engine was capable of 133.6 mph. The same year (1918) also saw the introduction of the Junkers D.I, the first all-metal monoplane fighter.

Giant steps had also been taken in bomber design. In 1915, still early in the conflict, bombing raids were carried out by aircraft such as the Caudron G.4 (twin 80-hp engines, top speed 82 mph, 250-lb bomb load); the Farman F.40 (single 160-hp engine, top speed 84 mph, 110-lb bomb load); and the Caproni

Ca.32 (three 100-hp engines, top speed 72 mph, 771-lb bomb load). Over the years, larger and more capacious aircraft were introduced. By the end of the war bombers were carrying highly respectable bomb loads: the Vickers Vimy (twin 360-hp engines, top speed 102.5 mph, 4,800-lb bomb load load) and the Handley Page V/1500 (four 375-hp engines, top speed 90 mph, 7,500-lb bomb load).

While the First World War increased the airplane's romantic appeal and legendary status, it above all favored the diffusion of aeronautical technology. During the five years of the conflict, Germany built 48,537 aircraft, Great Britain 58,144 and France no fewer than 67,987. Italy, the United States, Russia, and Austria contributed a further 45,000 aircraft. The air corps had expanded considerably: while in 1914 France had 138 front-line aircraft, by 1918 this total had risen

to 4,511. Great Britain's air strength rose from 113 aircraft to 3,300 and Italy's from 150 to 1,200. The size and importance of the new corps actually led Great Britain to create a third branch of its armed forces, the Royal Air Force, which in 1918 incorporated men and machines from the Army and Navy. Other countries shortly followed suit.

All aircraft had become much more reliable, robust and controllable than four years earlier. Thanks to technological developments and the surplus of airframes, engines and pilots, the post-war years were to see the establishment of the aircraft as a means of transport. At the end of the war aeronautical development was ensured by the thirst for adventure and glory of both the pilots and the manufacturers, who would turn to the fields of record breaking and aerial exploration.

61 center France also produced various types of bombers. Shown is a Caudron G.4 from 1915. It had twin engines of either 80 or 100 hp and could carry a bomb load of 248 lbs.

61 bottom The Vickers Vimy, introduced in 1918, was another British success. It was powered by two 360-hp Rolls Royce engines and carried a bomb load of up to 4800 lbs. Like the Handley Page V/1500, after the war it was used for civilian transport.

60 The Handley Page V/1500, a British bomber introduced in 1918, was an exceptional plane for its era. It was powered by four 375-hp engines, had a maximum take-off weight of 67,200 lbs (including a bomb load of up to 6780 lbs), and could remain airborne for 6 hours.

61 top An Italian air force Caproni Ca.3 in flight in 1915. This biplane bomber, powered by three 150-hp Isotta Fraschini engines, a 3100 lb bomb load. This successful plane was also made in France under license.

The Knights of the Air

While the Great War signified blood, suffering and death for millions of men condemned to an anonymous fate in the mud of the trenches, the new aerial warfare in which the individual courage, altruism, honor and heroism of the medieval knights were revived soon caught the imagination of the masses. Fighter pilots became the objects of unprecedented admiration and fame. Frequently exploited by the powers-that-be to boost public morale, the pilots themselves did their best to feed the legends, with audacious, bold and daring behavior on and off the field of combat. They were showered with honors to a degree that had not been seen for centuries, both during their lifetimes and after their deaths. Despite the ferocity of their aerial duels, they fought a different war, one ruled by a gentlemanly code and distinguished by mutual respect.

The greatest pilots became known as "aces," a term initially coined to describe someone who excelled, but it was then attributed only to those who had shot down five or more enemy aircraft.

The most famous of all was without question the German Manfred von Richtofen, the legendary "Red Baron," so named after the color in which he had his personal aircraft painted. Prior to his death, shot down by a Canadian, Captain Roy Brown, on 9 April 1918, von Richtofen set an unmatched record of 80 kills.

A list of the leading First World War Aces follows, subdivided by nation, and giving the number of enemy aircraft each brought down:
Germany: M. von Richtofen (80), E. Udet (62), E. Loewenhardt (53), W. Voss (48), F. Rumey (45), O. Boelcke (40). Austria-Hungary: G. Brumowski (40), J. Arigi (32), F. Linke-Crawford (30). Great Britain: E. Mannock (73), W.A. Bishop (72), R. Collishaw (60), J.T.B. McCudden (57). Italy: F. Baracca (34), S. Scaroni (26), P.R. Piccio (24), F.T. Baracchini (21), F. Ruffo di Calabria (20). France: R. Fonck (75), G. Guynemer (54), C. Nungesser (45), G. Madon (41). United States: E. Rickenbacker (26), W. Lambert (22), F. Gilette (20). Belgium: W. Coppens (37). Russia: A.A. Kazakov (17).

63 top left The German ace, Baron Manfred von Richthofen, better known as the Red Baron because his planes were painted that color. He commanded the 11th Pursuit Squadron (Jasta II) and was brought down behind British lines on 9 April 1918.

62 top Major Francesco Baracca, Italy's most successful war ace, posing in front of a captured enemy airplane. He knocked out 34 enemy planes before being brought down by anti-aircraft fire. His "rearing horse" coat-of-arms was handed on to certain Italian fighter squadrons; his mother also donated it to the car-maker Enzo Ferrari.

62-63 bottom Georges Guynemer, France's second most successful ace, shot down 54 enemy planes before being killed himself.

63 top right General Bongiovanni, Major Gabriele D'Annunzio and other pilots of the Serenissima Squadron's famous flight over Vienna, made on 9 August 1918. The purpose was to drop propaganda leaflets and bombs.

63 center right The funeral of Baron von Richthofen, held in Berlin in 1925. For seven years his remains had rested in a French cemetery.

63 bottom right Albert Ball, one of the most famous British aces. He died in combat after shooting down his forty-third victim.

Chapter 5

U p until the First World War, popular imagination had above all seen the airplane as the instrument of sporting bravado and a weapon for intrepid warriors; in both cases a vehicle of the élite, reserved for a few fearless souls.

The Great War radically changed this situation, in terms of numbers at least, if not the underlying concepts: by 1918 there were thousands of trained and experienced pilots, along with thousands of aircraft about to be sold off as military surplus. Flying had begun to spread and its commercial potential had begun to be appreciated.

The birth of civil aviation took place in post-war Europe and was the fruit of necessity rather than chance. The war had, in fact, destroyed many rail links, and routes which involved a sea crossing, such as the popular London-Paris route, were slow and complicated for any land-based means of transport. In contrast, America still benefited from an excellent and undamaged rail network, and the characteristics of contemporary aircraft meant that the railways still enjoyed a measure of superiority.

France, Great Britain and Germany all saw the birth of the first airline companies within a few months, early in 1919. The first scheduled service was actually established in Germany, with Zeppelin dirigibles linking Berlin and Weimar. The Paris-Brussels and Paris-London routes inaugurated by French and English companies operating airplanes soon followed.

64 top left The postwar period marked the beginning of many commercial aviation projects, like the then very sophisticated Caproni Ca.60 Transaereo hydroplane. Despite its eight 400-hp engines, this gigantic flying craft was too heavy to fly and was destroyed during trials.

PARIS·STRASBOURG·NÜRNBERG·PRAHA·WARSZAWA·WIEN·BUDAPEST·BEOGRAD·SOFIA·ISTANBUL·ATHÉNAI

FLÈCHE D'ORIENT

AIR FRANCE

64 bottom left A crowd gathers round a de Havilland DH.86 biplane during the opening of Gatwick Airport by Britain's Minister of Aviation.

64 right Two posters advertising KLM (Royal Dutch Air Services), the Dutch national airline.

65 left A splendid poster advertising Air France's "Arrow of the East" service, begun in 1933.

65 top right A twin-engined Air France Bloch 220 over France. The airline was formed in 1933 by the merger of Aéropostale, Farman and Air Orient.

65 bottom right The bare interior of the cabin of the Caproni Ca.60 Transaereo, which was designed to carry 100 passengers.

The first of the British companies were Aircraft Transport, Handley Page Transport, Instone Air Line, and Daimler Airway. They were emulated in Holland by KLM, in Belgium by SNETA, in France by Farman, Latécoère and Aéropostale, and in Germany by Junkers and Deutscher Aero Lloyd. As the years passed, many of the pioneering air transport companies disappeared or merged as a response to the demands of both the market and national governments. In 1924, the British companies merged to form Imperial Airways, directly supported by the government and charged with maintaining links with the far-flung corners of the empire. Two years later, all the German companies were brought together at the government's behest to form a single company, Deutsche Luft Hansa Akt engesellschaft, better known as Lufthansa. The year 1933 also saw the birth of Air France as a result of the merger of Aéropostale, Farman and Air Orient. Other companies sprang up throughout Europe: Det Danske Luftfartselskab in Denmark, Linee Aeree d'Italia in Italy, Sabena in Belgium, and so on.

Various constraints limited the individual companies' commercial initiatives, market capacity, and development potential. In fact, the aircraft themselves were the principal difficulty facing the nascent civil aviation industry: in the immediate post-war period there were no purpose-built passenger planes specifically designed to operate on commercial routes.

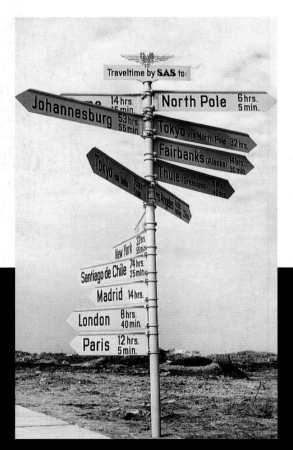

66 left The SAS sign in Bodø, Norway, indicates flight times to various destinations. With air travel, the world began to get smaller.

66 top right An 'air porter' of the German airline Luft Hansa helps a passenger board a Fokker F.II. This passenger plane entered service with the newly formed airline in 1926.

66 bottom right The luxurious passenger cabin in the four-engined, long-range Handley Page HP.42, in service with Britain's Imperial Airways from 1930.

67 top left Passengers disembark from a Luft Hansa Junkers G.24 at Berlin's Tempelhof airport in 1928. A shuttle bus took them right into the city center.

67 center left A poster advertising the 1927 Cologne air race, for civilian planes only.

67 bottom left Luft Hansa was the first airline in the world to serve food and drinks on board. Stewards are shown serving an in-flight meal in the cabin of a three-engined Junkers G.31 in 1928.

67 right With the advent of new and larger airplanes, on-board services increased. This Fokker F.XXXVI has couchettes, like KLM organized in 1935 for its night flights.

The first airliners were, in fact, perfunctorily converted multi-engined bombers or two- or three-seat single-engined planes with all the attendant discomfort and inconvenience of pioneering aircraft: noise, vibration, turbulence and freezing temperatures.

Among the most commonly used airplanes in this period were the Vickers Vimy, the Farman F.60, the Airco D.H.4, the Breguet Br.14 and Handley Page bombers such as the 0/10 and the 0/11, derived from the military 0/400 version.

The Vickers FB.27, named the Vimy after a First World War battle, completed its maiden flight on 30 November 1917. The three-bay biplane had two 203-hp Hispano-Suiza engines mounted on trestles between the two wings, a biplane tail with twin rudders, and a four-wheeled undercarriage equipped

with a front skid to prevent overturning. The plane had a maximum take-off weight of over 5.5 tons and a top speed of about 100 mph; it carried a crew of three along with twelve 110-lb bombs. A total of 235 Vimys had been recently ordered as heavy bombers for the Royal Flying Corps. The development of the Vimy was marked by setbacks: both the second and third prototypes were lost in accidents. By the end of the war (November 1918), the Royal Air Force had received just three Vimys, and the remaining 232 were built and delivered in the post-war period. The plane remained in service until 1933, when the last one was finally retired in Egypt.

The demands of commercial aviation convinced Vickers to produce a civil version of the Vimy. This version, named the Vimy Commercial, made its maiden flight on 13

April 1919. It featured a larger fuselage that could accommodate up to ten passengers in wickerwork seats. Behind the cabin was a baggage compartment that could carry a load of up to 2,500 lbs. The first prototype, registered as G-EAAV, was immediately followed by three production aircraft, all equipped with 456-hp Napier Lion or with 406-hp Lorraine Dietrich engines. The French company Grands Express Aériens purchased one, while the other two went to the British firm of Instone, and subsequently to Imperial Airways. Forty G-EEAVs were manufactured for China, but not all of them actually went into service, In total, 336 Vimy series aircraft were eventually built.

The French Farman F.60 Goliath was the most important transport aircraft of the early post-war period. The Goliath was originally designed as a bomber, but the

68 top: In the postwar period, the British Vickers Vimy bomber was converted to civil use. The commercial model seen here offered a complete passenger cabin.

armistice was signed before the first prototypes had been completed. With notable foresight, the company immediately set to work to convert the plane to passenger-carrying duties, replacing the original fuselage with one equipped with cabins in the nose and central section that was capable of accommodating a total of twelve passengers. The first F.60 Goliath made its inaugural flight in January 1919. Development of the military version continued, and it entered service in 1922. The F.60 civil version was first flown commercially on the London-Paris route by the Compagnie des Grands Express Aériens, on 29 March 1920. Shortly afterwards, the Farman line inaugurated the Paris-Brussels route, which late in 1921 was extended to Amsterdam and Berlin. Various airlines in France, Romania, Belgium and Czechoslovakia (where the F.60 was built under license) soon adopted the plane. A total of 60 commercial-use Farman Goliaths were manufactured. The aircraft featured a twin-engined biplane layout with a four-wheeled undercarriage and cruciform tailplanes. The two 260-hp Salmson C.M.9 radial engines provided it with a top speed of 87 mph and a range of 250 miles. The F.60 had a wingspan of 86.9 feet, a length of 47 feet, and a maximum take-off weight of 10,516 lbs.

The Airco D.H.4, designed by Geoffrey de Havilland, was introduced in 1916 as an advanced reconnaissance and bombing aircraft. It was a large twin-bay biplane initially equipped with a 200-hp BHP engine, providing for a top speed of over 87 mph at 15,000 feet, and a bomb load of over 660 lbs. The crew was composed of a pilot and a gunner. The D.H.4 immediately stood out as an aircraft with notable performance and specifications that could operate without a fighter escort. Some 1,450 of the aircraft were manufactured. After the armistice was signed, numerous civil versions were developed from the basic military D.H.4. The Aircraft Transport firm used the D.H.4 from 1919 for its first flights to the continent, and subsequently the company also operated the

D.H.4A, a version equipped with a closed cabin for two passengers. Handley Page, SNETA and Instone used other D.H4s. The best of them were those equipped with the 380-hp Eagle VIII engine that had a top speed of 143 mph and a maximum take-off weight of about 4,000 lbs. A majority of these aircraft, however, were fitted with less expensive and more common 12-cylinder, 203-hp RAF 3A engines, which provided significantly inferior performance.

A particularly important aircraft in this period was the German Junkers F13, the first all-metal monoplane designed for civil use. Derived from the J10 tactical support aircraft, the F13 completed its maiden flight on 25 June1919, powered by a 160-hp Mercedes D.IIIa engine. This first version had a closed cabin for four passengers and an open cockpit in the nose for the two pilots. Subsequently, the fuselage was modified to allow the crew to enjoy a closed cockpit. The original engines were replaced with BMW IIIa units producing 185 hp, and then by Junkers L-5s producing 210 hp. This small aircraft (a wingspan of 58 feet, a length of 31 feet 4 inches, and a maximum take-off weight of 4,410 lbs) was a great commercial success for the period: some 350 were manufactured and the plane remained in production until 1932. Over 60 variants were produced with wheeled undercarriages, skis, or floats. Junkers also derived two successful cargo planes from the F13, the W33 and the W34, which made their first flights in 1926.

In structural terms, these new aircraft were very similar to the F13 and were manufactured on the same production line. The major differences were a wingspan of just over 60 feet and an increase in maximum take-off weight to just over 7,000 lbs. The W33 was powered by the 314-hp Junkers L-5 engine while the W34 initially adopted the Gnome-Le Rhône Jupiter VI,

71 top *Luft Hansa maintenance and cleaning staff working on a Junkers F13. Note the corrugated surface of the fuselage, which gave greater strength to the whole.*

71 center *A British Airco DH.4 biplane in flight. The closed passenger cabin was located forward of the pilot, whose cockpit was open.*

71 bottom *A KLM Fokker F.VII on a Dutch airfield. This model, made in 1924, could carry up to 10 passengers. The 255-hp engine was increased to 530 hp.*

70-71 *The Junkers F13 hydroplane version. The small German aircraft was designed in 1919 to meet civilian air travel requirements. It could carry only four passengers.*

70 bottom *The conventional version of the Junkers F13 flying over Africa. The first monoplane made entirely of metal, it was a commercial success, selling 350 units.*

producing 425 hp. Subsequently, a longer, tapering fuselage was introduced, the overall length being increased to 33 feet 6 inches. In general, the W33 was used for carrying goods and mail, even though it could be fitted with seats for six passengers. The W34 was used as a passenger-carrying aircraft. In total, 1,990 planes of this family of aircraft (including the K43 military version) were manufactured.

Another famous German firm that successfully converted from military to civil production was Fokker, founded by the Dutchman Anthony Fokker. In 1924, the firm launched the F VII, a high-wing cantilevered monoplane with a fuselage structure in tubular metal and a 364-hp, in-line Rolls-Royce Eagle engine. In March 1925, after building five F VIIs, Fokker moved onto the F VIIA version. This retained the F VII's fuselage but featured numerous detail improvements, and was powered by a radial engine of various types with power outputs ranging from 355 to 550 hp. The aircraft had a wingspan of 71 feet, a length of 47 feet 6 inches and a maximum take-off weight of

11,685 lbs. It could carry a payload of 10 passengers (or about 2,200 lbs of goods) and boasted a top speed of 130 mph. In order to win the Ford Reliability Trial, Fokker transformed one his F VIIAs into a trimotor, with 243-hp Whirlwind engines. This version was extremely successful and was built in series as the F VII-3m. This plane, together with the F VIIB-3m with a larger wing, was widely adopted by European and American operators during the 1930s. The parent company built 74 of the planes; numerous others were built under license in Belgium, Great Britain, Italy, and Poland.

The Birth of Commercial Aviation

In the meantime, civil aviation had also begun to establish a foothold in America, thanks above all to the government's issuance of airmail contracts that gave the pioneering companies a much-needed boost. In fact, the Kelly Act of 1925 enabled American air transport to establish itself, and before long the United States outstripped Europe in this sector.

The first American carrier of the post-war period was Aeromarine West Indies Airways, which was founded in 1920 but ceased operations in 1923 owing to financial difficulties. After 1925 numerous companies began to appear, mainly competing for postal routes which they integrated with passenger transport. The period between 1925 and 1926 saw the birth of Stout Air Services, Florida Airways, Western Air Express and Pacific Air Transport, among others.

73 top Two pamphlets — one English and the other American — providing information on the growing air travel sector of the 1920s and 30s.

73 bottom A photograph from 1930 shows the first group of air hostesses, they worked for the American company, United Air Lines.

Henry Ford, the celebrated automobile manufacturer, also sought to establish himself in aviation. He founded Ford Air Transport Services and developed a modern transport aircraft: the Ford Tri-motor. It was soon carrying America into the skies while attaining legendary status.

The Tri-motor's origins lay in a 1922 design for the Stout 2-AT Pullman, an eight-seater high-wing monoplane equipped with a single 406-hp Liberty engine. In 1926, at Ford's request, Stout developed this design into the 3-AT, but the new aircraft proved to be unsuccessful and led to Stout's dismissal. However, that same year saw the appearance of the Ford 4-AT, an all-metal, high-wing, three-engined monoplane skinned in corrugated metal and seating eight passengers. This plane was very similar to the 3-AT, and first flew on 11 June. The first and most important client for the new plane was Maddux Air Lines of Los Angeles, which purchased 16 of them. In 1928, the 5-AT version was introduced; it was larger, more robust and featured a greater wing area. It had a wingspan of 77 feet 6 inches, a length of just over 50 feet, and a maximum take-off weight of 13,503 lbs. It was powered by three Pratt & Whitney SC-1 engines producing 425 hp. They provided a top speed of 143 mph and an operational range of about 550 miles. Between 1929 and 1931, 117 of these 17-seater 5-ATs were built, while a total of 198 Ford Tri-Motors in over 30 versions were sold to numerous air lines such as American British Columbia, Curtiss Flying Service, Eastern, Northwest, and Transcontinental. The American armed forces used the Tri-Motor for military purposes, as did Australia, Canada, Colombia and Spain. The aircraft proved to be so robust and reliable that a number were still being used for tourist flights in the 1980s.

74 top One of the first Ford Tri-Motors. The Tri-Motor first flew in June 1926 and was a development of the unsuccessful single-engined 3-AT.

74 center The passenger cabin of a Ford Tri-Motor 4-AT which could seat up to 12 passengers. The plane had two pilots.

74 bottom The Ford/Stout 2-AT Pullman of 1922, first of a series that led to the definitive Tri-Motor 5-AT of 1928. It could carry up to 17 passengers.

75 top A three-engined Fokker F.VII with French identification just after landing at a European airport, surrounded by a crowd. The F.VII was the Ford Tri-Motor's main competitor.

75 bottom An excellent photograph of a Ford Tri-Motor 5-AT belonging to American Airways.

A new generation of transport planes was emerging in Europe, the most common types were the Handley Page H.P.42, the Junkers Ju-52, and the de Havilland Dragon biplanes.

In Germany, shortly after the introduction of its successful W33/34 series, Junkers began work on a large new single-engined aircraft designed primarily for cargo work. Designated the Ju-52, the aircraft was completely skinned in corrugated metal, and at the wings' trailing edge had Junkers patented movable aerodynamic surfaces that acted as flaps and ailerons. The Ju-52 flew for the first time on 13 October 1930. Thanks to the power output of about 800 hp guaranteed by its engine, the Ju-52 could carry up to 17 passengers. In 1931, however, Junkers' design department decided to transform it into a tri-motor with the installation of 530-hp Pratt & Whitney Hornet engines. The prototype of this particularly fast version (188 mph) known as the Ju-52/3m took off in April 1932, and was an immediate commercial success. The Ju-52/3m had a wingspan of almost 96 feet, a length of 62 feet and a maximum take-off

weight of 23,148 lbs. The first two Ju-52s were delivered to Lufthansa before the end of 1932; the airline eventually purchased a further 230. Others were exported to Finland, Sweden and Brazil. In all, the Ju-52/2m saw service in over 25 countries in Europe, Africa, Asia, Australia and South America. It enjoyed continuing

success after the Second World War when numerous planes were built in France (as the AAC 1 Toucan) and Spain (as the C-352-L) and was used for both military and civil applications for many years. In 1934 the Ju-52/3mg3e military version was introduced, and thousands were built to serve as cargo planes and bombers.

In contrast to the Ju-52, the Handley Page H.P.42 was an aircraft with antiquated architecture built in response to the specific

76 bottom A de Havilland DH.89 Dragon Six belonging to Britain's Olley Air Service. A total of 930 Dragons were built in various versions for both civil and military use.

77 top The interior of a Handley Page HP.42 'Heracles' transport plane belonging to Imperial Airways. It was normally used on the London-Paris route and could carry 38 passengers.

76-77 A Misr Airwork's de Havilland DH.84 Dragon flies above the Pyramids in Egypt. The Dragon was first manufactured in 1932 to carry passengers on the London-Paris route.

demands of Imperial Airways and its need to maintain links with the distant British colonies. The aircraft was designed with mechanical reliability and passenger comfort in mind rather than speed and large payloads. The result was a four-engined metal biplane with a biplane tail and triple rudders. It was powered by Bristol Jupiter XIF engines that produced 500 hp and gave the plane a top speed of 127 mph. The wingspan was 130 feet, overall length was 89 feet 6 inches, and the plane had a maximum take-off weight of about 29,500 lbs. The first H.P. 42 took to the air in November 1930. Only eight were built; four 24-seater E versions for use on Asian routes and four 38-seater W versions (with 560-hp engines) for use on European routes.

The de Havilland Dragon series of twin-engined biplanes designed for short-haul work was far more successful. The first in the line, the D.H.84, was developed in response to a civilian airline's requirements for an efficient twin-engined passenger aircraft to link England with Paris. The

Dragon was an elegant, six-seat airliner with fixed undercarriage and two 132-hp de Havilland Gipsy Major engines. The plane made its maiden flight on 12 November 1932. A total of 115 were built in England, along with a further 87 constructed under license in Australia. The Dragon was the basis for the D.H. 89 Dragon Six, which was introduced in 1934. This model was equipped with two 203-hp Gipsy Six engines. The production version, which could carry up to ten passengers, was known as the Dragon Rapide. In total, 728 D.H.89 Dragon Rapides were built, with many of them seeing military service during

77 bottom left Seen from above, a Junkers Ju.52 flying Austrian colors. The Ju.52 first appeared in 1930 as a single-engined transport plane; it became successful when, from the seventh plane on, it was fitted with three engines.

77 bottom right A lovely view of the Handley Page 'Heracles' taking off. This four-engined plane could only just reach 130 mph and manage a distance of 500 miles.

the Second World War. The type went on to form the backbone of many post-war airlines such as Jersey Airways, KLM and Iraqi Airways. A number of Rapides were still in use in the 1980s.

In the United States, in the meantime, thanks to the Waters Act of 1930 which revolutionized the airmail contract system, the air transport scene was changing: the major monopolistic companies such as United Air Lines had to give up portions of their market to permit competition. It was within this environment of rationalization that TWA was born out of the merger between Transcontinental and Western Air Express. American Airways then acquired Southwest Air Fast Express, while on the East Coast, Eastern Air Transport took the place of Ludington Air Lines. In 1933, four major companies, American, TWA, Eastern and United Air Lines, dominated the American market, while Pan American monopolized the international routes.

The technical revolution that characterized the period leading up to the Second World War came about in the mid-1930s with the introduction of the first truly modern aircraft. These were to change the face of commercial air transport. The precursor of this new category of aircraft was the Boeing 247, designed toward the end of 1932. This airliner was derived from the Model 215 bomber, but was an all-new and highly innovative design that may rightly be considered as the first of the modern passenger planes. The 247 had a very aerodynamic shape, with a cantilevered low wing into which two engines were faired, and cruciform tailplanes. Moreover, the plane was of all-metal construction, had a retractable undercarriage and was equipped with a pneumatic de-icing system along the length of the wing and tailplane leading edges. The 247 had a wingspan of 74 feet, a length of just over 49 feet and a maximum take-off weight of 13,688 lbs. It was powered by two 600-hp Pratt & Whitney Hornet engines and could carry ten passengers over distances of up to 750 miles at a top speed of 200 mph; more importantly, it could maintain a cruising

speed of no less than 189 mph. The prototype first flew on 8 February 1933, and Boeing immediately received orders for 60 of the 247s from the four United Air Lines companies, while other firms ordered a further 15 planes. In 1934, Boeing introduced the 247D, an improved version of the 247. This variant adopted the new variable pitch propellers, new NACA engine cowlings and an aerodynamic windshield.

In spite of its avant-garde specifications, the initial Boeing 247 was simply too small to be economically viable, and Boeing's production capacity was too low to meet the initial demand for the plane. In 1932, Jack Frye of Trans World Airlines (TWA) was looking for a new plane to replace his Fokker Tri-Motors, but Boeing was obliged to quote a lead-time of two years for the 247. Frye thus invited other constructors to present designs, eventually selecting the one proposed by Donald Douglas. Although TWA's requirements were demanding, the Douglas engineers were determined to produce an aircraft that could out-perform the Boeing 247

while incorporating all the latest technological innovations such as a retractable undercarriage, NACA engine cowlings and flaps (a feature the Boeing lacked) to reduce landing velocity without penalizing cruising speed. The prototype of the new plane, the DC-1 (Douglas Commercial 1) was ready to fly on 1 July 1933. For that era it was an enormous machine, with a wingspan of over 85 feet, a length of 59 feet, and a maximum take-off weight of 17,361 lbs. Two 710-hp Wright Cyclone engines powered the DC-1; these were new and were fitted with the new variable-pitch propellers. The plane was capable of flying and climbing on just one engine. TWA was very satisfied and ordered 25 DC-1s. These were modified, however, to allow sufficient space for flexibility. The fuselage was lengthened by 23.5 inches, which allowed two more seats to be added, for a total of 14. The engines were also uprated. The DC-2 (as the modified plane was designated) stunned the aviation world. Anthony Fokker applied for distribution rights

78 top An American Airlines Douglas DC-2. The DC-2 was 25 inches longer than the DC-1 and could carry 14 passengers rather than 12.

78 bottom left TWA was the first company to introduce the revolutionary Douglas DC-1 in 1933. Here it is about to take off from an American airport.

in Europe, immediately placing a number of DC-2s with KLM, the Dutch national airline. In 1934, in order to satisfy an American Airlines request for an aircraft with couchettes, the Douglas DST was introduced. This variant, which featured 14 couchettes in a wider fuselage, entered service in 1936. However, the plane could also be fitted with up to 21 seats, and in this configuration was designated the DC-3. It was a plane significantly different to the DC-2 in that it had a hydraulic retractable undercarriage, new propellers, new dampers, a redesigned, thinner wing, and a wingspan extended by almost 10 feet.

The DC-3 was considerably easier to fly than its predecessor had been, but what particularly attracted the airlines was its ability to carry 21 passengers, a fact that made it the first airliner in aviation history able to pay its way on passenger ticket sales alone. A company

equipped with the DC-3 was much more likely to make a profit than a loss, and the DC-3 soon became the standard American transport plane. In 1939, 75 percent of all American passenger traffic was carried on DC-3s.

The Second World War saw the mass-production of the DC-3 for the American armed forces (as the C-47 Skytrain for the US Army, as the R4D for the Navy), as well as the Russian air force and the

British RAF, where it was known as the Dakota. Many historians have claimed that one of the principal factors in the Allies' victory was, in fact, the C-47, the indefatigable cargo and parachute drop plane. Its widespread use during the war ensured that once peace had been established there were countless C-47s in various forms and with various engines that continued to be flown successfully throughout the world – up to the present day.

78 bottom right A British European Airways DC-3. This definitive model of the DC family was developed from the DST model. It entered service in 1936 and could carry 21 passengers.

Chapter 6

Seaplanes and Marathon Flights

During the inter-war period the seaplane contributed more to the development and diffusion of aviation worldwide than any other type of aircraft. The fact that the seaplane required no particular infrastructure for take-off and landing operations, but could use any stretch of open water made it ideal for the development of aviation, for the great explorations of distant lands, and for the commercial linking of the continents.

Henri Fabre, a French engineer, built the world's first seaplane. Fabre, who was born into a Marseille shipping family in 1882, was infected with a passion for flight at a very early age. From 1906, he began devoting himself to his hobby, meeting with French aviation pioneers such as Voisin, Blériot and Farman and beginning to build the tethered float gliders he tested on the lake at Berre. In 1909, after developing working models

capable of take-off and landing, Fabre constructed a seaplane with three floats and three 125-hp Anzani engines. However, owing to its excessive weight and the poor hydrodynamic shape of the floats, the design proved incapable of flight. Fabre then built a new, smaller hydro-aeroplane, as it was known, with canard aerodynamic surfaces (i.e., with the main wing and the engine mounted at the rear and the stabilizers at the front). This new model also had three floats, but was powered by a single 50-hp Gnome engine. It took off for the first time on 28 March 1910. The era of the great seaplanes had dawned.

Significant developments soon followed, especially in the military field. In 1911, Italy saw the introduction of two new seaplanes built by the Italian navy officers, Alessandro Guidoni and Mario Calderara, and notable progress was made in France, Belgium and the United States. Glenn Curtiss of America

80 bottom Mario Calderara, an Italian Navy officer, was one of the first hydroplane pilots. Here he is in Brescia at the start of the Olofredi Prize race in 1909.

81 top The world's first hydroplane was built by the Frenchman, Henri Fabre. Here he is testing the plane on Berre Pond on 28 March 1910.

81 center Low over the water, Henri Fabre at the controls of his first successful hydroplane, following the botched attempt of 1909.

81 bottom left Henri Fabre next to one of his planes. He was born in Marseilles in 1882 and died in 1984, aged 102.

81 bottom right Another picture of Fabre's hydroplane, here seen over the Mediterranean near Monte Carlo in 1914.

was particularly successful in developing seaplanes, and his Triad first took off on 26 January 1911. In 1912, bolstered by this experience, Curtiss and his Triad participated in a rally in Monaco. In the same year, Curtiss also produced the Model F, a flying boat with a central hull. The Curtiss Company sold a150 of the Model Fs to the U.S. Navy, and additional ones to other navies, including Italy's.

The Schneider Trophy, instituted in 1912, greatly stimulated progress. The event was an air race reserved from seaplanes, and was the first competition of its kind. The debut race was held at Monaco in 1913, and the winning seaplane was won by a Deperdussin monoplane powered by a 160-hp engine, which managed to complete the course at an average speed of 61 mph.

By the outbreak of the First World War, the seaplane was already a fairly common type of aircraft. During the conflict, naval air services invested heavily in seaplanes, and thousands were manufactured around the world. The planes were particularly useful for spotting and patrol duties, especially in the North Sea and Adriatic regions. The most common types were the Austrian Lohner E and L, the Italian Macchi L.1 (based on a captured Lohner L), and the Anglo-French F.B.A.C. Subsequently, fighter floatplanes such as the Hansa-Brandenburg KDW, W.12 and W.29, the Sopwith Baby, and the Macchi M.5 made their appearance. Other successful seaplanes included the Curtiss H-1 and H-16, the N-9 trainers, the Macchi M.9 and the British Felixstowe F.2A patrol plane.

After the war, conflict no longer provided a stimulus for aircraft development. The armed forces set about promoting and completing great feats of aviation, aiming to demonstrate the aircraft's potential and overall worth. Prior to the war, aircraft capabilities were very limited and aeronautical exploits such as Blériot's crossing of the English Channel in 1909 and Roland Garros' trans-Mediterranean flight (from the Côte d'Azur to Tunisia) in 1913 were relatively tame. The Great War, however, had provided an enormous boost to aeronautical progress and by 1919 there were already land and seaplanes capable of crossing one of the world's traditional barriers, the Atlantic Ocean.

82-83 top Hydroplanes were used extensively during World War I. Here a French plane is being loaded onto a military ship for transportation overseas.

82-83 bottom The Curtiss Hydroaeroplane, first successful American hydroplane, developed in 1911.

83 top The German Arado Ar.196, one of the best-known military hydroplanes, first flew in 1937. More than 600 were built and used in World War II.

83 center After capturing an Austrian Lohner, Italy too was able to build hydroplanes in World War I, such as this Macchi M.5.

83 bottom right The Hansa-Brandenburg W.12, one of the first fighter hydroplanes, was used in World War I. This one belonged to the Austrian Navy.

On the 15 May 1919, the US Navy initiated the first trans-Atlantic flight. Three Curtiss seaplanes took off from Newfoundland to complete a coordinated naval mission with 41 destroyers deployed across the ocean that were to serve as route markers. The aim was to reach the Azores and then Portugal. Owing to a storm only one plane actually reached the Azores intact and was able to fly on to Lisbon, where it touched down on 27 May. The next great feat involving seaplanes was the round-the-world flight, organized by the American army's Air Service in 1923. For this event, the Douglas company built four examples of what it named the World Cruiser (DWC), which was derived from the DT-2 torpedo bomber. These two-seater biplanes were powered by a single 420-hp Liberty engine and were equipped with floats, but could also be fitted with a wheeled undercarriage to allow touch down on dry land. The four aircraft took off from Seattle on 6 April 1924, and followed a route that crossed Alaska, Japan, China, India, France, Great Britain and Newfoundland. Two of them made it through to Washington, D.C. on 9 September, and then on to the West Coast after a flight of over 26,500 miles.

In 1925, Francesco De Pinedo scored an even greater triumph. De Pinedo was an Italian naval officer and a veteran of the Italian-Turkish and Great Wars. With the creation of the Italian Royal Air Force in

1923, De Pinedo left the navy and became a promoter of the seaplane within the new service. It was in order to demonstrate the seaplane's potential that in 1924 he began planning an adventure that would outdo even that of the Americans. He plotted a route of 34,200 miles that took in Rome, Melbourne and Tokyo and included about 15,500 miles of flying close to the coasts, about 5,000 over the open sea, and 4,350 over dry land. Having received authorization to undertake his flight, De Pinedo chose to fly a standard Savoia Marchetti S.16ter seaplane, a biplane with a pusher propeller powered by a 400-hp Lorraine engine, which he baptized *Gennariello*. Lieutenant-Colonel De Pinedo, assisted by Marshal Ernesto Campanelli (a general mechanic), took off on 20 April 1925 from the waters of Lake Maggiore. The flight was not without difficulties. The major ones were due to problems with the lubrication system, but all the stages, from Baghdad to Java, Melbourne, Sydney and Tokyo were eventually completed and the *Gennariello*

84 top One of the US Navy's three three-engined Curtiss NC-4 planes that attempted to cross the Atlantic in 1919, but without success.

84 bottom Two Italian Navy FBA hydroplanes during World War I. Francesco De Pinedo, seated on the plane on the left, was to become famous in 1925 as an intercontinental flier.

successfully touched down on the waters of the Tiber in Rome on 7 November 1925, to great celebrations.

On 13 February 1927, De Pinedo set out on a new adventure aboard the Savoia Marchetti S.55 flying boat *Santa Maria,* accompanied by Captain Carlo Del Prete and engineer Vitale Zacchetti. During this second marathon, De Pinedo visited South America and Amazonia and then headed north toward the United States. At Phoenix, Arizona, the plane caught fire while refueling and had to be replaced. The three intrepid aviators eventually reached Ostia on 16 June, having covered almost 28,000 miles. With his promotion to the rank of general, De Pinedo subsequently organized two great formation cruises for military seaplanes, flying over the southern and eastern Mediterranean in 1928 and 1929. However, the Italian air ministry's upper echelons did not appreciate De Pinedo's his success and the popularity he enjoyed, and he was passed over for the most prestigious appointments.

84-85 In 1923, the US Army planned to circle the world with four Douglas DT-2 World Cruisers. Two managed to complete the trip, between April and September 1924.

85 center The Douglas World Cruiser could be fitted with floats for landing on water and with a conventional undercarriage for on land.

85 bottom De Pinedo and Campanelli on 'Gennariello', the Savoia Marchetti S.16ter they used for the Rome-Melbourne-Tokyo-Rome race.

The last great exploit in which seaplanes played the leading role occurred in 1933. Italo Balbo, the Italian Navy's under-secretary for aviation at that time, initiated the event, following up on the success of the 1930 aerial cruise from Italy and Brazil. In 1933, on the tenth anniversary of the founding of the Italian Royal Air Force, Balbo set about organizing a huge flight from Italy to the United States and back, involving an entire squadron of war planes. The aim was to demonstrate to the world at large the Italian air force's technical and military resources and its ability to dispatch not just one, but a significant number of aircraft to distant lands. After months of preparation at the Orbetello sailing school, the 25 twin-hulled Savoia Marchetti S.55X monoplane flying-boats, each powered by two 930-hp Isotta-Fraschini Asso engines, were ready. The expedition, composed of over 100 men including pilots and support staff, took off from Orbetello on 1 July 1933. Despite a tragic accident at the first stopover in Amsterdam, where an aircraft and one crewman were lost, the rest of the flight went perfectly. Thanks to the crews' training in close formation flying, they dealt brilliantly with the typically poor Atlantic weather. The 24 aircraft reached Chicago, site of the World's Fair, on 15 July and then proceeded to New York. Balbo and his men were given exceptional welcomes in both cities. The expedition then returned to

Rome on 12 August, with 23 aircraft, a second having been lost in the Azores on the way home. The exploit so impressed the English-speaking world that since then the term Balbo has been used in aeronautical jargon as a synonym for a large formation of aircraft.

In the 1920s and 1930s, however, the seaplane was by no means an exclusively military option; it was also used for commercial purposes. The S.55, for example, had made its maiden flight in July 1923 as a military plane but was soon converted to civilian use, given the Italian air ministry's

diffidence about what it saw as an overly innovative machine. In 1926, the S.55, converted to carry ten passengers, entered service with Aero Espresso Italiano and was subsequently exported to various countries. It was only later that the air ministry took an interest and purchased about 100 planes, using them until 1939. Prior to this, in 1919, the SIAI S.16 had been developed as a single-engined monoplane flying boat with a single central hull, built specifically for carrying passengers. It enjoyed considerable success with hundreds of planes were manufactured under license in France and Spain.

86 top North America was the Decennial Long-Distance Flight's goal. Here are some of the 24 Savoia S.55Xs that reached America, taking off from the St. Lawrence River, Montreal, Canada.

86 bottom left The formation of S.55Xs flies over the Statue of Liberty in New York in July 1933 during the Decennial Long-Distance Flight.

86 bottom right Italo Balbo, prime developer of the Italian air force and Under-Secretary of the new Armed Forces, was a great supporter of long-distance competitions which increased the prestige of Italy's government, air force and industry around the world.

87 top left *The Savoia X.55 was the Italian Air Force's most important plane in long-distance flights. It was a single-wing seaplane, with a double-hull, powered by two 930-hp Isotta Fraschini Asso engines that gave it a top speed of 175 mph and a flight distance of 2200 miles.*

87 top right *The goal of the Decennial Long-Distance Flight was the Chicago World Fair. Here Balbo receives an official celebratory welcome in the city.*

87 bottom *Some of the S.555 on the Decennial flight berthed at one of the stops.*

88 top The German Dornier Do.X, built in 1929, was the largest plane in the world at the time. This gigantic 12-motor seaplane was built for the Atlantic passenger routes.

88 bottom left The cross-section of the Dornier Do.X shows the plane's interior layout.

Dornier was another company that made a name for itself by building seaplanes, and in 1922 the Dornier J Wal, which many termed the greatest cargo seaplane of the Twenties, made its maiden flight. The J Wal had a twin-stepped hull, two short stabilizing wings, and a parasol main wing on which two engines were mounted in tandem. It carried a crew of four and had a rear compartment that could accommodate passengers or cargo, with various configurations available to suit purchasers' demands. The plane was designed for both civil and military use. As a clause in the Treaty of Versailles prohibited Germany from building heavy aircraft, serial production was entrusted to the Società Costruzioni Meccaniche in Pisa. The Do. J Wal was immediately successful and was also built under license in Switzerland, Spain, Holland and Japan. It was also used for a number of

geographical expeditions; in 1925, the explorer Roald Amundsen acquired two to use on a trip to the North Pole while in 1932 a number of Wals were used for a round-the-world flight. In 1934, Lufthansa used the seaplane to inaugurate an air mail service between Europe and South America, a route from Stuttgart to Natal in Brazil that took four days and required the presence of a support ship in mid-ocean.

In 1926, Dornier introduced a successor to the J Wal, the Do. R Super Wal. The new plane featured an elongated fuselage and a greater wingspan, and was powered by two 660-hp Rolls-Royce Condor engines. Like the J Wal, the Super Wal carried a crew of four, but passenger capacity was increased to 19 persons. The series continued with the Do. R4 which was introduced in 1927; it was equipped with four 525-hp Bristol Jupiter

engines enabling it to carry a 30% greater payload. The last of the seaplane line developed from the Wal was the Do.X, which at the time of its maiden flight on 25 July 1929, was the world's largest aircraft. The concept behind the Do X's design was that of creating an aircraft capable of carrying 100 passengers across the Atlantic while offering the standards of comfort found on liners and dirigibles. The aircraft had a single central hull, three decks, and was even equipped with cabins with bunks, salons, bathrooms and dining rooms. The fuselage was 131 feet long and the wingspan extended to over 157 feet. The original twelve 500-hp Siemens Jupiter engines proved insufficient to provide the plane, which had a maximum take-off weight of over 11,000 lbs, with an adequate safety margin. They were subsequently replaced with twelve 640-hp Curtiss Conqueror units that allowed the Do.X to complete a test flight with no fewer than 170 passengers. The inaugural cruise got underway on 2 November 1930, but was so dogged by accidents and mechanical problems that after visiting Amsterdam, the Canary Islands and Brazil the Do.X reached New York only after ten months – and became the object of much criticism and derision in the press.

While the magnificent but overly ambitious Do X seaplane never entered regular service this did not mean that the era of the great cargo and passenger carrying flying- boats was over.

Motorraum — Navigationsraum — Funkerraum
Führerraum — Eingang über dem Stummel — Hilfsmaschinenraum
Oberdeck = Kommandodeck — Maschinenzentrale — Küche
Hauptdeck = Passagierdeck

Unterdeck = Betriebsdeck — Treibstofftanks — Wasserruder
Ankerraum — Schlafkabine — Passagierkabinen
Bar — Rauchsalon — Aufenthaltsraum

Querschnitt durch das Flugschiff Do X.   A cross-section of the Do X flying boat.

Dornier GmbH, PR-Abt., Postfach 21 60, 8000 München, Tel. (089) 8 71 54 80

88 bottom right Designed in
1935 as a spotter and patrol
seaplane, the Dornier Do.24
was also used during World
War II. The German, Dutch,
Spanish and French air
forces all used it.

89 top left The Do.X's
elegant passenger cabin of
attempted to offer passengers
every comfort of the period.

89 top right The Dornier
Do.J Wal was perhaps the
best transport hydroplane of
the 1920s. It made its maiden
flight in 1922 and roughly
500 were built. This one is
being loaded on the German
ship 'Westphalen.

89 bottom The arrival of
the Dornier Do.X in New
York on its maiden flight.
Owing to various
difficulties, the trip lasted
from 2 November 1930
until 27 August 1931,
giving rise to largely
well-founded criticism.

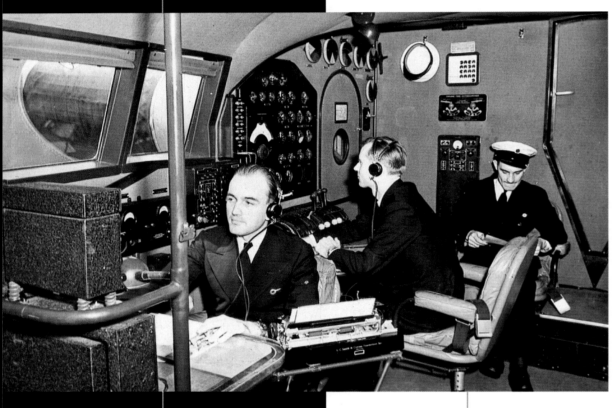

90 top The Boeing 314
Clipper was the largest
passenger seaplane in history.
It entered the trans-Pacific
and Atlantic services for Pan
America in February 1939.
It could carry up to 74
passengers and had a
maximum distance of 3500
miles.

90 center The interior of the
Boeing 314 was spacious and
comfortable. Shown is part of
the crew section where the
radio operator and flight
engineer were housed.

90 bottom The Sikorsky
S.42 was one of the B.314's
predecessors. Pan Am put the
S.42 into service in August
1934 on Caribbean routes,
and later on Pacific routes.

90-91 The Martin M-130,
the S.42's competitor, entered
service in September 1935; it
too was purchased by Pan Am
for use on Pacific routes. Here
it is taking off in San
Francisco Bay. Below, the
Golden Gate Bridge was still
being built.

In fact, in the United States during the 1930s, a number of new aircraft were developed to satisfy the demands of Pan American, the carrier that thanks to its American government contract enjoyed a monopoly on international airmail. In order to support the expansion of Pan Am's routes, Juan Trippe, the firm's managing director, asked Sikorsky (which had already produced excellent transport amphibious aircraft), for a new larger and more capacious plane. The result of this commission was the S-40, introduced in 1929. The S-40 was a single-hull amphibious flying boat with twin tail booms powered by four 580-hp Pratt & Whitney Hornet engines. The plane was capable of carrying 40 passengers on long-haul routes of up to 1,000 miles. The first S-40, named *American Clipper*, entered service in November 1931. The Pan Am consultant, Charles Lindbergh, was already working on proposals for an even better plane. Sikorsky came up with the S-42 while Martin's response was the M-130. Pan

Am purchased both. The S-42 was ready in August 1934, and was immediately put to work on the Caribbean routes.

Pan Am, however, also wanted to fly Pacific routes and to this end an S-42 was modified for use on path-finding flights. In 1935, the company began work on the construction of landing fields on the Central Pacific route at Honolulu, Midway, Wake and Guam. In the October of that year, the Martin M-130 also entered service, an enormous, elegant four-engined plane capable of flying for over 3,170 miles at 150 mph. During this period Pan Am acquired the last of the permits required to establish its network of routes, and the airline began to operate services to the Pacific regions and New Zealand. But in 1937 two accidents involving the loss of M-130s and many lives put the company under pressure. Juan Trippe's reaction was decisive: he unveiled a new strategy: the Atlantic route using the new aircraft he had commissioned the

previous year, the Boeing 314. This was without question the most beautiful commercial flying boat of its era, and through to the 1960s, the Boeing 314 remained the world's largest transport plane. The B-314 was derived from the XB-15 bomber design, from which it retained the broad wingspan of 152 feet coupled to a new twin-deck fuselage that was 106 feet long. The new plane was equipped with a huge centrally mounted cantilever wing and four 1,520-hp Wright R-2600 Cyclone engines. It too carried the name *Clipper*, and could carry 40 passengers in particularly comfortable couchettes or 74 in seats on routes up to 3,500 miles long, at cruising speeds approaching 186 mph. Its maximum take-off weight was a huge 82,122 lbs. The B-314 entered service on 22 February on both the Pacific and Atlantic routes. Shortly afterwards, however, the outbreak of the Second World War was to put a halt to all commercial transport aircraft development.

Seaplanes and amphibious aircraft had continued to find favor in the military sphere, at least with those sectors in which their particular capabilities were of use: maritime reconnaissance, patrol and rescue duties. During the war the Heinkel He-115, Dornier Do.18 and Do.24, Supermarine Walrus, Arado Ar.196, Kawanishi H6K and H8K and the Blohm und Voss Bv.138 all proved their worth. By the most famous examples of the breed were the CANT Z planes, the Short Sunderland, and the Consolidated PBY Catalina.

Thanks to the uncommon talent of the engineer Filippo Zappata, during the 1930s the Cantieri Riuniti dell'Adriatico (CRDA) company produced two successful series of military and civilian seaplanes, with hundreds of examples being constructed. The 7th of February, 1934, saw the maiden flight of the CANT Z.501, a single-hull, monoplane seaplane featuring a parasol wing and powered by a 900 hp Isotta Fraschini Asso XI engine. The aircraft was originally conceived for long-range reconnaissance and bombing duties and had a maximum speed of 171 mph and a range of around 1,500 miles. The Z.501 entered service in 1937 and was used in both the Spanish Civil War and the whole of the Second World War, remaining in service with the Italian air force through to 1948. The Z.501 was shortly followed by the CANT Z.506, which first flew on the 19th of August, 1935. Derived from the Z.505 postal aircraft, this plane was instead destined to carry passengers for the Ala Littoria company. The Z.506 was a low-wing tri-motor equipped with traditional tailplanes and two large floats below the wings. Its 750 hp Alfa Romeo 126 RC 34

radial engines provided it with a maximum speed of 227 mph and a range of around 1,700 miles. It had a maximum take-off weight of over 13 tons and could carry up to 14 passengers. The Italian Royal Air Force ordered the first 32 examples in 1937, adapting them for use as bombers, but with the outbreak of war the Z.506 was relegated to less hazardous duties such as reconnaissance, search and rescue and medical evacuation. The airplane remained in service in Italy through to 1960.

The Short S.25 was instead born in 1937 in response to a British ministry requirement for a new four-engined maritime patrol aircraft. The plane completed its maiden flight on the 16th of October that year while the production version, known as the Sunderland Mk. I, appeared in 1940. This large single-hull monoplane had a high wing in which four 1,024 hp Bristol Pegasus XXII engines were buried. It was crewed by no less than 13 men and its armament of eight 7.7 mm machine-guns earned it the nickname "flying porcupine". As the war proceeded, the Sunderland's general excellence ensured that continually improved versions were developed and it was also used in anti-submarine and anti-shipping roles. The last version, the Mk.V, was equipped with anti-shipping radar and powered by four 1,217 hp Pratt & Whitney engines providing it with a maximum speed of around 211 mph and a range of over 2,670 miles. It could carry a weapons load of up to 5,000 lbs of depth charges or mines and had a maximum take-off weight of around 33 tons. The Sunderland remained in production through to 1945, with around 740 examples being built.

Perhaps the most famous flying-boat (and amphibious aircraft) of all, however, was the Consolidated PBY Catalina, born in 1933 in response to a US Navy brief calling for a new patrol flying-boat.

The first prototype made its maiden flight on 28t March 1935; it was a monoplane parasol wing carrying the two radial engines, a tapering fuselage and a raised tailplane. That year the US Navy ordered the first 60 planes of the production version, the PBY-1. Prior to the outbreak of World War II, Consolidated had introduced a further three versions with gradual improvements, most relating to the engines and armament. The PBY-5A was introduced in 1940, and its amphibious capabilities made it particularly flexible. This version was powered by 1,217-hp Twin Wasp engines and flew at a top speed of 179 mph, with a range of about 2,500 miles. Armed with five machine-guns and carrying a load of up to 4,000 lbs, the PBY-58 had a maximum take-off weight of over 35,250 lbs. The Catalina was built at a frenetic pace in order to satisfy the demands of America and her allies (of whom the RAF took 700 planes), and was used as a spotter, a patrol plane, a bomber, and for search-and-rescue and anti-submarine duties. A total of over 4,500 Catalinas were manufactured, of which about 1,000 were built under license in the Soviet Union). The Catalina was an exceptionally robust and reliable aircraft, and numerous planes remained in service throughout the world into the 1960s. There are still a number of privately owned Catalinas in air-worthy condition.

The end of the Second World War nevertheless marked the onset of the seaplane's inexorable decline. In the field of post-war air transport, the great flying boats were replaced by more economical four-engined land planes which, thanks to their better aerodynamics and lighter weight, flew better and faster. Moreover, the demands of war had led to the widespread building of airfields, which meant that there was no longer any need for planes that could exploit economical stretches of water for take-off and landing operations.

The post-war period did however see the production of numerous seaplanes for specific duties, above all in regions such as Canada, Alaska and the Pacific Islands. A notable example is the Canadair CL214, a high-wing, twin-engined amphibian designed in the mid-Sixties as a specialist fire-fighting plane. Equipped with 2,129-hp Pratt & Whitney radial engines providing it with a top speed of 190 mph, the CL214 can scoop up no less than 5,450 litres of water, which can then be dumped on the nearest forest fire. The plane was updated in 1989 with the introduction of the CL215T version, which was equipped with turboprop engine in place of the original piston units. Then in 1993 the CL415, a production turboprop version featuring a number of aerodynamic and avionics innovations, made its first flight. About 200 planes of the Canadair amphibian series have been sold around the world, and the aircraft is still in production.

Land-based planes were also involved in marathon flights and important expeditions that contributed significantly to the widening of man's horizons and the development of aviation. Perhaps the two most famous exploits were John Alcock and Arthur Brown's flight in 1919, and Charles Lindbergh's solo flight in 1927.

Since 1913 the London *Daily Mail* had been offering the considerable sum of £10,000 for the first aviator to cross the Atlantic Ocean in less than 72 hours, and with at most one refueling stop. The prize lay forgotten during the First World War but the race to win it began immediately after the signing of the armistice, since by 1918 there were both pilots and airplanes capable of the feat. In the spring of 1919, only three weeks apart, two men, both ex-RAF officers, knocked on Vickers' door to propose themselves as candidates for an attempt. One was John Alcock, an expert pilot and instructor; the other

was Arthur Brown, an observer who had specialized in the modern techniques of astronomical and blind navigation. Vickers had an appropriate aircraft for the flight, the twin-engined Vimy bomber that had been modified with the installation of Rolls-Royce Eagle VIII power-units and enlarged fuel tanks that could hold over 750 gallons. After a single test flight, the pair, like the other competitors, decided to make their attempt by flying from

Newfoundland to Ireland to take advantage of the Atlantic's prevailing winds, which blow from west to east. On 14 June 1919, after completing a sea voyage, reassembling the aircraft in a field near St. John, and waiting for favorable weather forecasts, Alcock and Brown prepared for departure. After a nail-biting run and last-second lift-off, the Vimy headed through the fog in the direction of Ireland.

The flight was not trouble-free. First, the

The Great Land Plane Exploits

radio died, then one of the engines shed an exhaust manifold, and finally the crew's heated flying suits stopped working. Ten hours into the flight the pair encountered a storm; they had no choice but to fly straight into it. The Vimy was at the mercy of the air currents within the clouds and fell into a spin; Alcock managed to regain control just fifty feet above the ocean waves. Despite the dark and rain, he and Brown gradually managed to regain altitude, but then they started to meet problems with icing. When they finally emerged into the sunshine Ireland was there in front of them, no more than 125 miles away. The flight had a less than heroic conclusion as the Vimy finished nose-down in a bog near Clifden that, from above, had appeared to be a suitable landing site. However, the crossing had been made — and in just 16 hours and 27 minutes. The two were fêted throughout the country and along with the £10,000 prize, they also received knighthoods.

Charles Lindbergh's Challenge

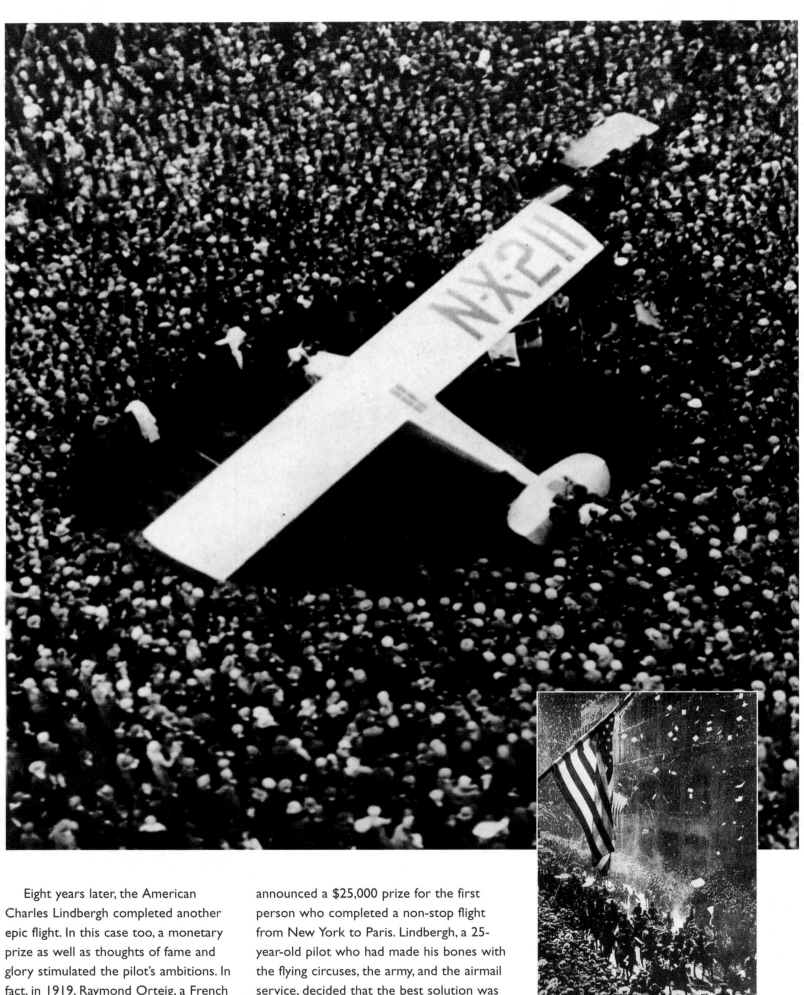

Eight years later, the American Charles Lindbergh completed another epic flight. In this case too, a monetary prize as well as thoughts of fame and glory stimulated the pilot's ambitions. In fact, in 1919, Raymond Orteig, a French entrepreneur living in New York, had announced a $25,000 prize for the first person who completed a non-stop flight from New York to Paris. Lindbergh, a 25-year-old pilot who had made his bones with the flying circuses, the army, and the airmail service, decided that the best solution was that of a special plane with a single pilot and no radio. The Ryan Company of San Diego built Lindbergh's aircraft, and it was named the NYP *Spirit of St. Louis* in honor of its financiers' hometown. The *Spirit of St. Louis* was a small high-wing monoplane dominated by an enormous 375-gallon fuel tank set between the engine and the minuscule cockpit. After meticulous preparations, Lindbergh took off from New York's Curtiss Field on 20 May 1927 at 7.52 in the morning; he had passed an almost sleepless night. The flight was relatively uneventful, apart from the continual attacks of drowsiness Lindbergh suffered for almost all of the 33.5 hours that it lasted before he reached Paris Le Bourget at 10.22 in the evening on 21 May. His flight of over 3,500 miles brought Lindbergh universal honors and an indelible place in the history of aviation.

97 top right Charles Lindbergh with his flying helmet. The 25-year-old American was the first to fly solo across the Atlantic, winning himself a place in history.

97 bottom left The cover-page of a famous song of the period illustrated with Lindbergh's Ryan NYP.

97 bottom right The 'Spirit of St. Louis' was an experimental plane. It was fitted with an enormous 450-gallon fuel tank, but had no radio and its single-seat cockpit offered no view directly forward.

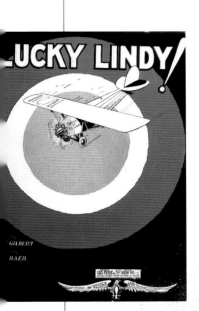

96 top After his arrival in Paris, Lindbergh stopped in London: here is the Spirit of St. Louis surrounded by a cheering crowd at Croydon airport.

96 bottom The City of New York gave Lindbergh an exceptional welcome. Here the pilot is receiving a traditional Lower Broadway ticker-tape reception.

97 top left The Ryan NYP in flight. Lindbergh completed the New York-to-Paris trip in 33 hours, 30 minutes.

The Schneider Trophy

The Coupe d'Aviation Maritime Jacques Schneider (the Schneider Trophy race) was instituted by Jacques Schneider, the son of an arms factory owner of the same name. He wanted the trophy to promote development of seaplanes, the aircraft he felt to be most worthy of attention given that seven tenths of the earth's surface is covered by water. The race was to be held annually at a location decided by the previous year's winners, and a nation winning the trophy three times in five years would retain it in perpetuity.

The first race was staged in Monaco on 16 April 1913, over an aerial circuit of 10 kilometers (6.21 miles) that was lapped 28 times. The winner was a Frenchman, Maurice Prévost, who flew a 160-hp Deperdussin floatplane. On 20 April 1914, the second race, organized by France, was also held in Monaco, and was won by the Englishman Howard

Pixton, flying a Sopwith Tabloid at an average speed of 86.82 mph. The First World War then interrupted the series, but in the post-war period, the spirit of competition and interest in the event were higher than ever. The third race was eventually staged at Bournemouth, England, on 10 September 1919. However, the weather was bad and only Italy's SIAI S.13 actually completed the full distance. As its performance could not be verified because of the fog, the organizers made the decision not to declare a winner but to entrust Italy with the organization of the 1920 race. This was held at Venice, with four aircraft competing, all Italian. Lieutenant Luigi Bologna, flying a SIAI S.12, won the contest. On 11 August 1921, again at Venice, three Italians and a Frenchman contested the trophy, which was won by De Briganti who, flying a Macchi M.7, average 117.91

mph. The sixth race was held at Naples, but the event did not go quite as expected: the Briton Henry Baird defeated the Italian and French teams. He was flying a Supermarine Sea Lion II powered to an average speed of 145.79 mph by a 456-hp engine. The 1923 race, held off the Isle of Wight, saw the first American victory thanks to XX Rittenhouse whose Curtiss CR-3 had the better of the British and French teams, finishing at an average speed of 177.1 mph. Owing to a lack of competitors, the race was not staged in 1924. In 1925 the British and the Italians were beaten by Lieutenant Doolittle, whose Curtiss R3C-2, powered by a 600-hp engine, completed the circuit at the stunning average speed of 232.67 mph. In 1926, both the French and the British chose not to participate. They had had only one year in which to develop new planes and believed that it would be impossible to compete with the Americans. The Italians instead pulled out all stops, with the full support of the Fascist régime, which was eager for a prestigious international victory. Macchi developed the M.39 while Fiat created the 800-hp A.S.2 engine. The race was held at Norfolk,

Virginia, and was an Italian-American challenge. The Macchi proved to be superior to the Curtiss, and the Italians finished first and third, with De Bernardi winning at an average speed of 246.6 mph.

The 1927 race was held at Venice, and this time the British were out in force with an excellent seaplane, the Supermarine S.5. This plane had been developed from the S.4, which had been unable to compete in 1926 because of an accident. Despite the Italian expectations placed on the new Macchi M.52, Captain S.N. Webster emerged victorious, flying an S-5 at an average speed of 281.79 mph. The Italians' defeat led to the founding of the Italian Royal Air Force's High Speed School at Desenzano, where one aim was to reclaim the trophy. After 1927, in recognition that the design of new aircraft was an increasingly complex affair, the race was staged every two years rather than annually. In 1928, however, in a non-Schneider trophy event, Italy did set a world air speed record at Venice, where De Bernardi reached a top speed of 297.96 mph with his Macchi M.52R.

In 1929 the Schneider trophy race was held at Calshot in England. The home team, with the new Supermarine S.6, won at a canter after the two Italian Macchi M.67s had to retire on the second lap.

Italy then plotted revenge with a fabulous new seaplane, the Macchi MC.72, but unfortunately it was not ready in time for the 12th race, held on 13 September 1931. Great Britain completed the event alone with Captain J.N Boothman flying the S.6B, powered by a 2,332-hp Rolls-Royce R engine. By winning this race, Bootham ensured that the Schneider Trophy would remain in Great Britain permanently.

Having lost her chance for victory in the Schneider Trophy race, Italy could take some consolation in the Macchi MC.72's victory in the 1933 Blériot Cup contest. Italy also set the world air speed record in 1934 when Sergeant-Major Francesco Agello achieved 440.90 mph, a record that remained unbeaten until 1939 and still stands as a seaplane record to this day.

98 top The first Schneider Trophy was held in Monte Carlo. It was won by Maurice Prévost piloting this 160-hp Deperdussin single-wing hydroplane.

98 bottom The most important plane missing from the 1931 Schneider Trophy competition was the Macchi MC.72, an exceptional plane for the period but not yet perfected. In 1934, it won a world

speed record for hydroplanes of 443 mph, still unsurpassed.

99 top An advertising poster for the Gloster announces the Model VI's victory in the King's Cup Race of 1929.

99 bottom The French businessman Jacques Schneider started the race that bears his name with the aim of developing hydroplanes.

The Winners

1913	France
1914	France
1919	No race
1920	Italy
1921	Italy
1922	Great Britain
1923	United States
1924	No race
1925	United States
1926	Italy
1927	Great Britain
1929	Great Britain
1931	Great Britain

Chapter 7

The Second World War: the Allies

It can hardly be said that the outbreak of the Second World War came as a surprise; in fact, the military planners had already been at work for some time. For years the winds of war had been blowing across Europe, Africa and Asia, and the 1930s had seen a series of conflicts. All shared a common cause: the extreme nationalism of a number of totalitarian regimes whose expansionism, power politics and, at times, pure greed, had ignited and fed conflicts of various types. The Sino-Japanese War, the Spanish Civil War and the war in Ethiopia had clearly demonstrated to the rest of the world that the regimes in Italy, Germany and Japan were determined to affirm their presumed superiority with the use of force.

In the late 1930s there was a true arms race in Europe, a process leading to the introduction of aircraft that were a great advance on their predecessors, even those designed just a few years earlier. In the United States this process occurred only after 1938, when Congress, alarmed by the military conquests of Japan and the ominous policies of Hitler in Europe, allotted funding for the modernization of the armed forces. In 1939, modernization efforts focused on the US Army Air Corps (USAAC) in particular; until then it had survived on a bare-bones budget, with a minimal number of pilots and only 1,100 obsolete combat aircraft.

In any case, the Great Powers most concerned involved in the military build-up were France and Great Britain. In September 1939, immediately after Hitler's invasion of Poland, they formally declared war on Germany. In the winter of 1939-40, the French air force and the British Expeditionary Force's aerial units were relatively inactive. Then on 10 May 1940, the Germans launched their great western offensive, and the true military and technological confrontation between the Axis and the Allies really began.

The French Armée de l'Air was able to respond to the German attacks with a number of fighters that were technically valid, but inferior to the enemy's planes, especially with regard to their tactical deployment. The French flew the Block MB.151 and 152 and the Curtiss H75 Hawk, the export version of the USAAC's P-36. Their front-line fighters were, however, the Morane-Saulnier MS-406 and the Dewoitine D-520. The former was the most numerous and in 1940 was in service with eleven fighter squadrons. Its origins lay in the MS-405, a modern, low-wing, all-metal fighter with a closed cockpit and retractable undercarriage, designed in response to a specific ministry brief issued in 1934. A total of 15 MS-405s were ordered in 1937, but production subsequently concentrated on the MS-406, which had a lighter wing and a more powerful Hispano-Suiza engine. The threat of war led to an order for 1,000 MS-406s, but the plane was never a match for the German fighters, in particular the more agile and more powerful Messerschmitt Bf-109E. The MS-406 was nonetheless employed in the defense of France, and purchased by other countries such as Switzerland and Finland, where it was used successfully in the war against the Soviet Union.

The French air force's best fighter was unquestionably the D-520, introduced in 1936 as a rival to the MS-406. This Dewoitine aircraft had modern lines and boasted avant-garde performance. In 1939 the French government decided to order serial production of 700 D-520s. However, the decision had been taken too late On the outbreak of war on the western front, even though 400 aircraft had been delivered, only one fighter group was equipped with the new plane, and this group was still working up to combat status. While the D-520 was a worthy rival for the Bf-109, it was unable to influence the outcome of the conflict. Following the armistice, the German and Italian air forces took over numerous D-520s and used them as advanced trainers and reserve fighters.

In the mid-1930s, Great Britain found that the Royal Air Force had fallen behind the times. In 1940, the RAF was still operating obsolete planes such as the Gloster Gladiator and the Fairey Battle light bomber. Thanks, however, to the process of rearmament that had been underway for some years, the RAF also had a reasonable number of modern aircraft such as the Hawker Hurricane fighter and the Bristol Blenheim bomber. The Hurricane, unquestionably one of the most famous and glorious of all Britain's fighters, was first mooted as early as 1933 when the Hawker designer, Sydney Camm, began work on the successor to the Fury biplane. The

new aircraft was extremely advanced for its day, equipped as it was with a low-set cantilever wing, a closed cockpit and retractable undercarriage. Moreover, the Hurricane was fitted with no less than eight 7.7 caliber machine guns and was powered by a 1,039-hp Rolls-Royce engine. The Hurricane completed its maiden flight on 6 November 1935, and flight-testing proved it to be a truly excellent, fast and maneuverable fighter. In 1936, the Air Ministry ordered 600 Hurricanes, which began to enter service in December 1937 and were eventually to constitute the RAF Fighter Command's backbone.

Following the unsuccessful French campaign, the Hurricanes assigned to 32 RAF squadrons were responsible for bearing the brunt of the German attacks during the Battle of Britain in 1940, managing to repel waves after wave of Luftwaffe bombers and their fighter escorts. In 1941, the Hurricane began to show its limitations when compared to the best of the British and German fighters, but it continued to operate in the skies above Great Britain and in the Mediterranean theater. Thanks to the introduction of a new, stronger wing, the hurricane also continued to enjoy success as a fighter-bomber. The Mk.IIC was armed with four 20-mm cannons, while the Mk.IV had 40-mm cannons and was able to launch bombs and rockets.

The Hurricane was built in about 20 different versions for a total of over 14,200 planes, and offered a naval version (the Sea Hurricane) that operated from aircraft carriers. The Hurricane and served in the Royal Air Force for the duration of the war and through to 1947; it was also used by 14 other air forces, including that of the Soviet Union, which received 3,300 planes.

100 top The British Fairey Battle bomber made its maiden flight in 1936. The RAF flew more than 1000 of them early in World War II, but the plane was dramatically and immediately superseded technically.

100 bottom The Hawker Hurricane was the mainstay of the British defense in 1939-1940. It entered service in 1936 and was still a valid fighter during the Battle of Britain. Shown here is the RAF's 71st 'Eagle' Squadron, formed by American volunteers.

101 first picture The Morane-Saulnier MS-406 fighter was the French air force's most numerous plane in 1940, but it was no match for the German Messerschmitt Bf.109.

101 second picture The Bloch MB.151 fighter and its MB.152 version were also used by L'Armée de l'Air, but neither was up to the tasks it was required to perform.

101 third picture The Gloster Gladiator biplane, another RAF fighter at the start of the war, was used in minor theaters, like the Mediterranean.

101 fourth picture Mk. I Hawker Hurricanes of the 111th Squadron in formation over Northolt, Middlesex. These fighters defended London in the first phases of the Battle of Britain.

The Hurricane's decline as a front-line fighter was not a major problem for the RAF as its successor had been available for some time. This was the famed Supermarine Spitfire, an aircraft so beautiful and effective as to gain the respect and envy of even enemy pilots.

The Spitfire, one of the greatest fighters in the history of aviation, was designed shortly after the Hurricane and completed its maiden flight on 5 March 1936. The aircraft was the triumph of Reginald Mitchell, a designer who had gained a solid reputation by creating the world's fastest planes, the winners of the Schneider Trophy. In 1931 he began work on a fighter, the Supermarine Type 224, but probably underestimated the complexity of the project. The resulting design was a failure. Mitchell then decided to shorten the wingspan and the fuselage and to adopt a retractable undercarriage. The result was the Type 300, which was still too slow when climbing. The solution to the problem arrived in 1934, when Supermarine reached an agreement with Rolls-Royce for the supply of a new engine,

the Merlin; with this power unit the Type 300, eventually to become known as the Spitfire, was transformed. After its maiden flight, the test pilot Joseph Summers exclaimed, "Don't touch anything."

The Spitfire was a sleek, elegant machine, but it was also innovative and highly efficient, so much so that a number of its features such as the elliptical wing and the semi-stressed skin initially caused production problems. In terms of both the structure and the engine, the Type 300 had grown out of work done on aircraft developed for the Schneider Trophy contest. The plane was equipped with the same armament as the Hurricane but boasted a more powerful engine and handled magnificently. The first production Spitfires were delivered in 1938, and by 1939 the Air Ministry had ordered 4,000 aircraft to be constructed by a number of companies. At the start of the war only nine squadrons were equipped with Spitfire Mk.Is, but their numbers grew rapidly. The Mk.V appeared in the March

102 top left The
Supermarine Spitfire was
Britain's most famous fighter
in World War II; it owed its
success to its manufacturer's
experience in the Schneider
Trophy.

102 top right A Spitfire Mk.
XII with trimmed wings
during an exercise over
Britain in 1944. The Spitfire
remained in production until
1948; in total, almost 23,000
were produced.

1941 with heavier armament and a more
powerful engine (the 1,440-hp Merlin). This
version, which was capable of over 373 mph at
19,500 feet, was also used as a fighter-bomber.

In July 1942 the Mk.IX was introduced to
meet the threat of Germany's new Focke-Wulf
190. In 1943, the Spitfire began to be equipped
with the 2,050-hp Griffon engine that, together
with a five-bladed propeller, made the Mk.XIV

one of the fastest aircraft in the world, capable
of matching the best the Germans could offer.

Production of the Spitfire continued
through to 1948 with over 22,800 planes being
built in some 30 versions. More than 20 air
forces, including those of the Soviet Union and
the United States, used the plane. Numerous
aces flew the Spitfire. From the RAF's
standpoint, the most important of them was

James "Johnny" Johnson, who shot down 38
enemy fighters. In no fewer than 515
missions, he was only hit once and survived
the conflict, continuing to serve with the RAF
in the post-war period. It is sad to record
that Reginald Mitchell, designer of the Spitfire,
was never able to enjoy his creation's success.
He died of cancer in June 1937, a year before
the Spitfire entered service.

102 bottom The Spitfire
production line,
Southampton, 941. Some of
the plane's most advanced
technical characteristics
initially gave problems when
mass-produced.

103 top Duxford airdrome,
1939: a squadron of Mk.
I Spitfires taking off in an
emergency exercise.

103 bottom A formation of
Mk. XII Spitfires in flight in
May 1944 before the D Day
landings in Normandy. This
model had the more powerful
2050-hp Rolls-Royce
Griffon engine.

Two other important Second World War British fighters were the Hawker Typhoon and Tempest. The Typhoon was developed in the late 1930s in response to an Air Ministry requirement for an eventual successor to the Hurricane fighter. Hawker came up with two prototypes, each of which was fitted with one of two new engines specified in the brief, the Rolls-Royce Vulture and the Napier Sabre. The design using the first of these engines, the Tornado, was abandoned, while the second, the Typhoon, went ahead, despite myriad difficulties encountered during the final development of the engine. The prototype first flew on 24 February 1940. However, problems with the engine were

20- mm cannons and 2,000 lbs of bombs or rockets, making it a deadly adversary for enemy vehicles. Assigned to the 2nd Tactical Air Force, the Typhoons could operate from advanced bases close to the front lines, frequently little more than fields with improvised runways, stands and maintenance hangers. Used in this way, the Typhoon could be kept in the air continuously and could easily support the land forces, among which there would have been an air force officer (the so-called FAC, Forward Air Controller). When required, the FAC would call up the planes and guide them to enemy groups that were obstructing the advance of the Allies' armor. It was above all with the Typhoon that

104 *The Gloster Meteor, Britain's first jet aircraft, first flew in March 1943. In 1945 it was sent to the Belgian and German fronts but was not up to the class of the Messerschmitt Me.262.*

105 top left *A formation of Mk. IA Typhoons on a training flight over England. Initially, the plane was supposed to be an aerial-defense fighter, but proved to be very dangerous to pilot.*

105 top right *A Hawker Typhoon fighter-bomber with four 20-mm cannons and eight air-to-ground underwing rockets, which were deadly against armored vehicles.*

105 center *Close-up of an RAF Gloster Meteor; it shows the central position of the wings, the two jet engines and the four 20-mm cannons in the nose.*

then compounded by certain structural failures, and after a number of fatal accidents shortly after the Typhoon entered service in 1941, it was threatened with withdrawal. Remedial work was doe on the design, and in 1942 the Air Ministry decided to continue using the airplane, not as an interceptor but as a fighter-bomber. In all, more than 3,000 of these fighter-bombers were manufactured.

The Typhoon's new career began in August 1942, and from 1943 on the plane proved to be an excellent tactical support weapon, known to be at its best in low-level flight. The Typhoon was never an easy plane to fly, but it built its reputation in the summer of 1944 when it participated in the Normandy landings and the Allied troops' advance across northern Europe into the heart of Germany. It was armed with four

the Close Air Support strategy was born and developed.

The Typhoon's successor was the Tempest, a variant design (initially known as the Typhoon Mk.II) intended to be operated as an interceptor. The Tempest Mk.I made its maiden flight on 24 February 1943, but continuing problems with the Sabre IV engine resulted in it being abandoned in favor of the Mk.V, which was equipped with the Sabre II engine. This version, which first flew on 21 June1943, was approved for serial production. It proved to be powerful and extremely fast at all altitudes. The Tempest Mk.II was then introduced with the Centaurus engine and improved aerodynamics, thanks to adoption of an annular radiator that made the nose more streamlined. More than 1,500 Tempests were built and the plane was retained in service in the post-war period until 1951.

The last of the RAF's famous Second World War fighters was the Gloster Meteor. Its fame derived largely from the fact that it was the first and only Allied jet fighter that actually took part in the war. The origins of the Meteor dated back to 1940 when the Air Ministry decided to press on with research on jet propulsion. The experimental Gloster E.28/39, propelled by a Whittle W.1 engine, was first British jet aircraft; it made its maiden flight on 15 May 1941. Gloster then built a Meteor equipped with a later version of this power unit, the Whittle W.2B/23, producing 1,697 lbs of thrust, with the twin engines buried in the mid-mounted wing. Eight such prototypes were constructed. The first new Meteor to fly, on 5 March 1943, was the fifth in the series. An initial batch of 20 planes of the production version was ordered, and they entered service in June 1944. They were

105 bottom The Typhoon's successor was the Tempest Mk.V, which could be used as a fighter or a fighter-bomber. It had the same armament as the Typhoon but its Centaurus 2550-hp engine gave it a maximum speed of 442 mph.

immediately employed over England to intercept German V1 flying bombs. About 200 planes of the subsequent Meteor F Mk.III version were built and assigned to number of squadrons. They saw action in 1945 in Belgium and Germany. The Meteor was not, however, a particularly fast aircraft and was generally inferior to the Messerschmitt 262, which it never actually met in combat. The Meteor had a highly successful post-war career. More than 25 different versions, including a trainer, were developed; a total of over 3,800 Meteors were built and were purchased by 14 different countries. The RAF employed the Meteor until 1961; it saw combat action in Korea and in the Arab-Israeli wars.

106 top The four-engined Halifax bomber entered RAF service in 1940. More than 25 versions were developed and over 6000 planes built. Shown here is a Handley Page HP.57 Halifax Mk.III.

106 center The Short S.29 Stirling was a contemporary of the Halifax. It first flew in May 1939 and entered service in August 1940, but was quite soon surpassed and in 1943 was relegated to secondary duties.

106 bottom A daytime bombing raid on Cologne, 18 August 1941. The RAF did not take long to take the war in the air directly to the heart of enemy territory.

107 Cold, uncomfortable and noisy: inside a Halifax bomber during a raid on Germany in October 1941. The machine-gunners search the sky for enemy fighters.

During the Second World War the RAF successfully employed various types of bombers. Heavy bombers included the Short Stirling, Handley Page Halifax and Avro Lancaster; light bombers included the Bristol Blenheim and Beaufighter and the de Havilland Mosquito. The Stirling and the Halifax had almost parallel careers, both being designed in 1936 in response to the Air Ministry's requirement for a new medium bomber. Both aircraft were equipped with four engines and both flew for the first time in 1939, the Stirling on 14 May and the Halifax on 25 October. The two planes' shared characteristics ended there, however. The Halifax was by far the more modern of the two and could reach a considerably higher altitude than the Stirling. The Halifax Mk.III version that went into service in 1943 was fitted with Hercules radial engines that improved its performance and ensured that together with the Lancaster, the Halifax remained in front line service throughout the war. In addition to use as a bomber, the Halifax was used for transport and glider-towing duties and for dropping parachutists. In total, 6,176 planes were built. From mid-1943 on, the RAF diverted the Stirling from bombing to transport and glider towing.

The most important British bomber of the war was in fact the Lancaster, an aircraft that evolved curiously out of an unsuccessful project. In response to an Air Ministry brief, Avro had built a heavy twin-engined bomber, the Manchester, powered by Rolls-Royce Vulture engines that proved to be insufficiently powerful and somewhat unreliable. In mid-1940, in light of this unsatisfactory performance, Avro decided on a complete and urgent redesign, focusing on a four-engined layout using Rolls-Royce Merlins, redesigned tailplanes and a greater wingspan. The result was the best British bomber of the war: nine factories built 23 different versions, for a total of more than 7,300 Lancasters.

The first Lancaster flew on 9 January 1941, and the type entered service in January 1942.

The Lancaster was also used for radar countermeasures, reconnaissance and maritime patrol duties, and remained in service until the 1950s. It was the RAF's principal bomber; it could carry the heaviest bombs and it shouldered most of the weight of the British night bombing offensive over Germany and occupied Europe. The Lancaster dropped several special-purpose bombs. They included the "Tallboy," an armor-piercing 12,000-pounder used, for example, to sink the *Tirpitz*; the 22,000-lb "Grand Slam" that achieved supersonic speed during descent; and a remarkable Barnes Wallis-designed bouncing bomb – a 9,250-lb cylinder bomb used to destroy the dams servicing the Ruhr's hydroelectric power stations. This delicate mission, perhaps the most famous of all those flown by the RAF during the war, was entrusted to 617 Squadron, the "Dambusters" as they became known, specially formed for the task and led by the veteran Lieutenant-Commander Guy Gibson. The mission was difficult because of the extreme precision required. The dam-busting bomb was set rotating at 500 rpm by a hydraulic motor before the drop; it had to be released at 250 mph from a height of 60 feet above the water and between 1,200 and 1,345 feet from the

dam. Only within these parameters would the bomb strike the face of the dam and sink to a depth of 40 feet before exploding. 617 Squadron had only six weeks in which to prepare for the raid. The squadron took off for Germany on the night of 16 May 1943. Results met expectations: two of the three dams were breached. Success had its price, however: eight of the 18 crews failed to return. Guy Gibson himself died in September 1944, shot down while returning from a raid over Germany. It was to have been his last mission.

The first of the famous British light bombers was the Bristol Blenheim, originally designed as a fast, twin-engined passenger plane. The Blenheim made an immediate impression during its maiden flight on 12 April 1935: it was faster than any fighter then in service. A military version of the plane was

developed and was flown for the first time on 25 June 1936. Bristol built almost 6,400 Blenheims, and the aircraft remained in service throughout the war, even though its performance advantage became eroded. The Bristol Beaufighter, a heavily armed twin-engined aircraft, made its first flight on 17 July 1939, and entered service in September 1940 as a night-fighter. Such was the quality of the design that day-fighter and Coastal Command strike versions were subsequently developed. The Beaufighter achieved its full potential in the Mk.VI and Mk.X versions, and the plane eventually carried rockets and torpedoes used against shipping and submarines. Almost 6,000 Beaufighters were built in 22 versions, and it remained in service for the duration of the war.

A plane almost as famous as the Spitfire, the de Havilland Mosquito, together with the Supermarine fighter and the Avro Lancaster, became a RAF symbol in the Second World War. The Mosquito came into existence in 1938; it was a product of de Havilland's private development program. Initially, the experts considered the plane to be too advanced: for this reason the Air Ministry

109 top right A two-engined Bristol Blenheim Mk.IV making a sharp turn early in the war. When introduced in 1935, it was the RAF's fastest fighter.

109 bottom Loading bombs into an RAF Lancaster. The air offensive against German cities and factories was one of the keys to Allied success in World War II.

rejected it no less than three times. Only the tenacity of Patrick Hennessy, a Ford manager seconded to the development of British aeronautical production, enabled the Mosquito to go into production. Once the Mosquito had demonstrated its merits in flight, there was no longer any question as to its suitability. In fact, following the outbreak of war, the authorities realized that an aircraft of this type, with a frame made of wood (a non-strategic material), would be extremely useful. Developed as a light bomber, the Mosquito first flew on 25 November 1940 and entered service in 1941. Thanks to its outstanding performance (a top speed of 400 mph, great

maneuverability, a rapid rate of climb, a 1,000-lb bomb load, a range of about 1,500 miles) and economical construction that earned it the nickname "Wooden Wonder," the Mosquito was soon developed for reconnaissance and night-fighter use. On 17 September 1941, the Mosquito undertook its first mission. Given its great speed, this was a reconnaissance flight extended as far into France as Bordeaux. More than 7,700 Mosquitoes were built in more than 40 versions, and the plane was used by the air forces of 18 countries. The Mosquito remained in service with the RAF through to the early 1960s.

110 top left The Bell P-39 Aircobra entered service in January 1941. It had several defects and was never appreciated by American pilots. The Russians, however, did like it and used about 4800 of the fighter-bombers, which they received from the United States.

110 The Curtiss P-40 Warhawk entered service in 1940. This fighter enabled the American air force to take on the Japanese in the first few months of the war; however, it was not up to scratch and was soon relegated to minor duties.

111 top The Japanese attack on Pearl Harbor on 7 December 1941 forced the United States to enter World War II. Here the NAS base on Ford Island is under enemy fire; in the background, the USS Shaw and USS Nevada are in flames.

During the 1930s and 1940s, the United States' aeronautical industry, like that of Great Britain, had to accelerate its output if it hoped to keep up with and eventually overtake the technical standards set by its adversaries. On the outbreak of the war in Europe, the USAAC's most modern aircraft were the Bell P-39 Airacobra and the Curtiss P-40 Warhawk, neither of which were top-drawer fighters. The former had aroused great enthusiasm when it first appeared in 1937, equipped as it was with a 37-mm cannon, a

turbocharged engine located centrally behind the cockpit, and the first example of a retractable tricycle undercarriage with a nose-wheel. However, after military modifications that included elimination of the turbocharged engine in favor of a more traditional unit, the P-39 proved to be a heavy, clumsy aircraft unsuited for use as a fighter. Nonetheless, the airplane was approved for serial production and entered service in January 1941. The Americans never loved it and the British rejected it, with only Russia appreciating its

qualities as a robust fighter-bomber. In fact, the Soviet air force received almost 4,800 of the 9,588 P-39s that Bell manufactured.

The Curtiss P-40 Warhawk fared better than the Bell P-39. It completed its maiden flight on 14 October 1938, and was immediately ordered into serial production, with the first Warhawks coming into service as early as 1940. The P-40 offered the advantage of immediate availability as well as respectable performance, and this allowed for high-volume production in a period of

111 bottom Innovative and unmistakable, the Lockheed P-38 Lightning fighter had exceptional performance and long-distance capability. It was used in the most important American assaults; more than 10,000 were made.

emergency. The P-40 was immediately adopted by the RAF as the Tomahawk, and was also used by the American volunteer "Flying Tigers" in China between December 1941 and July1942. Until the appearance of the new Bell P-38s and Curtiss P-47s, the P-40 was the best American fighter of the war, and it remained in production to satisfy the Allies' requirements. By December 1944, more than 13,700 Warhawks had been built.

After the United States entered the war following the Japanese attack on Pearl Harbor

on 7 December 1941, two new and significantly better fighters were introduced. The first was the Lockheed P-38 Lightning, designed in response to a brief issued by the USAAC in 1937 that called for a high-altitude interceptor capable of 528 mph at 19,500 feet and of climbing to its optimum operating altitude in 6 minutes. Many companies felt that these demands were impossible to meet, but Lockheed decided to make an attempt. The resulting design incorporated two turbocharged engines mounted in twin fuselages connected by the wing and twin tailplanes; the cockpit and the armament were set in a pod at the center of the wing. This was a decidedly innovative layout, but when the prototype made its first flight on 27 January 1939, its performance impressed the army and it was approved for serial production. The P-38, of which more than 9,900 were built, began to enter service at the end of 1941. The plane was at its best in the Pacific theater, where its great range was particularly advantageous.

The P-38 was flown by great American aces, such as Bong and McGuire. Richard Bong was sent to the front in November 1942, assigned to the 35th Fighter Group, then fighting in the Pacific. He completed a number of duty tours in this theater, attaining the rank of major and scoring a USAAF record total of 40 victories. He received the Congressional Medal of Honor, the highest American military award. Bong continued his career as a test pilot, but on 6 August 1945, while testing a Lockheed P-80, his aircraft crashed in flames and he was killed instantly.

In the second half of 1942, the P-38 began operating in Europe and Africa, but in these situations the Republic P-47 Thunderbolt proved to be the better of the two. This fighter developed out of a number of reworkings of a basic project headed by the aircraft designer Alexander Kartveli and the air force's own experts. Born as the AP-10, a light fighter, the plane was eventually enlarged, strengthened and equipped with the most powerful engine available at the time, the 2,000-hp Pratt & Whitney Double Wasp. In June 1940 it received approval as the XP-47B. It was to be the heaviest single-engined fighter of the Second World War, with a maximum take-off weight of almost 20,000 lbs. The P-47 completed its maiden flight on 6 May 1941, and went into production in February 1942. The 56th Fighter Group, stationed in England, was the first operational unit to use the p-47 in combat, and employed it as a bomber escort. In spite of its tubby, clumsy appearance, the P-47 was a fast, well-armed and robust fighter that proved its worth in dogfights as well as in fighter-bomber duties. By December 1945 more than 15,600 P-47s had had been built, and in the post-war years the plane remained long in service with numerous Allied air forces.

Of all the fighters flown by the US Army Air Force (as it was known from 1942 on), the North America P-51 Mustang was the greatest and most famous – a true thoroughbred of the air. This plane was the fruit of close collaboration between the United States and Great Britain. In April 1940, Britain was desperately seeking fresh arms with which to thwart the German offensive, and discussions with North American led to the definition of a project that was to use the same Allison V12 engine as the P-40, but mated to a better airframe. The only condition imposed by the British was that the aircraft should be ready in 120 days. North American actually took three days less than that, producing an extremely advanced plane equipped with a laminar wing. The RAF

named the new fighter the Mustang Mk.I. It first flew on 26 October 1940, and its performance was excellent at low level, but dropped off notably at higher altitudes. The British thus put it into service in April 1942 as a reconnaissance and ground-attack plane. Both the British and the Americans felt that the Mustang's performance could be improved by replacing the Allison engine with the more powerful Rolls-Royce Merlin, produced under license in America by Packard. The new version, designated as the P-51B, was decisively superior to any other fighter then in service and was immediately put into production: it first saw action in Europe in 1943. The definitive version, the P-51D, was introduced early in 1944 and adopted a new bubble cockpit canopy that reduced the dimensions of the fuselage. The Americans used this plane to escort their

bombers deep into the heart of Germany, and it proved to be a supreme interceptor. In 1944, the Mustang was the world's fastest fighter, with the exclusion of the first, very rare, jet aircraft. It was nonetheless a adversary to be reckoned with even by the Messerschmitt Me.262: on 7 October 1944 Lieutenant Urban Drew of the 361st Fighter Group swooped on two Me-262s as they were taking off, and shot them both down. On 25 February a formation of P-51s from the 55th Fighter Group came upon a German airfield just as an entire squadron of Me-262s was taking off and managed to shoot down six: the American pilots, confident of their P-51s' capabilities, were not easily intimidated by the new German jets. The Mustang's success is easily demonstrated by the statistics: over 15,400 were built and over 50 nations' air forces flew them until the 1960s.

112 top A North American P-51 Mustang is directed by a USAAF specialist before take-off on a mission escorting American bombers over Germany.

112 bottom left The Republic P-47 Thunderbolt looked heavy but was one of the fastest aircraft of the war, capable of 431 mph. Seen here is a reconditioned P-47D in the colors of the 366th Fighter Squadron, 358th Fighter Group, in France in 1944.

112 bottom right P-47D first series aircraft still featured the old-style cockpit canopies. The plane shown here has been restored and has the colors of the aircraft flown by Cameron Hart, 63rd Fighter Squadron, 56th Fighter Group, at Boxted in December 1944.

113 left A P-51D Mustang performing acrobatics. With two underwing, releasable fuel tanks, the Mustang proved an excellent fighter-escort plane able to accompany bombers into the heart of Germany.

113 right The North American P-51 Mustang was probably the best fighter of the entire Second World War and stayed in service with the USAF from 1943 till 1957. More than 15,400 Mustangs were built and more than 50 air forces round the world used the plane.

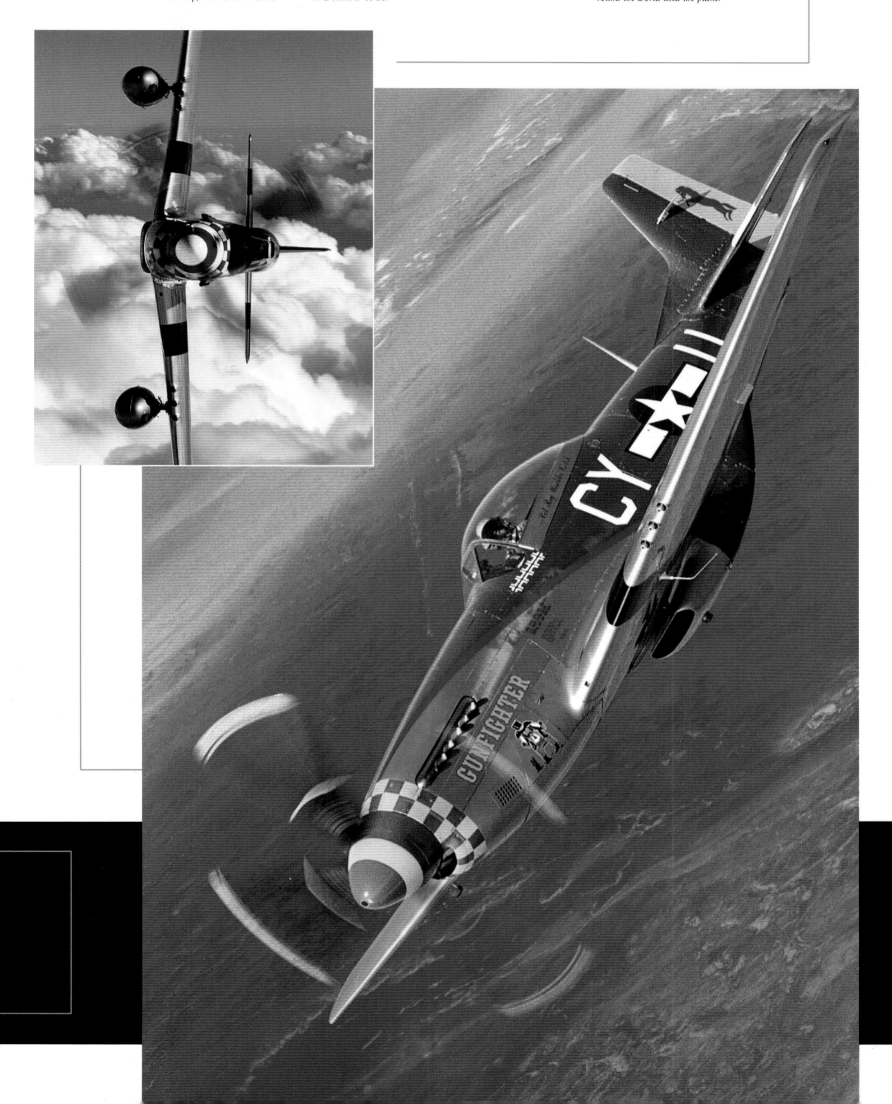

In fact, the planes saw action in a number of conflicts after the end of the Second World War. The American aviation industry also had to satisfy the navy's demands for carrier-borne fighters. In this field, Grumman seized the lion's share of orders, with the company turning out a series of increasingly advanced aircraft. The US Navy's first modern fighter was the Grumman F4F Wildcat, the firm's first all-metal monoplane. The F4F was developed in 1936 and completed its maiden flight on 2September 1937. After a number of modifications had been made, it entered service in 1940, first with Britain's Royal Navy (where it was known as the Martlet), and

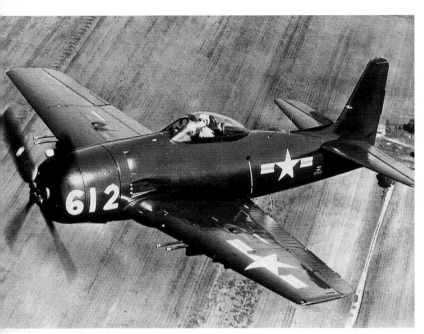

then from December of that year with the US Navy. The Wildcat, with production totaling 7,800 planes, was no better than the Japanese Zero, but thanks to the tactics developed by the American pilots, it managed to fend off the Zero until 1943, when it was replaced by the F6F Hellcat. Th F6F resulted from wartime experience that had shown the need for a more powerful engine, cockpit

armor, more ammunition, and more accommodating flying characteristics. The first Hellcat flew on 26 June 1942. Given the climate of emergency, the testing and development processes were extremely rapid; the plane was in fact pressed into service as early as January 1943. In total more than 12,200 Hellcats were built. The US Navy employed the F6F throughout the Pacific theater, where it proved to be superior to the various Japanese fighters, including the Zero. The Royal Navy also used the Hellcat.

At much the same time as it adopted the Hellcat, the US Navy introduced another carrier-borne fighter, the even faster Vought F4U Corsair, albeit after a more difficult period of gestation. The F4U's design dated from 1938, and the prototype made its maiden flight on 29t May 1940. During the course of the year the 4FU's stunning performance became

114 bottom The Grumman F4F Wildcat, which entered service in 1941, enabled the US Navy to compete during the first few months of the war. Though later surpassed in performance, it remained in service until 1943. Britain's Royal Navy also used the Wildcat, which it called the Martlet.

115 top The Grumman F6F Hellcat (another 'cat') was the Wildcat's successor on the American aircraft carriers, entering service in January 1943. Shown here is a Hellcat taking off from the USS Yorktown. The propeller-tip aerodynamic effects indicate the humidity of the air.

115 bottom A Hellcat fighter photographed on the deck of the USS Lexington on 13 July 1944, during the battle of Saipan in the Mariana Islands.

114 top The Vought F4U Corsair, an excellent fighter/fighter-bomber, was in service with the US Navy and Marines from 1943. Shown here is an F4U-1A in 1944, flown by Navy Lieutenant Ira "Ike" Kepford of Squadron VF-17.

114 center The Grumman F8F Bearcat, the US Navy's most advanced fighter during World War II, entered service in 1944. It had a 2129-hp engine providing a speed of 430 mph.

apparent; it was the first plane to break the 400 mph barrier in horizontal flight. However, modifications were required. These included the adoption of heavier armament and the relocation of the fuel tanks, with the consequent setting back of the cockpit to the detriment of forward vision. This last factor caused considerable problems in carrier-based use of the planes, and the first ones to enter service were actually assigned to the Marines, who from February 1943 flew them from land bases. It was only in April 1944 that the F4U was approved for carrier operations. The Corsair nonetheless proved to be an excellent fighter and fighter-bomber and remained in production until 1952, with over 12,500 being built.

The US Navy's best fighter, and indeed the best carrier-borne piston-engined fighter of all time, however, was the F8F Bearcat. A result of Grumman's policy of continual refinement of its successive models, the Bearcat was designed in 1943 and made its first flight on 21 August 1944. Compact, fast, maneuverable, and with an outstanding rate of climb, the Bearcat was immediately put into production, though the Allied victory in 1945 meant that many of the ordered planes were cancelled. About 1,260 Bearcats were built, and the plane remained in service with the US Navy until 1952 and throughout the 1950s with the navies of other countries, including France, South Vietnam and Thailand.

116 That aircraft-carriers played a major role in the US victory over Japan is an accepted fact. These ships were not, however, exempt from risk. Shown here is an incident from 1944: an explosion on a carrier deck, perhaps during fuel or weapons loading.

117 top left Two Curtiss SB2C Helldiver bombers fly over their ship before landing. Note the landing hook ready in position. Besides fighters, aircraft carriers also usually had attack aircraft such as Helldivers.

117 top right The Grumman TBF Avenger was another carrier-borne attack aircraft. It made its debut in the battle of Midway and was the US Navy's standard torpedo craft throughout the war.

117 bottom left Two Grumman Avengers, one ready to fly and the other with its wings folded, on the deck of an aircraft carrier under fire from Japanese bombers.

117 bottom right Douglas SBD Dauntless dive-bombers lined up on a carrier flight deck in 1942. It was the best American plane of its type and was also in service with the USAAF as the A-24.

The United States demonstrated its air power not only by the production of great fighters, but above all by production of the heavy bombers that contributed so decisively to eventual victory over Germany and Japan. Undeniably the Boeing B-17 Flying Fortress was most famous of these planes. The B-17 was a four-engined heavy bomber. Design work began in 1934 in response to the US Army's ambition request for a bomber that could defend the national territory against hypothetical enemy fleets. The new American bomber was to be capable of flying at 200 mph while carrying a 2,000-lb bomb load for 1,800 miles. The B-17 prototype first flew on 28 July 1935. For that period, it was a truly enormous airplane. Even though the first prototype had crashed, in 1938 the army ordered serial

production of a batch restricted to just 39 aircraft. This limitation was partly a result of opposition from the US Navy opposition, which saw its own role being subverted.

At the outbreak of war in 1941, the B-17 was the only truly modern plane in the American armament. Mass-production led to the formation of numerous strategic bomber squadrons that were given priority assignments in the European theater. With the B-17, the Americans developed long-range daylight-bombing strategies using "box" formations and enormous defensive firepower to create a wall of lead protecting the B-17 fleets from enemy fighters. These strategies initially led the Americans to believe that they could fly without fighter escorts, a decision that resulted in unacceptable losses. In contrast with the

RAF, the USAAF decided to fly by day to ensure greater precision when dropping bombs and to oblige the German defenses to labor round the clock. American losses thus continued to be high, but the devastation of the attacks the ever larger formations made was impressive. The definitive versions of the Flying Fortress were the B-17F and G, which fielded improved engines, armor and armament. Some 12,000 of these B-17s were built, and between 1943 and 1945, they carried out the greater part of the bombing raids on Germany, sustaining very heavy losses. The B-17 was an exceptional aircraft and much loved by its crews, above all because of its incredible robustness that allowed it to return to base even when badly damaged. Another famous bomber, the Consolidated

B-24 Liberator, could not boast this same degree of toughness and was also unstable, but it was built in greater numbers than any other allied aircraft, for a total of 18,188 planes, with production being shared with Ford, Douglas and North American. The Liberator, which was also a four-engined plane, first saw action in April 1942 and was used primarily in the Mediterranean and Pacific theaters. It was also used successfully in maritime patrol and reconnaissance, anti-submarine, training, and transport roles.

118 top A formation of Consolidated B-24 Liberator bombers during an attack on an oil refinery in Ploesti, Rumania, in 1944.

118 bottom Disaster! A B-24 loses part of its right wing to a bomb released by another plane above it in the formation. In a navigational error, the two planes managed to fly too close to each other.

119 top A formation of Boeing B-17 Flying Fortress bombers high over Germany. The escorting fighters engaged in dogfights with the German defense planes are creating condensation trails.

119 center left A machine-gun placement inside a British bomber.

119 center right A B-17G with hatches open a second before bomb release. The plane could carry up to 16,400 lbs of bombs and fly over 2000 miles without refueling.

119 bottom A B-24 in flames in the skies over Austria. Seconds later it exploded: the crew had no chance of escape.

The most advanced Allied bomber was, however, the Boeing B-29 Superfortress, which completed its maiden flight on 21 September 1942. The army required a bomber with extreme range that could be employed for strategic operations in the Asian theater; Boeing responded with an avant-garde airplane that even before that maiden flight had attracted 1,500 orders. The B-29 had a completely pressurized crew compartment, a retractable tricycle undercarriage, and four huge turbocharged engines, each producing 2,231 hp. However, the complexity of these engines caused major reliability problems and drastically reduced the B-29 squadrons' initial effectiveness. Nonetheless, the B-29 was the key to the rapid end of the war against Japan. The final thrust was marked by an incendiary bombing campaign started in March 1944 and culminated in the B-29s dropping atomic bombs on Hiroshima and

and heavily armed (up to ten 12.7-mm machine guns and 4,000-lb bomb load). The fact that it remained in service with the USAF until the Vietnam War and was used by a number of other countries is testimony to its worth. More than 2,400 Invaders were built.

A number of non-combat models featured among the most important Allied aircraft. For example, transport planes were crucial to the war effort, not only to maintain supply lines to troops scattered around the world, but also to play a key role in a various air transport operations – first and foremost the D-Day landings in Normandy. The leading transport plane was the twin-engined Douglas C-47 Skytrain, the military version of the famous DC-3. The civil airliner had completed its maiden flight on 1 July 1933, and in 1940, when it was selected as the standard military transport for the American armed forces, it

Nagasaki on 6 August and 9 August 1945.

The USAAF's strike forces were completed by a number of twin-engined planes for medium-light bombing and ground-support duties. The most famous models were the North American B-25 Mitchell, the Douglas A-20 Havoc, the Martin B-26 Marauder and the Douglas A-26 Invader. The best was unquestionably the Invader, which entered service in April 1944. This plane was extremely fast (over 350 mph), powerful (two 2,028-hp engines),

was the leading airplane on the civil market and already in service with the US Army and Navy. During the war, some 12,700 Skytrains were constructed, along with a further 2,000 built under license in the Soviet Union as the Lisunov Li-2. The Skytrain was a simple, rugged aircraft, but with features that made it an avant-garde design for its time. The RAF designated it the Dakota, and it has continued to fly with civil and military operators throughout the world, until the present day.

121 center The Douglas A-26 Invader was another medium bomber and assault aircraft was. It entered service in 1944 and was armed with ten 12.7-mm machine-guns and a bomb load of to 4,000 lbs.

121 bottom B-25 bombers from the 345th Bomber Group attack Japanese-held Dagua airfield in New Guinea in 1943.

120 top A Martin B-26 Marauder medium bomber during Operation Overlord, the assault on the beaches of Normandy in June 1944. The black and white stripes worn on the occasion are easily seen.

120 center A formation of USAAF Douglas A-20 Havoc bombers over the North Sea, looking for German ships. The RAF also used this aircraft, designating it the Boston.

120 bottom The Douglas C-47 Skytrain transport plane, the military version of the famous DC-3, was one of the main reasons for the Allied victory in World War II. This airplane was used with success in many roles, including medical transportation, as shown here.

121 top The Boeing B-29 Superfortress used against Japan was undoubtedly most powerful bomber of the war. The two 468th Bomb Group Superfortresses shown here are dropping incendiary bombs on targets in Burma in 1945.

122 top Mustered in front of their MiG-3s, Soviet pilots take an oath before combat. The MiG-3 was hurriedly brought into service in 1941.

122 center Soviet workers building aircraft during 1943. Despite dreadful work conditions and inferior technologies, the Russians managed to produce over 80,000 airplanes during the war.

122 bottom left The Polikarpov I-16, the standard Russian fighter at the start of the war, was an excellent aircraft in 1935 but heavily outclassed by 1941.

122 bottom right The Ilyushin Il-2M3 was the Soviets' best attack plane. Armed with 37-mm cannon and 2,200 lbs of bombs and rockets, it earned the name 'flying tank.' Including several postwar versions, a record number of 58,192 were built.

Mention should be made of the most important aircraft that the Soviet Union fielded during the Second World War. Stalin, who had signed a non-aggression pact with Hitler, was caught completely by surprise by Operation Barbarossa, the attack the Germans launched along the length of the Russian border on 22 June 1941. The Soviet armed forces were unprepared for conflict: their training was inadequate; their equipment too often obsolete and virtually useless. The situation was no better for the Soviet air force; in the first days of the war, it was almost annihilated on the ground and in the air.

At the outbreak of war, the Soviet Union's primary fighter was the Polikarpov I-16, a plane from 1933. In its day, it had been the first monoplane fighter with a retractable undercarriage, but by 1941 by the German Bf-109 outclassed it. However, in 1939, the Soviet Union introduced the MiG-1, a fast, modern aircraft equipped with an in-line engine, but which suffered from problems of instability. After just 100 MiG-1s had been built, the plane was replaced by the MiG-3, which incorporated a more powerful engine, greater range, and other improvements. The MiG-3 entered service in 1941, and it remained in use until 1943. During this period about 3,300 were built. However, the aircraft that enabled the Russians to compete on even terms with the Germans were those produced by the design departments of the Lavochkin and Yakovlev enterprises. Lavochkin, after having launched the LaGG-1 and 3 models, two relatively unsuccessful machines that were only lightly armed and dangerous to fly, in 1941 introduced a new model using the powerful 1,600-hp Shvetsov M.82 radial engine. The result was the La-5, which entered service in 1942. The design was soon uprated to La-5FN specifications (more powerful engine, composite wood-metal structure), and then to La-7 specifications (an even more powerful engine,

123 top Yakovlev Yak-9 fighter, an excellent aircraft that remained in production from 1942 to 1946. It was used in the Korean War in the 1950s.

123 bottom The Lavochkin La-5FN was another successful Soviet fighter. It was equipped with a 1700-hp engine and It could reach 400 mph.

123 center Yak-9 fighters on a training flight. In total, 36,000 were built.

heavier armament and a new all-metal wing), introduced in 1943 and 1944 respectively. The La series was produced until 1946, with a total of more than 22,000 units being built.

Yakovlev introduced its first design, the Yak-1 in 1940. This was a small, elegant fighter that entered service in 1942. Such was its success that its designer was honored with the Order of Lenin. This first model was gradually improved and modified, giving rise to the Yak-3 (an excellent low-altitude fighter-bomber), the Yak-7, and lastly the Yak-9, which entered service in 1942 and was to remain in production until 1946. Fast, well-armed and agile, over 36,000 piston-engined Yak fighters were built. Yak-9s fought in Korea between 1950 and 1953.

The most famous Soviet aircraft of the Second World War was, however, the Ilyushin Il-2 Shturmovik, the aircraft produced in the greatest numbers in the history of aviation. The USSR had been looking for a tactical support aircraft since 1938. A requrement was issued to which the Sukhoi and Ilyushin design departments responded. According to the Soviets the air force's duty was to provide tactical support for ground forces. The first Ilyushin prototype flew on 2 October 1939. In 1940, a second prototype, with an improved engine, armament, armor and maneuverability, was approved for production entered service in summer

1941. The Shturmovik, a single-engined, two-seat fighter-bomber with a low wing and a heavily armored engine and cockpit, became the scourge of the German armored divisions. There was no escaping the Shturmoviks: they were armed with 37-mm cannons, fragmentation bombs, bazookas and 132-mm anti-tank rockets. After having dropped their fragmentation bombs from about 2,500 feet, these aircraft would usually press home their attack by skimming over the ground, aiming directly at the armored vehicles. On the morning of 7 July 1943, during the famous Battle of Kursk, the greatest tank battle of the Second World War, the fighter-bomber provided a dramatic illustration of its offensive capabilities. Swarms of Shturmoviks attacked at dawn. Within 20 minutes, the 9th Panzer Division had lost 240 of its 300 armored vehicles, while 270 the 3rd Panzer Division's 300 vehicles had been hit.

The Il-10 Shturmovik, an improved model, first flew in 1944. It proved to be a truly excellent machine, equipped as it was with a 2,000-hp engine, four 23-mm cannons and up to 2,200 lbs of bombs and rockets. The Shturmovik series remained in production until the 1950s, being adopted by all the Communist countries. It was manufactured in the USSR and Czechoslovakia, and over 58,000 were built.

Chapter 8

Conditions imposed by the Treaty of Versailles that were designed to prevent the resurgence of German military power after the First World War made the rebirth of German military aviation a slow and clandestine operation. The Luftwaffe's official foundation dates back to 1 March 1935, and from that moment Germany's hectic race toward full rearmament became public. In August 1939, on the eve of the war, the Luftwaffe could claim about 4,300 aircraft: 1,180 medium bombers, 336 dive-bombers, 771 single-seat fighters, and 552 transport planes. There were also about 2,700 trainers. At that time, strengthened by the lessons learned from the Condor Legion's performance in the Spanish Civil War, the Luftwaffe was the world's strongest air force, both in terms of numbers and the quality of its aircraft. Its only defect was the German armed forces' conception of the use of air power: tactical deployment to support ground forces. What the Germans lacked was any strategic component; specifically, long-range heavy bombers that could strike the industrial and productive power of the enemy. Germany was to pay dearly for this oversight.

The Second World War began with the Blitzkrieg, or Lightning War, of which the Junkers Ju-87 was a perfect symbol. In fact, a group of three of these aircraft, led by Lieutenant Bruno Dilley, heralded the onset of the war in Poland at dawn on 1 September 1939. The group attacked virtually at ground level, emerging from the mists to strike the railway bridges over the Vistula on the outskirts of Dynów. They were not actually supposed to hit the bridges, but rather prevent their destruction by the Poles by cutting the cables linked to the explosive charges with which they had been mined. Even though the attack had not exploited the Ju-87s dive-bombers' capabilities, it was a success in that one of the two bridges remained intact, thus allowing the passage of the German troops.

The Junkers Ju-87 Stuka was a single-engined, two-seat dive-bomber, born in response to a 1933 ministry brief calling for a new bomber of that type. Four manufacturers submitted designs. In March

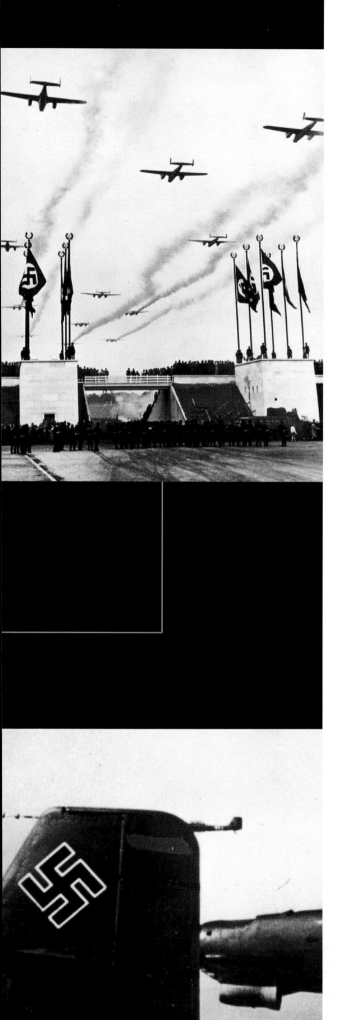

1936, Junkers was announced the winner, with a twin-rudder prototype powered by a Rolls-Royce engine. This prototype had first flown in 1935, but the plane was lost in an accident. A modified second prototype took on what to all intents and purposes was to be the definitive form, and featured a fixed undercarriage, the characteristic inverted gull's wing profile, and a single rudder. The Rolls-Royce engine was replaced with a Junkers Jumo unit driving a three-bladed metal propeller. The first production model was the Ju-87A-1 of 1937, which was sent to Spain for operational testing. The type reached its optimum configuration in the Ju-87B version. This aircraft was a bomber of deadly precision that also had a notable psychological effect on the enemy. By 1940, however, it was revealing its limitations, above all, its need to operate under conditions of aerial superiority given that it was particularly slow. Nonetheless, the Ju-87 remained in service throughout the war, thanks in part to its exceptional robustness.

The G-1, the last version of the Ju-87, was armed with two 37-mm cannons and was a fearsome anti-tank weapon. Ulrich Rudel, the so-called "Iron Flyer' and the Luftwaffe's most decorated pilot, earned his reputation flying a G-1. An indomitable fighter, Rudel was shot down and wounded on a number of occasions during the war and even suffered the amputation of a leg, but this did not prevent him from flying again in March 1945. During a wartime career begun in 1939 as a sub-lieutenant and ending in May 1945 as a colonel in command of the Schlachtfliegereschwader 2 (SD.2), Rudel participated in over 2,500 missions, destroying 519 enemy tanks, almost 1,000 vehicles of other types, and five warships. His renowned attack on the Soviet cruiser *Marat* in September 1941 demonstrated his absolute courage. The planes, which were carrying 2,200-lb bombs, barely managed to take off. Rudel pressed home his attack by diving at 90° straight into the anti-aircraft fire, overtaking even his wing commander. He dropped his bomb from a height of just 660 feet and desperately hauling on the stick just managed to bring up the nose of his plane, skimming barely six feet over the water. The bomb struck its target and broke the *Marat's* hull in two. In all, over 5,700 Ju-87 Stukas were built, and the air forces of Italy, Bulgaria, Romania, Slovakia and Hungary used the plane.

124-125 *A formation of Junkers Ju.87 Stukas on a training flight in April 1940. This dive-bomber was one of the Wehrmacht's most powerful support weapons in its blitzkrieg (air attacks).*

125 top left *A formation of Dornier Do.17 bombers in the ring at Nuremburg during a military parade in September 1938.*

125 bottom *Close up of a 510 lb bomb, the Stuka's main weapon. The photo taken in September 1939 during the German invasion of Poland.*

At the start of the war the Luftwaffe was also operating three well-known medium bombers that were responsible for most of the attacks on Poland, France and, above all, on the United Kingdom during the Battle of Britain. These bombers were the Dornier Do-17, the Heinkel He-111 and the Junkers Ju-88. As already mentioned, Germany never

built or used four-engined strategic bombers. This colossal error was largely due to Hitler's impatient insistence on the immediate creation of a large air force. Thus, in 1936 Goering cancelled two large bombers projects that would have required greater resources and longer lead times in favor of full scale mass-production of the proven Dornier Do-17 and the Heinkel He-111. At

the time Goering stated, "The Führer will not ask me how big the bombers are, but how many of them are there."

The twin-engined Dornier Do-17, that first saw the light of day in 1934, was designed to meet Lufthansa's demand for a fast airmail plane that could also carry six passengers. The plane was not particularly

well suited to these duties but, like all German aircraft of the era, its design was valid from a military point of view and it was soon transformed into a bomber. The first production versions (the E-1 bomber, the F-1 reconnaissance plane) were tested under operational conditions in 1937 during the Spanish Civil War. The experience gained there led to the development of the Do-17Z,

with its more spacious cockpit and improved armament. This version remained in production until 1940 and in service until 1942. Over 600 Dornier Do-17s were produced, and the basic design was also used to develop the Do-217, conceived specifically for military use in 1938. By 1944, more than 1,900 Do-217s had been built; the Luftwaffe used them for bombing, reconnaissance, anti-shipping and night-fighter duties.

The Heinkel He-111 had also been designed officially as a fast commercial plane, but it was soon – from the third prototype – adapted for its true vocation as a bomber. The He-111 completed its maiden flight on 26 February 1935. It too saw action in Spain. The He-111H version was then developed, fitted with the more powerful Jumo 211 engines. Early in the war, in the Blitzkrieg in Poland, over Scandinavia, and on the western front, the He-111 was used in massive formations and proved to be a fearsome instrument, completing the first carpet bombings of enemy cities. During the Battle of Britain, however, when the HE-111 came up against a determined defense, it began to reveal its shortcomings. From 1941 on, it was relegated to night bombing, glider- towing, and finally transport duties. If fulfilled this last role until the end of the war. In all, more than 7,000 Heinkel He-111s were built.

By 1941, the high-performance, twin-engined Junkers Ju-88 was recognized to be the Luftwaffe's best bomber. The Ju-88 was designed in 1935 as a fast bomber; the first prototype flew on 21 December 1936. The

126 bottom Heinkel 111s over France in May 1940. The plane began to show its limitations during the Battle of Britain in May 1940 and was relegated to secondary duties.

127 top left Though its design dated from 1934, the Dornier Do.17 was one of the Luftwaffe's strongest bombers at the start of the war and it remained in service until 1943. This is the Z version.

127 top right The Junkers Ju.88 was perhaps the best German bomber. It entered service in 1939 and proved flexible enough to be used as a night-fighter and even a glider puller. Almost 16,000 planes of the 88, 188, and 388 series were built.

production version, the Ju-88A-1, entered service in 1939, on the very eve of the war. It was initially used only as a pure bomber, but reconnaissance, night-fighter, anti-shipping, anti-tank, dive-bomber, ground attack, transport and glider-towing versions of the aircraft were subsequently developed, confirming the validity and versatility of the basic design. The Ju-88 was also built in France and Czechoslovakia; ultimately it was even transformed into the Mistel guided flying bomb. This program, developed in 1944, involved the installation of a Bf-109 fighter on the back of a Ju-88 with a modified nose containing an 8,350-lb explosive charge. The pilot flew the paired aircraft from the Messerschmitt as far as the target; he then uncoupled the Ju-88 and returned to base in the fighter. Having seen that the format worked, the Germans also created the Mistel 2, using a Fw-190 fighter. In all, about 250 Mistels were constructed in four different versions. By the end of the war, nearly 16,000 Ju-88s had been constructed in over 100 different versions. This production total includes 1,076 Ju-188 aircraft, a version with an extended fuselage and larger wing. The Ju-88 was used not only by the Luftwaffe but also by another five Axis air forces.

127 bottom left A Heinkel 111 during a raid on Warsaw during the Polish campaign in September 1939.

127 bottom right This Heinkel 111 was photographed over London during the Battle of Britain. The 111H could fly 1220 miles but carry only 1,250 lbs of bombs.

128 top *The Messerschmitt Bf.108, undoubtedly the most famous German fighter, seen here is the B-1 version. As this and other models were improved, the Bf.108 remained the backbone of the German fighter force from 1939 to 1945.*

128 bottom *Derived from the civil transport plane of the same name, the Junkers Ju.52/3mg was adopted by the Luftwaffe as a bomber but most of all as a transport plane. It remained in production until 1944 and was used in many support roles.*

129 left *A formation of heavy Messerschmitt Bf.110 fighters during the Battle of Britain in 1941. Unsuited to the job it was designed for, the Bf.110 was developed and put to other uses like night-fighting and reconnaissance.*

129 top right *Willy Messerschmitt, the brilliant German engineer who designed several successful military aircraft, including the Bf.108, Bf.109, Bf.110 and Me.262.*

Another very famous aircraft from the early years of the war was the Junker Ju-52 transport plane, a solid, reliable machine, affectionately known as "Tante Ju" (Auntie Ju) by its crews. The aircraft was originally designed in 1930 as a single-engined cargo plane, but its fate was transformed in 1932 when the seventh model (the Ju-52/3m) was built in what was to become the definitive configuration, with three radial engines, a fixed undercarriage, and characteristic ribbed metal skinning. International civilian sales success was repeated in 1934 in the military sphere when the Luftwaffe ordered a version for use as a bomber and transport plane. Following the Spanish Civil War, the Ju-52/3mg3 went into mass production, and by the outbreak of the Second World War the Luftwaffe was already using 1,000 Ju-52/3mg2s to transport troops and materials and for dropping paratroopers. These planes were fundamental to the success of the invasions of Denmark, Norway, Holland and Greece. The Ju-52/3mg2 was also used in the airborne invasion of Crete, during which it suffered extremely heavy losses, and in the airlift during the tragic battle of Stalingrad. The plane, which remained in production until mid-1944, was also used for towing gliders and as an air-ambulance, operating with wheels, skis or floats. More than 5,400 Ju-52s were constructed, some of them under license in Spain and France.

Germany's fortunes waned after three years of war, and after 1942, the Nazis were obliged to fight a defensive battle. In spite of Hitler's wishes to the contrary, the Luftwaffe's most important aircraft began to be the fighters needed to combat the Allies' devastating bombing raids on the Fatherland and the occupied territories. The Germans had begun the war with two principal fighters, the singe-engined Messerschmitt Bf.109 and the twin-engined Bf.110.

The first is still the aircraft most closely associated with the Luftwaffe and, with almost 35,000 built, it was the most numerous plane of the Second World War; it was also one of the most famous fighters in the history of aviation. In 1934, the German Air Ministry had issued a requirement calling for a new monoplane, single-seat interceptor to replace the biplanes currently in service. Willy Messerschmitt responded. In just 15 months he designed his first great aircraft, the Bf.109. This was a small, light, all-metal plane with extremely advanced features and the most powerful engine then available, the 695-hp Rolls-Royce Kestrel V. The Bf.109 was not a particularly innovative fighter, but for the first time a fighter combined a number of advanced features. They had a retractable undercarriage, a closed cockpit, a metal fuselage and wings and Handley Page-type slats on the wings' leading edges. The prototype first flew in September 1935. It was soon put into limited production at the expense of its three competitors: the Arado Ar-80, the Focke-Wulf Fw-159 and the Heinkel He-112. This last was in practice the equal of the Bf-109, but lost out because it was more complicated to mass-produce. The Luftwaffe tested the aircraft in the Bf.109G form, powered by the German-built Jumo 210 engine, in air operations in the Spanish Civil War, where it proved to be the best fighter in the world at that time. The 109 design achieved full maturity with the E (Emil) version. It was the first Messerschmitt to be mass-produced (from 1939 on) and introduced significant improvements, including the powerful and reliable new Daimler-Benz DB-601 engine. The Bf.109E participated in the opening phases of the war, above all during the Battle of Britain, when many of its pilots distinguished themselves and became celebrated aces. However, in 1940 the Bf.109 met its eternal rival, the British Spitfire, the aircraft against which it was to be matched throughout the war as designers on both sides searched for ever greater performance.

The most important version of the 109 was the G (Gustav), which boasted significant improvements to its 1,800 hp DB-605 engine and armament. It entered service at the end of 1942. Eleven versions of the 109G were developed, and almost 20,000 planes were constructed built. The Bf-109 was the favorite aircraft of Germany's greatest aces, including Gerhard Barkhorn, who accumulated 301 kills, and Eric Hartmann, the most prolific ace of all time, with 352 victories. Hartmann arrived on the Russian front as a sergeant and undertook his first combat mission in October 1942. After his first victory on 5t November 1942, Hartmann developed a refined, ruthless combat technique in which his great success was based on the initial decision to accept or refuse the fight according to the situation at that moment. A year later he had already accumulated 148 victories. In March 1944 Hartmann was promoted to lieutenant; by the end of the war, after receiving the foremost honors (such as the Knight's Cross with Oak Leaves, Swords and Diamonds), he had reached the rank of major and was in command of the 1st wing of the JG.52. After some time, Hartmann's plane began to sport a black tulip as a personal insignia, its petals covering the whole nose of his Bf-109. For this reason he was nicknamed by the Russians the "Black Devil of the Ukraine" and was soon avoided by all enemy pilots. In the later stages of the war he only managed to reach his eventual total of victories by flying an unmarked aircraft.

Toward the end of the war, production difficulties imposed various modifications designed to simplify and accelerate assembly of the Bf-109. The final model was the K-4, introduced in 1944. It had a 2,000-hp engine,

and its maximum take-off weight was almost double that of the first series, a testimony to the basic design's underlying excellence and versatility.

The career of the other pre-war Messerschmitt fighter, the Bf.110, was less successful. This aircraft was designed in 1934 to meet the requirement for a long-range, heavy fighter. Despite early successes in the Polish campaign, the Bf.110C was out-classed during the Battle of Britain, unable to match the British fighters in terms of maneuverability and acceleration. In 1941, the Luftwaffe began to use it in other roles. It performed best as a night-fighter, especially in Bf.110G form, equipped with Lichtenstein radar from 1942 on. The 110s were also used as reconnaissance planes and fighter-bombers. By 1945, German factories had built more than 6,000 of the Bf.110s.

appeared early in 1944, characterized by a new, longer and tapering nose that housed a 1,800-hp in-line Jumo engine. With this model, the German pilots were able to fight on even terms with the best Allies' best fighter aircraft of 1944-45, even though training possibilities and fuel supplies were no longer adequate to allow the Luftwaffe to conduct effective and continuous operations. The last of the FW-109 line was the Ta-152, an extremely fast and heavily armed high-altitude interceptor, of which only 150 were produced. A total of about 20,000 planes in the FW-190 series were built before the war ended.

The German munitions industry's desperate efforts toward the end of the war gave rise to revolutionary aircraft that might have been able to change the conflict's eventual outcome. These were the first operational aircraft to be powered by jet and rocket engines, designs that impressed the Allies but which, for various reasons, were ultimately unable to alter the course of history. The first jet aircraft in the history of aviation to see active service was the Messerschmitt Me.262, the origins of which actually dated back to before the war. The delays in its introduction were largely due to the developmental problems encountered with the BMW engines. In fact, the Messerschmitt Me.262 made its first flight on

Together with the Bf.109, the greatest German fighter of the war was unquestionably the Focke-Wulf 190; it was in fact superior in many respects to its Messerschmitt stable-mate. In 1937 the German Air Ministry asked Focke-Wulf to create a new interceptor to join the Bf.109. At that time Kurt Tank led the Focke-Wulf design department. He was an engineer who had ventured into aviation in 1924 to design a seaplane. Tank, who was also a fine test pilot, wanted a less extreme airplane than the Bf-109 and the Spitfire; a fast fighter but one that would be larger, more robust and heavier, a true war machine. He succeeded in his intent thanks to BMW's 139 14-cylinder radial engine that produced an impressive 1,550 hp. The prototype first flew on 1 June 1939, immediately demonstrating great promise. After 40 pre-series planes had been built for operational testing, the FW-190A went into production in 1941. From its very

first encounters with the Spitfire Mk.V, it proved to be superior, offering attractive flying characteristics and great speed and maneuverability. In 1942, the FW-190A fighter version was followed by the F and then by the G versions. Both were dedicated to the fighter-bomber role. In that same year, General Douglas of the RAF stated, "I have no doubt, and nor do my pilots, that the FW-190 is today the world's best fighter." The last mass-produced version, the FW-190D

130 top The German Arado Ar.234, the first jet bomber in history, is shown here during trials without an undercarriage. Powered by two Jumo 004 motors producing 890-hp of thrust, it flew at 462 mph and carried 1,250 lbs of bombs. It was also used for reconnaissance.

18 April 1941, with a piston engine mounted in the nose. The third prototype, the first to be fitted with the final version of Junkers Jumo 004 engines, flew on 18 July 1942, and immediately showed exceptional qualities in terms of performance and handling.

The Me-262 nonetheless suffered from a serious drawback: the conventional layout of its undercarriage and tail-wheel meant that during take off the jet exhaust flow interfered with the elevators, preventing the plane from gaining altitude. In order to get round the problem, the test pilots developed a procedure as simple as it was dangerous: a short squeeze on the brakes during the take-off run that dipped the nose, modified the gas flow at the tail, and allowed the elevators to function efficiently. Clearly, this was not an option in normal conditions and so the airplane had to be modified with the nose-

wheel adapted to align the plane with its aerodynamic requirements. Flight testing also revealed another problem: the engines. They had to be treated very gently because they tended to flood and on occasion catch fire. Moreover, at certain engine speeds anomalous vibrations set in that could cause cracking in the turbine blades.

In order to resolve this problem, the Messerschmitt company turned to a professional violinist who "played" each blade with his bow. He thus identified their natural frequency and the fact that they began resonating at the plane's cruising speed. A decision was made to reduce the blades' thickness and to vary the engine speed at cruising velocity, two measures that effected a miracle cure. Nonetheless, Hitler's insistence on making a bomber of the Me.262 meant that development and

production were delayed; the first pre-series planes did not actually fly until spring 1944. In total, 1,433 Me.262 s were actually constructed, but in too many versions and sub-versions (17 in all): including single- and two-seat reconaissance, ground attack, day-fighter and night-fighter variants. Efforts were thus diluted and dispersed, and the Me.262 had little operational effect despite the fact that it in technical terms it was unrivalled.

The Messerschmitt Me.163 Komet was a small rocket-powered interceptor that came out of the engineer Lippisch's pre-war research into tailless gliders. The aircraft's period of gestation was nonetheless lengthy because the technical difficulties associated with using highly unstable dual-component fuels were considerable. Early in the war the Me.163 became a low-priority project. The rocket-powered plane made its first test flight 13 August 1941, and the Me.163B pre-series model first flew on 23 June 1943. Production began in February 1944 and the plane went into service in the summer of that year. The Komet, which was armed with two 30mm cannons, was powered by a Walter HWK rocket engine that gave it a top speed of almost 600 mph, but for a mere 7.5 minutes. After the rocket engine had burned out the plane had to glide back to base and make a belly-skid landing. At the end of 1944, however, Germany was facing defeat and the 400 or so Komets that had been produced could do little to help the aerial defense of the Fatherland.

Another German aircraft, the Arado Ar.234 Blitz, was the first jet bomber in history. This plane, which used the same Jumo engines as the Me.262, also went through a troubled development period; two years elapsed between design and the maiden flight made on 15 June1943. The Blitz went into service with an experimental squadron in summer 1944, but saw only limited action in 1945 as a bomber and reconnaissance plane. A total of 200 Blitzes were produced in 22 different versions. The jet had a maximum take-off weight approaching 22,000 lbs, and was flown by a single pilot. It could fly at 460 mph for 1,000 miles, with a 4,400-lb bomb load.

130 center The Focke-Wulf Fw-190, a fast, manageable and sturdy airplane, was the German fighter forces other arm. It created serious difficulties for the Allies when introduced in August 1941.

130 bottom The Messerschmitt Me.262, the first jet fighter in history to be used in combat. Its troubled development resulted principally from Hitler's decision to use it as a fighter-bomber.

131 top The Messerschmitt Me.163 Komet jet interceptor was an unusual aircraft developed to counter Allied bombing raids on Germany. It was, however, difficult and dangerous to fly.

131 bottom A row of Me.262-B Messerschmitts, the two-seater training version. The U-1 version of this model was equipped with a Liechtenstein radar unit in the nose and used for night fighting.

Germany's principal European ally was Italy, a country that in the 1920s and 1930s had been at the forefront of aeronautical technology, thanks to the exploits of various record-breaking planes and the great ocean-crossing flights organized by the Italian Royal Air Force. Italy had, however, been notably weakened by its involvement in colonial wars and the Spanish Civil War, and in 1940 its aging air force could count on fewer than 1,800 serviceable aircraft. During the course of the war this situation worsened: given the excessive variety of types in service, the national aeronautical industry was unable to produce either a sufficient number of new aircraft or the modern engines needed to power them.

Early in the conflict, the Italian Royal Air Force's main fighter was the Fiat CR.42 Falco biplane. This had a fixed undercarriage already obsolete upon introduction on 23 May 1938. There was, however, still conviction in Italy that a light, maneuverable biplane was preferable in aerial combat. As a result, while Germany initiated production of the Bf.109, Italy began to

turn out the Falco, which was powered by an 840-hp radial engine, had a top speed of 267 mph, and was armed with two 12.7-mm machine guns. Thus Italy's CAI (Corpo Aereo Italiano), in accordance with Mussolini's wishes but against German advice, participated in the attack on Great Britain with planes such as the CR.42. Their pilots had to compete with superior airplanes in a fighter that was conceptually outdated and even had an open cockpit that resulted in a number of frostbite cases. Up through 1943, a total of 1,782 CR.42s were built – a significant number for Italy. They were built despite all evidence to the contrary and the availability of better aircraft, on which production should have been concentrated. From 1941, however, the plane was relegated to less demanding duties such as ground attack, reconnaissance and night-fighting.

On 26 February 1937 (a year earlier than the Falco's introduction), another Fiat fighter had made its first flight, the G.50 Freccia, an all-metal monoplane with retractable undercarriage. In 1938, the G.50 lost out to the Macchi MC.200 in the competition for the

air force's new interceptor, but it was nonetheless approved for serial production. This plane, equipped with the same engine as the CR.42, was not however, a success; its performance, with a top speed of 292 mph, was only slightly better than that of the Falco. A total of 780 G.50 Freccias were built.

The Macchi MC.200 Saetta was a far superior machine. It had made its maiden flight on 24 December 1937, and entered service in the summer of 1939. The Macchi fighter, despite being penalized by a not particularly powerful radial engine (870 hp), boasted excellent performance and flight characteristics. A total of 1,151 Saettas were constructed up to July 1942, when the model was replace by the MC.202 Folgore. This last was none other than the Saetta re-equipped with the German Daimler-Benz DB.601 engine (built under license by Alfa Romeo), an in-line unit producing 1,100 hp that gave the Folgore a top speed of 373 mph. After its maiden flight on 10 August 1940, the MC.202 went into production: a total of 1,070s were built. The planes operated successfully on all fronts.

133 center right A machine-gunner in an Italian bomber in his aft defensive placement during a mission over the Mediterranean.

133 bottom Despite its defects, the CR.42 was agile and reliable and continued to be used by the Regia Aeronautica even after 1941 as a light attack craft and night-fighter.

133 top In the foreground, the Macchi MC.202 Folgore fighters of the 97th Squadron on an Italian airfield. The MC.202 was the best Italian fighter before the advent of the 'Serie 5' fighters.

133 center left A Macchi MC.200 Saetta in the 74th Squadron. The MC.200 was an excellent plane but suffered from a radial motor of little power and just two machine-guns.

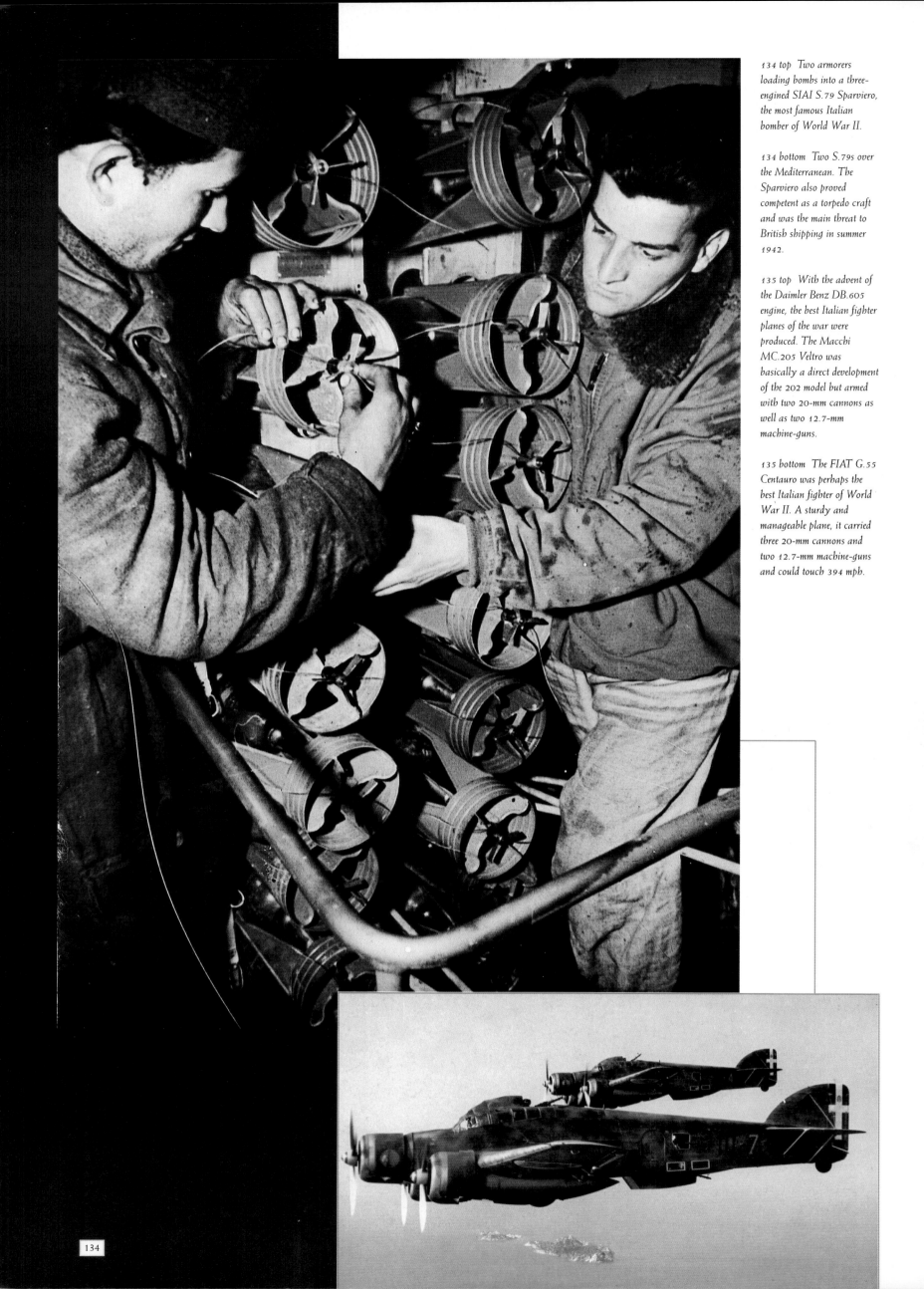

134 top Two armorers
loading bombs into a three-
engined SIAI S.79 Sparviero,
the most famous Italian
bomber of World War II.

134 bottom Two S.79s over
the Mediterranean. The
Sparviero also proved
competent as a torpedo craft
and was the main threat to
British shipping in summer
1942.

135 top With the advent of
the Daimler Benz DB.605
engine, the best Italian fighter
planes of the war were
produced. The Macchi
MC.205 Veltro was
basically a direct development
of the 202 model but armed
with two 20-mm cannons as
well as two 12.7-mm
machine-guns.

135 bottom The FIAT G.55
Centauro was perhaps the
best Italian fighter of World
War II. A sturdy and
manageable plane, it carried
three 20-mm cannons and
two 12.7-mm machine-guns
and could touch 394 mph.

The final version of this Macchi MC family was the MC.205 Veltro, which completed its maiden flight on 19 April 1942. This model was designed to overcome the main weaknesses of the 202: it was more powerful and was more heavily armed. The Veltro thus used the 1,475-hp DB.605 engine and carried two 20-mm cannons along with the traditional two 12.7-mm machine guns. It was an excellent aircraft, capable of matching its Allied counterparts, but only just over 200 were built and the plane did not enter service until April 1943. Following the armistice between Italy and the Allies that was signed on 8 September 1943, the National Republican Air Force (ANR) used a further 112 in the north of the country.

Perhaps the best Italian fighter of the war was the Fiat G.55 Centauro, which flew for the first time on 30 April 1942. The Fiat fighter was powered by the DB.605 engine (again built under license by Alfa Romeo), and armed with three 22mm cannons and two 12.7-mm machine-guns. It was robust and maneuverable and could reach a top speed of 391 mph. The ANR used it primarily in

attempts to fend off the Allies' bombing raids on northern Italy. Only just over 250 were manufactured before the already reduced production capacity collapsed entirely. The last aircraft of the famous "5 Series" (fighters equipped with the DB.605 engine) was the Reggiane Re.2005 Sagittario that flew for the first time on 9tMay1942. Though it was an excellent plane, only 29 Sagittarios were built before the armistice.

Among other aircraft Italy used during the war, special mention should be made of the SIAI S.79 Sparviero, a traditional profile trimotor that remained in service for various duties for the duration of the conflict. The aircraft had been conceived as an eight-seat

civilian transport plane and was equipped with three 750- hp radial engines, a low wooden wing and retractable undercarriage. The S.79 first flew on 8 October 1934. It immediately distinguished itself for its speed, setting six world records. This performance alerted the military authorities to the potential for a

bomber version. Production began in October 1936; subsequently, the aircraft performed well during the Spanish Civil War. At the outbreak of the Second World War, almost 600 S.79s were in service. Torpedo-launching duties were soon added to the traditional bombing missions, and enhanced the S.79's reputation thanks to a number of heroic operations in the Mediterranean. Some of the Italian Royal Air Force's most glorious Second World War achievements featured the 132nd Group's S.79s, first based in Sicily and then at Pantelleria, under the command of Major Carlo Emanuele Buscaglia. Other famous pilots such as Giulio Cesare Graziani and Carlo Faggioni flew with this autonomous

unit. It earned great distinction in maritime operations in summer 1942, in particular in the battles of "Mezzogiugno" and "Mezzagosto" (Mid-June and Mid-August), when its pilots succeeded in sinking or damaging numerous Royal Navy warships and cargo vessels.

The setting for these two battles was the struggle for Malta. The S.79 crews displayed great courage in the face of withering anti-aircraft fire. Deetermined British fighters slipped in a few feet below the S.79s' wings and above the waves as they lined up to drop their torpedoes. During the battle of Mezzagosto, the Italian aircraft, in collaboration with the Germans, managed to sink a Royal navy destroyer and five cargo vessels, and hit two aircraft carriers and a further five cargo ships. This was the Italian torpedo planes' last successful mission: the war in the Mediterranean was by now going against the Axis forces. Major Buscaglia was shot down on 12 November and was presumed dead. In fact, he was alive and a prisoner of the Allies. In early in 1944 he returned to command the 132nd Group, now equipped with British twin-engined Baltimores, in the Aeronautica Cobelligerante (the Italian post-armistice airforce assisting the Allies). Shortly thereafter, on 23 August 1944, Buscaglia was killed in a flying accident at Camp Vesuvius. The S.79, nicknamed the "hopeless hunchback" because of the shape of the fuselage behind the cockpit, was also used by the ANR after 1943 as a torpedo plane; more than 1,300 were produced. Exported and constructed under license abroad, in the post-war period the S.79 was used as a cargo plane until the 1960s.

On the other side of the world, the third Axis ally, Japan – a country that had no great aeronautical tradition – had gone into the war with an excellent fighter. This was the Mitsubishi A6M Zero which, thanks to gradual improvements and modifications, was to remain in service throughout the war. The Zero was designed in the late 1930s as a new carrier-borne fighter for the Imperial fleet, and had been developed in response to a very demanding brief that Mitsubishi's rival, Nakajima, had judged to be impossible to meet. The A6M1, which first flew on 1 April 1939 responded perfectly to all requirements save that of top speed, which was lower than hoped-for 310 mph. After the engine had been replaced with a more powerful unit, the A6M2 went into serial production.

The Zero entered service in July 1940, and up to mid-1942 it was probably the best fighter in the Pacific theater. It was fast and maneuverable; its weaknesses were lack of armor plating and self-sealing fuel tanks, making it vulnerable to enemy fire. The best version of the Zero was the A6M5, which was deployed in 1943 to counter the threat of the American Hellcat and Corsair fighters. This model, armed with two 20-mm cannons and two 13.2-mm machine guns, had a 1,130-hp engine and could reach a top speed of 351 mph, but it was still no match for the American designs. A total of 10,499 Zeroes, code-named "Zeke" by the Americans, had

been produced by August 1945, but its decline had already become apparent two years earlier, in parallel with the loss of Japan's best pilots. The introduction of the last version, the 16M8 with a 1,560-hp engine, did nothing to improve the situation.

Another Japanese fighter that remained in service throughout the war was the less well-known Nakajima Ki-43, the army's front-line combat plane. This aircraft was commissioned directly from Nakajima without an open competition being held. The Ki-43 made its first flight in January 1939. It was an all-metal monoplane with retractable undercarriage, a low wing and a radial engine that initially proved to be heavy and clumsy. Like the Zero, it subsequently became light and agile; early in the war it actually gave the impression of being invincible. Constantly improved, especially with regard to its engine, the Ki-43 ("Oscar" to the Americans) was nonetheless overtaken by the Allied fighters, above all because the Japanese aeronautical industry proved incapable of producing sufficiently powerful engines. A total of 5,919 Ki-43s were built.

A third famous aircraft employed by the Japanese armed forces was the Mitsubishi G4M. This was a twin-engined bomber that completed its maiden flight on 23 October 1939, and went into production in 1940. Though designed for the navy, the

136 top A Japanese
machine-gunner in 1942.
Japan did not produce any
particularly advanced planes
after 1942 but their crews'
courage was never doubted.

136 center right The
Mitsubishi A6M Zero was
unquestionably the best-
known Japanese plane. An
excellent fighter, its only
weak point was lack of
armor-plating and of self-
sealing fuel tanks.

G4M was in fact a land-based long-range
bomber capable of carrying a 2,200-lb bomb
load or a torpedo for up to 2,500 miles. It
had a top speed of 292 mph and was armed
with four 20-mm cannons and two 7.7-mm
machine guns. Nonetheless, the G4M
(designated "Betty" by the Americans) was
only lightly armored and also lacked self-
sealing fuel tanks. Because of this, the
Americans nicknamed the G4M " The One-
shot Lighter." This was the most numerous of
the Japanese bombers; 2,466 were built and
the plane remained in service until August
1945.

136 bottom Japan had more
Mitsubishi G4Ms, known as
'Betty' by the Allies, than
any other plane but it too
was poorly armored. The
Americans nicknamed it "the
flying lighter."

137 top A Japanese torpedo
plane crashes into the sea
after being hit by the 127-
mm anti-aircraft guns of the
USS Yorktown aircraft-
carrier on 25 October 1944.

137 center Japan had a
powerful navy equipped with
naval aviation. These Zeros
are preparing for take-off
from an aircraft carrier.

137 bottom Toward the end
of the war, the Japanese could
find no better tactic to stop
the American fleet than
kamikaze attacks. In this
photograph of 4 May 1945,
a Japanese fighter is hit as it
tried to crash into the
aircraft-carrier escort, USS
Sangmon.

Chapter 9

The First Jets and the Korean War

By the early 1940s, traditional aircraft characterized by piston engines driving one or more propellers had reached the limits of their potential. During the Second World War, the fastest fighters came up against the 500-mph barrier beyond which propellers begin to lose efficiency. In order to go faster, far more powerful engines would be required, but they would be so large and heavy as to be unacceptable. In addition, their weight would eventually offset any theoretical increase in their performance, bringing the practical speed and efficiency values back down to the levels already achieved.

For some time, however, two men, Frank Whittle in Great Britain and Hans von Ohain in Germany, had been working independently on the development of an engine that to most observers appeared as revolutionary as it would be impossible to construct: the gas turbine engine.

The concept underlying gas turbines was very simple; in fact, these turbines were already being used in industrial applications. Air entered from the front and was compressed and forced into a combustion chamber where it mixed with the fuel; the mixture was then ignited, and the gases exited at high speed from the rear jet, driving as they did so a turbine which actuated the front compressor.

The difficulties lay in creating a turbine sufficiently compact, powerful and light to be mounted successfully in an airframe.

Von Ohain, a Heinkel aeronautical company an engineer conducted an initial demonstration of his turbine engine in February 1939. The test was successful, and Ernst Heinkel became a supporter of the new power unit, with his firm building the world's first jet aircraft, the He-178. This small, simple all-metal monoplane had a feature that in a few years became very common: an air intake in the nose where a propeller would normally be found. The He-178 flew for the first time on 27 August 1939, inaugurating aviation's modern era.

In Great Britain, Whittle, a RAF engineer, first had the idea of a gas turbine engine in

1929, but he could only begin to work seriously on the project from April 1937. In June 1939, he was ready to stage a demonstration of his WU engine for the Air Ministry, whose representative received the new invention enthusiastically. The Gloster Company was immediately commissioned to build an experimental plane using the W.1 engine. The result was the Gloster E.28/39, a low-wing, experimental model featuring a tricycle undercarriage and a nose air intake. It flew for the first time on 15 May 1941.

138 top The Heinkel He-178, which flew in August 1939, was the first jet plane. Its development was made possible by perfection of the jet engine by the German engineer, von Obain.

138 bottom The de Havilland Vampire was the first successful jet aircraft. A total of 19 versions and more than 3700 planes were built. In addition to Britain, 25 countries used the Vampire. Shown here is a two-seat training model.

139 top The Italian Caproni Campini N.1 was, together with the German and British attempts, another early jet-engined plane. It made its first flight on 28 August 1940 but its top speed was just 220 mph, and only two prototypes were built.

139 bottom With the advent of jet engines, aerodynamic tests became increasingly important. In this 1945 photograph, two men stand inside a wind tunnel.

In Great Britain, this line of research led to the construction of the Gloster Meteor fighter powered by Rolls-Royce engines (see Chapter 7), while in Germany, the development of airframes and engines took the form of a race between two industry groups; Heinkel and Messerschmitt, and BMW, Bramo and Junkers. The German Air Ministry ordered Heinkel and Messerschmitt to produce a jet fighter design to be powered by one of the three other firms involved in the project. Heinkel was the first to complete its design (in September 1940), but as no jets were yet available, its twin-engined He-280 first flew in March 1941 with engines built by Heinkel itself. The He-280 was an attractive aircraft that featured a number of interesting innovations such an ejector seat and a tricycle undercarriage. Even with its provisional engines, the He-280 was capable of 485 mph. However, for technical and political motives, the German authorities preferred the Messerschmitt Me.262, despite the fact that it was not ready until later and did not fly until July1942. Its finalized Jumo 004 engines produced 1,984 lbs of thrust. Hwever,

the Me.262It had a longer range and greater firepower than the He-280 (see Chapter 8).

In Great Britain, Gloster continued to improve and build the Meteor (before its withdrawal in 1954, about 3,900 had been built, with many exported). The second British jet was the de Havilland Vampire (initially named the Spider Crab). The plane was commissioned in 1941, and made its maiden flight on 26 September 1943. The vampire was small, equipped with mid-mounted metal wings with air intakes at the roots, and a short wooden fuselage; the undercarriage had a tricycle layout with a nose wheel. The tailplanes, similar to those of the Lockheed P-38, were carried on twin booms extending backwards from the wings. A single de Havilland Goblin engine producing 2,700 lbs of thrust powered the new aircraft, and gave it a top speed of around

500 mph. Though the Vampire proved to be an excellent fighter, it was not ready in time to play an active part in the war; in fact, the first production model, the Vampire F Mk.I, reached the RAF squadrons in April 1946. The F Mk.I, which was armed with four 20-mm cannons, had a Goblin 2 engine, producing around 3,100 lbs of thrust and guaranteeing a top speed of 540 mph. The Vampire was continuously upgraded, and specialized versions were introduced. These included the new fighter (F), fighter-bomber (FB), night-fighter (NF), trainer (T), and naval (Sea Vampire) versions. A new wing and new tailplanes gave rise to the Venom and the Sea Venom. More than 3,700 planes were built, with purchases made by 26 different countries around the world. The last Vampires, those used by the Swiss air force, were only withdrawn in the 1980s.

140 *Two photographs of a Lockheed T-33A Silver Star. This jet plane was derived from the P-80 Shooting Star fighter as a training plane for the new type of engine. It first flew on 22 March 1948.*

The United States was also involved in the development of jet fighters. Thanks to the exchange of technological information with Great Britain during the war, General Electric (which already had considerable experience with turbines) was chosen to develop a new engine based on Whittle's research. On 5 September 1941, Bell was commissioned to construct the prototype of a plane to be propelled by the new engine, the General Electric I-A turbine, which produced 1,250 lbs of thrust. Bell came up with the Model 27, a twin-engined plane of traditional lines, with a straight, mid-mounted wing, a tricycle nose wheel undercarriage, and engines buried in the wing roots. This aircraft, designated the XP-59A Airacomet, first flew on 1 October 1942, from Rogers Dry Lake to Muroc Field in California. In 1944, the three prototypes were followed by 13 pre-production examples of the YP-59A, powered by I-16 engines producing 1,650 lbs of thrust. These new engines nonetheless failed to provide an answer to the plane's chronic slowness (a top speed of only about 400 mph) and its instability. A total of 20 of the P-59As

were then ordered along with 30 of the P-59Bs, the latter powered by the J31-GE-5 engine, which produced 2,000 lbs of thrust. All these planes were, however, used for a vast series of test and evaluation flights and for training by the US Army and Navy. In spite of its relative lack of success, the Airacomet made a significant contribution to the development of jet aircraft technology, and the second American jet plane was an immediate winner.

While Bell was struggling with the troublesome P-59, Lockheed was assigned the task of producing an operational jet fighter. The firm prepared the design in just six months and the XP-80 prototype, equipped with a de Havilland Goblin gas turbine engine, flew for the first time on 8 January 1944. However, the decision was made not to proceed with production under license of the British engine. June 1944 thus saw the maiden flight of the XP-80A powered by a General Electric J33 unit. Operational testing began in October 1944, once the first 13 pre-production YP-80As had been completed. and orders were then placed for manufacture of the large total

of 5,000 P-80A jet fighters, but the end of the war drastically reduced the USAAF's need for new planes, and the order was cut back to just 917. The P-80A Shooting Star had a wingspan of 39 feet 6 inches and a maximum take-off weight of 14,500 lbs. The GE J33 engine produced 3,850 lbs of thrust and a top speed of 560 mph. The Shooting Star carried the same armament as the propeller-driven fighters; six machine guns and up to 2,000 lbs of bombs. In 1948, the improved F-80C was introduced, and a total of 798 were built; they saw action in the Korean War. (It should be noted that in 1947, with the

141 *top left The USAF's "Acrojets" acrobatic team used F-80 fighters. The plane entered service at the start of 1945 but not in time to be used during World War II.*

141 *top right This formation of Bell fighters was photographed in 1944. From top down: an XP-77, a P-39Q, a P-63A, and the first American jet airplane, the P-59 Airacomet, here in the pre-production version, the YP-59.*

141 center In 1947 McDonnell introduced a new jet fighter, the Banshee, derived from the Phantom. Shown here is the XF2H-1 prototype.

141 bottom left The prototype of the Ryan FR Fireball, 1944. A hybrid between jet and propeller propulsion, it was the first jet aircraft used by the US Navy.

constitution of the United States Air Force as a separate armed service, the designation of fighter aircraft was changed from P = Pursuit to F = Fighter.)

The excellent F-80C also formed the basis for an exceptional two-seat trainer that flew for the first time on 22 March 1948. Initially designated the TP-80C, it then became the T-33A Silver Star, with over 6,500 being built, serving in over 40 countries around the world. A number of T-33s are still being flown today by various air forces, a testimony to the validity and robustness of the design.

In the meantime, the US Navy had also taken cautious steps in the direction of jet propulsion, but due to the greater reliability required of carrier-borne aircraft, its first plane of this type was actually a hybrid. The Ryan FR Fireball, which completed its maiden flight on 25 June 1944, was in effect an experimental airplane, being equipped with a 1,350-hp Wright Cyclone radial engine and a General

Electric I-16 turbojet producing about 1,600 lbs of thrust. The end of the war again led to production being restricted; in this case to just 66 planes, with deliveries being made in 1945. By this time the Navy was already looking at its first true carrier-borne jet, the McDonnell FH Phantom, which had been designed in 1943. The Phantom flew for the first time on 26 January 1945, powered by two Westinghouse 19XB-2B engines producing about 1,150 lbs of thrust (in the production version, these were replaced by J30 units producing 1,600 lbs of thrust). On 21 July 1946, the Phantom became the first American jet aircraft to land on an aircraft carrier. Production was gain restricted, and only 60 of the FH-1s were produced; they were delivered between 1947 and 1948.

Progress in the field was continuous, and McDonnell was already working of the FH-1's successor the XF2H-1 Banshee, which took to the air in January 1947. This plane closely resembled the Phantom, but was significantly better in all respects, including its two Westinghouse J34 engines that produced 3,250 lbs of thrust and guaranteed a top speed of about 580 mph. The plane was also more heavily armed, with four 20-mm cannons and two 500-lb bombs. The F2H Banshee went into service in March 1949.

141 bottom right The McDonnell FH-1 Phantom was the US Navy's first full jet, adopted in 1945. It was the first jet aircraft to land on an aircraft carrier.

It should be noted that only in very late 1940s were the Americans able to field an operational fighter that was an improvement on Germany's Second World War Messerschmitt Me.262. However, a number of planes were already in the flight-testing stage, and a number of excellent jet fighters were ready in time to participate in a new international war. Though it was geographically restricted to Korea, this new war was in effect a confrontation between the great Western and Eastern powers, and risked plunging the world into another disastrous global conflict.

At 0400 hours on Sunday, 25 June 1950, the North Korean army made a mass attack on the border with South Korea. The opposing forces were mismatched, and the North Koreans easily broke through the defensive lines and penetrated deep into South Korea. A few days later, the UN Security Council approved the use of force to repel the invaders and re-establish the border on the 38th parallel. The United States assumed responsibility for this military action and, together with 16 other countries, intervened drastically. For its part, North Korea could count on the initially indirect and then open support of the People's Republic of China, and then that of the Soviet Union. The result was a long, hard and bloody war that lasted for three years, into 1953.

The United States went into the war with the planes of the 5th Air Force, stationed in Japan.

These were mainly F80 jet fighters and F-82 Twin Mustangs, the USAF's last propeller-driven fighters. The North Koreans opposed these with inferior planes, the Soviet Yak-9 piston-engined fighter and the Ilyushin Il-10 Shturmovik fighter-bomber. Early in the war, the Americans introduced new combat jets, the USAF's Republic F-84 Thunderjet

142 top Two Grumman F9F Panther fighters fly over the USS Princeton on 28 May 1951 during the Korean War. They are discharging excess fuel from their wing tips before landing.

142 center A Grumman Panther prototype photographed during one of its first flights. The Panther made its maiden flight 24 November 1947 and the fighter entered service with the VF-51 in May 1950, shortly before the outbreak of the Korean War.

142 bottom The two Republic reconnaissance prototypes from the 84 series with swept wings. The aircraft behind had the definitive RF-84F Thunderflash nose design.

and the Navy's Grumman F9F Panther. Work began on the Thunderjet project in 1944 when the Republic designer Alexander Kartveli started thinking about a replacement for this P-47 Thunderbolt fighter-bomber. The prototype appeared in 1945 and was designed to use the General Electric J35 engine. The XP-84 first flew on 28 February 1946, and testing demonstrated that the design was valid. The fuselage was large and robust, with an air intake in the nose, and a mid-mounted wing was employed, along with a tricycle undercarriage and traditional cruciform tail. In summer 1947, the operational squadrons began to receive the first production F-84Bs. The plane was subject to development, with subsequent versions featuring improved engines and airframe characteristics. The definitive straight-wing version, the F-84G appeared in November 1950, and 3,025 were built. Numerous allied countries purchased and flew the F-84B. The G version (which had a nuclear capability) had a wingspan of 38 feet, and a maximum take-off weight of 23,500 lbs. It was powered by an Allison J35-A-29 engine, which developed 5,600 lbs of thrust and provided a top speed of 620 mph at sea level. The G version was armed with six 12.7-mm machine guns and 4,000 lbs of bombs or rockets. The last version of this aircraft was the F-84F Thunderstreak, which never saw action in Korea. The Thunderstreak was very different to the original Thunderjet, primarily because it had adopted a 45° swept wing and tailplane and had a redesigned cockpit canopy. The prototype flew on 5 June 1950, and production began to reach the squadrons in 1954. Over 2,700 Thunderstreaks were built, and the plane was supplied to a number of allied countries. The RF-84F Thunderflash reconnaissance version was distinguished by twin air intakes at the wing roots given that the nose was occupied by the photographic gear.

The US Navy's leading fighter was the Grumman Panther, which had made its first flight on 24 November 1947, designated the XF9F-2. The plane was originally commissioned during the war as a four-engined night-fighter. However, its development was delayed by various problems and, in accordance with the navy's mutating requirements, it was redesigned as a day-fighter. The F9F prototypes were powered by a Pratt & Whitney J45 engine producing about 5,000 lbs of thrust (the J45 engine was a version of the Rolls-Royce Nene built under license) or the Allison J33 of 4,600 lbs of thrust. The best version was however the one fitted with the J42 engine and produced in series as the F9F-2 and later as the improved F9F-5. This fighter entered operational service in May 1949 as the Panther, and more than 1,300 were built. The F9F-5 had a Pratt & Whitney J48 engine developing 6,250 lbs of thrust and a top speed of 602 mph. The plane had a maximum take-off weight of 18,700 lbs, and was armed with four 20-mm cannons and 2,000 lbs of bombs or rockets. In Korea, the Panther was used by both the Navy and the Marines, and was generally employed as a ground attack fighter, but also distinguished itself in aerial combat, scoring a number of victories.

Thanks to the availability of information regarding swept wings, Grumman decided to modify its Panther, just as Republic had uprated the F-84G. On 20 September 1951, the XF9F-6 Cougar made its maiden flight. It was powered by a J48 engine that produced 7,250 lbs of thrust; it boasted a 35° swept wing with flaps and slats. The Cougar entered service in November 1952. It provided no clear improvement over the Panther given that it carried the same armament and had a top speed of 646 mph. Nonetheless, more than 1,000 Cougars were produced, and the plane remained in service up until the end of the 1960s.

143 top Two Republic F-84G fighters during the early 1950s. The Thunderjet was the first USAF fighter-bomber designed to carry atomic bombs.

143 bottom The F-84 was widely used by the USAF during the Korean war as a fighter-bomber due to its 4000 lb bomb-load and its rockets. Here a F-84G launches a salvo of rockets against North Korean gun emplacements.

With these aircraft, the Americans succeeded in halting the North Korean advance and moving into the offensive. By 29 September 1950, the South Korean and ONU forces had once again regained the 38th parallel. However, the General MacArthur, the Allied commander, decided to pursue the enemy beyond the border in order to inflict a definitive defeat. The Allies' northwards advance finally provoked the direct intervention of Chinese forces and on 25 October an army of 180,000 men launched a counterattack on the Americans, forcing them to retreat. As if this was not enough, on 1 November a deadly new threat appeared in the skies of Korea, catching the western world by surprise. It was an agile, extremely fast swept-wing jet: the MiG-15.

The benefits of extremely advanced German technological research in the Second World War had not been the exclusive prerogative of the Americans. The Russians too, as they advanced from the East, had managed to capture and take back to the Soviet Union a notable quantity of research material and designs, as well as prototype and production examples of jet aircraft, together with a number of German engineers. Then, in 1946, Great Britain's labor Government gave the USSR the production plans and a number of examples of the Rolls-Royce Nene turbojet, at that time perhaps the most advanced jet engine in the world. These factors, combined with the great progress the Soviet aeronautical industry had made by the end of the war, soon

enabled the USSR to bridge the technological gap that separated it from the Americans and to produce, in great secrecy, excellent aircraft.

The first Russian jet fighters were the MiG-9 and the Yak-15, both equipped with German-designed engines. The prototype of the MiG-9, derived from 1944 F project, was a fighter with a mid-mounted straight wing and a nose air intake powered by two RD-20 engines (the BMW 003A unit delivering around 1,750 lbs of thrust). This fighter flew for the first time on 24 April 1946. The plane had a wingspan of 32 feet 8 inches, a length of 32 feet, and a maximum take-off weight of 11,150 lbs. It was armed with one 37-mm and two 23-mm cannons. After certain structural problems had been resolved, more than 1,000 MiG-9 fighters were produced in various versions including a trainer (MiG-9 UTI).

The Yak-15 also flew for the first time on 24 April 1946. It was a hurriedly designed machine, the result of combining a Junkers Jumo 004 engine (designated the RD-10 by the Russians) complete with nacelle and as many components as possible from the propeller-driven Yak-3 fighter. The Yak-15 was armed with two 23-mm cannons and could attain a top speed of 488 mph. Fewer than 300 were built over a period of two years. The Yak-15 was then used as the basis for the Yak-17, which was powered by the RD-10A engine, a unit that produced 2,200 lbs of thrust and was capable of providing a top speed of 516 mph.

These initial Soviet planes were relatively modest and overall their capabilities were inferior to the German aircraft on which they were based. The turning point came with the arrival of the Nene engine that was adopted for the MiG project for a swept-wing aircraft initiated in 1945 as Project S but never developed because of lack of a suitable power unit. Designated the I-310, the prototype made its maiden flight on 30 December 1947. The MiG-15 (known as the "Faggot" by NATO) had a fairly short fuselage with a nose air intake and 35° swept wings and tailplanes. It was powered by the RD-45F, a copy of the Nene engine, which produced 5,000 lbs of thrust and provided a top speed of 640 mph. The 32-foot long plane had an identical wingspan (to what), and a maximum take-off weight of 10,595 lbs. It was armed with one 37-mm and two 23-mm cannons. The MiG-15 entered service with the Soviet air force in late 1948; it was continually improved and over 9,000 were produced, including trainer and all-weather interceptor versions. Thousands of MiG-15s were built under license in Poland (as the Lim-1 then the −2 and −3), in Czechoslovakia (as the S-102 and 103) and in China (J-2), and the fighter was exported to over 30 countries. It remained in service until the 1980s.

On 8 November 1950, the first dogfight between jet aircraft in the history of aviation took place. A MiG-15 dueled with the F-80

144 top A MiG-15 displaying the Soviet Union's colors. This airplane popped up out of nowhere in the Korean War, giving UN forces serious difficulties.

144 bottom The Soviet Yakovlev Yak-15 fighter, was the outcome of a rushed Russian program to equip its air force with a jet aircraft. The plane combined the German Jumo 004 engine with the Yak-3 fuselage. It first flew in 1946.

145 top The North American F-86D interceptor version, with radar from the daytime fighter. It proved itself during the Korean War. Shown here is the F-86K export model, flying French colors.

145 bottom The F-86A Sabre entered service with the USAF in February 1949 and was used in Korea with the 4th Fighter Interceptor Wing from December 1950. It became the NATO fighter plane of the 1950s.

flown by Lt. Russell Brown, who had the better of the encounter. Nonetheless, neither the F-80 nor the F-84 were a match for the MiG-15, and the USAF decided to send the North American F-86 Sabre, its most advanced fighter, to Korea. The plane (the NE134), from which the F-86 Sabre derived dated back to 1944 and was an experimental fighter for the US Navy, subsequently designated as the XFJ-1 Fury. It featured a straight wing, an engine mounted in the center of the fuselage and a nose air intake. North American also offered the airplane to the army, which designated it the XP-86. The prototype's performance was not particularly impressive, however, and in June 945, after having received technical information regarding swept wing technology, the company suggested delaying the project so that the new type of wing could be adopted. The swept-wing prototype (powered by an Allison J53 engine producing 3,750 lbs of thrust) first flew on 1 October 1947; such was the improvement that the Air Force immediately ordered 221 of the P-86A version, soon redesignated as the F-86A, They planes began to enter service in February 1949. The F-86A version was equipped with the General Electric J47-GE-13 engine, producing 5,200 lbs of thrust, sufficient to guarantee a top speed of 671 mph.

On 13 December 1950, the 4th Fighter Interceptor Wing arrived in Kimpo, Korea, with its new Sabre fighters. Things began to change.

The MiG-15 retained an advantage in terms of rate of climb, could reach a higher ceiling, and was more maneuverable, but it also had major defects: at high speeds it became very unstable and when turning to starboard its pilots could on occasion lose control. Moreover, its gun-sight was inferior to those of the Sabres, and its pilots were not issued with G-suits. Lastly, the tactics the American pilots employed were frequently superior to those of their adversaries. By late December 1950, the Sabres had achieved a success ratio of 8 to 1 and dominated "MiG Alley" a corridor stretching 100 miles along the Yalu River (marking the China-N. Korea border), that the F-86As patrolled to prevent China-based MiGs from attacking. The Sabres flown by the Americans were gradually uprated; the E version, fitted with fully mobile tailplanes, first flew in September 1950, while the F-86F introduced the new "6-3" type wing with no slats, which made the plane more maneuverable at high speeds. The F-86F had a wingspan of 37 feet and a length of 37 feet 5 inches. It was armed with six 12.7-mm machine-guns and could carry an external load of up to 2,000 lbs and had a maximum take-off weight was 20,350 lbs. It was powered by the J47-GE-27 engine, which developed 5,900 lbs of thrust and provided a top speed of 634 mph. Other versions of the Sabre included the F-86D, an all-weather interceptor equipped with radar mounted in the nose, the computerized Hughes

fire control system for its 24 unguided rockets and a J47-GE-17B engine with an afterburner that produced 7,650 lbs of thrust. The D proved to be troublesome to develop and entered service only in March 1951; however over 2,000 were eventually built. The F-86K was a simplified version for use by NATO countries, and had a simplified armament composed of four 20-mm cannons. This plane first flew in 1954; subsequently 341 were built for use by the French, West German, Dutch, Norwegian, and Italian airforces. The last versions of the Sabre were the F-86H and L, both equipped with improved avionics, engines and airframes. The F-86 was an exceptional fighter for its time, and about 9,800 were constructed including all the various versions and those built under license in Canada, Australia, Italy and Japan. It was used by the air forces of over 30 countries around the world, and in some case remained in service until the 1980s. For its part, the US Navy, after the brief aside of the FJ-1, also flew a plane derived from the F-86; this was the FJ-2, similar to the F-86E apart from modifications required for carrier-borne use and an armament composed of four 20-mm cannons. The FJ-2 entered service in 1954, and was followed by the FJ-3 and 4 versions; about 1,000 Furies were built, and they remained in service until the early Sixties.

Chapter 10

The Era of the Great Transport Aircraft

The Second World War brusquely interrupted the development of air transport, but the hiatus was not wholly detrimental. The 1930s saw the continued rivalry of land and seaplanes, the latter being preferred primarily for transcontinental routes. The war led to considerable changes thanks both to the construction of numerous airfield facilities around the world and the technical developments that allowed for the introduction of multi-engined aircraft of exceptional range, reliability and payload capacity.

At the end of the war, it was only natural that civil air transport should be revived using the machines and airfields (and in certain cases the routes) already developed by military transportation during the war. The lion's share of the new business was naturally conducted by the Americans, who had had to develop the best cargo planes in order to link their homeland with the distant war theaters in Europe and the Pacific. Even before the war, the main major American airlines had actually been searching for new and more capacious aircraft; the design of the

Lockheed L-049 Constellation dated from 1939, while that of the Douglas DC-4 went back to 1936, at least in embryonic form. Both aircraft entered service with the US Army Air Force, the first designated the C-69 and the second the C-54 Skymaster.

In the immediate post-war period, America and its enterprising airlines began to look to the international markets once again and in particular to the transoceanic route linking the USA and Europe. In 1947, Boeing, Lockheed and Douglas were all producing long-range aircraft with pressurized cabins. Thus was born the era of the great piston- engine airliners, the Douglas DC-6 and DC-7, the Lockheed Constellation and Super Constellation, and the Boeing 377 Stratocruiser.

The Douglas DC-6 resulted from a USAAF requirement for an aircraft with an

even larger capacity than its successful C-54. The prototype of the new airplane (designated the XC-112A) completed its maiden flight on 15 February 1946, too late to contribute to the war effort, but just in time to be sold to the civilian airlines. The first of the 50 ordered by American Airlines flew on 29 June 1946, and entered service on the New York-Chicago route in April 1947. In design, the plane retained the wing of the DC-4 but introduced new and more powerful engines and a stretched fuselage that could accommodate up to 86 passengers in its high-density configuration. The DC-6B (a version with more power and more interior space that appeared in 1948) was equipped with four Pratt & Whitney R-2800-CB17 Double Wasp radial engines, each producing 2,535 hp, and the plane had a maximum take-off weight of about 107,000 lbs. It could sustain a cruising speed of 315 mph at 25,000 feet and had a maximum range of 4,725 miles. Like the C-118A Liftmaster (or R6D for the US Navy), the DC-6 also served with the US armed forces, with over 160 being ordered. A total of 704 DC-6s were built in various configurations. The development of its successor, the DC-7, was a result of

146 top A four-engined Breguet Provence belonging to Air France is guided to a halt by ground staff at Marignane Airport, Marseilles, February 1954.

146 bottom A KLM
Lockheed Constellation
landing at Schiphol Airport
shortly after the end of the
Second World War. Note the
temporary, makeshift
buildings in the background.

147 top The control room at
Northolt Airport in 1948.
Postwar development of air
transport required the
development and expansion of
ground services.

147 center This TWA
four-engined Douglas DC-4
was photographed in 1954.
The model was developed
from the military C-54
version, which first flew
in 1942.

147 bottom A Douglas
DC-6, British Eagle
Airways. This aircraft was a
development of the C-54/DC-
4; it kept the same wings but
had a new, larger fuselage
and new engines.

American Airlines' desire for an aircraft with
performance superior to that of the Super
Constellation used by its rival TWA. The
prototype of the new plane first flew on 18
May 1953, and was in effect a DC-6B with a
stretched fuselage and the same 3,295-hp
Wright R-3350 Turbo-Compound engines
that powered the Super Constellation. As the
first DC-7s lacked sufficient range to cross
the Atlantic safely when fully laden and facing
head winds, the DC-7C was thus developed
with an increased wingspan, more powerful
engines, and a fuselage stretched by 3 feet,
which allowed 105 passengers to be carried.
The same Wright engines uprated to
produce 3,447 hp provided a top speed of
406 mph at 21,500 feet and fully laden range
of 4,600 miles. Maximum take-off weight was
about 143,000 pounds.

*148 top The Lockheed
Constellation was originally
a military aircraft introduced
in 1943, but after the war it
was transformed into a
civilian plane. Shown here is
one belonging to Eastern
Airlines.*

Boeing's large civil transport aircraft derived from a military design. The Model 377, which completed its maiden flight on 8 July 1947, was closely related to the C-97 transport plane of 1944; this in turn had been derived from the B-29 bomber design. The 227 Stratocruiser could be ordered in various configurations, and was first used by Pan Am and BOAC, but only 55 were ever built. The Super Stratocruiser model with fuel tanks modified for operating on the Atlantic routes was equipped with four 3,549-hp Pratt & Whitney R-4360 Wasp Major engines and cruised at 340 mph at 25,000 feet. The maximum take-off weight was 145,800 lbs, and the aircraft boasted a maximum range of 4,200 miles.

After a brief military career during the war (just 22 entered service between 1944 and 1945), the Lockheed Constellation was developed essentially as a civil aircraft from December 1945, when it received the appropriate certification. The airplane immediately entered service with Pan Am

and TWA who in February 1946 began operating a scheduled service between the United States and Paris. The first true civilian Constellation was, however, the L-649 that had a more luxurious cabin and could carry up to 81 passengers (48-64 in the normal configuration). In 1949, as air transport became established and spread, increasing numbers of carriers required a larger aircraft. Lockheed responded with the Super Constellation (L-1049) that had a fuselage stretched by 18 feet 4 inches, and could carry up to 109 passengers. A total of 856 Constellations were built, including the military versions of the post-war period. The last model in the line was the L-1649 Starliner, equipped with four 3,447-hp Wright 988TC-18EA-2 engines that provided a top speed of 377 mph at 18,700 feet, with a range of 4,950 miles. This model was not a great commercial success owing to the emergence of jet aircraft.

In the second half of the 1940s, jet propulsion began to gain a foothold in the

military sphere, but in the civil sector it was seen as little more than a pipe-dream. The jet engines of the era were extremely thirsty and were thus considered to be unsuitable for commercial applications. However, in Great Britain another factor came into play: the jet engine was the only aeronautical technology in which the British had an advantage over the Americans. In order to regain a leading position in the world of aviation, the British decided to build a commercial jet airliner that would outclass all its propeller-driven rivals. This was recommended by the Brabazon Committee, a government study group charged with the task of reviving the British aeronautical industry in terms of commercial transport. There was only one company in the United Kingdom with the capacity undertake such a project, de Havilland, the firm already having experience in the design and production of an airframe and related jet engine, specifically with the Vampire fighter.

Work began in 1947 and was guided by a key concept: the jet engines had to return acceptable fuel consumption figures at altitudes of 32,000 feet and above, and the reduction in thrust due to the altitude had to be compensated by lower drag. The problem of pressurization also had to be resolved, given that at 32,000 feet a pressure would be exerted on the airframe the like of which had never been experienced before. The chosen architecture was traditional, with a 20° sweep to the wings and tailplanes. The four engines were to be buried in pairs in the wing roots. The project was designated the D.H.106 Comet. Recognizing the design's potential and driven by national pride, British Overseas Airways Corporation (BOAC) immediately ordered eight planes, with an option on the planes constructed after the fourteenth to be built.

The Comet, built with ample safety margins and subjected to unprecedented endurance testing, made its maiden flight on 27 July 1949, and immediately proved to be fast and highly promising. Further orders then arrived from British Commonwealth Pacific, Air France, Union Aéromaritime de Transport, Canadian Pacific, Japan Air Lines, the Royal Canadian Air Force, and even Pan

Am. On 2 May 1952, Comet service was inaugurated, with a flight from London to Johannesburg, South Africa.

The jet airliner unquestionably represented the future; piston engines had by now reached the limit of their potential and were frighteningly complex. Moreover, the noise and vibration they generated in the large four-engined planes made the flights uncomfortable for passengers who were now pleasantly surprised by the quietness and smoothness of the new jet engines.

The Comet was immediately successful and in the first year BOAC's planes carried 28,000 passengers with 88% of seats being filled. In 1953, de Havilland had orders for 50 more planes and were negotiating a further 100 orders. The Comet was capable of 485 mph, had a ceiling of 36,000 feet, and a range of over 3,100 miles. Despite certain accidents considered to be within the norms, the plane's career began to decline on 10 January 1954, when a Comet flying out of Rome's Ciampino airport mysteriously crashed into the sea near the island of Elba, with 35 people aboard. BOAC immediately grounded its fleet, and the British aviation authorities set up investigations. Despite their efforts, however, they found no clues as to the cause

of the disaster. It was thus decided to make 50 modifications of various kinds; all were intended to improve safety and would, it was thought, resolve any problems. The Comets resumed operation in the March of that year, while work continued on the recovery of the crashed Comet's wreckage, which was taken to Farnborough for the examination at the Royal Aircraft Establishment.

Then, on 8 April, another Comet unaccountably crashed while flying from Rome to Cairo. The fleet was grounded once again, and the RAE was put under intense pressure to find a solution to the mystery quickly. After conducting tests of various kinds, the RAE put forward the hypothesis of structural failure. At the end of a simulation carried out in a large tank of water with a complete fuselage, the sought-after proof was revealed. Following a certain number of pressurization cycles, the fuselage of the Comet would crack at the square corners of the windows, a feature that had already been criticized by the American aviation authorities. It was not only the angular design of the windows that caused the problems, but its combination with a fuselage that had been lightened as much as possible to allow the plane to fly higher and thus extend its range. The accidents undermined the passengers' faith in the aircraft, and de Havilland hastily made significant modifications. In the third series, oval windows were introduced along with other changes that made the Comet ever better, but its fate had already been decided. American manufacturers had taken full advantage of the time lost by the British and had begun to turn out their own jet airliners. The Comet continued to carry passengers up to 1980, but only about 80 Comets were built. Great Britain had lost forever its supremacy in the field of commercial aviation.

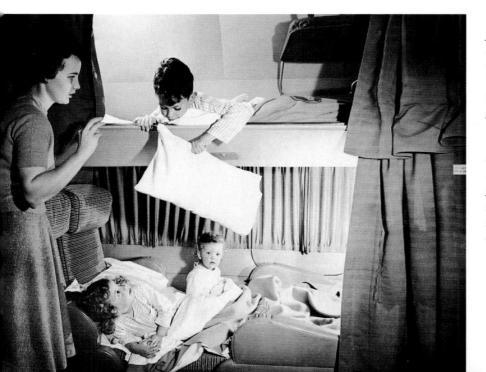

The American firms had certainly not been standing idle, but it was Boeing, the producer of the least successful piston-engined airliner, that was most committed to the creation of a jet plane. Boeing was, in fact, the only major firm to have experience with large jets, having built the B-47 Stratojet, a six-engined bomber with swept wings that first flew in December 1947.

From the outset, the Boeing engineers were convinced that one of the errors made with the Comet was its size: it was too small to be economical. The new Boeing was designed to carry twice the number of passengers. Initially the company considered developing the new jet on the basis of the Stratocruiser, but it soon became clear that this was not a viable option. The design was completely revised even though, for reasons of "disinformation" with regard to its rivals, Boeing maintained the original serial designation 367. In reality, within the restricted circle of those working on the project, the aircraft already had another name: 707, because it was Boeing's 707th project. The aircraft had an accentuated 35° sweep to its wings, which carried four separate pods for the four engines. The fuselage was slim and streamlined and the

risk; the 707 project meant success or outright failure for the company. The design and development work was carried out with the utmost thoroughness, and the resulting aircraft was above all safe and extremely robust. The fuselage, for example, had stood up to a grueling sequence of 50,000 pressurization cycles.

The first Boeing 707 was a truly large airplane for its time: it was 128 feet long and weighed around 160,000 lbs. It completed its maiden flight on 15 July 1954, powered by four Pratt & Whitney JT3P engines each producing 9,500 lbs of thrust. The plane immediately displayed great handling characteristics. Boeing initially aimed for a military clientele, and the company demonstrated the prototype (equipped with a rigid probe for in-flight refueling) to the USAF in order to underline its potential as a jet tanker. In March 1955, the USAF ordered a preliminary batch of 29 of the KC-135As, the military tanker version of the 707, eventually the Air Force acquired a total of more than 800. Having received military approval, Boeing then modified prototype and fitted it out for civilian use. In this configuration, the 707 immediately made all other transport aircraft

Douglas suffered a severe shock in 1955 when Pan Am's management declared that with the appearance of the Boeing 707, Douglas risked missing the boat. Pan Am wanted the competition between the two giant manufacturers to result in better, more economical aircraft, and a Boeing monopoly of the four-engined jet market would not have been at all welcome. The task facing Douglas was difficult, the DC-8 would have to be launched fully developed if it was going to better its rival. The company naturally took advantage of the experience accumulated and the defects identified with the 707. The design process was painstaking; given the costs and delay Boeing had experienced, the Douglas plane had to be right first time. The passenger cabin was larger and the aircraft had a longer range than the 707. Douglas's audacity was rewarded, and less than five months after the announcement of the launch of the program, Pan Am announced that it would be purchasing 25 DC-8s and 20 707s. Two weeks later, United also made public its intention to acquire 30 DC-8s. Boeing was stunned: Douglas was selling more jet liners than it was without even

tailplanes were also swept.

Irrespective of its final form, William Allen, Boeing's president, wanted the new design to be appropriate for both commercial transport and military tanker applications. He knew, in fact, that the Air Force would soon need new jet tankers to replace the old propeller-driven Boeing KC-97s, whose performance was inadequate to service the B-47 and the future B-52.

The American airlines also started to take an active interest in jet airliners. Unfortunately, however, at that time they were carrying heavy debts resulting from expansion programs that had led to the acquisition of hundreds of propeller-driven planes. The USAF also lacked the funds to replace its KC-97s. Boeing would have to start up and finance the 707 program on its own. In April 1952, the board of directors authorized the investment of $15 million in the project. At this point Boeing was running a truly enormous

of the era seem obsolete. On 13 October 1955, Pan Am ordered the first six planes of the production version, the 707-120.

In reality, the 707 did not have an entirely trouble-free birth; early on there were problems with the brakes, the thrust provided by the engines was insufficient when the aircraft was fully laden, and the range was inadequate for fully laden transatlantic flights. The 707-120 was therefore immediately equipped with JT3C-6 engines producing 13,500 lbs of thrust. At this time, Douglas was the largest company involved in building civil aircraft, and it had by no means been resting on its laurels. Its confidential DC-8 project for a 560-mph, four-jet airliner had not, however, attracted much interest from the airlines to which it had been shown secretly in 1952. They had preferred to order the most recent propeller-driven transport aircraft, the DC-7.

having built a single plane, and the airlines appeared to be more attracted to the DC-8 than the to the 707. The DC-8 prototype first flew on 30 May 1958: the aces in hand with respect to the 707 were more powerful engines, a greater range, and a larger cabin. All that Boeing could do was redesign the 707.

Thus was born the 707-320 Intercontinental, which first flew on 10 October 1959. This was the first transoceanic version; it was followed by the 707-320C version, which had JT3D-7 engines producing 19,000 lbs of thrust. These engines provided a top cruising speed of over 600 mph, a ceiling of 39,000 feet, a maximum range of 5,750 miles with 147 passengers, and a maximum take-off weight of about 333,500 lbs. With this aircraft, and thanks to the design flexibility of the 707 fuselage, Boeing regained supremacy over Douglas. In the meantime, the international airlines had come to accept the need to operate jets. American Airlines purchased 30 707s, with an option for a further 20. Delta, Eastern, Trans Canada, Western, Japan Air Lines, KLM, SAS, Alitalia and Swissair all went for the DC-8, while the 707 was ordered by Lufthansa, Air France, Sabena, Continental, Western, TWA and Air India. More than 1,000 707s and more than 550 DC-8s were built.

The airlines appreciated the new jets' low running costs, while passengers were more than happy with the increased convenience: greater comfort and speed and, with the increase in the number of flights, even cheaper tickets. The world truly had become a smaller place, and even distant lands and the VIP life-style now seemed to be available to all.

While the struggle for supremacy in the long-range sector was going on in America, in Europe there were those who had recognized the potential market for a medium-short range jet. On the old continent, in fact, large jets were still superfluous and overly expensive. In 1951, the French government announced a competition among the nation's aeronautical firms for the design of an aircraft with a range of less than 1,250 miles and seating about 60 passengers. Six companies responded, and in 1952 the design submitted by Sud-Est (SNCASE) of Toulouse was announced as the winner. The Caravelle as it was named, had an innovative layout, characterized by the positioning of the engines at the tail, either side of the fin.

The Caravelle was equipped with two powerful Rolls-Royce Avon RA.29 Mk.552 engines producing 10,500 lbs of thrust. This allowed the plane to fly on a single engine in cases of emergency. The fact that the engines were at the rear provided additional advantages such as a cleaner, more efficient wing and a quieter cabin. The first client to purchase the new aircraft was naturally Air France.

The Caravelle completed its maiden flight on 27 May 1955 and soon it proved to be a successful design. Continuously developed and improved (up to 140 passengers eventually

150 A Sud-Est Caravelle belonging to the Swiss airline Air City about to land. The Caravelle project was prompted by the French government; it became the first successful European jet, eventually sold to 35 airlines.

151 top The DC-8 was Douglas's answer to the Boeing 707 and was initially an improvement on its rival. Note the DC-8-63 of 1967, which had various improvements in terms of streamlining, engines, flight range and flaps and slats.

151 center A three-engined British Airways Hawker Siddeley HS.121 Trident in descent. This airplane was designed for short journeys but was not popular with airlines; only 117 were built.

151 bottom A Lufthansa Boeing 707 in flight. The 707 originated as a military aircraft, covering its development costs with US government orders.

being seated), 281 Caravelles were constructed, and it was used by more than 35 airlines.

Having seen the success of the Caravelle and given market demands, the British also focused on the medium-small jet sector. The result was the introduction in 1956 of the de Havilland DH.121, which with Hawker Siddeley's acquisition of de Havilland, was soon to become known as the H.S. 121 Trident. It first flew on 9 January 1962. However, despite a number of interesting features (it was the world's first aircraft with automatic landing gear), the Trident was never particularly successful, by 1975, only 117 had been built. On the other hand, the American firms were now also looking at the medium- and short-haul sector, and a number of the most successful and famous airliners in the history of aviation were beginning to take shape.

Chapter 11

The Great Fighters of the Fifties

Probably no period in aviation history saw such a proliferation of avant-garde aircraft as did the 1950s, especially in the United States. Many factors explain this phenomenon. Aeronautical research, spurred on by the demands of the Second World War, had continued to set new objectives, above all developing the jet engine and the swept wing, and breaking the sound barrier. Moreover, the Cold war's ominous context stimulated this progress. The confrontation between the Western powers and the Communist world, particularly the Korean War, encouraged governments to approve vast funds for military and aerospace research and development. While there was no open conflict between East and West (owing to the presence of the nuclear deterrent), there was nonetheless a very real technological confrontation as the adversaries attempted to intimidate one another.

The Korean War had shocked the Americans. The introduction of the MiG-15 and its advanced capabilities had come as a complete surprise to western aeronautical experts and had clearly demonstrated that the Soviet Union was capable of producing aircraft with performance very similar and even superior to that of the best American jets. Any American advantage demonstrated in the contested skies was insufficient to reassure the USAF and the Navy. America needed aircraft that were clearly superior to those of its enemy. In short, thanks above all to the experience and data accumulated by the NACA (subsequently NASA) and the USAF from the X series experimental planes, the American aviation industry was able to produce aircraft with ever more remarkable features. Within just four years, no fewer than six new fighters were introduced, the famous "Century Series" planes.

The first of these was the North American F-100 Super Sabre, an airplane designed as the heir to the extremely successful F-86

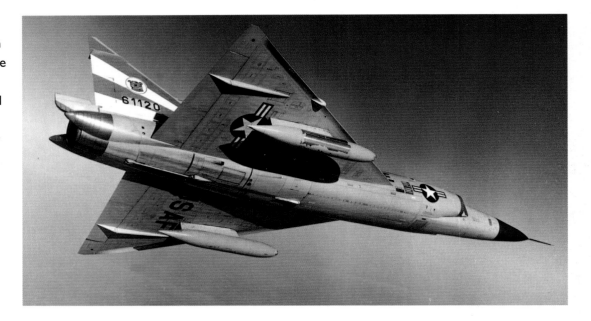

produced by the same company. The program was launched in 1949, departing from the previous Sabre design by adopting a 45° swept wing and a J57 engine with an afterburner. In both performance and weight the new aircraft was far superior. With the outbreak of the Korean War, the USAAF accelerated the program, and the first prototype flew on 25 May 1953. Despite certain problems with inertia roll coupling, the Super Sabre proved to be the world's first aircraft designed for operational use capable of exceeding Mach 1 in level flight. It was thus approved rapidly and put into production as the F-100A, with the first planes reaching the operational squadrons in September 1954. After a number of incidents involving inertia roll coupling, however, the Super Sabre was grounded, and the F-100C version was developed. This version had longer wings and fins, as well as a probe for in-flight refueling.

The definitive Super Sabre model was the F-100C. It had a substantially modified wing and avionics and a weapons system that could include nuclear bombs. This version was 46 feet 11 inches long and had a maximum take-off weight of about 34,850 pounds. Its Pratt & Whitney J57-P-21A produced 17,000 lbs of

thrust, which was sufficient to provide the plane with a maximum speed of about 865 mph. Last, it was armed with four 20-mm cannons and up to 7,500 lbs of external auxiliary tanks, bombs, missiles and rockets. The final version of this plane was the two-seat F-100F that was successfully employed in the Vietnam War to attack enemy anti-aircraft defenses. A total of 2,294 Super Sabres were produced, with the plane also being exported to Denmark, France, Taiwan, and Turkey. The fighter was highly regarded within the USAF. As well as equipping the Thunderbirds' aerobatic team, it was also extensively used in the early phases of the Vietnam War. The USAF's last Super Sabres were finally decommissioned in the 1980s, after service with the National Guard.

The second of the Century Series planes was the Convair F-102 Delta Dagger, a design derived from the experimental XF-92A of 1948 and influenced by research into supersonic flight. The first prototype, characterized by a delta wing and an absence of stabilizers and elevators at the tail, made its first flight on 24 October 1953, but its performance was disappointing: the aircraft was unable to achieve supersonic speed.

152 The Convair F-102A Delta Dagger was the first supersonic fighter with a delta wing. It made its maiden flight in October 1953. More than 1000 were built, some as the two-seater TF-102A.

153 top and center The F-102 was the first fighter to which 'area rules' were applied to improve performance during trans-sonic and supersonic flight. Note the different form of the fuselage in the first prototype (above) and after modification (below).

153 bottom The North American F-100 Super Sabre fitted with a turbojet and afterburner. This was the first fighter in the world to fly horizontally at supersonic speed. This is a two-seater F-100F.

Thanks to recently completed wind tunnel experiments concerning the laws of aerodynamics (they scientifically codified the most appropriate forms and volumes for breaking the sound barrier), the XF-102's fuselage was redesigned. It assumed a distinctive "Coke-bottle" shape, becoming slimmer in the area where it joined with the wing. The YF-102A prototype built on the basis of the new calculations first flew on 19 December 1954. From this very first flight, the plane proved easily capable of exceeding Mach 1.

The production F-102A entered service in 1956. Even though it was a transitional fighter, it was characterized by advanced engineering features (such as honeycomb elements), and its interceptor armament was composed of radar-controlled firing associated with GAR-1D Falcon air-to-air missiles. The Delta Dagger was just over 68 feet long, had a wingspan of 38 feet and a maximum take-off weight of about 31,250 lbs. Its Pratt & Whitney J57-P23 turbojet engine produced 17,200 lbs of thrust on afterburn, sufficient to provide the plane with a maximum speed of 825 mph or Mach 1.25 at 35,000 feet. Around 1000 F-102As were produced, including the two-seat TF-102A training version, and it remained in service with the National Guard through the 1960s before subsequently being converted to PQM-102A radio-controlled target drone specifications.

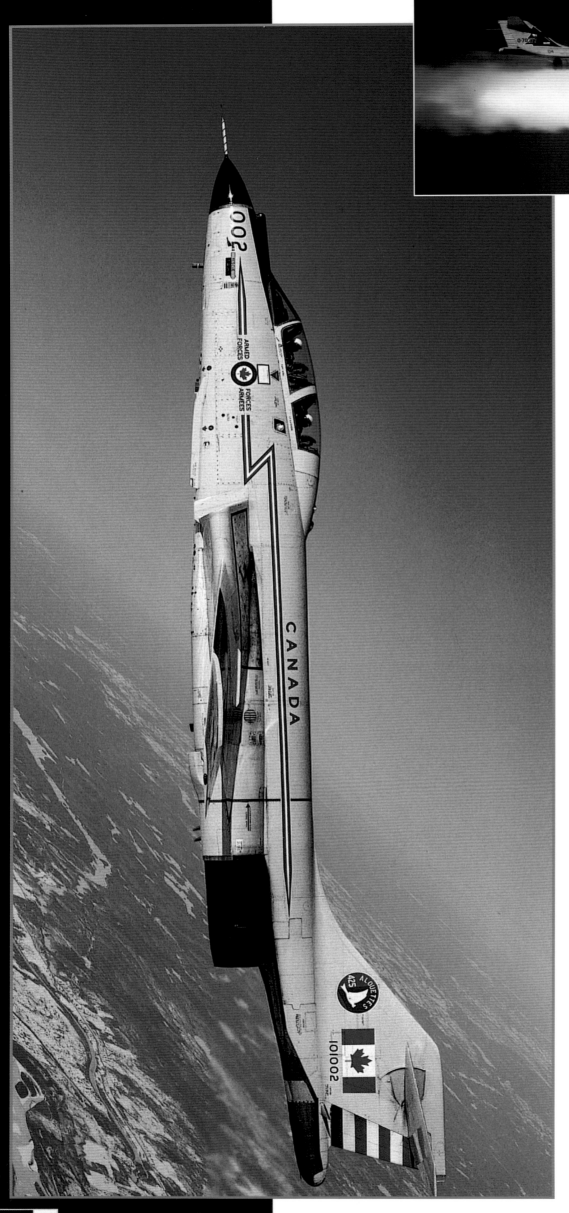

The third of the Century Series jets in chronological order of introduction was the Lockheed F-104 Starfighter. It completed its first flight as the XF-104 on 7 February 1954. The Starfighter, whose design drew upon the experience and suggestions of pilots fighting in the Korean War, was the first operational fighter capable of reaching Mach 2, and breaking the sound barrier while climbing. In effect, what the USAF demanded of this plane was acceleration and outright speed, and in order to achieve these objectives Lockheed's chief designer, Clarence "Kelly" Johnson (the "father" of the P-38 and F-80), was uncompromising. The F-104 had a stubby laminar-profile wing and a long, aerodynamic fuselage little bigger than the engine it housed. The pilot and the armament, radar and avionics systems were all crammed into the restricted space of the nose.

The F-104A entered service with the USAF on 26 January 1958; it was 54 feet 5 inches long, with a wingspan of 21 feet 7 inches, and a maximum take-off weight of 22,000 lbs. A single General Electric J79-GE-3B producing 14,800 lbs of thrust powered the aircraft to a maximum speed of 1367 mph, or Mach 2.2. The F-104A was typically armed with two AIM-9B Sidewinder air-to-air missiles and an M61 Vulcan 20-mm cannon. While its performance was exceptional, the plane as a whole did not satisfy the armed forces because it was too difficult to fly, had a restricted range, and was only lightly armed: it was soon passed on to the reserve squadrons. The successor F-104C, fitted with a more powerful engine and optimized as a fighter-bomber, was no more successful; both versions saw limited action in Vietnam but were in practice rejected, although the Starfighter continued to fly with the National Guard up until the 1970s.

The export version of the aircraft, the F-104G Super Starfighter (and the two-seater

154 left The McDonnell F-101A Voodoo fighter's development was long and difficult, and when the plane entered service, it was assigned the role of interceptor. Canada purchased this aircraft, calling it the CF-101, and kept it in service until the start of the 1980s.

154 top right As an interceptor, the F-101A was able to fire Genie nuclear air-to-air missiles, as seen in the photograph of the National Guard launching the aircraft's weapons in Maine.

TF-104G) enjoyed better fortunes, thanks above all to the fact that America's allies were offered the opportunity to construct it themselves under license, an offer taken up by Germany, Holland, Belgium, Italy, Canada and Japan. The F-104G completed its maiden flight on 7 June1960. The plane featured a strengthened airframe (the maximum weight had risen to around 28,750 lbs), improved avionics and a new engine, the J79-GE-11A producing 15,800 lbs of thrust on afterburn and providing a top speed in excess of 1,350 mph at 36,000 feet. The armament remained the same as that of the F-104C with the Vulcan cannon and the external load of up to 4,000 lbs, which could include supplementary fuel tanks, bombs and rockets or a nuclear bomb. Sixteen countries adopted the Starfighter, and a total of 2,576 (including all variants) were built.

In 1966, Italy decided to develop an advanced version of the Starfighter designated the F-104S. This variant entered service in 1969; it had improved avionics, an even more robust airframe (which featured two new underwing pylons) allowing a maximum take-off weight of 30,850 lbs, and a heavier weapons load. The plane's maximum speed was about 1,500 mph and the principal armament consisted of the semi-active radar-guided AIM-7 Sparrow air-to-air missile. Modernized on a number of occasions, the F-104S.ASA-M is still in service with the Italian Air Force.

plane was therefore adapted as a two-seater all-weather interceptor for the tactical command. It entered service early in 1957 as the F-101B. The B model was 67 feet 3 inches long, had a wingspan of 39 feet 4 inches, and a maximum take-off weight of 52,400 lbs. It was powered by two Pratt & Whitney J57-P-55 engines producing 14,880 lbs of thrust on afterburn, which gave it a maximum speed of 1,222 mph, or Mach 1.85. The armament consisted of two GAR-2 Genie rockets with nuclear warheads or up to six AIM-4 air-to-air missiles. More effective planes soon replaced the Voodoo for interceptor duties, while the reconnaissance versions (RF-101A and C) remained in service longer. Just over 800 Voodoos were produced, of which 132 were sold to Canada, where they were kept in service as CF-101 interceptors until 1984.

The Republic company built the fifth aircraft in the Century Series on its own initiative, in the hope that it would be selected to replace its own F-84s, which were already in service. Getting underway in 1951, the project involved the creation of a large, single-seat fighter-bomber capable of supersonic performance while carrying a large, potentially nuclear, weapons load. The USAF approved the project in 1954, and the first YF-105A prototype flew on 22 October 1955. As was traditional with Republic, the plane had a large fuselage housing a single Pratt & Whitney J57

turbojet, a mid-mounted wing with air intakes at the roots, and swept tailplanes. The new and more powerful J75 engine was soon available, however, and the plane was re-engined and designated as the YF-105B, making its maiden flight on 22 May 1956; the production version, the F-105B Thunderchief, began to enter service in May 1958.

After 75 F-105Bs had been built, production shifted to the F-105D, which had a length of 64 feet 4 inches, and a wingspan of 34 feet 5 inches, an uprated engine and new avionics that gave the plane all-weather capability. The engine was the J75-P-19W, producing 24,500 lbs of thrust and offering reach 1,250 mph at the plane's operating ceiling. Maximum take-off weight was 52,850 lbs, of which external loads – auxiliary tanks, bombs, rockets and missiles – accounted for 14,000 lbs. A 20-mm Vulcan cannon completed the armament. The model D was followed by the two-seater F-105F, which featured a stretched fuselage. This model proved to be of great use in combating enemy anti-aircraft defenses and led to the development of the EF-105F and F-105G versions, both used in the "Wild Weasel" role with special electronic equipment and Shrike and Standard anti-radiation missiles. All these models were widely used in Vietnam and were withdrawn from service only in the early 1980s.

The fourth of the Century Series was the McDonnell F-101 Voodoo, which made its first flight in definitive form on 29t September 1954. In reality, the original design for the aircraft dated back to 1946, when the USAAF issued a requirement for a jet-powered escort fighter for long-range operations. MacDonnell built the XF-88 prototype in 1947, but owing to a change of policy by the armed forces and the strategic command (as well as problems associated with the engines and the financing) the program was suspended and only revived in the face of the developing war in Korea. The new project was designated the F-101 and was to be a large, swept-wing aircraft with twin engines and a T-tail. However, it proved ill suited to the bomber escort role owing to its insufficient range. It

155 top The Lockheed F-104 Starfighter was the first standard fighter to fly at speeds in excess of Mach 2. Everything in this no-compromise project was designed to boost acceleration and speed. However, the USAF never liked the plane.

155 bottom The Republic F-105 Thunderchief was designed as a supersonic fighter-bomber able to carry 14,000 lbs of bombs and rockets. Shown here are two refueling over Vietnam.

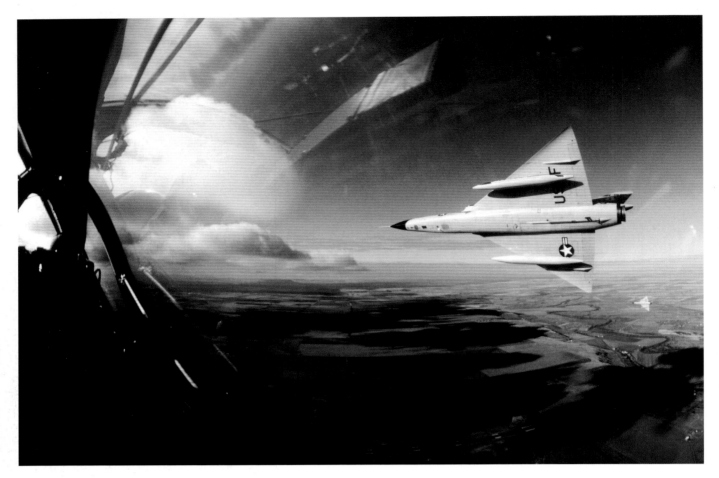

The last of the Century Series was the Convair F-106 Delta Dart, basically the direct descendent of the earlier F-102. This last had never fully satisfied the USAF, which required an all-weather supersonic interceptor with computerized fire control. The F-012B was intended to be the definitive version, but in June 1956, the in-development plane was redesignated the F-106. This aircraft was equipped with a new and far more powerful engine (the J75) and a Hughes MA-1 computerized fire-control system that finally seemed to have been debugged. The first Delta Dart flew on 26 December 1956. It had very similar lines to its predecessor, with a length of 70 feet 9 inches, a wingspan of 38 feet 4 inches, and a maximum take-off weight of about 41,830 lbs. The J75-P-17 engine was almost identical to that of the F-105, and provided the Delta Dart with a maximum speed of 1,525 mph, or in excess of Mach 2.3, at its operational ceiling. The armament comprised an AIR-2A Genie or 2B Super Genie missile with a nuclear warhead and four AIM-4F/G Falcon air-to-air missiles. The armaments system was initially unconvincing, but the USAF nonetheless acquired a total of 277 single-seat F-106As and 63 two-seat F-106Bs that entered service in October 1959. Over the years the Delta Dart proved to be an effective, reliable plane and remained in service as an interceptor with the National Guard until the second half of the 1980s. The Dart has subsequently been used as a radio-controlled target drone after numerous planes had been converted to QF-106 specifications.

While the USAF acquired a notable variety of advanced fighters to perform various roles, the US Navy was lagging behind in this process of modernization. A number of carrier-based combat aircraft such as the AD-1 Skyraider were actually still propeller driven, while the fighter ranks had seen a proliferation of different models, all of modest performance. Early in the 1950s, the Panther, Cougar and Fury were joined by aircraft such as the Vought F7U Cutlass (first flight in 1948), the McDonnell F3H Demon (1951) and the Douglas F4D Skyray (1951). These planes shared innovative technical features, but also problems regarding the efficiency and performance of their engines, which were frequently underpowered. None of these fighters had supersonic capabilities.

Things began to change with the advent of the Grumman F11 Tiger, a development of the Panther and Cougar line. The aircraft was,

however, completely new and adopted a thin-profile wing, swept tailplanes and a more powerful engine. The first prototype took to the air on 30 July 1954, but in January 1955 a second prototype was introduced. This had an afterburner-equipped J65 engine that made the Tiger the Navy's first supersonic fighter, with a top speed of 752 mph. The F11F entered service in March 1957, but its operational career was fairly brief. It was immediately overshadowed by a brilliant new design: the Vought F-8 Crusader, the US-Navy's first true superfighter:

The F-8 Crusader resulted from a requirement issued by the US Navy in 1952 for a new supersonic carrier-borne plane. Vought won the competition (designated VAX) the following year, and received an order to build two XF8U-1 prototypes in keeping with its design. The aircraft was muscular single-seater characterized by a high swept wing with a variable angle of incidence that could be adjusted during the take-off and landing phases so that the pilot could avoid giving the plane an excessively nose-up stance. The prototype first flew on 25 March 1955. It was equipped with a Pratt & Whitney J57-P-11 engine producing 14,800 lbs of thrust, and immediately proved to be an excellent, fast, and maneuverable airplane. A total of 318 F8U-1s were ordered, and serial production was rapidly initiated. The first F8U-1s were already in service by March 1957. The plane was gradually improved to give it more power, strength and firepower as well as all-weather and reconnaissance capabilities.

The definitive version, the F8U-2NE appeared in 1961. (From 1962 on, following the rationalization of US military designations, the Crusader became the F-8 and the F8U-2NE model became the F-8E.) The F8U-2NE was powered by a J57-P-20A turbojet producing 18,000 lbs of thrust on afterburn

and could reach 1,120 mph, the equivalent of about Mach 1.7. It had a maximum length of 54 feet 5inches, a wingspan of just over 35 feet and a maximum take-off weight of 33,995 lbs. The weapons system retained the original four 20-mm cannons – which, with the advent of the F-4, earned the plane the nickname of "The Last of the Gunfighters." To this armament was added the possibility of mounting up to four AIM-9 Sidewinder air-to-air and bombs or rockets on the two underwing pylons for a maximum total of 5,000 lbs. A total of 1,259 Crusaders were built, and the plane fought successfully in Vietnam. In RF-8G form, the Crusader remained in service until the early 1980s. A number of Crusaders were sold to the Philippines air force, while 42 F-8Es (FNs) were delivered to the French navy in January 1965. These were actually the last operational Crusaders, though they were withdrawn from service only in December 1999.

The aircraft discussed above were the principal American designs of the 1950s. However, aeronautical engineers on the other side of the Iron Curtain were similarly prolific. Following the success of the MiG-15 fighter, the MiG factory (led by the designers Mikoyan and Gurevich) soon began work on a new design that would eradicate the defects identified in the earlier plane, particularly with regard to its aerodynamics. The I-330 prototype appeared in January 1950. In terms of overall lines, the I-330 resembled the earlier design, but introduced a longer fuselage, larger tailplanes, a 45° swept wing and, of course, a more powerful engine. The plane went into production in 1951 as the MiG-17, reaching the first operational squadrons the following year. A Klimov VK-1A engine producing 5,950 lbs of thrust enabled the I-330 to reach a top speed of 690 mph. It had a length of 36 feet 8 inches, a wingspan of 31 feet 5 inches, and maximum take-off weight of 13,400 lbs. The first model (known to NATO as "Fresco-A") was followed by the MiG-17P, which had a VK-1F engine fitted with an afterburner that produced 7,450 lbs of thrust, giving the plane to reach a top speed of 693 mph. The MiG-17 was more heavily armed than the MiG-15. It fielded three 23-mm cannons, one 37-mm cannon, and free-fall weaponry weighing up to 1,100 lbs. Next followed the MiG-17FP, which was equipped with Izumrud interception radar; then came the MiG-17PFU, which was stripped of its cannons but could carry up to four AA-1 "Alkali" radar-guided air-to-air missiles.

The MiG-17 remained in production in various forms up until 1958, with about 9,000 planes being built (about 3,000 of these were built under license in China as the J-5 and in Poland as the LIM-5). Simple and robust, the MiG-17 served with the air forces of all the Soviet bloc countries, as well as the USSR, in some cases up to the present day.

The next development was the MiG-19, an aircraft born out of the I-350 project that was intended to provide the Soviet Union with a supersonic airplane capable of competing with the new American fighters. The prototype, which first appeared in 1953, had a strong 55° sweep to its wings, new tailplanes with low-set horizontal surfaces. The MiG-19 was equipped with two AM-5 engines with no afterburners. This plane first flew on 18 September 1953, and went into service in 1954 with afterburner-equipped AM-5F engines. (NATO designated it "Farmer-A.") However, the plane was not yet fully developed and demonstrated serious instability at high speeds. The MiG-19S version was consequently developed, featuring new, completely mobile tailplanes. This version was followed by the SF, powered by new Turmansky RD-9BF engines producing 3,300 lbs of thrust, sufficient to propel the SF to a top speed of 901 mph. The plane was 39 feet 7 inches long, had a wingspan of slightly over 30 feet, and a maximum take-off weight of just over 20,000 lbs. It was armed with three 30-mm cannons and up to 1,100 lbs of external weaponry.

The MiG-19P all-weather interceptor version was introduced in 1958, equipped with radar and two 23-mm cannons. This was followed by the MiG19PFM, which featured radar and four AA-1 air-to-air missiles, then the PF interceptor with two 30-mm cannons, then the MiG-19R reconnaissance version, and finally the two-seater MiG-19UTI trainer. About 2,500 MiG-19s appear to have been built in the USSR, while double that number were built in China, which acquired a production license for the MiG-19S. China built the MIG-19 and exported it numerous countries as the J-6/F-6 and, in two-seater form, as the FT-6. These last and their derivatives are still in service in a number of Asian countries.

The introduction of the MiG-21A gave Soviet aviation a decisive technological and operational boost. The new MiG was the Warsaw Pact countries' first aircraft capable of Mach 2; it came as a disagreeable surprise to the West, one with similar impact to that of theMiG-15's introduction. Work on a new, lightweight, supersonic fighter had begun as early as 1953. The first configuration (E-2) was the logical development of what had gone before and featured a swept wing. Subsequently, however, the E-5, which introduced a delta wing, was preferred. It first flew on 9 January 1956. Out of this

experimental aircraft came the E-6; in effect the prototype MiG-21, which first flew on 20 May 1958. While featuring a delta wing, the jet retained strongly swept traditional tailplanes and had a nose air intake with an antishock cone to feed the afterburner-equipped Turmanski R-11 turbojet. Put into production in 1959 as the MiG-21F ("Fishbed-C" to NATO), the new fighter boasted excellent level flight and climbing performance and was sufficiently agile, but was only lightly armed with two 30-mm cannons. It was 43 feet 10 inches long and had a wingspan of 23 feet 3 inches, and a maximum take-off weight of 16,700 lbs. The engine produced 12,765 lbs of thrust, giving the plane a top speed of about

1,245 mph at its operational ceiling.

The following year, the MiG-21F's first mass-produced version, the MiG-21F-13 was introduced. This plane was equipped with radar and two K-13 (AA-2 "Atoll") air-to-air missiles, the Soviet copy of the AIM-9B Sidewinder. Over the years, this aircraft was continuously developed and improved. The four principal versions followed. The MiG-21PF featured a more powerful engine, larger fuel tanks, and new radar system): the MiG-21PFM

(from 1964 on) featured a new system of flaps, an enlarged fin, new weaponry and avionics. The MiG21R, the reconnaissance version, featured a pod and larger dorsal fairing; and the MiG21S and SM both featured a more powerful engine, new radar, four underwing pylons and an internal cannon. The MiG21S had an export version designated MiG-21MF). Then in 1972 the MiG21BIS ("Fishbed-L") appeared, introducing a larger dorsal avionics pack, new R-13M, R-55 and R-60 air-to-air missiles, and a new Soyus-Gavrilov R-25-300 engine producing around 16,535 lbs of thrust, sufficient to provide the plane with a top speed of 1352 mph, or Mach 2.05. The plane's maximum take-off weight

rose to 22,928 lbs, with 2,650 lbs accounted for by the external weapons load.

The MiG-21 design gave rise to various two-seater training versions, starting with the original MiG-21U (based in the MiG-21F-13 and designated "Mongol-A" by NATO), and proceeding to the MiG-21US and lastly to the MiG-21UM. Over 11,950 MiG-21s were produced in the USSR and, under license, in China (as the J-7/F-7), Czechoslovakia, and India. During the 1960s and 1970s, it was in service with all the Soviet bloc countries, in close to fifty air forces. It is estimated that about 3,000 Fishbeds are still in service today; in fact, in the 1990s two projects were introduced to modernize MiG-21s that were still flying. Modernization involved extensive improvements to the airframe, the avionics, and the weapons system. The Soviet MAPO-MiG project developed the MiG-21-93, which India has adopted. IAI, the Israeli project, offers the MiG-21-200, the version chosen by Romania and designated the Lancer. Other countries are likely to take advantage of the updating to continue using an aircraft that even forty years after its first flight remains a fairly effective weapon.

Chapter 12

The precarious alliance between the United States and the Soviet Union lasted only until the defeat of their common Nazi enemy. Even during the conflict, despite the incessant flood of military aid dispatched by America to the USSR (planes, trucks, tanks and prime materials in vast quantities), Stalin was never particularly friendly toward his western Allies, either politically or militarily. A number of American bomber crews who had made emergency landings behind the Russian lines in 1944 and ad 1945 were, in fact, jailed as common prisoners and only released many months later; their planes,

Communist, recognized that the USSR's undeclared aim was that of exploiting the war to take control of as much of Europe as possible.

In the United States, the attitude toward the Soviet Union was still one based on trust, but this changed after the President Roosevelt's death in April 1945, when the

"Free World" in the West and the Communist states in the East, in a perennial state of confrontation and tension. The conflict, though never openly declared, came to be known as the Cold War.

Apart from political and ideological propaganda and international espionage,

especially the B-29 bombers, were confiscated by the Russians. During the battle of Warsaw (August and September 1944) Russian strategy was made clear to the western Allies. Following the Warsaw Uprising against the Germans, the Russian troops failed to advance from their positions just a few miles outside the Polish capital. This effectively allowed the rebels to be caught and massacred – because the Polish Government-in-Exile in London had refused to accept the authority of Moscow. The Allies' attempts to supply Warsaw from the sky were unsuccessful, resulting in heavy losses. Churchill, a convinced anti-

Potsdam Peace Conference brought to light the progressive deterioration of the Allied-Soviet relationship. Other factors also came into play in this gradual dissolution of the wartime alliance. These included the United States' possession of the atomic bomb (1945), followed by the Soviet Union's (1949); creation in Eastern Europe of satellite governments subject to the Soviet Union; formation of the NATO military alliance (1949); the outbreak of the Korean War (1950); and formation of the Warsaw Pact (1955). All these events contributed to the creation of two distinct and contrasting power blocs, the so-called

the principal Cold War weapons were aeronautical; in particular, strategic aircraft, nuclear bombers, in-flight refueling tankers, and reconnaissance planes.

From the outset, Cold War tactics hinged on bombers with a nuclear capability. The first aircraft of this type was the Boeing B-29, the bomber used in the attacks on Hiroshima and Nagasaki. After the war, beginning in 1947, the B-29s began to be replaced by an advanced version known as the B-50, which featured structural modifications designed to increase both its weapons load and its range. As early as 1950, however, the B-50 remained in service until the end of the 1950s.

In the meantime, in 1948 the Strategic Air Command (SAC), responsible for nuclear bombers and their in-flight refueling tankers, came under the command of General Curtis LeMay. He was a hardliner who had distinguished himself during the war, above all during the bombardment of Japan. By means of grueling and unrelenting training exercises and thanks to the acquisition of new planes, he managed to revive the forces from the dangerously low level of efficiency to which they had sunk, making of the SAC an efficient, reliable and fearsome unit. The United States' Cold War strategy demanded that armed bombers with a global strike capability be in flight at all times, ready to respond rapidly and decisively to a nuclear attack by the USSR. The introduction of jet-powered bombers and in-flight refueling tankers made this capability possible.

had already been rendered obsolete and was relegated to less demanding reconnaissance and refueling duties. Convair built the first true strategic bomber in response to a USAAF requirement issued in 1941 calling for an intercontinental bomber capable of carrying a weapons load of about 10,000 lbs for a distance of 5,000 miles. Owing to the technical difficulties involved and the ongoing Second World War, project development was slow, and the prototype did not fly until August 1947. At 162 feet in length and with a wingspan of 230 feet, the B-36 Peacemaker was a truly enormous aircraft; it was powered by six 3,800-hp Pratt & Whitney radial engines and had a maximum take-off weight of over 165 tons. The plane's performance was disappointing, however, and 1949 saw the introduction of the B-36D, fitted with four J47 turbojets each producing 5,200 lbs of thrust. That same year also saw the introduction of the first strategic reconnaissance version, the RB-36D. This plane's definitive version was the B-36J, which first appeared in 1953. It had a maximum take-off weight of 410,000 lbs, a maximum range of 6,800 miles, a weapons system composed of 86,000 lbs of bombs and sixteen 20-mm cannons, and a crew of 15 men. A total of 383 Peacemakers were built, and the aircraft

160 The Avro Vulcan strategic bomber was developed after 1947 to provide the RAF with a nuclear-capability carrier and to make Britain militarily independent of the US. The Vulcan, which entered service in 1956, had a typical delta wing and was the second in the triad of British nuclear bombers, the other two being the Vickers Valiant and the Handley Page Victor.

161 top The strategic superbomber, the Convair B-36, was developed following futuristic specifications drawn up in 1941 that required an airplane able to fly over 10,000 miles at a speed of at least 244 mph. Shown here is the B-36J, which combined six propeller engines with four turbojets, making it capable of reaching 413 mph.

161 bottom The four-engined Boeing B-50, developed from the B-29, entered service at the end of World War II, though only 79 planes were built. It was more powerful and carried a larger payload than its predecessor.

162 top The Boeing B-47 Stratojet, which entered service in 1950, was the USAF' first really modern bomber. It had swept wings, flew at 609 mph and carried up to 10 tons of bombs. The photograph shows a rapid take-off assisted by jet engines.

162 bottom The B-52H, often considered washed up, is still in service more than 50 years after its first flight. It was used recently in the Kosovo and Afghanistan conflicts.

163 top In-flight refueling of a Boeing B-52 Stratofortress by a Boeing KC-135 Stratotanker over the mountains of the Sierra Nevada in California in 1958. This combination gave the USAF a strategic component that could span the globe.

163 bottom A B-47 flies above the clouds with a three-man crew (the pilot and navigator are in tandem in the nose cockpit). The Stratojet remained in service until 1966. Roughly 1,800 were built.

The B-36's role had already been revised by the appearance of the first jet-powered strategic bomber, the Boeing B-47 Stratojet. This project first saw the light of day in 1944 when Boeing, together with Convair, Martin and North American, set to work on the creation of a jet-powered bomber. After considerable research, initially focused on straight-wing models, the Air Force accepted the Boeing Model 450, which featured an innovative wing with a 35° sweep (derived from acquisition of German know-how), a single-track undercarriage below the fuselage aided by two underwing stabilizers and six engines slung from underwing pylons. The first prototype, the XB-47, took to the air on 17 December

1947, powered by Allison J35 turbojets, which in the second prototype were replaced by more powerful General Electric J47 units. The first production B-47A flew on 25 June 1950, the very day war broke out in Korea. The most significant version of the Stratojet was the B-47E, which appeared in 1951; a total of 1,614 were built, of which 255 were the RB-47E reconnaissance version. The B-47E had a length of 109 feet 5 inches, a wingspan of 115 feet 9 inches, and a maximum take-off weight of almost 200,000 lbs. It was armed with two 20-mm cannons 22,000-lb bomb load. Powered by six J47-GE-25 turbojets, each producing 7,200 lbs thrust, the plane had a top speed of 606 mph and a range of 4,000 miles that could be extended through in-flight refueling. The three-man crew were provided with ejector seats. The B-47 was a much smaller than the B-36, but far more up-to-date, faster and better suited to the changing operational scenario. This model formed the basis for the RB-47E/H/K

reconnaissance variants, and remained in service with the USAF until 1967.

In the meantime, with respect to ultra-heavy bombers, Boeing had been working since 1945 on the replacement for the B-36, an aircraft that had never been wholly satisfactory. The new aircraft was equipped with a 20° swept wing and was powered by turboprop engines. Given the B-47's success, however, and the availability of the new J57 jet engines (powerful, reliable, and less thirsty), Boeing decided to redesign the plane. It did so, making the new bomber a kind of "big brother" to the Stratojet. The new bomber retained a more highly developed version of the 35° swept wing, engines slung from underwing pylons, an in-flight refueling capability, a fuselage-mounted main undercarriage and (on the prototype at least), a cockpit with tandem seating. Thus was born the Model 464-67 or XB-52, a plane that flew for the first time six months after the YB-52's maiden flight on 15 April, 1952. The B-52 Stratofortress was

another gigantic machine, 60 feet 8.5 inches in length with a wingspan of 184 feet 8 inches, and a maximum take-off weight of over 220 tons. It was powered by eight jet engines and could carry a load consisting of about 22 tons of nuclear or conventional weapons. The first production model, the B-52A, was introduced in 1954 and was followed by a series of uprated versions that culminated in the B-52H of 1961. This last model introduced the new Pratt & Whitney TF33-P-3 turbofan engines producing 17,000 lbs of thrust, had a maximum take-off weight of about 485,000 lbs, a top speed of 595 mph, a range of about 9,950 miles, a weapons load of 60,000 lbs, and a crew of five.

Other significant versions had appeared earlier, including the B-52G in 1958, which incorporated a new wing and a lower fin (also fitted to the B-52H) and the B-52D in 1956, which had a greater maximum take-off weight than the preceding B and C variants. Moreover, 1955 saw the introduction of the RB-52B reconnaissance version. In total, the USAF ordered 774 of the various versions of the Stratofortress. Over the years this aircraft, at times criticized and written off as obsolete, has always proved to be up to the job. In 2001, five squadrons of the USAF were still flying updated versions of the B-52H, a plane that has survived two cost-cutting programs in which its retirement from service had been planned. Fifty years on from its maiden flight, B-52H is still enjoying rude good health.

With the B-47 and the B-52, the USAF, or rather the Strategic Air Command, could count on a highly effective nuclear bomber force, but the organization's weak point was in-flight refueling.

Owing to the nature of their missions, the bombers required constant service from air-borne tankers: this was an essential element of the overall strategy. In the mid-1950s, however, the USAF was still flying obsolete propeller-driven aircraft on refueling flights, the KB-50 and above all the KC-97 whose slowness obliged the bombers to refuel perilously close to their stalling speed. It was again Boeing that presented a valid response to the SAC's dilemma. In the early 1950s, the Seattle-based company had begun work on the first large passenger jet, the 707 (broadly based on the B-47 bomber), a model that was to become an extremely popular airliner. In order to cover itself against the risk of eventual commercial failure, however, Boeing wanted to recoup its development costs before launching the civilian 707 by selling a military version, the Model 367-80, to the government as a refueling tanker and transport plane. The USAF approved the design that featured a narrower diameter fuselage (lacking most of the windows), an upper deck for passengers and cargo and a lower section that housed the fuel and the refueling gear. Boeing also designed a refueling system employing a rigid probe that could be actuated by an operator located in the tail so as to facilitate the coupling operation. The first KC-135A Stratotanker flew on 31 August 1956, and deliveries of the production version began just three months later. The aircraft was 134 feet 6 inches in length, had a wingspan of 130 feet 11 inches, and a maximum take-off weight of 316,000 pounds. It was powered by four Pratt & Whitney J57-P-59W engines producing 13,750 lbs of thrust, sufficient to provide it with a top speed of 584 mph and allow it to carry about 25,000 gallons of fuel.

The Stratotanker represented an enormous advance for the SAC, improving on the KC-97's performance from every point of view, including the fuel transfer rate. Naturally, the KC-135 also proved to be of great use for refueling the Tactical Air Command's (TAC) fighters and fighter-bombers. The USAF purchased 820

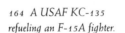

164 A USAF KC-135 refueling an F-15A fighter.

164-165 In-flight refueling by a KC-135 photographed from the cockpit of a USAF twin-seat F-15B Eagle over the Pacific Ocean.

165 bottom A formation of F-106A interceptors being refueled in flight by a KC-135. This procedure has been almost routine for American pilots for 50 years.

Stratotankers, many of which (incorporating updated E and R specifications) still constitute the backbone of its tanker fleet. The most recent version currently in service is the KC-135R, which first appeared in 1982. This variant is in reality an update of the previous models, with a strengthened airframe, new main systems and new CFM International F108-CF-100 turbofan engines producing 22,000 lbs of thrust. The 135R can carry more than 6.5 tons of additional fuel, and thanks to the new engines, has improved take-off characteristics, a greater range, and the capability of transferring 150% more fuel to other aircraft, compared to the original KC-135A.

Needless to say, the Soviet Union was also active in developing new bombers, although its progress was slower than that of the United States. After the four-engined propeller-driven Tupolev Tu-4 (a copy of the Boeing B-29), the first jet bombers to appear in the USSR were not aircraft with strategic capabilities, but rather tactical twin-engined planes. These included in 1947 the Tupolev Tu-14 (code-named "Bosun" by NATO) and in 1948 the Ilyushin Il-28 "Beagle," this last being particularly successful, with production of more than 10,000 planes. The Il-28 entered service in the USSR in 1950, and adopted by many Soviet bloc countries, remaining in service until the 1960s.

The USSR's first jet-powered strategic strike bombers were the Myasishchev M-4 and the Tupolev Tu-16. The M-4 was a four-engined plane with swept wings and tailplanes, designed in 1949 in response to Stalin's requirement for a bomber capable of attacking the United States. The first jet bomber appeared in 1954, and was designated the "Bison" by NATO. While incorporating interesting specifications, the M-4 was never a great success: when fully laden it was unable to provide the required performance. The M-4 was 154 feet 8.5 inches long, had a wingspan of 165 feet 3.5 inches, and a maximum take-off weight of about 350,000 lbs. It was propelled by four Mikulin AM-3D turbojets producing about 21,000 lbs of thrust and could reach a top speed of about 620 mph at its operating ceiling. It could carry almost 20,000 lbs of bombs, was armed defensively with ten 23-mm cannons, and had an eleven-man crew. The M-4 was in service, it was diverted to less demanding duties such as reconnaissance and in-flight refueling, a role

it performed through to the 1980s.

The Tupolev 16 derived from the Tupolev Works' prototype No. 88, which had been initially developed from the four-engined prop-driven Tu-4. The project was, however,

166 center A Soviet air force Tupolev Tu-16 on a reconnaissance mission is escorted by two F-4 fighters as it flies over the USS Kitty Hawk aircraft carrier during an exercise in the Pacific in 1963.

166 bottom A pair of Tu-16 bombers on a surveillance mission is intercepted by an F-4 and F-8 having landed on an American aircraft-carrier in the north Pacific in January 1963. During the Cold War, these close encounters were common.

167 top and bottom The Tu-22M3 had a swing-wing, could reach 1,250 mph and carry up to 24 tons of bombs and missiles, both conventional and nuclear. It entered service in 1975, and 500 were built. This one belongs to the Ukrainian air force.

radically modified, introducing a swept wing and tailplanes, with engines buried in the roots of the wings and improved aerodynamics. In general terms the plane resembled the M-4. It completed its maiden

166 top The crew of a Soviet Ilyushin Il-28 bomber embark for a mission. This twin-engined plane was the Soviet Union's first jet-engined bomber.

flight on 27 April 1952, and production of the definitive Tu-16 version began a year later. The aircraft made its public début in 1954, and was codenamed "Badger" by NATO. The Tu-16 remained in production in the Soviet Union for about ten years and some 1,500 were built (together with those built in China as the Xian H-6). The Tu-16 was powered by two Mikulin AM-3M turbojets producing 21,000 lbs of thrust (engines virtually identical to those used in the M-4), had a top speed of 609 mph, and a range of over 4,500 miles. Its maximum take-off weight was about 167,000 lbs; its armament comprised a bomb load of about 20,000 lbs and seven 23-mm cannons. The Tu-16 was 118 feet 8.5 inches in length and had a wingspan of 107 feet 11 inches. The Tu-16 was developed in a number of variations for anti-shipping strike roles (equipped with AS-2 "Kipper" or AS-6 "Kingfish" missiles), reconnaissance, electronic warfare and in-flight refueling. A number are still in service with the Chinese air force today.

The Tupolev Tu-20 was built at the same time and designed in response to the same requirement as the Myasishchev M-4. It made its first flight on 12 November 1952. The Tu-20, however, reflected a different approach to the problem of meeting the great range requirement; it was fitted not with jets but with more economical turboprop units. The Tu-20 went into service in 1956, and was soon adapted to carry the AS-3 "Kangaroo" nuclear missile. This made it a fearsome adversary for NATO, which named it the "Bear." The Tu-20 was 161 feet long, with a wingspan of 167 feet. Its maximum take-off weight was 340,000 lbs (increased in successive versions up to about 408,000 lbs); its weapons system comprised 44,000-lb bomb load and six 23-mm cannons. Four Kutznezov NK-12MV engines, each producing 14,795 hp and equipped with contrarotating propellers, powered the Tu-20 to a top speed of 528 mph and provided it with a range of about 7,500 miles. It was crewed by ten men. Production of the Tu-20 continued until 1965, and was then revived in 1983 with the redesigned Tu-95MS version capable of launching cruise missiles. A number of reconnaissance, strategic, electronic warfare and maritime patrol and spotting versions of the Bear were developed, and the Tu-142 variant was built

for anti-submarine and communications duties. A total of over 300 Tu-2os were built; many are still in service.

The Soviet Union developed its first supersonic bomber, a Tupolev, in the mid-1950s, and the prototype completed its maiden flight in 1959. The plane, initially designated the Tu-105, eventually became the Tu-22 (known as the "Blinder" to NATO), a sleek, highly aerodynamic design with strongly swept wings and tailplanes, and with two turbojet engines located at the base of the fin. The new bomber's afterburner-equipped engines each provided a maximum of 27,000 lbs of thrust and gave it a top speed of 932 mph. It had a range of 1,400 miles, and carried a crew of five men. The

Tu-22's armament consisted of a 23-mm cannon for short-range defense, and the plane carried a bomb load of nearly 20,000 lbs. Some 250 Tu-22's were built, including reconnaissance, training and missile assault versions. Both the Libyan and Iraqi air forces used the plane.

Some years later, the Tupolev Works developed a new bomber based on the Tu-22 design; NATO code-named it the Tu-26 "Backfire, but it was officially designated the Tu-22M. This aircraft, which flew for the first time on 30 August 1969, had a number of new features, including engines located within the fuselage with lateral air intakes and a new variable-geometry wing. The Tu-22M was a very superior aircraft. Its two Samara NK-25 turbojets produced about 55,000 lbs of thrust, and it was capable of a top speed of about 1,245 mph, with a range of about 3,750 miles, carrying an offensive load of up to 53,000 lbs of nuclear and conventional bombs and missiles. The plane entered service in 1975; some 500 were built, a number of which are still flying today.

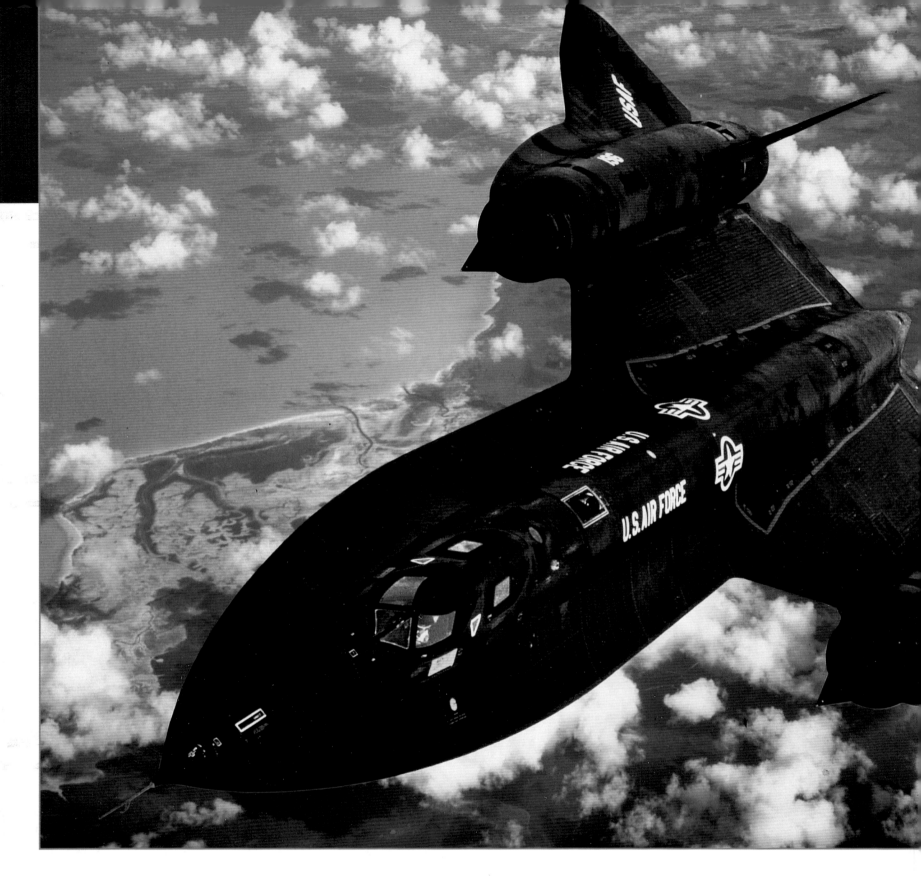

This Cold War chapter would not be complete without mention of two aircraft that have become symbols of the era, the United States' Lockheed U-2 and SR-71 spy-planes.

Lockheed designed the U-2 in the early 1950s in order to provide the American government (or rather the CIA) with an aircraft capable of completing strategic reconnaissance missions deep into Soviet territory. Led by Kelly Johnson, engineers employed in the "Skunk Works" (the California-based company's secret R&D facility) came up with a hybrid machine, midway between a glider and a powered aircraft. The fuselage housed the pilot, the electronic systems and the engine, a Pratt & Whitney J57-P-13 producing 11,200 lbs of thrust. The U-2 had a relatively immense wing span of almost 80 feet that guaranteed the plane lift at altitudes of over 65,500 feet, where it would

be beyond the reach of enemy anti-aircraft fire. The U-2A completed its maiden flight on 1 August 1955 and entered operational service the next year. On 1 May1960, a Soviet SA-2 missile downed a U-2 flown by Gary Powers. This U-2's loss revealed the plane's vulnerability and led to a revision of strategic reconnaissance tactics. Subsequently, numerous improved versions of the aircraft were introduced, with NASA and the USAF operating flights in addition to the CIA. The new models included the U-2C electronic surveillance version and the U-2R, which had a wingspan extended to over 101 feet, new wing pods for surveillance gear, an increased maximum take-off weight, and a new J75 engine producing close to 17,000 lbs of thrust. In 1981, the TR-1A was introduced; it as in effect a variation on the U-2R, which was dedicated to radar reconnaissance and used

primarily in the European theater. Last, in 1994, the U-2S entered service. It was equipped with the most advanced electronic surveillance gear, a satellite data-link, and a new General Electric F118-GE-101 engine producing 19,000 lbs of thrust. Ever since Lt. Gary Powers had been shot down in 1960, the United States had continued to employed the U-2 in numerous crisis-and-war theaters to collect data and information. However, the Powers' episode had convinced the American authorities of the need for an aircraft with far superior performance and features, one that could operate safely on a global scale, even above hostile territory.

Once again the Lockheed Company was commissioned, and it produced from scratch a truly exceptional airplane. The form, dimensions and materials employed (titanium, for example) were exotic and unusual, dictated by the

168-169 *The Lockheed SR-17A Blackbird strategic reconnaissance plane was one of the most secret and interesting aircraft in history. It first flew in 1962 and remained in service until 1997.*

169 top An SR-71A being rolled out at dawn for a mission. The size of the two Pratt & Whitney J58 engines is clear. Together, with the afterburners, they provided almost 30 tons of thrust.

169 center A Lockheed U-2S reconnaissance aircraft on a training flight over the Californian mountains. Thanks to constantly updated models, this airplane, which first flew in 1955, is still in service today.

169 bottom Thanks to what were science-fiction techniques for the period, Lockheed was able to produce the SR-71A, an aircraft able to cruise at over 2,000 mph at heights up to 85,300 feet.

extreme conditions of use and the heat developed during supersonic cruising at over 1,865 mph. In order to achieve such performance, two enormous Pratt & Whitney J58 engines producing 32,500 lbs of thrust on afterburn were used. They were designed to operate at maximum power for hours rather than for a few short minutes, as was normally the case with fighters. A special fuel named JP-7 was developed, with an extremely high ignition point that required a tetraethyl borane additive (which explodes on contact with air), in order to start up the engines. The first prototype, initially designated the A-12, took to the air on 30 April 1962, from the ultra-secret Area 51 Base in the Nevada desert. All the A-12's early flight-testing (which was entrusted to the 1129th SAS, a CIA-controlled squadron) was conducted from this base. Subsequently, the SR-71A Blackbird (as the production A-12 was designated) was flown by the USAF's specially constituted 4200th Strategic Reconnaissance Wing based at Beale Air Force Base in California, and by its operational units in Japan and Great Britain. The Blackbird was 107 feet 2.5 inches in length and had a wingspan of 55 feet 5 inches, and had a maximum take-off weight of 170,000 lbs. The Blackbird could be equipped for each mission with interchangeable systems packs with photographic, infrared and electronic

surveillance gear. Crewed by a pilot and navigator, the plane had a top speed of over 2,000 mph (Mach 3) at altitudes of over 85,300 feet, while its maximum range of about 3,000 miles could be extended with in-flight refueling. KC-135A tankers were modified to KC-135Q specifications in order transfer the special JP-7 fuel. Some 50 Blackbirds were built (including the prototypes and experimental versions such as the A-12B, the YF-12, and the M-21) served successfully until 1990, with NASA also using it. It was in service from 1995 to 1997, when it was finally withdrawn without being replaced by an aircraft of similar capabilities.

Chapter 13

Helicopters

What to some may today appear to be a "peculiar" way to fly, taking off and landing vertically, even hovering stationary in mid-air, was for many European children from the 14th century onward a popular and highly enjoyable game. The toy that was involved (which probably originated in China) consisted of a kind of spinning top equipped with leather blades that would rise vertically into the air as the result of a cord being tugged. In about 1480, Leonardo da Vinci investigated the underlying principle vertical lift. In one of his notebooks, he drew an aircraft equipped with a mechanically actuated spiral air screw that appeared to be capable of lifting itself into the air, thanks to an autonomous propulsive thrust.

The principle of vertical flight became increasingly clear to many, but from 1700 until the beginning of the 20th century, pioneers and researchers such Cayley, Phillips, Pènaud, Forlanini and Edison were limited to building only scale models of vertical take-off flying machines. This limitation was due largely to lack of an

170 top What may be considered as the first vertical flight project in history was unquestionably Leonardo da Vinci's "vite aere" (air screw).

170-171 center The Frenchman Etienne Oehmichen was one of the pioneers of vertical flight machines. Here he is at the controls of one of his first designs in 1923.

170 bottom Paul Cornu's helicopter before take off at Lisieux, France, 13 November 1907. This was the first such attempt with any machine of this kind. Despite its success, Cornu abandoned the project.

engine capable of developing sufficient power to allow a full-size, manned prototype to fly.

The first aircraft to lift a man vertically was Breguet-Richet's Giroplane No. 1, a complex machine equipped with a 32-blade rotor driven by a 40-hp Antoinette engine. On 29 September 1907, this machine lifted itself about 2 feet off the ground for one minute. The aircraft was not a true helicopter as the passenger on board had no control whatsoever over it. Nonetheless, Breguet and Richer had taken an important step in the right direction. Paul Cornu then took Louis Breguet's work further, and on 13 November he successfully flew a similar but more sophisticated machine. In 1909, another pioneer of vertical flight arrived on the scene when Igor Sikorsky, aged twenty and fresh from his technical school studies in Russia, began work on his first helicopter. He devoted himself enthusiastically to research and development on his designs

No. 1 and then No. 2, but both suffered from problems of instability, vibration, power and control that could not be solved at the time. Sikorsky thus turned to airplane design, a field in which he enjoyed notable success, and many years passed before the supremely talented Russian designer went back to helicopters.

Another three interesting designs appeared in the 1920s. In the United States, George de Bothezat designed a machine featuring a 38-blade rotor driven by a 220-hp engine; in France, Raul Pateras Pescara, a Spaniard, built a helicopter with two twin-blade rotors; and Etienne Oemichen, a Frenchman, built a controllable aircraft with six large rotors. All three machines managed to fly successfully, but technical obstacles meant that they were fragile, dangerous and unsuitable for any serious use at a time when the relatively fast and reliable airplane had already made enormous progress.

171 top The Gyroplane I designed by Louis Breguet and Richet was first vertical flying machine that succeeded in lifting a man. The flight took place in Douai on 29 September 1907 but was not considered a free flight because of the attached safety lines.

171 bottom Raoul Pescara's 16-blade helicopter as it lifts off in Issy-les-Moulineaux, France, on 23 January 1924 during a duration-record attempt.

Thanks to the airplane and the talent of the Spaniard, Juan de la Cierva, the helicopter principle was able to be developed in a new direction. De la Cierva, an enthusiastic aviation pioneer since his youth, recognized that the problem of in-flight safety (in particular the phenomenon of stalling) could be resolved by a horizontal rotor that could the problem by adopting blades that were free to oscillate and adapt themselves to the forces in the various rotation phases. On 9 January 1923, he flew his C.4 model for the first time, and found that it behaved perfectly.

The autogyro was propelled by an engine driving a front-mounted propeller and flew

provide the necessary lift at any speed. Far from looking to develop the helicopter, de la Cierva was instead interested in creating a hybrid machine, an airplane that was also equipped with a rotating wing. De la Cierva patented his idea in 1920, calling it an autogyro. In effect, the solution of a rotor free to revolve above the vehicle gave rise to the phenomenon of auto-rotation, which guaranteed a continual source of lift even in the absence of engine power and therefore torque to be counteracted. In order to overcome the problem caused by the difference in lift provided by the freewheeling blades, de la Cierva constructed two counter-rotating rotors installed one above the other. His new aircraft, named the C.1, was ready to fly in October 1920, but like successive models suffered from severe problems of stability in balancing the lift. After repeated studies and experiments. De la Cierva managed to solve

like other aircraft, taking off when the rotor blades provided the necessary lift, but could land vertically, with a minimal runway. The aircraft was truly astounding and was warmly received abroad. In fact, after careful evaluation, the British government acquired the autogyro, while demonstrations were performed in various European countries. De la Cierva's invention was soon a commercial success and by the late 1920s his autogyros were being constructed under license in Germany, Russia, France, Japan and the United States. Technical development continued, and in 1933 s de la Cierva introduced the "jump start," which allowed the rotor to be actuated by the engine. This permitted vertical take-off, with the angle of incidence of the blades controlled by the pilot. Initially the implications of this innovation were unclear, but it soon became fundamental to the evolution of the true helicopter. While ingenious, the autogyro lacked the payload-carrying capabilities that commercial and military applications required, and its performance was by no means exceptional.

The Italian Corradino D'Ascanio was another pioneer of vertical flight. He was an aeronautical engineer who left the fixed-wing field in 1926 and constructed his first helicopter in that same year. In 1927, he designed a new helicopter powered by an 85-hp engine. The machine was designated the DAT-3, partly in honor of his financier, Baron Pietro Trojani. The helicopter, which was equipped with two coaxial rotors and control surfaces at the tail, was presented to the Air Ministry, which in 1928 commissioned a prototype for experimentation. The aircraft's maiden flight was staged in Rome on 8 October 1930, and was a great success. The DAT-3 set world records for altitude, range and duration for that type of aircraft, and the future of the first Italian helicopter briefly appeared to be rosy. However, the Fascist regime's technical experts, military personnel, and politicians were skeptical about the helicopter's potential, and the project was deliberately

172 top Two autogyros flying over New York in 1930. At the start of the 1930s, Harold Pitcairn bought the US construction rights for the Cierva autogyro, but the craft did not catch on.

172 center The autogyro invented by the Spaniard, Juan de la Cierva, was a compromise between a plane and a vertical flight machine and opened the way to the development of the helicopter.

172 bottom The Italian engineer, Corradino d'Ascanio, dedicated himself in 1926 to designing a helicopter; he constructed a craft with two counter-rotating blades on the same axle but the Fascist regime had no faith in the new machine.

173 top The Cierva C.30 autogyro abandoned conventional wings in favor of just the rotating blade to provide lift.

173 bottom The German Focke-Achgelis Fa.61 helicopter was derived from the autogyro even though its two rotors were powered by an engine, as in a helicopter.

ignored. The same fate awaited the PD.2, a two-seater equipped with a main rotor and an anti-torque rotor at the tail, built in 1939 by D'Ascanio and the Piaggio Company. Italy's opportunity to take a lead in helicopter design thus evaporated.

Such was not the case in Germany. Henrich Focke, a First World War pilot who had subsequently founded the Focke-Wulf aeronautical company, had been removed from the head of the firm in 1933 because of his anti-Nazi views. He then devoted himself to the construction of the autogyro under

license, and soon began to explore the machine's potential for development, primarily in the application of power to the rotor to create a true helicopter. On 26 June 1936, his first aircraft, the Fa-61, took to the air. Within a year it had proved to be so effective that it broke all standing records and attracted the interest of that famous aviatrix, Hanna Reitsch, a darling of the Nazi régime. Reitsch made numerous demonstration flights in Germany and the Nazi government approved the formation of a new company, Focke-Achgelis, which it

commissioned to build a new, more powerful helicopter capable of lifting a payload of 1,500 lbs. The new machine, the Fa-223, was ready by 1940 and featured a 1,000-hp engine, two tri-blade rotors mounted side-by-side and a closed, four-seat cabin. It could achieve a top speed of 115 mph, climb to a ceiling of almost 23,000 feet and lift a load of just over a ton slung beneath the fuselage. Focke-Achgelis continued to develop the aircraft, but the bombing of the factory by the Allies prevented production, though at the end of the war, the British were able to capture a Fa-223 there.

Anton Flettner was another German engineer working on helicopters; he built his first one in 1930. In 1937, after developing various experimental designs, including one for an autogyro. Flettner built the Fl-265, a true helicopter equipped with two contrarotating rotors. The machine attracted the attention of the German navy, and in 1938 the admiralty ordered a small batch. In 1940 Flettner's company produced the improved Fl-282 Kolibri version that could fly at about 108 mph and carry a total load of about 800 lbs. The navy approved the design and placed orders for 1,000 Fl-282s. About 20 pre-production Fl-282s saw operational use in the Mediterranean theater from 1943, but the planned mass-production program was cancelled as a result of the Allies' continuous bombardment of Germany.

On the other side of the world, however, another famous engineer was about to lead the helicopter to maturity. Having abandoned Russia after the end of the revolution, Igor Sikorsky settled in the United States in 1919 where, after overcoming a series of problems, he had founded the Sikorsky Aero Engineering Corporation on Long Island. The company initially concentrated on manufacturing successful fixed-wing air- and seaplanes, but economic success meant that Sikorsky was able to devote himself to his passion for vertical flight. The opportunity to apply his research came in 1938, when he began work on an aircraft that featured an invention he had patented in 1935: a single rotor combined with an anti-torque rotor mounted vertically at the tail. On 14

174 top The VS-300 of 1939 was first helicopter Igor Sikorsky built. This is the second version, with two horizontal tail rotors.

174 center The American Arthur Young was one of the most famous pioneers of the helicopter. Here he is shown with members of his team during a full-load test flight of his Model 30, the first helicopter produced for Bell.

174 bottom Before developing actual size aircraft, Young experimented with scale models like this radio-controlled craft of 1938, with a 20-hp motor.

September 1939, his design, the VS-300, began to make its first cautious hops lasting just a few seconds. After a seemingly endless series of adjustments and modifications, the VS-300 made its true maiden flight on 13 May 1940. By the end of the year, it was competing with other designs for a US Army contract for a new military helicopter, designated the XR-4. In December 1941, with control problems resolved thanks to the adoption of a cyclical system, the VS-300 was ready to fly in its definitive configuration. Subsequently, the slightly larger XR-4, equipped with a 185-hp engine and incorporating all the advances made with the earlier model, undertook its first flight on 14 January

1942. The American army approved Sikorsky's design and ordered the XR-4 into serial production as the R-4. Two larger models were commissioned during the war. By 1945, the Sikorsky Company had produced over 400 helicopters, placing it at the forefront of the field.

By the end of the Second World War it was clear that the helicopter had a brilliant future and some engineers like Sikorsky himself, predicted that helicopters would come to cost little more than cars and would enjoy widespread popularity. In 1947, in the United States alone, more than 70 companies were working on the development of the new technology; few however managed to establish themselves with successful products. Among those that did was Piasecki, which developed the tandem rotor layout with its PV-3, HRP-1 and H-21 (Flying Banana) models, and Bell, which entrusted its rotating wing sector to an up-and-coming engineer, Arthur Young. Young's first project was the Model 30, a single-engined, single-rotor design with architecture similar to that of the Sikorsky VS-300. It flew for the first time in June 1943. Numerous improvements and modifications were made to this first helicopter, and in the December of 1944 it was redesignated as Model 47 and soon went into serial production. The Bell 47's strong suit was the civil certification obtained in 1946 that accelerated its diffusion in the commercial field. This machine had a characteristic side-by-side two-seat cabin in the form of a transparent Plexiglas bubble, lift being provided by a single twin-blade rotor responsible for the unmistakable noise that led to the "chopper" nickname. The Bell 47 was extremely versatile, and was well suited to numerous civilian and military transportation, search-and-rescue and air-ambulance roles. It was the first modern helicopter. The USAF acquired 28 Bell 47s in 1947 and the US Army acquired 65 in 1948, while further orders flooded in from other forces in America and throughout the world. Over 5,000 Bell 47s had been built before production ceased in 1973, some of them under license in Italy by Agusta and in Japan by Kawasaki. The Bell 47G variant was powered by a 270-hp Lycoming engine and had a top speed of 121 mph and a ceiling of 10,500 feet. With a main rotor diameter of just over 32 feet and a maximum take-off weight of about 2,850 lbs, the helicopter could carry two passengers.

175 top One of the first Bell Model 47s as soldiers prepare to load wounded soldiers during the Korean War. This aircraft marked the beginning of the modern helicopter era.

175 bottom Frank Piasecki invented the tandem rotor configuration featured in his PV-3 model. Because of its shape, this craft was soon called the "flying banana." Shown here are three Piasecki HRP-1s landing troops during the Korean War.

176 top *The concept of the tandem rotor was developed by Piasecki with new, larger and more reliable models like the H-21. Two USAF H-21s are shown during a matériel transportation exercise.*

Two other brilliant American designers were Stanley Hiller and Charles Kaman, who established their reputations in the late 1940s when founding companies carrying their own names. In the meantime, Sikorsky launched the first true cargo helicopter in 1948 in response to a U.S. army requirement, the S-55 prototype being given the military designation YH-19. This aircraft adopted an all-new configuration in which the engine was located in the nose and the cockpit and the transmission system were placed above the cargo hold, which was thus spacious and located close to the ground. The helicopter flew for the first time on 10 November 1949, and soon went into production as the H-19. It was 43 feet 3.5 inches long and its tri-blade main rotor had a diameter of 52 feet 9.5. Powered by a Wright R-1300 piston engine producing 800 hp, the H-19 could achieve a top speed of 112 mph. With a maximum take-off weight of about 7,900 lbs, the aircraft could carry a crew of two and up to ten soldiers or eight stretcher patients. The air force and the army, and subsequently the US Navy, the Marines, and other operators throughout the world ordered the H-19. Almost 1,300 H-19s were built, some under license by Mitsubishi and Westland.

War broke out in Korea on 25 June 1950, with the western democracies, above all the United States, being drawn into the conflict. This war saw the establishment of the helicopter as extremely versatile tool for the armed forces. Initially, however, the principal duty entrusted to the rotary wing aircraft, one that it performed admirably, was that of the air ambulance: Bell 47s equipped with two external stretchers were supplied to the army's famous MASH (Mobile Army Surgical Hospital) units. The Sikorsky S-51 used by the USAF and the Marines was also adapted for use as air ambulances. With the arrival in Korea of the H-19 and the H-21, however, the use of helicopters became more widespread. First the Marines and then the army began to exploit the helicopter's air mobility capabilities, using it for the rapid transportation of troops, particularly in emergency situations. Operation Bumblebee on 11 October 1951 saw the

176 bottom left *A USAF Sikorsky H-19 during operations at an advance camp in Korea in March 1951.*

176 bottom right *The first helicopters led inevitably to the first accidents. Here a Sikorsky S-51 Dragonfly, in service in the Korean War, hits the island of a British aircraft-carrier and falls into the sea.*

177 top Helicopters were soon employed on rescue missions. Here a USAF Sikorsky S-55 saves the crew of a US Army tow-boat sinking off Okinawa in 1956.

177 center The French army rapidly acquired helicopters for their armed forces. Here an S-55 (H-19 for the armed forces) evacuates wounded men from the outskirts of Dien Bien Phu, Vietnam, March 1954.

177 bottom An S-51 belonging to the Marines takes off with a wounded soldier during fighting near Seoul on 25 September 1950. Evacuation of the wounded was one of the first duties assigned to helicopters.

first large-scale operation in which a battalion of Marines (almost 1,000 men) was dispatched aboard a dozen H-19s to relieve another front-line unit located on a mountain top.

The decade that followed the Korean War saw the most intensive period of helicopter development. Designs were refined and differentiated to meet the requirements demonstrated by the military and civilian sectors, and the turbine engine was introduced--a technical and operational revolution that promised to increase both performance and on-board comfort.

The first of the new generation of helicopters was a Kaman K-22 that had been modified in 1951 to accommodate a 177-hp Boeing YT-50 gas turbine engine. However, the first helicopter to successfully exploit the new turbine units was actually French rather than American.

The Sud-Est Company entered the helicopter field following the Second World War, thanks in part to the consultancy of Heinrich Focke, who was attempting to improve on his Fa-223 design with its SE 3000 model. Sud-Est began to establish its reputation with the SE 3120 Alouette, a two-seat helicopter with a single engine and a single rotor. The Alouette completed its maiden flight on 31 July1952. This model was used as the platform for the installation of a Turbomeca Artouste I turbine developing 360 shp (shaft horse power). The turbine engine offered enormous advantages when used in helicopters; it provided significant power while weighing only half as much as an equivalent piston engine. The new helicopter, the SE 3130 Alouette II, flew for the first time on 12 March 1955. Once it had obtained civilian certification, it aroused immediate interest and was a great commercial success. In 1957, following the merger of Sud-Est and Sud-Aviation, the model was redesignated the SE 313B. This helicopter had a top speed of 115 mph, could carry up to three people, and had a maximum take-off weight of 3,527 lbs, compared with a dry weight of 1,973 lbs.

Subsequently, the SA 318C variant was created with the introduction of the more economical Astazou IIA engine. The Alouette II series remained in production until 1975, with about 1,300 being sold around the world. Sud-Aviation (later known as Aérospatiale) expanded its family of French helicopters with the introduction of the SA 316 Alouette III (in 1959), the SA 321 Super Frelon (in 1962), the SA 330 Puma (in 1965), and the SA 315 Lama (in 1969). These aircraft helped make Aérospatiale one of the world leaders in the helicopter field.

In the United States, however, Bell had by no means been resting on its laurels. On the strength of experience gained during the war, the company immediately developed a multipurpose turbine-powered helicopter in response to a US Army requirement issued in 1955. The resulting Bell Model 204 was to remain a milestone in the history of rotary wing aircraft, winning acceptance in June of the same year, even before it had made its maiden flight. That flight took place on 22 October1956, and the helicopter demonstrated its huge potential. It featured the classic Bell layout of a single, twin-blade main rotor with

an auxiliary rotor at the tail. The fuselage housed the two-man crew in the nose, with the loading bay behind it, capable of holding six soldiers or two stretchers accessed via two large sliding doors. In 1959, when it entered service with the US Army as the UH-1A Iroquois, the helicopter was powered by an Avco Lycoming T53 turbine developing 710 shp, but this output was soon increased to 1,115 shp with the UH-1B model, and eventually reached 1,419 shp with the Fuji-Bell 204B-2. This helicopter was almost immediately followed by an improved version, the Model 205, offered to the US Army as early as 1960. To all intents and purposes a stretched version of the 204, the Model 205 could accommodate 14 soldiers or 6 stretcher patients, for a maximum payload of 4,000 lbs. The prototype flew on 16 August 1961, and the aircraft was in service by August 1963, designated the UH-1D. It was powered by the same engine as the UH-1B and had a maximum take-off weight of 9,500 lbs. This version was soon followed by the UH-1H powered by the same 1,419-shp engine as the Model 204-B-2. Like the 204, the 205 was also built under license by Agusta and Fuji, and in all, more than 10,000 of the two versions were built.

Mainly used for military duties, the UH-1 series reached the height of its fame during the Vietnam War. It became something of a symbol of the American cause and was used extensively for air-borne cavalry and troop transportation, these being the great innovations of the Southeast Asian conflict. Vietnam also saw another helicopter produced by Bell, the Model 209, which privately developed by the American company to provide the army with a dedicated combat helicopter. The 209 used the 204's mechanical elements, incorporating them within a narrower fuselage that was equipped with two tandem seats and wing stubs to which the armament was attached. After the 209 had completed its maiden flight on 7 September 1965, the US Army ordered an initial batch, designating the model the AH-1G Cobra. It entered service in 1967 and was immediately dispatched to Vietnam. The lightweight, single-engined Bell Model 206, also designed for military use as a reconnaissance helicopter, completed its maiden flight on 10 January 1966; it also enjoyed great commercial success in the civilian field. In fact, the 206 is still in production after a long sequence of versions and modifications, and over 9,000 have been built. The Bell multipurpose helicopter series continued with other machines, whose design can be traced back to the 204/205. These were the twin-engined Model 212, the Model 412 with a four-blade main rotor, the Model 214, and the Model 222.

178 top The French Aerospaziale SA.315B Lama was developed for Indian forces that needed a helicopter able to operate at high altitude and low temperatures. The photo also shows a Pakistani army vehicle.

178 bottom left The Agusta-Bell 205 (this is a Greek army model) was developed from the Model 204 and was one of the most popular military helicopters.

178 bottom right A Sud-Est SE.313 Alouette II belonging to the Belgian army. This machine made its maiden flight in 1952 and the turbine version arrived in 1955.

178-179 bottom The heavy Sud-Aviation SA.321 Super Freon was produced to meet French military requirements and first flew in 1962. Here, commandos disembark on the flight deck of a French aircraft carrier.

179 top A formation of three Bell AH-1 Cobra attack helicopters. This aircraft was derived from the UH-1 transport model for use in the Vietnam War.

179 center An Aerospaziale SA.330 Puma (built by Westland) flying British army colors. It first flew in 1965 and was the result of experience gained from the Super Freon.

179 bottom right A Sud-Aviation SA.316 Alouette III of the Portuguese air force flying at low altitude. This helicopter made its maiden flight in 1959, and more than 1,800 were produced.

Sikorsky, a still active American colossus, concentrated largely on satisfying the requirements of the US Navy. In the late 1950s, following the S-58 model of 1954 (still powered by a piston engine and designated by the military as the HSS-1 Seabat and then--from 1962--as the H-34), the Sikorsky company introduced the S-61, a truly remarkable helicopter still widely used throughout the world. The company developed the S-61 in response to a US Navy brief calling for an anti-submarine helicopter with both search and assault capabilities. Sikorsky designed a large twin-engined machine equipped with a five-blade main rotor, folding tail boom and a large fuselage capable of housing the crew and the mission systems. The prototype first flew on 11 March 1959, and the helicopter, designated as the HSS-2 ("Sea King") proved to be an immediate success. The first production examples went into service in

Navy requirement. The Model S-65 was designed for the Marines corps as a heavy transport helicopter, capable of transporting troops and munitions from ship to shore during landing operations. While retaining the basic mechanical elements of the S-64, Sikorsky redesigned the fuselage along the lines of that of the HH-3E. Designated the CH-53 Stallion, the new helicopter began entering service in 1966, and was immediately sent to Vietnam, where there was great need for such an aircraft. Other versions were developed from basic S-65 for minesweeping duties and for the USAF (for search and rescue and special operations), as well as for other armed forces. In all, more than 730 S-65s were built in over 20 versions.

The most recent Sikorsky success story was the S-70, which flew for the first time on 17 October 1974. In this case, however, the helicopter resulted from a requirement issued by the US Army, which sought a new multipurpose tactical transport helicopter to replace the UH-1 series. The Sikorsky model was declared the winner of the competition, and its production model was designated the UH-60A Black Hawk in December 1976. The first Black Hawks began to enter service in 1979. Subsequently, numerous different versions were developed from the basic model; these included the naval SH-60B, F and R (and the export S-70B and C variants), and the MH-60, EH-60 and HH-60 designed for rescue, electronic warfare, and special operations. The US Army and the USAF used these versions, as did a further twenty or so countries around the world.

181 top The Sikorsky S-65 (designated the H-53 from 1964) was the American forces' largest helicopter. Here a US Marines' CH-53A is on a transport mission in South Vietnam.

181 bottom The Sikorsky H-3 was widely used by the US Navy and the Marines. This is a VH-3D version operated by the HMX-1, the Marines' section involved in flying the President.

September 1961. Mitsubishi, Westland and Agusta acquired production licenses, and the powerful and robust aircraft was subject to continued development. The year 1960 saw the introduction of the S-61L passenger version for the civilian market, while an amphibious version dedicated to search and rescue duties made its début in 1963. This version, designated the S-61R by the company, had a much larger fuselage and was equipped with a rear-loading door. It was initially produced as the HH-3E Jolly Green Giant and adopted by the USAF; the more advanced HH-3F Pelican model was introduced later. In total, the Sea King, since 1962 known to the American armed forces as the H-3, had a production of over 1,300 planes in almost 40 different versions. It is still in use throughout the world.

In the early 1960s Sikorsky developed yet another large helicopter in response to a US

180-181 Westland produced the Sikorsky S-61 under license as a naval helicopter, the Sea King, derived from the SH-3A, for the US Navy. It was also built under license by the Italian Agusta company.

180 bottom An RAF Sea King HA3 on a search and rescue mission in extreme weather conditions.

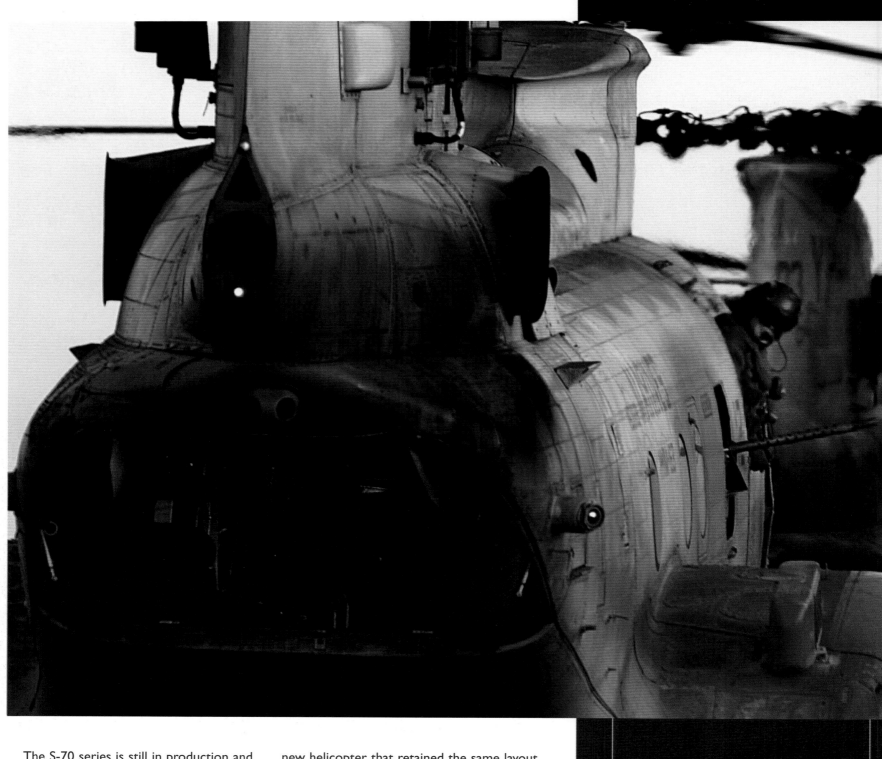

The S-70 series is still in production and has attracted over 2,300 orders to date. The company's most recent projects have included the multipurpose S-76 model and the S-92 heavy transport helicopter.

Vertol (later known as Boeing-Vertol) was another American company that established a reputation in the field of large transport helicopters. Within a few years Vertol introduced two notable models still widely used today. The Model 107, a twin-turbine helicopter with two rotors mounted in tandem, designed for commercial transportation, was presented on 22 April 1958. The H-46, as the 107 was designated, was powered by two General Electric CT58 turbine engines, each developing 1,400 shp. It had a maximum take-off weight of over 21,000 lbs. The CH-46's success, however, was largely as a result of its acquisition by both the US Navy and the Marines. In all, 624 H-46s were ordered during the 1960s.

At much the same time, Vertol built a new helicopter that retained the same layout as the H-46, from which it clearly derived, but was scaled up in size. The Model 114 completed its maiden flight on 21 September 1961. Its characteristics made it particularly well suited to the requirements of the US Army, and the Army adopted it as the CH-47 Chinook in place of the smaller CH-46. The Chinook was powered by two Avco Lycoming T55 engines, each developing 3,800 shp, and had a maximum take-off weight of about 38,500 lbs. Seven different versions of the Chinook were developed and were used by about twenty different countries. Over 1,150 Chinooks were built, with production licenses being acquired by Agusta and Kawasaki. Subsequently, Boeing and Sikorsky joined forces to create a new armed reconnaissance and assault helicopter for the American army, the RAH-66 Comanche, an extremely advanced machine that completed its maiden flight on 4 January 1996. The helicopter is currently in development and is due to enter operational service in 2006.

183 center Two CH-46s turning before landing on the amphibious assault ship USS Peleliu in the Arabian Sea. This was during Operation Enduring Freedom in November 2001.

183 bottom A pair of US Army UH-60A Black Hawk helicopters during Exercise Bright Star in Egypt in 1983. The Black Hawk entered service with the American army in 1979 and has been used by more than 20 countries.

182-183 The Boeing-Vertol CH-46 Sea Knight has long been the Marines' standard transport helicopter. It is due to be replaced by the new V-22 Osprey tiltrotor aircraft.

182 bottom A Boeing-Vertol CH-47 Chinook, here displaying RAF roundels, prepares to lift an armored vehicle. The Chinook first flew in 1961 and has been used by roughly 20 countries around the world.

183 top The SH-60 Sea Hawk is the naval version of the Black Hawk and was developed at the same time for the US Navy. Here an SH-60 from HS-4 squadron is shown firing a torpedo.

184 The AH-64D, the most recent version of the Boeing Apache, is the equipped with Longbow radar, seen above the main rotor. This one belongs to the British army.

185 top A formation of National Guard UH-60As and AH-64As flying over Kuwait in 1998 during Operation Southern Watch.

185 center A Boeing AH-64A Apache assault helicopter launching air-to-ground missiles during a shooting exercise. The Apache is armed with a single 30-mm cannon and a mixture of rockets and anti-tank and air-to-air missiles.

185 bottom Three AH-64A Apaches at dusk before a night mission. This aircraft entered service with the US Army in 1986 and since then more than 1000 have been built, some for eight other countries.

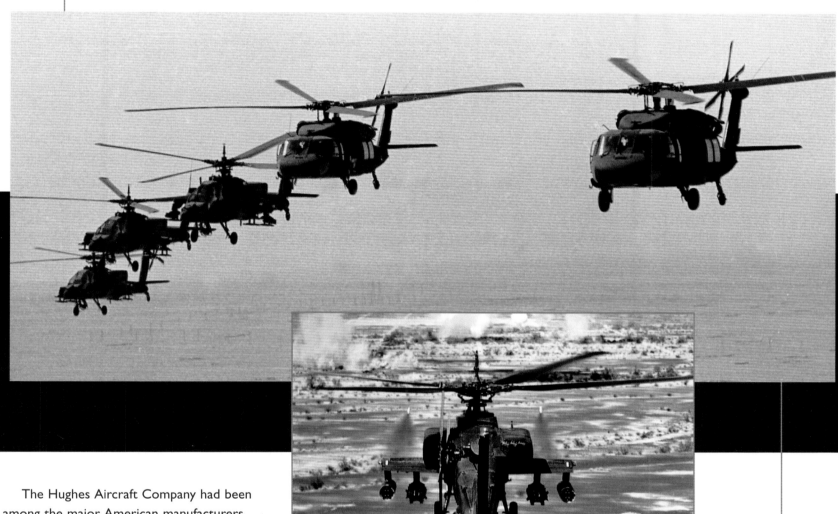

The Hughes Aircraft Company had been among the major American manufacturers until it was absorbed by McDonnell Douglas, which was in turn was absorbed by Boeing. In the early 1960s, Hughes introduced the Model 369 in response to a US Army requirement for a new reconnaissance and scouting helicopter. It flew for the first time on 23 February 1963, and designated the OH-6A Cayuse. In 1965, the US Army began ordering OH-6As. The civil version was known as the Hughes 500. These two helicopters marked the beginning of an enormously successful program that through

development of numerous and gradually improved versions resulted in the manufacture of about 5,000 helicopters to date, some being built under license in various countries. One of the most recent versions, the 520N NOTAR, is characterized by the absence of an auxiliary tail rotor. Powered by an Allison 250 turbine producing 450 shp, it is capable of a top speed of 175 mph. With a dry weight of about 1,600 lbs and a maximum take-off weight of 3,850 lbs, the 520N can carry up to five people, including the pilot. The most famous Hughes helicopter is, however, the AH-64 Apache, which in 1976 the US Army selected as its new assault and combat helicopter. A powerful, robust and large aircraft, the Apache flew for the first time

on 30 September 1975. After McDonnell Douglas absorbed Hughes, the AH-64 began to enter service in its "A" specification in 1986. The AH-64D (a version equipped with radar) was characterized by a classical layout with a tandem two-seat cockpit in the nose together with the navigation and weapons sensors, and well-separated engines in a higher, better protected location. It was fitted with a four-bladed rotor driven by two General Electric T700-GH-701C engines, each developing 1,890 shp, providing the helicopter with a top speed of 226 mph. Maximum take-off weight was about 22,250 lbs, and the armament comprised anti-tank missiles, air-to-air missiles, rockets and a 30-mm cannon. The American army bought 820 of the AH-64Ds, which has also been bought by the armed forces of Great Britain, The Netherlands, Greece, Israel, Kuwait, the United Arab Emirates, Egypt and Saudi Arabia.

Along with the United States and France, the Soviet Union for obvious reasons also invested heavily in the design and construction of its own series of helicopters. Two factories in particular have specialized in this sector, Mil and Kamov. The first was founded by Mikhail Mil in 1947 and in the following year presented its

first design for a light, multipurpose helicopter equipped with a 575-hp Ivchenko piston engine, a tri-blade main rotor, and an auxiliary rotor at the tail. This helicopter, subsequently designated the Mi-1, was later developed into the Mi-2 that used two Isotov turbine engines producing 450 shp. This model appeared in 1961; more than

6,500 were built, and production licenses were granted to other manufacturers. Mil then produced a number of other designs for increasingly powerful and more specialized helicopters. These included, among other models, the Mi-6 in 1957 (then the world's largest helicopter, with a 13-ton payload capability) and the Mi-24 in 1969, a combat helicopter of notable strength and power that strongly cemented its reputation during the Soviet invasion of Afghanistan. Conceived virtually as a flying combat vehicle, the Mi-24 carried a two-man crew and considerable firepower, but also featured a loading bay that could accommodate up to eight soldiers or stretchers for the evacuation of wounded personnel. Built in over 20 different versions, the Mi-24 (like the Mi-25 and Mi-35 versions) was exported to over 30 countries in the former Communist bloc, in all, more than 2,300 of these helicopters were built. Such are the merits of this plane that a great many are still in service, and a number of programs

186 top Two Russian Mil Mi-24s landing near the Chechen capital Grozny in 1999, during fighting to repress the local rebellion.

186 bottom A Mil Mi-24 belonging to the Czech Republic flying in an air show. The Mi-24 has a maximum speed of 210 mph and can carry eight armed soldiers.

have been developed to update the basic model platform with advanced avionics and armaments.

The most recent Mil combat helicopter is the Mi-28, which flew for the first time on 10 November 1982. The definitive prototype, a tandem two-seat assault helicopter, did not appear until 1988, however; the economic and organizational difficulties resulting from the Soviet Union's collapse to date prevented large-scale government orders, and the machine has yet to go into serial production.

The Kamov design department built its reputation with the creation of a broad range of helicopters built for naval use, especially in anti-submarine roles. Distinguished by a characteristic layout with dual contrarotating coaxial rotors, the Ka-25, the first in Kamov's line of small naval helicopters, made its maiden flight on 26 April 1961. A number of different versions followed, designed for anti-shipping missile,

search and rescue, mine sweeping and intercontinental ballistic missile data transmission duties. Then came the Ka-27, 28 and 29 models for transportation and assault purposes, the Ka-31 air-borne radar helicopter and the Ka-32, a multirole helicopter used in both the military and civil sectors. The most recent and best known Kamov design is the Werewolf K-50 attack helicopter; it retains the typical Kamov dynamic layout, but combines it with a slim, streamlined fuselage with a single-seat cockpit equipped with an ejector seat. The K-50 is thought to have flown for the first time in June 1982, but it probably entered operational service only in 1996. It has a top speed of 217 mph, thanks to the 2,220 shp supplied by each of its two Klimov turbine engines, and a maximum take-off weight of about 23,800 lbs. This model formed the basis of the K-52, a side-by-side two-seater used for training, reconnaissance and combat.

187 top left The Mil Mi-24 is one of the most common and effective assault helicopters in the world. It entered service in 1972 and over 2,300 have been produced and sold to 30 countries.

187 top right The Mil Mi-28 is a latest generation Russian attack helicopter. It first flew in November 1982, but various development difficulties slowed its entry into service.

187 bottom The Russian Kamov Ka-50 Werewolf attack helicopter has a dual coaxial rotor and an ejection seat for the pilot. It can fly at 219 mph.

Two other European companies have
established solid reputations in the helicopter
field over the years, Westland in Great
Britain and Agusta in Italy. The former has,
among other models, produced the Wasp
and the Lynx, while the latter, after a number
of attempts, produced its first truly successful
model with the A.109, which first flew on 4
August 1971. A twin-turbine craft with clean,
elegant lines, the A.109 was designed for
civilian use and over 700 have been sold,
primarily for use in shuttle services, VIP
transport and air ambulance, search and
rescue and police duties. The A-109 has also
enjoyed considerable sales success in the
military sphere. The current best-selling
version of the A.109 is the Power version.
Introduced in 1996, it has already attracted
over 100 orders. The A.129 Mangusta
completed its maiden flight on 11 September
1983. This is the first European-built assault
helicopter; it was designed specifically to
satisfy the requirements of the Italian army,
which has ordered 60 of them. The most
advanced version of the Mangusta
International (the firm's export model) is
powered by two Rolls-Royce Gem turbine
engines, each producing 825 shp, and is capable
of a top speed of 171 mph. It has a maximum
weight at take-off of just over 9,000 lbs, and
can carry a weapons load of 2,645 lbs.

Following a significant decision in the
1980s, the Agusta and Westland groups
combined forces to produce a new three-
engined heavy-duty helicopter, the EH-101,
which completed its maiden flight on 9
October 1987. This powerful machine,
optimized for both civilian and military use,
has to date attracted about 100 orders and is
already in service with the Italian and British
navies and the Canadian air force. Agusta and
Westland officially merged in February 2001.

Another colossus of the aviation world is
the German-French group Eurocopter, created
in 1992 by Aérospatiale and Daimler-Benz.
Today, this group offers the AS 332 Super
Puma and AS 532 Cougar, the AS 350 and 355
Ecureil, the AS 550 and 555 Fennec, the AS
365 Dauphin and AS 565 Panther, the SA 342
Gazelle, the Bo. 105 the EC 135 and the Tigre,
the future combat helicopter for the French
and German armies. After the maiden flight
was made on 27 April 1991, prototypes were
subjected to intensive development and

testing, and the helicopter is now approaching operational status. The Tigre is equipped with extremely advanced avionics and two Turbomeca/Rolls-Royce turbine engines, each producing 1,170 shp. It has a top speed of 200 mph and a maximum take-off weight of about 13,200 lbs.

The most advanced helicopter currently under development in Europe is also the result of cooperative planning. This is the NH-90, built by the multinational NHI consortium that Eurocopter France, Eurocopter Deutschland, Agusta and Fokker instituted in 1992. The first prototype flew on 18 December 1995, and the consortium currently has more than 700 orders for the aircraft. Two basic versions are available: the TTH for tactical transportation, and the NFH

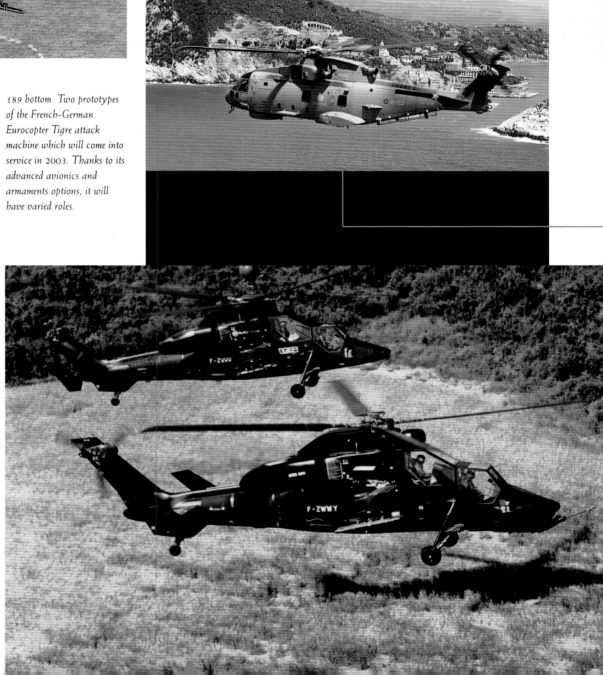

for naval use (being developed by Agusta). The NH-90 is an extremely versatile machine with state-of-the-art features and avionics; it was designed to cover a vast range of tactical transportation, search-and-rescue, air-ambulance, parachute-dropping, electronic warfare, anti-shipping strikes, anti-submarine and mine dropping roles. The helicopter is equipped with two Rolls-Royce Turbomeca RTM322 turbine engines producing 2,100 shp or two General Electric FIAT Avio T700 units producing 2,400 shp each. It is capable of a top speed of about 186 mph and has a maximum take-off weight of just over 19,000 lbs. Along with its two-man crew, the TTH transport version of the helicopter can carry up to 20 troops or a payload of 5,500 lbs.

189 bottom Two prototypes of the French-German Eurocopter Tigre attack machine which will come into service in 2003. Thanks to its advanced avionics and armaments options, it will have varied roles.

189 top The NHIndustries NH-90 is one of the most advanced multi-role helicopters in the world. Developed in land and sea versions, it will enter service in 2004.

189 center left The Italian Agusta A.129 Mangusta is the first European-built

assault helicopter. This is the A.129CBT version bought by the Italian army.

189 center right The Agusta Westland EH-101 is the new craft planned to replace the Sea King used by the British and Italian navies. The project has been so successful that the helicopter will also be exported.

Chapter 14

Trainers

The claim could be made that the most significant aircraft in a pilot's life are trainers: they are the aircraft that enable novices to complete that all-important first flight, to gain experience and obtain a license, whether civil or military. In fact, the trainer is the airplane that allows any budding pilot to realize the dreams of flight. Yet, strange though it may be, at the dawn of aviation, when the need was particularly acute, there were no planes designed specifically for pilot training. Intrepid pioneers frequently began their careers perched behind their instructor, barely able to reach the joystick yet expected to pick up at least rudimentary notions on how to control an aircraft. The earliest aviators of all were of course self-taught, taking off alone with scarce or non-existent theoretical notions – and with results that are all too easily imaginable.

Pioneering aviation was however a field reserved for a few adventurous enthusiasts willing to try anything. The outbreak of the First World War was to transform flying radically, from an elitist sport to an activity of the masses. Military demands and rapid

technological development provided enormous impetus to powered flight, and during the conflict the belligerents had to produce tens of thousands of aircraft and, naturally, tens of thousands of pilots capable of flying them. Initially, practical approaches were limited, and training was conducted with aircraft no longer effective as front-line military machines, generally spotters and bombers such as the French Farman, the German DFW B.1 and the early Avro 504s. From 1916, however, airplanes expressly designed for the delicate task of pilot training began to appear. These machines were characterized by dual controls and "forgiving" handling.

Among the first great trainers from this period, the British Avro 504J was of particular note. The original model, a two-seater biplane with a front-mounted engine and control surfaces at the tail, completed its maiden flight in July 1913. The British War Ministry then ordered it for use as a spotter and light bomber. The aircraft, which was also used as a fighter for a time, soon proved to be obsolete in terms of front-line combat, and in 1916 Avro decided to revive its fortunes by

developing the 504J version as a purpose-built trainer. The aircraft enjoyed notable success, so much so that to overcome problems with standardization of the engine, Avro developed the 504K version. This featured an engine mount that could accept three different types of power unit in use at the time. The 504 had a wingspan of 35 feet 6.5 inches, a length of 29 feet 2 inches, and a maximum take-off weight of about 1,830 lbs. The principal power unit was a Le Rhône rotary engine producing 110 hp, providing the plane with a top speed of just over 90 mph. Also built under license in Australia, Belgium, Canada, Denmark and Japan, the 504 continued to be used well after the end of the war. The 504N version was introduced in 1925; it featured a new undercarriage and a radial engine producing 162 hp. The Avro 504 remained in service with the Royal Air Force as a trainer up until 1932, but was widely used in the civilian sphere until the outbreak of the Second World War. Over 10,000 504s were produced, and the aircraft was employed in over 25 different countries around the world. It remains one of the most

190 top The Curtiss JN-4 Jenny was one of the commonest and most famous airplanes between the two World Wars. More than 6,500 were built and many were used in civil aviation.

190 bottom left Training simulators came into use before the 1940s. Here, in 1938, a Royal Navy cadet is undergoing a flight preparation session at the RAF school at Netheravon.

190 bottom right German air force cadets during a lesson on

engine mechanics in February 1914.

191 top In this RAF propaganda photograph from 1940, RAF student pilots receive last instructions on flying in formation before a mission.

significant aircraft in history thanks to the contribution it made to the diffusion of flying.

Another "giant" in this sector was the American Curtiss JN, of which more than 6,500 were built. The most famous of the series was the JN-4, which resulted from development of the JN-2 and JN-3 models, and was affectionately nicknamed "Jenny" by its pilots. The JN-4 flew for the first time in July 1916. Britain's RAF immediately purchased 105 planes. Shortly thereafter, in view of the need to produce ever greater numbers of pilots, the American army also began to order the plane. The JN-4D, which incorporated improvements made to JN-4s built in Canada and the USA, was introduced in June 1917. This aircraft had a wingspan of 43 feet 6 inches, a length of 27 feet 2 inches, and a maximum take-off weight of about 1,920 lbs. The Jenny was powered by a Curtiss OX-5 engine producing 90 hp, sufficient for a top speed

of about 75 mph. War-time production forced output to ever higher levels, and the plane was also built by a further six American firms.

In 1917, Curtiss launched an advanced training version, the JN-4H, which was powered by a 132-hp engine and could be armed with bombs and machine guns. Subsequently the slightly improved JN-6 was introduced. In the post-war years, a number of Jennies remained in service, being subjected to numerous refits, but a considerable proportion of the military aircraft were sold on the civilian market and made a notable contribution to the diffusion and development of flying. The Jenny's military career continued up until 1927, but the plane continued to be a mainstay of civil aviation for much longer, and even today a number of Jennies can be found in airworthy condition.

191 center A student pilot is prepared for ejection using a Martin-Baker seat. The year is 1949, and with the advent of new equipment, training activities were expanding.

191 bottom Britain's Avro 504T was one of the first real training aircraft in aviation history. It flew in 1913 as a spotter but was used as a trainer after the outbreak of the Second World War.

Italy also produced a notable training aircraft during the First World War, the SVA 9, one of the successful SVA series of planes. Production of these aircraft (designed by engineers Savoia and Verduzio of the Ansaldo company, hence the initials SVA) began in 1917 with the appearance of the SVA 4, a biplane originally developed as a fighter for the Italian army, but soon relegated to reconnaissance duties, given its limited maneuverability. Later in 1917, the SVA 5 bomber version spawned the SVA 9, a two-seater with dual controls for pilot training. This aircraft had a wingspan of 28 feet 9.5 inches, a length of 26 feet 6 inches, and a maximum take-off weight of 2,315 lbs. It was powered by an in-line SPA 6A engine developing 265 hp, and had a top speed of about 124 mph. The SVA 9 began entering

192 top The Caproni Ca.100 – better known as the 'Caproncino' – was a popular and common Italian touring plane and trainer between the wars. It first flew in 1929 and its 130-hp engine could take it to 116 mph.

192 center and 193 top Shown here are two Avro Tutors. The photograph on the right shows a restored Avro Tutor still flying today. The Armstrong Siddeley Lynx radial motor produced 243 hp and a top speed of 123 mph.

192 bottom The Avro 621 Tutor first flew in 1929. Designed to replace the Avro 504 in the RAF's flying schools, it remained in service for ten or so years until the outbreak of World War II.

service early in 1918, and proved to be unquestionably more successful that its predecessors. Adopted by a dozen countries, the SVA biplanes remained in production until 1928, with more than 2,000 being built. The most famous feat involving a SVA 9 was undoubtedly Lieutenant Arturo Ferrarin's 1920 expedition from Rome to Tokyo with a group of 6 two-seaters, a journey of 9,500 miles completed in less than three months. The year 1928 also saw

the introduction of another famous Italian trainer, the Caproni Ca.100, nicknamed the "Caproncino." About 700 Ca. 100s were constructed between 1930 and 1937, and the plane proved to be a well-designed, versatile machine. It was, in fact, able to accept about fifteen different engines (from the 86-hp FIAT A50 through to the 132-hp Colombo S63), and was also transformed into a seaplane and was fitted with skis to that it could fly from snow-covered runways.

Exported to numerous countries for civilian and military uses, the Caproncino also gave rise to the Ca.100bis version, which had a 136-hp Gipsy engine and featured a closed cabin.

The RAF flying schools' retirement of the Avro 504N in 1930 coincided with the Air Ministry's purchase of the new Avro 621 Tudor biplane as its training aircraft. Though about 800 Tudors were built, the plane was soon competing with the de Havilland DH.82 Tiger Moth, another two-seater that was to enjoy far greater success. This aircraft, which completed its maiden flight on 26 October 1931, was developed from the civil Gipsy Moth, but featured new wings, a new engine and a reinforced frame. The RAF immediately ordered the Tiger Moth, and it began to enter service in 1932. Not long thereafter, Avro introduced the DH.82A version, which was equipped with the more powerful Gipsy Major engine, producing 132 hp. The Tiger Moth was to become one of the most widely used and successful trainers in aviation history. About 8,000 were built and production licenses were granted for Australia, Canada, New

193 bottom left The de Havilland DH.82 Tiger Moth was without doubt one of the most successful and commonest trainers. It first flew with the British forces in 1931 but was then licensed for construction and used in many countries around the world.

193 bottom right The Polikarpov U-2 biplane first flew in 1928 but, thanks to its sturdiness, remained in service for many years and many purposes, including night-time bombing raids during the Second World War.

Zealand, Sweden, Norway and Portugal. For many years, and well past the end of the Second World War, the Tiger Moth was to remain the standard military basic trainer for all the Commonwealth countries. Still widely used in the civilian field for recreational flying, the Tiger Moth is now considered to be a classic.

The Soviet Union, which was a leader in aeronautic design in the 1920s and 1930s, also produced a particularly interesting trainer. It is probably still the most widely constructed aircraft of its type, with more than 33,000 being built. The merit for this success goes to the designer Polikarpov, who radically modified the U-2TPK design (for an aircraft that was actually never built) to produce a robust, conventional biplane that was easy to produce and fly. The U-2 flew for the first time on 7 January 1928, and proved to an excellent plane. It was immediately ordered into mass production.

During the Second World War, the U-2 was used in diverse roles such as reconnaissance, tactical support, night bombing, target towing, transport and air-ambulance, and remained in production up until 1952. On Polikarpov's death the aircraft was renamed in his honor as the Po-2.

The early 1930s saw the birth of another great aircraft, this time in Germany There, with the support of the Nazi regime, aviation was rapidly regaining ground lost after the restrictions imposed by the Treaty of Versailles. The newly formed Buckner firm made its debut in 1934 with the Bu-131 Jungmann, a two-seat biplane of compact dimensions, built from wood and aluminum covered in canvas, and featuring a moderate sweep to the wing. The Bu-131, powered by an 82-hp Hirth engine, made its maiden flight on 27 April. In this case too, the aircraft achieved sales success in both the military and civilian fields, being adopted the nascent Luftwaffe, by aero clubs, and purchased by numerous other countries. The Bu-131B model was powered by a Hirth HM 504 engine developing 106 hp, and had a wingspan of 24 feet 2.5 inches, a length of 21 feet 7 inches, a maximum take-off weight of 1,500 lbs, and a top speed of about 113 mph. The Jungmann was also produced in Czechoslovakia and Japan, with 1,254 being built in the latter nation alone. The total production figure is unknown but is certainly in the order of some thousands. A single-seater, the Bu-133 Jungmeister, was also developed from the Bu-131. It was basically a scaled-down version but equipped with a more powerful Hirth engine producing 137

hp. In the C version, this engine was replaced by a Siemens Sh 14 engine, producing 162 hp. This truly agile and lively aircraft was used as an advanced trainer for fighter pilots. Finally, in 1939 Buckner produced the last of its famous planes, the Bu-181 Bestmann, a basic trainer with modern features. A low-wing monoplane with a closed two-seater cabin, the Bu-181 had the same Hirth engine as the Bu-131 but a top speed of about 134 kph. During the Second World War, some thousands of Bestmanns were produced in Germany, Holland and Sweden and subsequently in Czechoslovakia and Egypt.

Another trainer to earn a place in the history of aviation was the American Stearman 75 Kaydet, which flew for the first time in 1935 and was used to train thousands of American pilots during the Second World War. Developed from the X-70 prototype, the Model 75 was initially ordered by the US Army and it began to enter service in 1936 as the PT-13. In 1939, Stearman was bought out by Boeing, a firm capable of meeting the enormous demands that the army and navy made for aircraft with the outbreak of war. In 1940 the PT-17 (known as the N2S to the US Navy) was

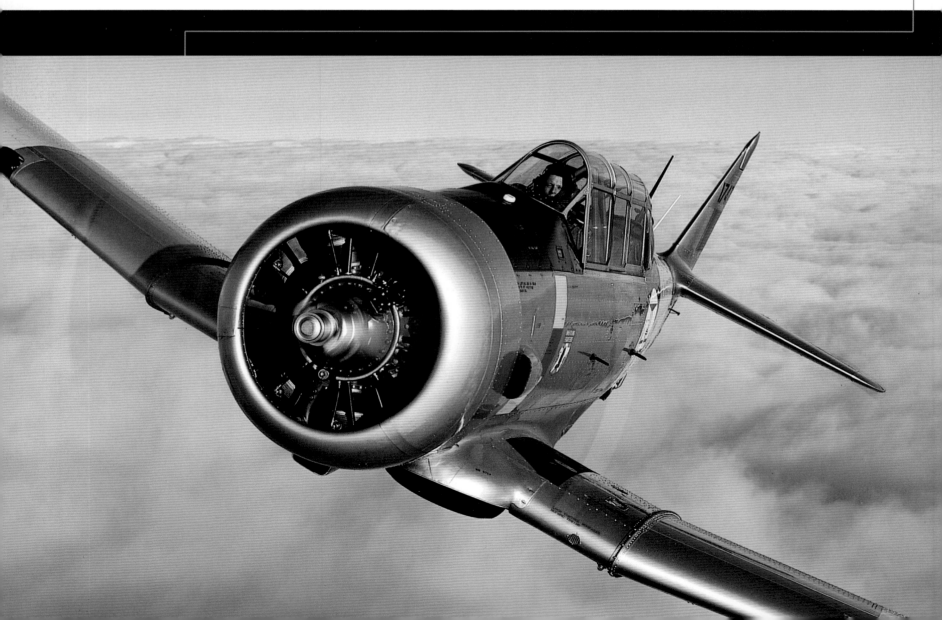

introduced; this most successful version of the aircraft had adopted the Continental R-670 engine, producing 220 hp. The PT-17 had a wingspan of just over 32 feet, a length of 24 feet 11 inches, and a maximum take-off weight of 2,710 lbs, and was capable of a top speed of about 125 mph. By 1945 Boeing had produced 10,436 PT-17s, and the plane continued to fly in great numbers in the military and civilian spheres for many years after the war.

The General Aviation Company (shortly to become North American) introduced another great military trainer, the T-6 Texan, which was used in the United States and then throughout the world from the 1940s to the 1960s and beyond. The plane, which was redesignated the NA-16, flew for the first time in April 1935. The US Army appreciated features such as the aircraft's all-metal construction, monoplane architecture, two-seat tandem cockpit and 405-hp Wright engine, and ordered an initial batch of 42 that year, designating the plane as the BT-9. This aircraft was then the basis for the BC-1 (the SNJ-1 for the Navy), introduced in 1937 and featuring a retractable undercarriage, a more sophisticated airframe and a new, more powerful engine developing 550 hp. In 1940, the BC-1 was redesignated the AT-6. Output of the airplane increased constantly as war loomed and finally broke out. The basic design was gradually improved

195 top The US Navy called the T-6 Texan the SNJ. Shown are two splendid restored SNJs in their official colors before the US entered the Second World War in December 1941.

195 center left The Bearing-Stearman 75 Kaydet, another famous trainer, was used by the flying schools of the USAAC and US Navy from 1936, and after the war by many other forces. Over 10,000 were built.

195 center right Germany too built excellent trainers during the 1930s, including the Bucker Bu-133 Jungmeister, a small acrobatic, single-seat biplane with a 160-hp engine and top speed of 137 mph.

195 bottom Designed to be a touring plane, the Bucker Bu-181 Bestmann first flew in 1939. It was very advanced for its time and, after the war, was used by various countries, including Egypt, flying the one depicted here.

194 top A North American T-6A Texan flown by the Canadian air force. Built under license, it was given the name Harvard H4M in the Commonwealth countries.

194 bottom A T-6A flown by the Portuguese air force. The Texan was a great success and was sold to many of America's allies after World War II. More than 21,000 T-6s were built and used in over 60 countries.

and adapted to meet diverse needs with the introduction of specific versions. Baptized by the British as the Harvard, the AT-6 was known to the Americans as the Texan, given that it was built in a new factory in Dallas. The AT-6A was equipped with a Pratt & Whitney R-1340-49 engine producing 607 hp, and was capable of a top speed of 210 mph. It had a wingspan of 42 feet, a length of 28 feet 9.5 inches, and a maximum take-off weight of about 5,150 lbs. Designated the T-6 in the post-war period, the plane was built under license in Australia, Sweden, Spain, Canada and Japan. Taking into account all the versions of the T-6 (over 260), it appears that a total of more than 21,000 were built. After

the war, far from being withdrawn from service, the T-6 was adopted by over 60 different air forces and used throughout the world as a standard military trainer, in some cases until the 1980s.

Perhaps the most significant expression of technological progress in aviation to emerge from the Second World War was the jet engine and the aircraft powered by it: the Messerschmitt Me-262, the Arado Ar.234, the Gloster Meteor and other experimental designs. In the post-war years it became clear that with the rapid spread of jet aircraft, traditional propeller-powered trainers were no longer adequate. A new generation of jet-powered trainers was thus introduced, some of which were actually used for the basic training of student pilots. The first to appear and the most famous was (like others in that period) derived from a fighter, the Lockheed F-80. On the basis of this excellent jet, the California-based manufacturer created a two-seater model that conserved the architecture of the original plane. Designated the TP-80C, the airplane flew for the first time on 22 March 1948, and was immediately approved for serial production. The TP-80C had a wingspan of 38 feet 8.5 inches, a length of 37 feet 8.5 inches, and a maximum take-off weight of about 14,450 lbs; it was equipped with an Allison J33 turbojet that produced 5,400 lbs of thrust, sufficient to give it a top speed of 600 mph. The TP-80C trainer was soon renamed the T-33A Silver Star and enjoyed exceptional sales success: Lockheed and other firms that manufactured it under license produced a total of 6,557 planes. These were purchased by the armed forces of more than 40 different countries around the world. Such was the

quality of the design that over fifty years later, a number of T-33s are still flying operationally in a number of countries.

Following the United States' lead, jet-powered basic trainers began to be designed in Europe too. Apart from the British de Havilland Vampire T, derived from the well-known fighter, the first true trainer from the Old World was designed in response to a requirement issued by the French Air Force. This was the Fouga CM-170 Magister, which completed its maiden flight on 23 July 1952. The Magister boasted highly streamlined, elegant lines with a straight wing, a tandem cockpit layout with no ejector seats, a characteristic "V" tail and two Turboméca Marboré turbojets buried in the wing roots, each developing about 880 lbs of thrust. The plane had a wingspan of 39 feet 7 inches, a length of 32 feet 9.5 inches, a maximum take-off weight of 7.050 lbs, and a top speed of 444 mph. It could be armed with two 7.62-mm machine guns and up to 220 lbs of external weaponry in the form of bombs or rockets. As it was one of the first jet trainers to be produced in series, the Magister sold very well and was used by no less than 22 different countries. It was also built under license in Germany, Finland, and Israel. A total of 929 Magisters were produced, some of which are still flying today. Fouga also produced the CM-175 version for the French navy as a trainer for deck-landing operations.

Another two significant aircraft appeared

two years after the Magister. The first to fly, on 16 June 1954, was the British Hunting P84 Jet Provost, developed from the propeller-driven Provost trainer in the hope of meeting the RAF's requirements for an instructional jet. Maintaining the wing and the tailplanes of the Provost, Hunting designed a new fuselage featuring side-by-side ejector seats and two air intakes in the wing roots that fed a Bristol Siddeley Viper turbojet producing 2,500 lbs of thrust, sufficient to provide the plane with a top speed of 440 mph. The Jet Provost had a wingspan of 35 feet 1 inch, a length of 33 feet 8.5 inches, and a maximum take-off weight of about 9,200 lbs. The RAF ordered 201 of the T. Mk.3 version, which was followed by a further nine production versions, many of which were exported. In all, about 530 P84s were built, and the aircraft was adopted by seven air forces. It remained in service with the RAF through until the late 1980s.

On 12 October 1954, the Cessna Model 318 made its maiden flight. It was the company's response to a USAF requirement for a new jet-powered basic trainer. The plane, which won the USAF contract, was a compact twin-engined design, with parallel seating and a low undercarriage. The Model 318 then received the military designation T-37A. It had a wingspan of 35 feet 8.5 inches, a length of 28 feet 2.5 inches, and a maximum take-off weight of about 6,395 lbs, and was powered by two Continental J69 engines, each producing 920 lbs of thrust. In 1974, after 534 T37-As had been constructed and the plane had begun to enter service, the T-37B version with more powerful engines (1,025 hp) was introduced. Then followed the T-37C and the A-37A and B Dragonfly versions, equipped with new engines, a maximum take-off weight of 14,000 lbs, armament and wingtip tanks. In the main, these planes were sold to Allied air forces as light strike aircraft. Subjected to an updating program and prolongation of its operational life, the T-37 (with over 1.230 built) remains the USAF's basic trainer, although it is gradually being replaced by the Beech T-6A Texan II.

196 top left The Lockheed T-33A Silver Star, derived from the F-80 fighter, was the first US Air Force jet trainer. It first flew in 1948.

196 bottom left A pair of RAF Hunting P.84 Jet Provosts. This plane was a jet-engined development of the propeller-driven Provost trainer.

196 right Two Cessna T-37As belonging to the Pakistani Air Force. With two side-by-side seats and straight wings, this plane first flew in 1954 and over 1,800 were made.

197 The French Fouga CM.170 Magister was one of the first airplanes designed to train new pilots on jet aircraft; it first flew in 1952. This one is flown by the Irish air force.

The Aermacchi MB.326, another trainer that was to be sold successfully throughout the world, completed its maiden flight in Italy on 10 December 1957. With a traditional layout and tandem seating, the 326 was a simple, reliable and robust aircraft. However, it featured a number of innovative features, and in 1962 the Italian air force (the AMI) began ordering it for use by its flying schools. The plane had a wingspan of 34 feet 5 inches, a length of 34 feet 8.5 inches, and a maximum take-off weight of 8.300 lbs. and was powered by a Rolls-Royce Viper turbojet producing 2.500 lbs of thrust, providing a top speed of 500 mph. A number of important production contracts granted in South Africa, Australia and Brazil confirmed the MB.326's sales success. A total of 763 planes were manufactured, and they were used in twelve

different countries. The MB 326 formed the basis of a single-seat strike version, the MB.326K. In 1972, in order to create a 326 series replacement for the AMI, Aermacchi began work on the MB.339. This was a radical development of the preceding model, equipped with a more powerful Viper engine producing 4.000 lbs of thrust (the same unit used in the MB.326K), and a completely redesigned nose with a tandem cockpit featuring stepped seats. This aircraft flew for the first time on 12 August 1976. It was a commercial success; the air forces of nine countries adopted the plane, and over 220 were built in a number of different versions. The advanced FD/CS version of the 339, with digital avionics, is still in production today.

The Soviet bloc countries had their own basic jet trainer: the Czech Aero L-29 Delfin, a single-engined plane with a tandem cockpit, a straight wing and a T-tail that flew for the first time on 5 April 1959. This plane had a Motorlet M701 engine producing about 1,960 lbs of thrust, sufficient to provide it with a top speed of 407 mph. It had a wingspan of 33 feet 9.6inches, a length of 35 feet 4.8 inches and a maximum take-off weight of about 7,230 lbs. Over 3,500 of the L-29s were built, with 2,000 acquired by the Soviet air force for its flying schools. In the 1960s, Aero decided to produce a successor to the Delfin, but initially the L-39 Albatros project encountered difficulties, apparently due to the combination of the new airframe and the Soviet Ivchenko engine. The Albatros completed its maiden flight on 4 November 1968, and entered operational service in 1974. The Albatros

198 top The Northrop T-38 Talon was the USAF's first supersonic trainer. It entered service in 1961 and was used for advanced training. Shown here is a Talon belonging to the Turkish air force.

198 center The Anglo-American McDonnell-Douglas (Boeing)/Bae T-45A was developed from the BAe Hawk for the US Navy. Though it still has the general lines of the Hawk it was in fact an entirely new airplane.

198-199 The Alpha-Jet, introduced in 1973, was the result of a French-German collaboration to build a multi-role aircraft that could act both as a light fighter-bomber and as a training airplane.

199 top The Aermacchi MB.339A, which first flew in 1976, was a direct successor of the MB.326. This model is the MB.339C belonging to the New Zealand Air Force and is shown during an acrobatic display.

had a wingspan of 31 feet 1.2 inches, a length of 39 feet 7.2 inches, and a maximum take-off weight of about 10,360 lbs. Powered by an Ivchenko Progress engine that produced about 3,790 lbs of thrust, the plane had a top speed of 470 mph. The Albatros was extremely successful; over 2,800 were built and exported to over 18 different countries, the majority to the Soviet Union. The L-39 basic training version was followed by ground-attack version and, in 1986, by the improved L-59 with uprated avionics and engine. The L-139, a collaboration with the American aviation industry, which provided the power unit and avionics, made its maiden flight in 1993, and the L-159, a single- or two-seat fighter based on the L-59, was introduced in 1997.

The American firm Northrop produced the first supersonic trainer: its two-seat N-156 made its maiden on 10 April 1959. The USAF then took delivery of the plane in 1961, designating it the T-38A Talon. The plane was a slim tandem two-seater, with twin engines, it featured a short, moderately

swept wing. The USAF used it as an advanced trainer to which pilots graduated after basic training with the T-37. The T-38 had a wingspan of 25 feet 2.4 inches, a length of 46 feet 2.5 inches, and a maximum take-off weight of about 13,000 lbs. Its two General Electric J85 turbojets each produced 3,850 lbs of thrust and powered the plane to a top speed of Mach 1.23. A total of 1,187 Talons were built; many went into service with the US Navy, NASA and the air forces of Portugal, Turkey and Taiwan. The original model formed the basis of the AT-38B gunnery trainer. The T-38 is also the subject of a modernization program that involves replacement of the avionics and redevelopment of the airframe, upgrades designed to allow the plane continue in service with the USAF until 2020.

199 bottom left The Aero L-29 Delfin first flew in 1959 and was for many years the standard training aircraft of the Warsaw Pact countries and allies of the USSR. More than 3500 were built.

199 bottom right The Aermacchi MB.326 was the greatest Italian success after the Second World War. This plane belong to the South African acrobatics team.

In Europe in the mid-1970s two other successful modern trainers came into being. Together with the MB.339, they represented the new generation. The three were the Franco-German Dassault-Breguet/Dornier Alpha Jet and the British Hawker Siddeley (later British Aerospace) Hawk. The former was introduced in 1969, and was the outcome product of combining the French need for a trainer and the German need for a light fighter-bomber. The resulting Alpha Jet was, however, closer to the French requirement than to the Luftwaffe's: it was a tandem two-seater with a high swept wing and two low-mounted engines that were not equipped with afterburners. The Alpha Jet E trainer had with a wingspan of 29 feet 10 inches, a length of 40 feet 3.6 inches, and a take-off weight of about 16,500 lbs. The plane's twin Larzac 04 turbofan engines produced 2.975 lbs of thrust, giving it a top speed of 572 mph. The Alpha Jet completed its maiden flight on 26 October 1973, and

since then over 500 have been produced and sold in eleven different European, Asian and African countries. In 1982, the Alpha Jet 2 followed, equipped with modern avionics and specific ground-attack weaponry.

The BAe Hawk, which flew for the first time on 21 August 1974, also enjoyed considerable sales success. The plane was an advanced trainer with tandem seating and a low wing, and was designed to provide the RAF with a replacement for its Folland Gnats and Hawker Hunters. The fast, maneuverable Hawk entered service in 1976, and soon proved to be a fine strike aircraft. Its export success was largely due to this versatility. The Hawk T Mk.1 had a wingspan of 30 feet 9.6 inches, a length of 38 feet 8.4 inches, and a maximum take-off weight of about 17,000 lbs. Powered by an Adour turbofan engine producing 5,200 lbs of thrust, the plane was capable of a top speed of 646 mph.

After 1980, with the introduction of

various export versions (the Mk. 50, 60 and 100 series), the Hawk was sold to about fifteen European, Asian, African and North American countries. The Mk. 200, a single-seat version expressly designed for combat roles, was introduced in 1986, and the Hawk Mk. 60 was chosen as the basis for McDonnell-Douglas/BAe joint venture advanced trainer for the US Navy. Designated the T-45A Goshawk, this plane flew for the first time on 16 April 1988, and entered service in 1992. The US Navy has placed orders for a total of 174 of the T-45A's, which by 2003 will have replaced the T-2 Buckeye and the TA-4 Skyhawk. The T-45A is a substantially different aircraft from the Hawk; it features significant avionics, structural and aerodynamic modifications enabling it to respond to the navy's particular demands, including those of carrier-borne operations. A total of over 700 of all versions of the Hawk have been built to date.

200-201 The Italian Frecce Tricolori, one of the three most appreciated acrobatic teams, has flown ten Aermacchi MB.339s since 1982. The Frecce, known as the 313th Group, are also trained as a fighter-bomber unit.

201 top The Patrouille de France, another of the world's top acrobatics teams, uses nine Dassault-Breguet/Dornier Alpha Jet E. The French use this plane only as a training aircraft, but the Germans also use it as a light fighter-bomber.

201 bottom The RAF Red Arrows acrobatics team uses nine BAe Hawk trainers. The Hawk first flew in 1974 and can be used as a light attack aircraft carrying bombs and

rockets. It has been exported to a dozen or so countries as a trainer and light, multi-role fighter. A single-seat version, known as the Hawk Mk.200, was also developed.

In the post-war years, production of propeller-driven trainers continued alongside that of the jet models as the former were required for the initial phases of flight training. In this category, of particular note were the Yak-18, the Beech T-34 Mentor, the North American T-28 Trojane and the SIAI-Marchetti SF.260.

In the Soviet Union, the Yak enterprise had designed a single-engined prop trainer before the outbreak of the war, but the project remained frozen until 1945 as a result of more urgent wartime priorities. The Yak-18, characterized by a radial engine, a tandem cockpit and a tricycle undercarriage with a tail-wheel, thus first appeared in 1947. In 1955, however, it was replaced by the Yak-18U, equipped with a nose-wheel tricycle undercarriage, and then by the model A with a 260-hp engine and further refinements. By 1968, more than 6,750 Yak-18s had been produced; the plane was the principal basic trainer of the Soviet air force and those of its various allies and satellite states. In 1976, the

202 left The North American T-28 Trojan was the US Navy's replacement for the SNJ Texan. Mass production started in 1950 and almost 1,200 were built. This is a restored Trojan wearing USAF colors.

202-203 The Beech T-34 Mentor replaced the T-6 Texan prviously used by the USAF. The T-34 mentor took to the skies in December 1948 and was also used by the air forces of 16 other countries.

203 bottom The Russian Yakovlev Yak-18A was a famous Eastern European propeller-driven plane, first seen in 1946 as a tandem two-seater design. In 1967 it was developed into the four-seater Yak-18T (shown here), used for light transport and as an air-ambulance.

Yak-18 formed the basis of the single-seat Yak-50 aerodynamic plane. The Yak-18 also formed the basis of the Yak-52 two-seater, which was powered by a Vedneyev M14 radial engine producing 360 kph. The Yak-52 had a semi-retractable undercarriage, was capable of a top speed of 186 mph, and had a maximum take-off weight of about 2,865 lbs. Externally the plane appeared very similar to its predecessors. To date, over 1,700 Yak-52s have been built.

In the United States, the Beech 45 was introduced in 1948. Based on the 35 Bonanza model, it was designed as a new basic trainer for the USAF. It featured a nose-wheel tricycle undercarriage and a tandem cockpit, and flew

for the first time on 2 December 1948. The military authorities designated it the T-34A Mentor and ordered 450 for the USAF, with a further 423 going to the US Navy (as the T-34B). The T-34A had a wingspan of 33 feet 1.2 inches, a length of 28 feet 6 inches and a maximum take-off weight of 4,320 lbs. It plane was powered by a Continental O-450 engine that produced 225 hp and gave it a top speed of 188 mph. Later, the USAF adopted a jet aircraft, the T-37, while the US Navy decided to uprate its B models to C specifications, equipping these with Pratt & Whitney Canada PT6A turboprop engines that produced 400 shp and provided an increase in top speed to 246

mph. Over 1,200 of the T-34s were produced (a number under license in Japan and Argentina). They served and continue to serve in over 15 countries.

The North American XT-28, a robust monoplane with a tandem cockpit and a low wing flew for the first time on 26 September 1949. It was designed to replace the T-6, and was approved in 1950, designated the T-28A Trojan for the USAF and the T-28B for the US Navy, which also acquired the T-28C, a version equipped with a deck-landing hook. The Trojan was fitted with a powerful Wright R-1820 engine producing 1.445 hp and capable of a providing the plane with a top speed of 340 mph. It also proved to be an effective light strike aircraft, and was used in the conflicts in Algeria and Indochina. A total of 1,194 XT-28s were built, and the plane was used by more than six countries.

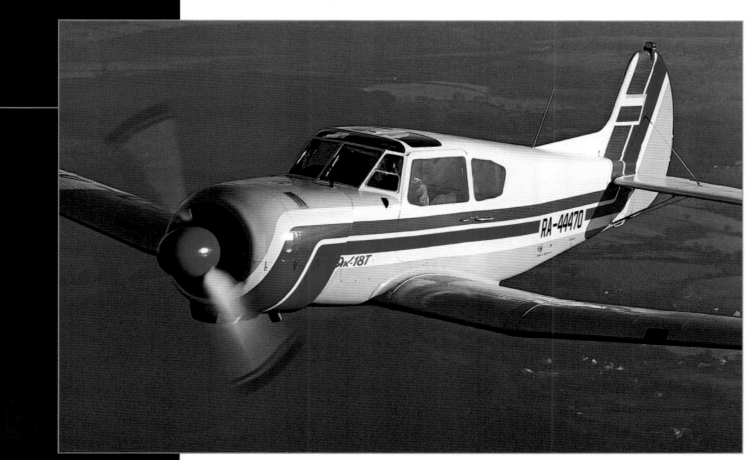

The Italian SIAI Marchetti SF-260, designed as a recreational aircraft, flew for the first time on 15 July 1954. The aircraft was derived from two designs of the engineer Stelio Frati, the F.8 Falco and the F.250. SIAI Marchetti acquired and developed the F.250, and adapted it for serial production. After its initial success in the civilian market, civil and military flying schools took the plane into consideration, thanks to its notable capabilities as a trainer. As a result, toward the end of the 1960s, the SF.260M was developed for military applications; this version bwas followed by the SF.260 Warrior, which could be lightly armed. The airplane featured very clean, elegant lines with a laminar profile wing, side-by-side cockpit seating and a retractable undercarriage. It was powered by a Lycoming AIO-540 engine producing 260 hp and could reach a top speed of 215 mph. It had a wingspan of 27 feet 4.8 inches, a length of 23 feet 3.6 inches, and a maximum take-off weight of about 2,645 lbs. A TP turboprop version SF.260 was developed, and overall the SF.260 has been a great commercial success: more than 900 have been produced, and the military version has served in 31 different countries. Aermacchi is still building the plane.

In the 1970s a third type of training aircraft fitted with turboprop engines began to become established. The turboprop combined the high performance of jet-powered alternatives with lower running costs. Along with the Marchetti SIAI T-34C and the SF.260TP, the most successful trainers of this type were designed in Switzerland and Brazil. In the 1960s, the Swiss company Pialatus, which already produced the P-3 piston-engined aircraft, decided to revitalize its range with the introduction of a turboprop-engined plane. The new plane, designated the P-3B, flew for the first time on 12 April 1966, but the definitive PC-7 Turbo Trainer version did not appear until 1978. It had a wingspan and length of 33 feet 1.2 inches and a maximum take-off weight of about 7,050 lbs. The PC-7 was powered by the classic 700-shp Pratt & Whitney Canada PT6A engine, which provided a top speed of 345 mph. The PC-7 entered service with the Swiss air force in 1982; 15 or more countries have adopted it, and more than 450 PC-9s have been built. It also formed the basis for the PC-9, which flew for first time on 7 May 1984. This version featured a more powerful PT6A engine (950 shp), better performance, and ejector seats for the crew. More than 160 PC-9s were built; the model in turn formed the basis for the Beech Mk.II, which in 1995 won the JPATS competition for a new trainer for the American armed forces. Designated the T-6A Texan, the plane features a 1,250-shp engine together with new avionics, a pressurized cabin, and other modifications. More than 700 T-6A Texans will be built for the USAF and the US Navy.

In the mid-1970s, the Brazilian manufacturer Embraer focused on development of new turboprop trainer, producing a prototype that flew for the first time on 16 August 1980. The plane, named the EMB-312 Tucano, has a wingspan of about 36 feet, a length of 32 feet 3 inches, and a maximum take-off weight of about 7,000 lbs. The Tucano was powered by the Pratt & Whitney PT6A engine, capable of producing 760 shp but restricted to 590 hp, giving the plane a top speed of 270 mph. The plane entered service with the Brazilian air force in 1982, and has been successfully exported, in particular to two countries notoriously reluctant to import aircraft, Great Britain and France. Both have assigned the Tucano to their flying schools. The Tucano is still in production (as is the A-29/EMB-312H assault version), and to date over 680 have been delivered to 14 countries around the world.

204-205 bottom The SIAI Marchetti (today Aermacchi) SF.260 was one of Italy's most successful postwar light trainers. Introduced in 1964, it is still in production, and more than 900 have been sold to 30 or more countries.

205 top The Swiss Pilatus PC-7, introduced in 1978, is another successful turboprop trainer. More than 500 have been sold to 16 countries, including Malaysia, which owns the three shown here.

205 center Two of the RAF's Shorts Tucanos (the British version of the Brazilian EMB-312, built under license). At the end of the 1970s, with the aim of reducing training costs, turboprop airplanes began to be used instead of the more complex jets.

205 bottom The Pilatus PC-9, a natural development of the PC-7, was an excellent twin turbo-prop trainer and was the winner of the JPATS competition to re-equip the flying schools of the American forces.

Chapter 15

The term "general aviation" is relatively recent, being coined as the result of the ever-increasing differences and specialized categories that were becoming established in the world of powered flight. Prior to the Second World War, in many cases there was no clear distinction between aircraft for civil use and those designed for military purposes. At that time sectors such as training, passenger services and transport and even bombing saw the use of aircraft that had never been designed with an exclusive role in mind; civilian aircraft were frequently converted with only minor modifications for military purposes and vice versa. In the post-war era, with the advent of jet engines and increasingly sophisticated technology in aerodynamics and avionics, aircraft could be designed to respond more closely to end-users' specific demands, and the differences between them became increasingly

well defined. In the 1920s in America, the Curtiss JN was used by both military flying schools for training and by civilian pilots for recreational purposes; nowadays the differences between the military T-37 or T-45 jets and the Cessna 172s flown by numerous American aero clubs are self-evident.

General aviation thus comprises all those aircraft for private use that do not fall into the military, commercial and airliner categories. In practice they are light training, tourism, or business planes, the highest expression of which are the business or executive jets which the largest corporations and most rushed VIPs use to carry their staff around the world.

Among the companies representing the pillars of this sector are the American firms Piper and Cessna, responsible for introducing millions of people around the globe to the world of aviation.

In this context, the Piper J-3 Cub, which

first flew in September 1930 as the Taylor Cub, may be seen as the progenitor of modern general aviation planes. This was a lightweight aircraft covered in canvas with a high, braced wing, a closed, two-seat, tandem cabin, a tricycle undercarriage with a tail-wheel and a 41-hp Continental engine. In 1937, the newly founded Piper company took over development and production. It increased the Cub's engine power output to 66 hp, a modification that increased the plane's popularity. In 1949, Piper decided to introduce an improved, more robust version, the PA-18 Super Cub, the relative weight and performance figures of which were increased. The Super Cub was initially equipped with a 91-hp engine, but a number of variations of the Cub theme were produced; some models equipped with skis and floats and powered by engines of up to 152 hp. The PA-18-150, equipped with a 150-hp Lycoming unit, had a maximum take-off weight of 1,750 kg and a top

206 *The Piper Pa-28 Cherokee is one of the commonest tourist flight planes. Since January 1960, more than 30 versions have been built and the plane is still widely used today.*

207 top *A Piper Pa-18 Super Cub at low altitude over Maryland. The Pa-18 was the natural evolution of the J-3 and was developed from 1949 on.*

207 center left *A Piper J-3 Cub, the progenitor of a long line of modern touring aircraft. Designed in 1929, the Cub originally had just a 41-hp engine and weighed less than 1,100 lbs on take-off.*

speed of 210 kph, but compact dimensions: a wingspan of 32 feet 9.5 inches and a length of 19 feet 7 inches.

Military versions of both the Cub and the Super Cub were constructed for personnel transport and observation purposes (the L-4, L-18 and L-21 models) and were used by the armed forces of numerous countries. Albeit with a number of interruptions, the Super Cub remained in production through to the mid-1990s and together with the Cub, production exceeded 26,000 planes. A heavier tourist airplane, powered by a 150-hp Lycoming engine, completed its maiden flight on 14 January 1960: this was the PA-28 Cherokee, an attractive low-wing monoplane with a fixed undercarriage and a four-seat cabin.

The PA-28 went into production in 1961 and is still available today, having enjoyed an enormous commercial success that led to the construction of over 19,000 planes to differing specifications. Among the more than 30 thirty models that have been produced are the Archer, Arrow, Dakota and Warrior series, variously equipped with carburettor, fuel-injected and turbocharged engines, retractable undercarriage systems, and power outputs of up to 235 hp.

In October 1977, Piper introduced the PA-38 Tomahawk, a new single-engined, two-seat light trainer characterized by a T-tail and a fuel-efficient 114-hp engine. Although carefully designed with advice from some 10,000 flight-instructors, the Tomahawk never enjoyed commercial success; up until 1982, fewer than 2,500 had been built.

Another of the Piper company's major strengths is twin-engined aircraft, the first being the PA-23 Apache, a low-wing monoplane with a retractable undercarriage, a four-seat cabin, and engines faired into the wings. The Apache made its first flight on 2 March 1952 and remained in production until 1965, when the Aztec replaced it. The new model featured a larger cabin, a greater carrying capacity, and two 250-hp engines. Next came the Turbo Aztec, which was powered by two 253-hp turbocharged Lycoming units, had a top speed of 253 mph, and a maximum take-off weight of 5,600 lbs. It had a wingspan of 37 feet 4.8 inches, a length of 31 feet 1.2 inches, and could carry five passengers and a pilot. Over 2,800 PA-23's were built.

207 bottom left The Pa-38 Tomahawk was produced by Piper in 1977 to equip flying schools with a new light, single-engined plane, but it did not meet with the hoped-for success.

207 bottom right The four-seater Pa-23 Apache was the first twin-engined plane designed and built by Piper. It made its maiden flight in 1952 and remained in production until 1965.

The PA-31 Inca completed its maiden flight on 30 September 1964; three years later this model became the Navajo. This was a larger, heavier airplane that, with its eight-seat capacity and 300-hp engines, was closer to the business aircraft and air taxi sector. Piper developed various versions of the PA-31, offering a pressurized cabin and turbocharged engines, and in 1972 introduced the Navajo Chieftain, which had an elongated fuselage and even more powerful engines. The company also introduced another new plane in 1972, the PA-42 Cheyenne, powered by turboprop engines. The plane was developed in various more advanced versions. The Cheyenne III had a wingspan of 47 feet 6 inches, a length

208 top Pa-31-350 Navajo Chieftain introduced in 1972 was one of the planes in the Pa-31 family. It had a lengthened fuselage and 335-hp engines.

208 center The Piper Pa-34 Seneca appeared in 1972 as a development of the single-engined Cherokee Six. Shown

here is the 1975 Seneca II with turbocharged engines.

208 bottom The Piper Pa-31 Inca, renamed the Navajo in 1967, was the basic model from which 20 versions were developed. It had turbocharged engines, a pressurized cabin and a lengthened fuselage and wingspan.

of 43 feet 3.6 inches, and a maximum take-off weight of 1,200 lbs, and was powered by two 730 shp engines guaranteeing a top speed of 342 mph. The Cheyenne IV featured eleven seats, a power output of 1,014 shp per engine, and a top speed of about 398 mph.

Yet another successful Piper model was introduced in 1972, the PA-34 Seneca developed from the single-engined Cherokee Six, This airplane featured typical Piper styling with a low wing, a six- or seven-seat cabin and two 230-hp Lycoming engines. Then came the Seneca II, equipped with turbocharged engines and contrarotating propellers, and then the Seneca III. The latest in this line is the Seneca IV powered by twin 220-hp Teledyne Continental engines that provide a top speed of 224 mph. The model has a wingspan of 36 feet, a length of 26 feet 2.4 inches and a maximum take-off weight of 4,740 lbs. More than 4,600 Senecas have been built to date, and the model remains in production.

The other American colossus in this sector, Cessna (founded in 1927), launched its most successful product in 1948 with the introduction of the Model 170, a four-seater with a high, braced wing and a fixed tail-wheel tricycle undercarriage derived from the earlier Model 120. True success came, however, some years later, first with the introduction of the 170 B (powered by a 147-hp engine and equipped with Fowler slotted flaps) and then, on a larger scale, with the Model 172 of 1955 that introduced a nose-wheel tricycle undercarriage. A total of 1,170 planes in this series were sold in 1956 alone. Since then the range has been continuously improved and developed, with numerous different 172, 175 and 182 versions being introduced with turbochargers and a retractable undercarriage

(RG). The Cessna 172 had a wingspan of 35 feet 8.5 inches, a length of 26 feet 2.5 inches, a maximum take-off weight of 2,500 lbs, and a Teledyne Continental engine producing 213 hp, sufficient to provide the plane with a top speed of about 152 mph. A total of 730 of the 172s were built to T-41 military trainer specifications. Fifty years later, the 170 and its successors are still in production (albeit after a number of interruptions), and over 58,000 have been built.

In parallel with the Model 170 series, Cessna also produced the Model 180 series, in practice a heavier and more powerful version of the 170B that used the same wing. The 180 Skywagon first flew in 1953. Seven years later came the six-seat Model 185, which was powered by a 300-hp engine producing a top

fuselage. This general-purpose plane was particularly well suited to airdrop, air taxi and air-ambulance duties. Over 8,000 Model 207s have been built, with some equipped with turbocharged engines.

Another exceptionally successful aircraft was the Model 150, in which generations of pilots learnt to fly. Equipped with the typical Cessna braced high wing, a fixed nose-wheel undercarriage, the two-seat 150 was introduced in September 1957 as a low-cost light aircraft for flying schools and aero clubs. The Model 150 had a wingspan of 32 feet 9.5 inches, a length of 22 feet 11 inches, and a maximum take-off weight of 1,600 lbs. It was powered by a 100-hp Continental engine and could attain a top speed of about 125 mph. The Model 150 enjoyed great commercial

209 top The Cessna 172, perhaps the most famous touring plane of all time. It was first produced in 1955, and more than 60,000 of the three-wheeler front undercarriage planes were built.

209 bottom The Cessna 206 Super Skywagon hydroplane version. It first flew in 1964, and is highly suitable for general work tasks.

speed of about 178 mph. The plane had a maximum take-off weight of 3,350 lbs. A military version was also developed from the 185, equipped with a more powerful engine and a nose-wheel tricycle undercarriage. This was the Cessna 206 Super Skywagon, introduced in 1964 and followed in 1969 by the Model 207, which had a stretched

success throughout the world, and was also built under license in France by Reims. Model 152 was introduced in 1977; version, the only significant difference being the adoption of the 112-hp Avco Lycoming engine. A total of more than 27,000 of the 150/152 series were built, and the planes are still very common today.

210-211 A twin-engined
Cessna E310P flying over
the sea. Cessna has produced
an enormous series of twin-
engined touring and business
planes, which has culminated
in the 425 turboprop model.

feet 6 inches, and a maximum take-off weight of about 4,630 lbs. Two Continental engines, each producing 213 hp, powered the 337 to a top speed of about 206 mph. The 337 was built under license by Reims. Two military versions were developed (the 0-2A and FTB337) for observation and light ground attack duties. In all, by 1980, a total of 2,678 Super Spymaster 337s had been manufactured.

Cessna also built a noteworthy series of successful twin-engined planes. The first, the Model 310, made its maiden flight in January 1953. The 953's low-wing design incorporated supplementary wing-tip fuel tanks, a retractable tricycle undercarriage, a six-seat cabin and two 228-hp Continental engines (replaced by 264-hp units when production began).

In February1961, Cessna introduced an aircraft that was to a certain degree revolutionary: the Model 336 Skymaster, characterized by the "push-pull" layout with one engine in the nose and the other in the tail. The plane featured a four-seat cabin, the traditional Cessna braced high wing, a twin-boom tailplane, and twin-rudder assembly. Not only was the plane original but it also handled very well; nonetheless, owing in part to its out-dated fixed undercarriage, it never achieved great success. The 337 Super Skymaster was introduced in 1965, featuring a needed retractable undercarriage, an optional belly luggage compartment, and a cabin that could now accommodate six in comfort. The plane had a wingspan of 36 feet, a length of 29

In July 1962, Cessna introduced the first of a long line of traditional twin-engined planes featuring a low wing, a retractable undercarriage and six-, eight- or ten-seat cabins. These Cessna 411 series aircraft were very similar to the earlier 310, but slightly larger and more powerful. The 411 was followed by the more economical 401 and 402. 1965 saw the introduction of the 421 Golden Eagle, developed from 411, and with a pressurized, air-conditioned cabin that could accommodate up to ten passengers. The 421 was powered by two Continental turbocharged engines developing 370 hp, and providing a top speed of almost 300 mph.

In 1968 the Cessna 414 Chancellor was introduced, incorporating the 401's wing type and the 441's fuselage. In the 1970s the company introduced the 441 Conquest and the 404 Titan; they were outwardly similar and both were equipped with positive dihedral tailplanes. The 401 was powered by turboprop engines and could accommodate up to eleven passengers, while the 404 was powered by turbocharged piston engines. These two models were followed by the 425 Corsair, another turboprop plane that combined the 421's airframe with Pratt & Whitney Canada PT6A engines.

In the late 1960s, Cessna took a significant step in the direction of twin-engined business jet, developing the Model 500, which flew for the first time on 15 September 1969. This aircraft, named the Citation, had a classical layout with a straight wing and the engines paired at the tail, and immediately won a position as a valid competitor in the executive jet sector. Over the years, the Citation family has been expanded with the introduction of ever more sophisticated and powerful models. In 1982, the Citation III became the first to be equipped with a swept wing. The next models were the Citation V (replacing the II), then VI and the VII, and finally in 1993, the Citation X, a VIP jet for intercontinental flights that can accommodate up to twelve passengers. The Citation X has a wingspan of 62 feet 3.5 inches, a length of 72 feet, and a maximum take-off weight of 34,500 lbs. The plane is powered by two Allison turbofan engines that each provide 6,400 lbs of thrust, giving a top speed of about 565 mph.

210 bottom This Cessna 321 Golden Eagle has British markings. It can seat up to 10 people and fly at 300 mph.

211 top A German twin-jet Cessna 525 Citation about to land. This plane first flew in 1969 and was one of the first relatively cheap business planes within the reach of a fairly large market.

211 bottom The Cessna 336/337 was undoubtedly a revolutionary plane, characterized by the in-tandem or "push-pull" twin engines. This is a F337F model with retractable undercarriage.

Beechcraft is another major American firm operating in the general aviation sector. Among its best-known products are the Bonanza, the Baron and the King Air. The Bonanza took to the air on 22 December 1945 as Beech Model 35, and with its highly successful and advanced configuration contributed to the post-war revival of civil aviation in America. Characterized by a low wing, a retractable nose-wheel tricycle undercarriage and a V-tail, the Bonanza enjoyed enormous success; within just two years from its launch over 1,000 had been sold. Subsequently Beechcraft introduced models 33 and 36; both featured traditional tailplanes. Fifty years later, more than 15,000 have been built, and they are still available on the market. Model 55 was by contrast a small plane with twin piston engines that first flew in February 1960. Named the Baron, the plane was derived from the

Model 95 but used more powerful Continental engines that produced 263 hp. The aircraft was subjected to continuous development, resulting in the B55 (six-seat cabin), the C55 (289-hp engines), the 56TC and the 58 of 1969, featuring a stretched fuselage. The 58, which is still in production, has a wingspan of 36 feet, a length of 25 feet 6 inches and a maximum take-off weight of

6,200 lbs. Its two Continental turbocharged engines each produce 329 hp, and provide the plane with a top speed of 300 mph.

January 1964 saw the maiden flight of another, heavier type of twin-engined plane equipped with turboprop engines, and suitable for transport and training roles. This was the Model 65-90T, derived from the Model 65-80 Queen Air in response to a requirement from the US Army. Named the King Air, the plane had a traditional layout with turboprop engines and a pressurized ten-seat cabin. Subsequently, a series of uprated versions with improved specifications and performance were introduced; these included the 99, the 100 with a 15-seat cabin and, in 1972, the 200 Super King Air, which was equipped with a T-tail, a longer wing and new engines. The B200 had a wingspan of 52 feet 6 inches, a length of 42 feet 7inches, and a maximum take-off weight of 12,500 lbs. It was powered by two Pratt & Whitney Canada engines developing 850 shp, and could attain a top speed of about 323 mph. The last of the series, the Super King Air 350, was introduced in 1990. This plane features winglets at the main-wing tips, an even longer fuselage that can accommodate up to 17 passengers and PT6A engines developing 1,050 shp. Beech also

212 top Known first as the Mitsubishi Diamond, the design of this twin-jet was subsequently bought up by Beechcraft, which produced it as the Beechjet 400A.

212-213 The Beechcraft C90 King Air is one of the most flexible families of twin-engined planes. The series has so far reached the 17-seat Super King Air 350.

213 top The Beechcraft 35 Bonanza was one of the most successful single-engined planes in general aviation. It first flew in 1945 and introduced the innovative V-shaped tail unit.

213 center The Beechcraft Model 55 Baron. In 1960 Beechcraft decided to relaunch itself in the twin-engine tourist and business market with this plane, which was more powerful than its predecessor, the Model 95 Travel Air.

213 bottom The MS.880 Rallye, produced by the French company Morane-Saulnier in 1959, was one of Europe's most successful tourism planes.

produces a useful executive jet, the Beechcraft 400. This plane was actually introduced as the Mitsubishi Diamond II, but the American firm acquired the rights to the design, and since 1986 the Mitsubishi original has been marketed under the Beechcraft name. The ten-seat Beechcraft 400 has a maximum take-off weight of 16,000 lbs and a top speed of about 537 mph.

In Europe, France led in the executive jet sector, producing numerous successful light aircraft in the post-war period. The Morane-Saulnier single-engined MS.880 Rallye first flew in June 1959. This was an all-metal, low-wing monoplane with flaps and slats that provided short take-off and landing capabilities. The nose-wheel tricycle undercarriage was fixed and the cabin could accommodate four people beneath an ample glazed canopy. In 1965 Sud Aviation absorbed Morane-Saulnier, and went on to found SOCATA the following year. The Rallye series saw the introduction of diverse models, including the 88B, the 885 Super Rallye, the 100T, the Rallye 180 and the more powerful 235; they differed mainly in terms

of engines and their two- or four-seat cabins. In 1979, SOCATA, then part of Aérospatiale, changed the name of the Rallye series, assigning the names Galopin, Garnament, Galèrien, Gaillard and Gabier to the principal versions. The Gabier (formerly the 235GT) was the top of the range; it had a wingspan of 29 feet 6 inches, a length of 22 feet 11 inches, and a maximum take-off weight of 2,645 lbs.

In 1975 SOCATA introduced a new series of more modern airplanes, of which the TB.10 Tobago led the way, completing its maiden flight on 23 February 1977. This low-wing monoplane had a fixed undercarriage, a spacious four-seat cabin and a Lycoming O-320 engine producing 160 hp. This first model was followed by a variant equipped with a180-hp engine. At this point Aérospatiale decided to call the first type the TB.9 Tampico and to introduced its most famous aircraft: the DR.400, characterized by its forward-sliding canopy. The DR 400's first model was the DR.400/125 Petit Prince, powered by a 125-hp engine and designed to carry two adults and two children. The Petit Prince was followed in close succession by other models with power outputs of up to 180 hp, four-seat cabins and glider-towing capabilities. The Robins are also popular among with the flying schools and

assign the TB-10 designation to the more powerful version that could carry up to five people. A third version appeared in 1980, characterized by an even more powerful engine (250 hp) and a retractable undercarriage; it was designated the TB.20 Trinidad. This last model could attain a top speed of 192 mph; it had a wingspan of 29 feet 6 inches, and a length of 22 feet 11 inches, and had a maximum take-off weight of about 3,085 lbs. Still later, the XLTB.200 Tobago, powered by a 200-hp engine, and the TB.21 Trinidad equipped with a turbocharged engine, were introduced.

The Jodel/Robin family of light aircraft was another successful series. The first model to make its mark was the Jodel DR.100, which went into production in 1958. This airplane, designed by Jean Delemontez and Pierre Robin, was a three-seat with a fixed two-wheeled undercarriage, a 96-hp Continental engine and a low wing with upturned outer sections, a feature that was to become a characteristic of the series. In 1961 the aircraft was renamed as the DR.1050 Ambassadeur, and various versions were developed with engines of up to 106 hp. Two other firms were engaged in building the planes: Avions Pierre Robin and the Société Aéronautique Normande (SAN). This last built the D.140 Mousquetaire model with a 180-hp engine and up to five seats in the cabin. SAN went out of business in 1969, with Robin taking over its activities. In1972, Robin

aero clubs, and more than 1,400 have been built. Seven versions of the DR.400, with engines producing between 110 and 200 hp, are still in production.

France also saw the establishment of a major national aircraft manufacturer, namely the Mudry firm, founded in 1958. Its CAP 10, introduced in 1968, was the first of a successful series of aerobatic aircraft. The CAP 10 was a low-wing monoplane with side-by-side seating, a 180-hp engine, and a fixed undercarriage. It had a wingspan of 26 feet 2.4 inches, a length of 22 feet 11 inches, and a maximum take-off weight of 1,830 lbs. It was capable of a top speed of about 168 mph. In 1969 the CAP 20, a competition single-seater, was introduced. The series continued with the CAP 21 (featuring a new wing) and then the CAP 230, 231 and 232.

In the 1960s, Dassault pioneered the way in the business plane sector, introducing increasingly successful models. Today the company remains a leading manufacturer in this sector. The Mystère 20, a particularly elegant twin-engined jet with swept wings and tailplanes, completed its maiden flight on 4 May 1963. Subsequently named the Falcon 20, the plane enjoyed considerable success, and a number of different versions were developed. The Falcon 20 was followed by the smaller Falcon 10 (later replaced by the 200 and 100 models, respectively), while in 1976,the Falcon 50m, a long-range tri-jet with a new wing and tailplanes and a stretched fuselage accommodating up to twelve passengers. In 1984, Dassault introduced the Falcon 900, a tri-jet with an intercontinental range and able to accommodate up to nineteen passengers. In the mid-1990s, the firm rejuvenated its product range rejuvenated with the introduction of the Falcon 2000 (twin engines) and the 50EX and 900EX models. Falcons have also been produced for military purchasers, and more than 1,200 have been built.

214 top The three-engined Dassault Falcon 900EX, which can carry 19 passengers across oceans, is one of the largest and most successful business jets.

214 bottom The fixed wheel DR.400, the most famous plane built by the French manufacturer Avions Pierre Robin. It is shown here with Italian registration.

214-215 Two two-seater CAP.10Bs during an air acrobatics display. This 1968 plane is still one of the best acrobatics trainers.

215 center Two Robin DR.500/200I Presidents shown over the French coast. These aircraft derived from predecessor designs, adopting the typical Jodel/Robin rising wing.

215 bottom The TB.9 Tampico, the TB.10 Tobago and the TB.20 Trinidad, a family of tourism planes, were produced by SOCATA during the 1970s. All were developed around the same cell.

In Italy, SIAI Marchetti was the most famous firm in aircraft manufacturing. Along with the SF.260, Marchetti also produced the renowned S.205/208 series. The first to fly was the S.205 on 4 May 1965. This monoplane, which had a roomy four-seat cabin, could be ordered with various engines (180, 200 or 220 hp), and with a fixed or retractable undercarriage. In 1967 the five-seat S.208, which was equipped with wing-tip tanks and used a more powerful O-540 engine producing 260 hp (the same unit fitted to the SF.260), made its maiden flight. Over 520 planes of the two models were built, and many are still flying in Italy and abroad.

The Czech firm Zlin has also been an important light aircraft manufacturer. The first plane in its most successful series was the Zlin 42, which flew for the first time in October 1967. This small two-seater, powered by a 137-hp Avia 137 engine, featured a side-by-side cockpit, a fixed undercarriage and a characteristic wing with a slight negative sweep, ad had been designed to meet the demands of Eastern European flying schools and aero clubs. The Zlin 42 formed the basis of the Zlin 43, a four-seat version, and then the Zlin 142, a two-seater with a 213-hp engine. This latter had a wingspan of 29 feet 6 inches, a length of 22 feet 11 inches, and a maximum take-off weight of about 2,400 lbs. It could attain a top speed of about 143 mph. Today the Zlins are produced in the Czech Republic by Morovan, the top of the range being the Zlin 143L with a 235-hp engine, while the most advanced trainer is the Zlin 242L, powered by a 200-hp engine.

Morovan has also produced a very popular series of aerobatic planes that began with the Zlin 526 (in both single- and two-seat versions) and continued with the Zlin 50L, introduced in 1975. In 1978, the 50L won the world aerobatics championship. The Zlin 50LS is

216 top left A Gulfstream III landing at the international airport in Tucson, Arizona. This model, with a new wing design and a lengthened cabin, first flew in December 1979.

216-217 The Mystère 20, later renamed the Falcon 20, was first of the Dassault business twin-jets. It appeared in 1963. This particular plane has Swiss markings and is shown at dusk over the Alps.

216 bottom A SIAI Marchetti S.208 with a 260-hp engine and five seats. The SIAI Marchetti S.205/208 series accounted for the commonest tourism planes in Italy. More than 500 planes of the series were built.

217 top A Learjet 45 twin-jet in flight. This 12-passenger plane dates from 1995 and is the most recent in the Learjet line. Learjet is today owned by Bombardier.

217 bottom Zlin has proved one of the most successful producers of competition acrobatic aircraft and has won several titles. Thephotograph shows a single-seater Zlin 50 during a competition.

the Gulfstream II, which was derived from the original turboprop model. The Gulfstream II was a large aircraft with transatlantic capabilities and could accommodate up to 19 passengers; the low, swept-wing and T-tail architecture was similar to that of the Learjets. A total of 258 Gulfstream IIs were built. In 1978 Grumman sold the rights to the plane to Gulfstream American, which a year later introduced the Gulfstream III. This plane featured a stretched fuselage and a new supercritical wing profile. In 1985 the Gulfstream IV, which had more economical engines, was launched. Further improvements to the airframe and avionics helped make the Gulfstream IV into a more versatile plane, suited to military and governmental roles as an air-ambulance and a search and rescue plane, as well as for electronic warfare, surveillance and transportation duties. The Gulfstream V, introduced in 1995, is the most recent model.

currently in production, powered by a 300-hp engine and with a maximum take-off weight of about 1,345 lbs. Other aerobatic planes built in the Eastern Bloc countries include the Soviet Yak-50 and 55 and the Sukhoi Su-26/29 series, all winners of various world championships.

In the business jet field, a number of the major players are still located in the United States. Learjet (founded by William Lear) was the first to produce a modern executive jet capable of offering both speed and comfort. Model 23, the progenitor of the Learjet line) first flew on 7 October 1963, and was an immediate success. It was a small twin-engined jet with attractive, fighter-like slim lines, and it that handled like a fighter. The low, straight wing was derived from a design for the Swiss P16 fighter-bomber (never produced in series), while the engines were carried at the rear of the fuselage, along with a T-tail. The Model 23 formed the basis for the stretched models 24 and 25; the 35 and 36 had an even longer fuselage and greater wingspan. The models currently in production are the Learjet 31A, 35A, 45 and 60. The most recent is the Learjet

45, which completed its maiden flight on 14 September 1995. It has a wingspan of almost 48 feet, a length of 55 feet 8.5inches, and a maximum take-off weight of 19,500 lbs. Two AlliedSignal TFE731 turbofan engines producing about 3,500 lbs of thrust give the Learjet 45 a top speed of about 540 mph.

In 1965, Grumman began work on a high-end twin-engined executive jet, giving rise to

It is an even larger aircraft with an intercontinental range (over 7,500 miles) and a cabin that can accommodate up to nineteen passengers. It has a wingspan of 91 feet 9.5 inches, a length of just over 95 feet, and a maximum take-off weight in the order of 45 tons. The two Rolls-Royce BR710 turbofans each produce about 14,750 lbs of thrust, and provide the plane with a top speed of approximately 580 mph.

Chapter 16

European Fighters

Duuring the 1950s and 1960s, the USA and the Soviet Union's dramatic Cold War confrontation overshadowed the world. The hostility between the Western and Eastern global superpowers was also evident in military aviation as their aeronautical industries designed and mass-produced some of the world's most effective aircraft, many of which were sold to the two blocs' various allies. Nonetheless, even during those difficult years Europe proved capable of maintaining a degree of independence, and produced a number of aircraft of significant technological specifications and performance.

The French aeronautical industry emerged from the Second World War in a very poor state, but found its inspiration in Marcel Dassault. Born in 1892 (with the name of Marcel Bloch), Dassault was soon caught up in the world of aviation, and as early as 1917 he was building his first industrial aircraft, the SEA4. During the 1930s, his factory produced diverse military and civil aircraft, but with the imposition of the German occupation Bloch was arrested, interred and finally deported to Buchenwald, after having refused to collaborate with the invaders. In 1945, following the liberation, the family changed its name to Dassault and began once again to produce increasingly successful aircraft. The first post-war fighter was the MD 450 Ouragan, which completed its maiden flight on 28 February 1949. This was the first French jet aircraft, and its specifications had much in common with other contemporary jets and engines, including the Rolls-Royce Nene engine, which produced 5,000 lbs of thrust.

The MD 450's design featured a straight low wing with tip tanks, air intakes at the nose and cruciform tailplanes. It was armed with four 20-mm cannons and about 1,920 lbs of bombs and rockets and flew at a top speed of about 585 mph. In total, 493 of the MD 450s were built; they were used by the air forces of France, Israel and India. The plane had only a brief front-line career as Dassault soon introduced its natural successor, the MD 452 Mystère, which in effect combined the MD 450 Ouragan's fuselage with a new 30° swept wing. The Mystère fighter first flew on 23 February 1951, but the development program led to the creation of diverse variants (with different engines) prior to the introduction of the Mystère IIC production model. In 1952, after 1,250 Mystères had been built, the Dassault introduced the definitive IVA version. This version was powered either by a Hispano-Suiza 250A engine producing 6,283 lbs of thrust or by a Hispano-Suiza 350 Verson unit delivering 7,716 lbs of thrust. The aircraft had a wingspan of 36 feet and a length of 39 feet 4 inches, and was armed with two

218 top A Dassault Mystère IV of the French air force. This fighter was introduced in 1952 and perormed well for its era, including its weaponry of two 30-mm cannons and 2,200 lbs of bombs and rockets.

218-219 The Dassault Mirage III was an exceptional fighter for its time and produced a family of 1,400 aircraft sold to more than 20 countries worldwide. This is the two-seat Mirage IIIB.

219 top Three Dassault MD.450 Ouragans of the French air force photographed in formation in 1956. The Ouragan was the first French jet fighter.

30-mm cannons and 2,200 lbs of bombs or rockets. Maximum take-off weight was about 20,950 lbs, and top speed was 696 mph.

By now, the Mystère's similarities to the Ouragan were minimal: the Mystère's fuselage had an oval section, the wing was thinner and stronger and had a 41° sweep, and a different engine had been fitted. A total of 411 Mystères were built and were sold to Israel and India as well as to the French air force. The IVA was followed by a new version designated the Mystère IVB, which first flew in December 1953. The IVB was a significant step forward: it was the first French supersonic jet, thanks to installation of an afterburner-equipped Atar 101G engine.

Serial production concentrated, however, on the Super Mystère B2 that was introduced in March 1955. This was a further development of the basic design, featuring an improved fuselage with an oval air intake in the nose and a thin wing profile with a saw-tooth leading edge and a 45° sweep. The plane had a wingspan of 32 feet 9.5 inches and a length of 45 feet 11 inches; it carried two 30-mm cannons, a container for 55 65-mm rockets and 2,200 lbs of bombs or rockets slung beneath the wings. The maximum take-off weight rose to just over 22,000 lbs. This version too was powered by the Atar 101G engine, which produced 9,920 lbs of thrust and provided a top speed of Mach 1.12. The Super Mystère was Europe's first operational fighter with a supersonic capability; a total of 180 were built, of which 32 were sold to Israel.

The Super Mystère IVB is fighter had barely completed its maiden flight before Dassault was working on a completely new and interesting concept: a high performance fighter with a delta wing. The MD.550 Mirage, which first flew in June 1955, featured a 60° delta wing and two Armstrong Siddeley Viper engines producing 2,200 lbs thrust, along with an auxiliary rocket that allowed a top peed of Mach 1.3 to be attained.

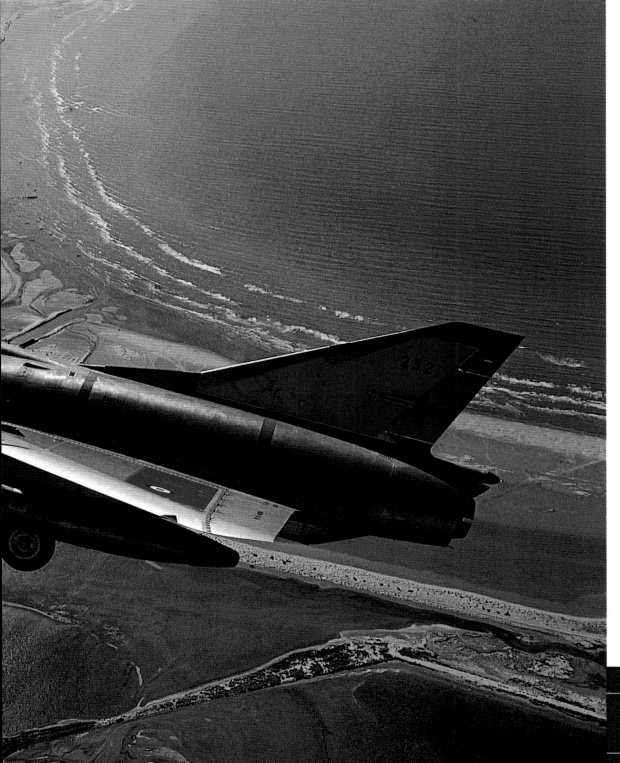

Following the Mirage II project, which used an engine that never actually went into production, the Mirage III flew for the first time on 18 November 1956. This version was powered by an Atar 101G engine equipped with an afterburner and also carried a detachable rocket propulsion unit. After a number of improvements and modifications had been introduced, Dassault finally launched the production version, the Mirage IIIC, that was later joined by the two-seat Mirage IIIB trainer. The Mirage III was 42 feet 7 inches long, had a wingspan of 26 feet 3 inches, and a maximum take-off weight of about 26,000 lbs. Its afterburner-equipped SNECMA

increased fuel load and five weapon-mounting points. Given its versatility, this version was particularly well suited for export.

The Mirage III airframe was also used as the basis for the IIIR reconnaissance version, the IIIS (exported to Switzerland) and the two-seater IIID. Apart from the Mirage 5 version built for Israel but never delivered for political reasons, the last of the line was the Mirage 50 introduced in 1979, but this plane failed to attract the same sales success. A total of more than 1,420 of the Mirage III and 5 were built and exported to around 20 different countries throughout the world; they fought successfully in diverse

had nonetheless demonstrated its potential, and the government authorized construction of three pre-series aircraft. Deliveries of the F.1 C interceptor, the production version began in 1973. The plane had a wingspan of 26 feet 3.5 inches, a length of 49 feet 3 inches, and a maximum take-off weight of about 35,700 lbs. It could attain a top speed of Mach 2.2 and its armament comprised two 30-mm cannons and a load capacity of up to 8,800 lbs, carried externally on seven mounting points. The basic design also gave rise to the F.1A ground attack, the F.1B two-seater, and the F.1E multi-role export versions. Subsequently, Dassault

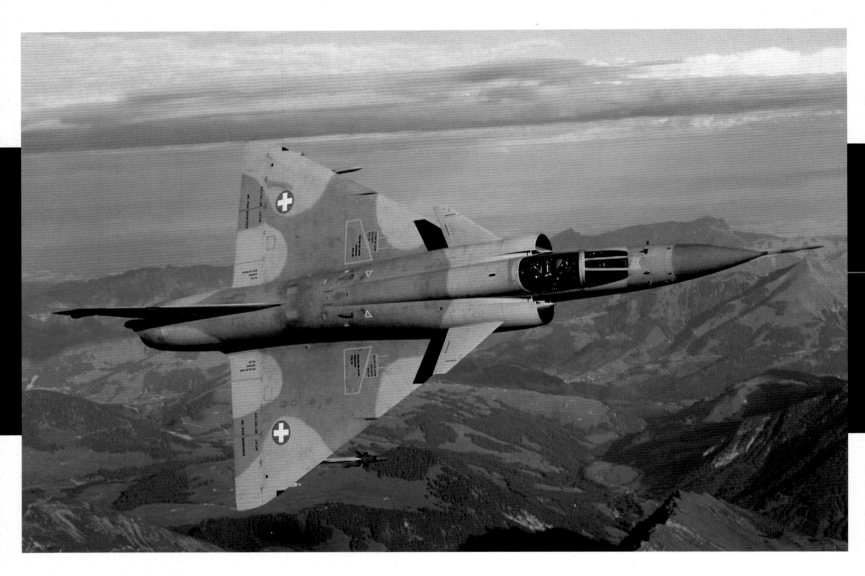

Atar 9B engine delivered up to 13,225 lbs of thrust, sufficient to power the Mirage III to a top speed of Mach 2.1. Armament comprised two 30-mm cannons and an external load of almost 3,000 lbs, including air-to-air missiles and supplementary fuel tanks. Thanks to its dramatic aerodynamic shape, the Mirage III caused a sensation; it also provided the French air force with an excellent Mach 2 interceptor that attracted significant orders from Africa and Israel. Well aware of the fundamental quality of the design, Dassault exploited it to the full and soon introduced the IIIE model, which was modified for a ground attack role. Equipped with a slightly more powerful Atar 9C engine, the IIIE completed its maiden flight in April 1961. It featured a new fire control system, an

conflicts in the Middle East, Asia and South America. A number of these planes are still in service, following modernization.

In the early 1960s Dassault was already working on the successor to the Mirage III. In 1964 the firm obtained French government approval, and the new Mirage F.1 was in the air by 23 December 1966, after the parallel F.2 project (a large aircraft weighing almost 20 tons) had been shelved. The F.1 broke with the Mirage delta wing tradition and featured a fuselage very similar to that of the series III together with a swept wing and an Atar 9K engine producing almost 16,000 lbs of thrust. The plane was equipped with the new Cyrano IV radar and new Matra air-to-air missiles. The first prototype was destroyed in a crash but

produced the F.1C-200 with an in-flight refueling capability, the F.1CR reconnaissance plane, and the F.1CT multi-role version for the French air force. This last plane was delivered by converting 55 of the F.1C-200s. The Mirage F.1 series was also commercially successful; a total of 731 planes were purchased by the air forces of eleven different countries.

220 A Mirage IIIS interceptor of the Swiss air force. The plane given a complete overhaul featuring canard fins on the air intakes to improve maneuverability, and its new aerodynamic profile is clearly shown.

221 A Mirage F.1CJ of the Jordanian air force climbing at high altitude. With this airplane, Dassault returned to a more conventional aerodynamic design that was also more effective in terms of the technology of the period.

In the meantime, across the Channel, Great Britain, another pre-war aeronautic colossus, continued to be a player. In the field of military aircraft, domestic firms produced numerous fighters and strike aircraft for the Royal Air Force and the Royal Navy. The pioneering jets developed during the war were the Gloster Meteor and the de Havilland Vampire, but it was Hawker that gave rise to the first true post-war success, the P.1067, developed out of the Sea Hawk naval fighter. This aircraft was developed in response to a RAF statement issued in 1948 that required a swept-wing aircraft to replace the Meteors; performance was to match that of the American F-86. Named the Hunter, the new aircraft encountered certain teething troubles. However, because of global crisis that the Korean War represented, serial production had been authorized even before the plane's maiden flight on 20 July 1951.

The Hunter featured a long, slim fuselage, a swept wing with an ample chord, and engine air intakes at the root. The F Mk.6 fighter version was powered by a Rolls-Royce Avon Mk. 207 engine producing just over 10,000 lbs of thrust, sufficient to ensure a top speed of 700 mph. The Hunter was 45 feet 11 inches long and had a wingspan of 32 feet 9.5inches; maximum take-off weight was about 23,800 lbs. Because initially fighter and then bomber versions were being developed, the Hunter was armed with four 30-mm cannons and an external bomb and rocket load of 3,000 lbs. The Hunter entered service in 1954, but it was no match for the jets flown by the Americans: they already had the supersonic F-100. Nonetheless the Hunter enjoyed a long and successful career with the RAF through until the 1970s. Also built in reconnaissance two-seater training and export versions, the reliable, well-armed Hunter was a great international success. In all, 1972 Hunters were built, and they were sold in 18 countries

The Hunter's replacement as interceptor was developed by English Electric (later BAC), with the company using a design on which they had actually been working since 1947. The prototype P.1A first flew on 4 August 1954, and featured innovative lines with a stubby swept wing and two Sapphire engines mounted one above the other. In 1957, the P1.B appeared, featuring notable improvement; the RAF ordered 20 pre-series planes. Deliveries of the first production model, the F Mk.1, began in 1959. The Lightning (as the fighter had been named) was a truly exceptional aircraft for its time, capable of flying at twice the speed of sound, with a fantastic rate of climb, good handling and an armament comprising radar-guided Firestreak air-to-air missiles. The principal version of the Lightning was the F Mk.6, which appeared in 1965. It had a length of 52 feet 6 inches, and a wingspan of 32 feet 9.5 inches, and was armed with two air-to-air missiles and an optional pair of 30-mm cannons in a belly pod; it had a maximum take-off weight at take-off of 50,000 lbs. The F

Mk.1 was powered to a top speed of Mach 2.27 by two afterburner-equipped Rolls-Royce Avon 30 engines producing 16,300 lbs of thrust. Ten RAF air defense squadrons few the Lightning, and in Mk. 53 form it was also exported to Saudi Arabia and Kuwait. Together with the two-seater models of the T series, 334 of these fighters were produced. This figure by no means reflects the quality of the aircraft; however, the Lightning was competing on the global markets with other European planes such as the Mirage III and the F-104, against which it had little chance.

In the meantime, the British aerospace industry had ventured into a wholly new field of great technical complexity: that of vertical flight. A joint venture between Hawker Siddeley and Bristol had been set up as early as 1957 in order to design a fighter with vertical take-off and landing capabilities. The engine-builder came up with the new BS.53 Pegasus turbofan, which was well suited to the particular demands of the project. The first prototype, the P.1127 completed its maiden flight on 21 October 1960. It was a

222 top An RAF English Electric Lightning. The plane, which first flew in 1954, was unusual in shape but very effective. Shown here is a Lightning fitted with auxiliary fuel tanks above the wings and Firestreak missiles in the fuselage.

222 bottom An RAF Hawker Hunter F Mk.6 fighter. This aircraft was a great commercial success for British industry, with more than 2,000 being built and sold to 18 countries.

223 top In the foreground a Sea Harrier F/A Mk.2 armed with missiles. This model was introduced in 1988 and features Blue Vixen radar on the nose.

223 bottom An RAF Harrier Mk.1 firing air-to-ground missiles. This British fighter-bomber entered service in 1969, its vertical take-off and landing capability revolutionized tactical air-support procedures.

single-seat aircraft characterized by a high, swept wing, below which were located four directional nozzles that allowed the plane to fly vertically and to hover. The six prototypes were followed by nine Kestrel pre-series planes destined for evaluation by a combined British-American squadron. The first British Harrier flew on 31 August 1966, and the first production examples, designated the Harrier GR Mk.1, entered service with the RAF as fighter- bombers in April 1969. The Harrier offered new opportunities in the field of tactical support: it could be operated from advanced positions with no airfield infrastructure whatsoever. The Mk.3 version (equipped with laser telemetry systems in the nose) was equipped with a more powerful engine, the Pegasus Mk. 103 engine, producing 21,500 lbs of thrust and providing a top speed of about 735 mph. The plane had a wingspan of 22 feet 11 inches and a length of 45 feet 11 inches. Maximum take-off weight was 26,000 lbs, of which 8,000 were accounted for by external loads in the form of bombs, rockets, fuel tanks and pods for two 30-mm cannons.

Despite its great potential, the Harrier never enjoyed significant sales success and only 305 were actually built and operated by Great Britain, the US Marines (designated the AV-8A) and Spain (AV-8S), this last purchaser subsequently selling its planes to Thailand in

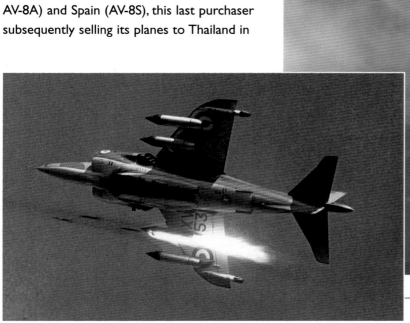

1997. In 1975, British Aerospace (born out of the merger of various companies including Hawker) began to develop a naval version of the Mk.3 in response to a Royal Navy requirement for a multi-role carrier-borne fighter with a V/STOL (Vertical/Short Take-Off and landing) capability. The Sea Harrier, as it was named, made its first flight on 20t August 1978. It featured a multi-role radar system, Sidewinder air-to-air missiles and anti-shipping missiles. The plane entered service in 1979 as the FRS Mk.1. Two-seater and export versions of the plane (the Mk.51

for India) were also developed, and it distinguished itself in 1982, during the Falklands War, when it shot down a number of Argentinean fighters without suffering any losses. A modernization program initiated in 1988 brought the aircraft up to F/A Mk.2 specification with a new Blue Vixen radar system and the potential for employing AMRAAM and ALARM missiles. In all, 106 Sea Harriers were built. From the mid-1970s, British Aerospace and McDonnell Douglas worked jointly on the development of the new AV-8B Harrier II.

Despite traditional national rivalry, in the mid-1960s France and Great Britain managed to collaborate on the development of a new military jet, an advanced training and strike aircraft. In May 1965, the Breguet 121 was selected as the most promising design, and to further develop it, BAC and Breguet set up a joint company, the Société Européenne de Production de l'Avion d'École de Combat et d'Appui Tactique, better known by its initials SEPECAT. The resulting aircraft had twin engines, a high wing, a slim fuselage and a high undercarriage suitable for operation from improvised airstrips. It completed its maiden flight on 23 March 1969. Great Britain insisted that the aircraft should have increased operational potential and eventually the Jaguar (as the plane was named) developed into a true supersonic fighter-bomber. The Jaguar GR Mk.1, the basic version produced for the RAF, had a wingspan of 26 feet 2.5 inches and a length of 49 feet 2.5 inches. It was powered by two Rolls-Royce/Turboméca Adour 104 turbofans delivering about 8,000 of lbs thrust on afterburn and was capable of a top speed of Mach 1.6 or about 1,056 mph. The plane had a maximum take-off weight of close to 34,600 lbs, of which about 10,000 lbs were accounted for by external loads. Two 30-mm cannons made up the plane's armament. The RAF also had a two-seater version, designated the T Mk.2.

The French versions, the Jaguar A and the two-seater E, though characterized by simpler

avionics than the British models, were fitted with laser telemetry, a sophisticated inertial navigation system, a mission computer, and HUD equipment. An international version of the Jaguar was also built, and sold to four countries including India, where 91 Shamshers were build under license. The British continued to update the design to new standards with the GR Mk.1A, Mk.1B, Mk.3, and most recently the Mk.3A, a truly modern and capable aircraft which

entered service in January 2000. In total, SEPECAT has to date built 588 Jaguars.

Sweden was the third European country to distinguish itself in building excellent fighter aircraft in the post-war period, primarily through Saab, its principal aeronautical firm. Following the Saab 21, 29 Tunnan and 32 Lansen jets, the company produced the 35 Draken, a highly innovative fighter that was actually the first European fighter capable of exceeding twice the speed of sound. The origins of the design dated back to the early post-war years, when the Swedish air force identified the need for a high- performance interceptor to defend the country against possible raids by enemy jet bombers. The research gave rise to an unconventional design featuring a double delta wing and no tailplanes. Testing was conducted using a 7:10 scale aircraft, the 210 Lilldraken, which first flew in 1952. The first Saab 35 prototype subsequently completed its maiden

flight on 25 October 1955, with its futuristic lines and cutting-edge performance causing an immediate sensation. The 35 Draken entered service with the Swedish air force in 1960. In all, including the J35A, B, C, D and F fighters, the E reconnaissance version, and the two-seat Sk35C version, a total of 525 Drakens were built.

In the 1980s, Saab introduced the J35J Draken. This version was basically an improved model F. The J35J had a wingspan of 29 feet 6 inches, a length of 49 feet 2.5 inches, and an afterburner-equipped Volvo RM6C engine delivering 17,200 lbs of thrust and providing a top speed of Mach 2 or about 1,321 mph. The plane's maximum take-off weight was about 27,550 lbs, and the armament comprised a 30-mm cannon and up to 6 air-to-air missiles. Although the Draken had exceptional characteristics and performance, for political reasons it was exported only to allied or neutral countries such as Finland and Denmark and, in 1988, to Austria, the last country in which the plane is still in service. Had the Draken been built in France or Great Britain it would have been a formidable rival for the Mirage and the F-104 in the global markets of the 1960s. Nonetheless, including export versions, 606 Drakens were built, a highly respectable figure.

During the 1960s Saab was working on a

224 top left The Swedish SAAB Viggen, which first flew on 8 February 1967, was the Swedish air force's basic combat aircraft until the advent of the Gripen. Shown here is the improved model AJS37.

224 top right A SAAB 35F Draken fighter flown by the Finnish air force is shown landing. This aircraft was the first European plane to reach Mach 2, and more than 600 were built.

224 center A FIAT G.91R/1 of the Italian air force's 5th Air Brigade in 1959 at Treviso air field. The G.91 was the first true attempt by NATO at standardization but it did not meet with its expected success.

224 bottom A SAAB 350E of the Austrian air force performing acrobatics. The typical form of the Draken's delta wing without tailplanes is clearly shown.

224-225 A SEPECAT Jaguar E of the French air force's 7th Squadron. France introduced the plane to service in 1972, two years before Great Britain did so, and bought 200 of them.

successor to the Draken. This had to be an aircraft exhibiting excellent performance but adapted to the Swedish defense strategy that, in the case of war, featured (and continues to feature) the dispersal of forces in the forests. A robust aircraft was needed, with short take-off and landing capabilities and operable with minimal technical-logistical support. This requirement led to the development of the Saab 37 Viggen, a large single-engined, single-seater featuring a double delta wing with canard control surfaces, with an engine equipped with a thrust-reverser to reduce the runway length required for landing. The Viggen made its maiden flight on 8 February 1967, and the production aircraft entered service in June 1971. The first version to be developed was the AJ37 ground attack model with secondary air defense capabilities. The SF37 reconnaissance version, the SH37 maritime reconnaissance version, and the Sk37 two-seater version followed. In 1979, Saab introduced the JA37 interceptor. It had a wingspan of 32 feet 9.5 inches, a length of 52 feet 6 inches, and was equipped with a Volvo RM8B turbofan engine producing about 28,000 lbs of thrust on afterburn and providing a top speed of 1,368 mph. The plane's armament was a 30-mm cannon, up to six air-to-air missiles,

and air-to-ground weapons (bombs, rockets and missiles. Maximum take-off weight was about 22 tons,

The potential market for the Viggen was restricted to an even greater degree than with the Draken, and Sweden remains the only country to operate the aircraft. Since 1993 the Swedish air force has been flying the AJS37 version with uprated avionics that make it an extremely versatile aircraft capable of flying interception, attack or reconnaissance missions as required. Saab has constructed a total of 329 Viggens.

This overview of the most significant European fighters of the 1950s and 1960s could hardly be complete without mention of the Fiat G.91. This plane resulted from one of NATO's first attempts to adopt standardized weaponry among its member states. NATO requirement NBMR-1 (1953) called for a light fighter-bomber capable of operating from advanced bases. The Fiat team, led by led by engineer Gabrielli, developed the G.91, an aircraft with a low swept wing and an air intake beneath the nose, a layout that recalled the general architecture of the F-86K (which Fiat built under license). The first of three prototypes flew on 9 August 1956. Despite the loss of that first prototype, within a few months the design proved to be fully

responsive to NATO requirements, and the G.91 was approved for production in January 1958. The G.91 attracted numerous favorable opinions, but because of the usual political-economic maneuvering of national governments, it was never adopted by the majority of NATO air forces, but only by Italy and Germany.

Italy adopted the base model G.91R/1. This model had a wingspan of 26 feet 3 inches, a length of 32 feet 9.5 inches, and was fitted with a Bristol Siddeley Orpheus engine producing about 4,050 lbs of thrust, providing a top speed of 640 mph.

It had a maximum take-off weight of 12,125 lbs, and was armed with four 12.7-mm machine-guns and up to 2000 lbs of bombs and rockets carried on two underwing pylons. This model formed the basis for the two-seater G.91T and the G.91R/3, which was built for Germany and equipped with improved avionics, two 30-mm cannons and four underwing pylons. The Portuguese air force also flew the G.91, receiving 66 of them from Germany. In total, despite the ostracism of various countries (above all France, whose rival to the Fiat model had been rejected), over 760 of the G.91R and T models were built, and the plane remained in service until the 1990s.

Chapter 17

Vietnam

Although Vietnam had been engaged in guerrilla warfare and fighting since the 1930s, first against the French and then against the Japanese, the Vietnam War properly refers to the war fought from about 1960 to 1975. This conflict involved the Vietcong and the North Vietnamese army on one side and the South Vietnamese army, supported by the United States, on the other. From an aeronautical point of view, the Vietnam War was a hugely significant conflict, given that it saw the application of new aircraft, new weaponry, and new tactics that have made their mark on the history of aviation.

The Vietnam War began as a fight by South Vietnam's government against the attempted insurrection urged by North Vietnam's government (with large-scale material support from the Soviet Union). The crisis heightened with the direct involvement of the American armed forces; it culminated in 1968 when the US troops in the area numbered some 550,000. The United States Government made grave political errors: on the one hand global public opinion (and also that of a section of American society) came down in favor of the North Vietnamese, on the other, military operations were ultimately unsuccessful despite the enormous resources expended.

Initially, the United States restricted its intervention to the dispatch of advisors

226 top left A CH-54 helicopter transports a Marine Corps 155-mm howitzer to a hilltop during operations around Khe Sanh in January 1969.

226 bottom American fighters fly over a burning ship during the Vietnam war. The shadow on the water is from a US Navy F-8 Crusader.

226-227 The Vietnam War is remembered as "the helicopter war." Shown here is a formation of Bell UH-1s supporting South Vietnamese troops during an attack on the Vietcong, March 1965.

227 bottom A US Navy Douglas A-4E Skyhawk fighter-bomber drops a Mk. 84 high-explosive bomb on a Vietcong troop emplacement in January 1966.

and armaments to the government of South Vietnam. The goal was to form the first nucleus of the South Vietnamese air force, equipped with A-1 Skyraiders, T-28 Trojans, B-26 Invaders, C-47 Skytrains, and C-123 Providers. In Agust 1964 following the Gulf of Tonkin incident (an attack by North Vietnamese patrol boats on the destroyer *USS Maddox*), the US Navy began to play a direct role in the conflict, conducting bombing raids using its own carrier-borne aircraft. Early in the war, the Navy's aircraft carriers were generally equipped with F-8 and F-4 fighters and A-4 and A-6 fighter-bombers.

The US Navy's most modern fighter at the time was the McDonnell F-4 Phantom

II, which had entered service in December 1960. This plane was designed and built following a naval requirement for a large interceptor (designated the AH-1), derived from the F3H model and to have a three-hour in-the-air time frame and the capability to launch the new Sparrow missiles. The navy ordered two prototypes of the F4H-1 Phantom, the first of which took to the air on 27 May 1958. The twin-engined design featured a trapezoidal wing and tailplanes with negative dihedral, was equipped with radar, and carried a second crewmember to operate the weapons system. The Phantom immediately proved to be an exceptional multi-role fighter, and in December of that year the US Navy ordered an initial batch of 375. In 1962, the fighter was redesignated the F-4, and the first mass-production version was the F-4B. Its two General electric J79-GE-8 engines delivering 17,000 lbs thrust on afterburn powered it to a top speed of Mach 2.2. Moreover, the plane also featured an APQ-72 multifunction long-range radar system (which allowed it to fly interceptor missions without the need for ground radar), a redesigned cockpit, and the ability to operate as a fighter-bomber

carrying bombs and rockets. While the F-4A and B versions began to fly with the US Navy and the Marines, the USAF also showed an interest in the design, given that it was well suited to its own requirements. McDonnell thus built a specific version of the fighter for land-based operations, the F-4C (initially designated the F-110A), fitted with a different undercarriage and tires, self-starting, J79-GE-15 engines, APQ-100 radar,

228-229 A USAF RF-101Cs at low altitude over the My Dug road bridge in North Vietnam, which has just been bombed. Its shadow is reflected on the river.

228 bottom A row of A-4Es waits to take off from the USS Oriskany off Vietnam in 1968. An A-3D Skywarrior has just been launched.

dual flight controls and a rigid-probe in-flight refueling capability. The USAF acquired 583 of the various F-4s between 1963 and 1966. These versions were soon followed by reconnaissance variants (RF-4B and RF-4C), the F-4D for the USAF and the F-4J for the Navy powered by J79-GE-10 engines producing around 18,000 lbs of thrust and fitted with AWG-10 fire control systems. The final version for the USAF was the F-4E, introduced in 1966. Its design drew on experience gained during the war and introduced more powerful engines, new wing flaps and a redesigned nose equipped with APQ-120 radar and, finally, the M61 20-mm Vulcan cannon. The RF-4E reconnaissance version then followed. The F-4E had a wingspan of 36 feet, a length of 62 feet 3.6 inches and a maximum take-off weight of about 61,650 lbs. The two J79-GE-17 engines provided about 17,900 lbs of thrust

on afterburn and propelled the aircraft to a top speed of about 1,485 mph. The weapons system comprised an external load of up to 16,000 lbs. A powerful, robust and reliable plane, the Phantom also shone in the arduous Indochinese theater once the air force and the navy had developed appropriate tactics. The F-4 proved to be a solid base for the creation of specialist versions and innovative applications. Thee included the F-4G anti-radar strike version, the F-4K for Britain's Royal Navy, and the F-4N and S, modified and rebuilt versions of the F-4B and J. The Phantom was also sold to numerous allies, NATO states and otherwise, such as Israel, Iran, Japan, Egypt and South Korea. A total of 5,195 of the various F-4 versions were built; many have been modernized and are still in operational use.

The smallest of the carrier-borne fighter-bombers at that time was the Douglas A-4 Skyhawk, a plane privately developed by the Californian firm in order to offer the US Navy a jet replacement for the manufacturer's own A-1 Skyraider. The A-4 was a small, single-engined plane with a delta wing and a cruciform tailplane. It had surprising technical and performance characteristics. As it was built in one piece, the A-4 was notably robust and light; the small wing, for example, did not need to be folded for the aircraft to be

parked aboard a carrier. The Skyhawk flew for the first time as the XA4D-1 on 22 June 1954, and with only a few modifications required, it entered service two years later, equipped with the J65-4B engine producing around 7,700 of lbs thrust.

In 1962, the Skyhawk was redesignated the A-4, and numerous and continuously improved versions were introduced. The A-4E was the first of a new series that introduced the more efficient J52 engine, producing 8,500 lbs of thrust (while consuming less fuel), and was equipped with five underwing pylons rather than three, raising the potential weapons load to 9,150 lbs. The F model saw the first appearance of the dorsal "hump" containing new avionics, while the TA-4F was the first two-seater advanced training version.

Fast, maneuverable, robust, and capable of carrying a considerable weapons load, the Skyhawk performed extremely well in Vietnam, operating both from aircraft carriers and the Marines' land bases. The plane remained in production until 1979; 2,960 were constructed and sold to ten countries around the world. Among the last American forces to fly the Skyhawk were the Marines' Aggressor units, which used them in combat training to simulate the agile and deadly MiG-17s and MiG-19s.

The US Navy also flew the Grumman A-6 Intruder, which could be considered the diametric opposite of the A-4. The A-6 Intruder was a large, carrier-borne all-weather bomber then considered to reflect the height of avionics sophistication. The basic model, the Grumman G-128, which was approved in 1957, had been designed in response to a requirement for a new carrier-borne strike aircraft. The plane was to reflect the lessons of the Korean War. The G-128 was a twin-jet aircraft featuring a large nose housing the radar system and a two-man cockpit with parallel seating. The prototype made its first flight on 19 April 1960, and the first production planes, designated the A-6A, began entering service in 1963. The Navy and the Marines used them in Vietnam from 1965 on. The Intruder's strengths included a significant weapons load (fully freighted, the plane weighed in the region of 27.5 tons) and sophisticated strike and navigation systems (APQ-146/148 radar and ASN-92 inertial navigation) that allowed it to find and hit targets even in conditions of zero visibility. Subsequent versions included the A-6B anti-radar aircraft, the A-6C night attack variant, the KA-6D in-flight refueling tanker, and the EA-6A electronic warfare plane.

The definitive version of the Intruder was the A-6E (most versions were built around converted A-6A airframes), which boasted even more advanced avionics. The A-6E had a wingspan of 52 feet 6 inches, a length of 62 feet 4 inches, and a maximum take-off weight of 60,450 lbs. It was powered by two Pratt & Whitney J52-P-8B engines without afterburners, producing around 9,300 lbs of thrust, and was capable of a top speed of around 650 mph. An updated version of the A-6E was equipped with the TRAM (Target Recognition Attack Multi-sensor) system composed of FLIR (Farward Looking Infra-Red) sensors and lasers for navigation and strike operations. A total of 710 A-6s were built, all for the exclusive use of the US Navy and Marines. The aircraft was withdrawn from service in the mid-1990s.

The Vietnam War saw the use of another two carrier-borne bombers. The first of these was the Douglas Skywarrior, which made its first flight on 28 October 1952. When it

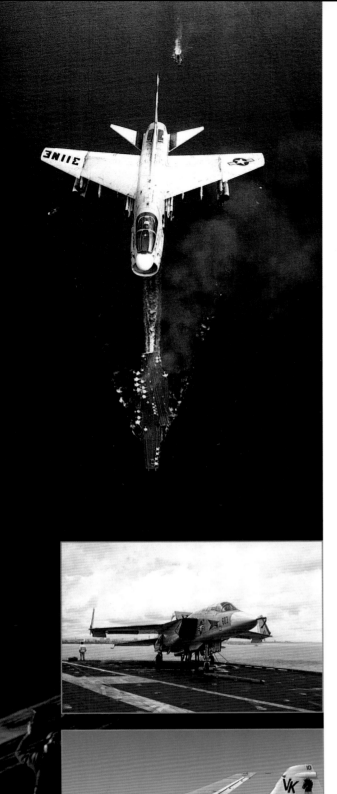

entered service in 1956 as the A3D, the plane was the largest ever built for carrier-borne operations. Equipped with a high wing to which the two Pratt & Whitney J57 jet engines were attached, the aircraft was designed as a nuclear bomber, but was subsequently converted to perform diverse specialist roles such as reconnaissance, electronic warfare, in-flight refueling and training. In 1962 the plane was redesignated the A-3; the B model had a wingspan of 72 feet 2 inches, a length of 75 feet 6 inches and a maximum take-off weight of about 82,000lbs, of which the internally stored weapons load amounted to about 12,000 lbs. The engines delivered about 15,615 lbs of thrust, giving the plane a top speed of 610 mph. The USAF also used the plane, which it designated the B-66, and beginning in the mid-1950s purchased 290 for the reconnaissance and electronic warfare roles in which it was employed in Vietnam in the 1960s.

The second Navy bomber, the A3J-1 Vigilante (redesigated the A-5 in 1962), was also used for reconnaissance in Vietnam in its RA-5 version. This aircraft had been designed in the mid-1950s as the supersonic successor to the Skywarrior, and featured highly futuristic lines with fully mobile tailplanes and variable-geometry air intakes. The Vigilante had a wingspan of 52 feet 6 inches, a length of 75 feet 6 inches, and a maximum take-off weight of 66,000 lbs. It was powered by two General Electric J79-GE-10 engines and could attain a top speed of Mach 2.2.

The pressures of war led to the development of a new fighter-bomber for the US Navy, the response to a requirement for a successor to the A-4. In order to accelerate development time, the requirement specified that the proposed designs should be derived from planes already in service. Ling-Temco-Vought (LTV) developed a project loosely based on the Vought F-8 Crusader, but the resulting plane was in effect all new. It was a subsonic aircraft with a fixed wing and an enlarged fuselage that could carry a notable weapons load on six underwing pylons. The navy declared this plane to be the winner of the competition. Designated the A-7 Corsair II, the new fighter-bomber flew for the first time on 27 September 1965 (ahead of the contract-specified date) and in 1966 entered service as the A-7A; by the following year it was already seeing combat duty in Vietnam. The A7-A was equipped with a TF30-P-6 engine delivering 5150 lbs of thrust; the B and C versions received slightly more powerful units. The USAF also took an interest in the plane. In 1968 the A-7D version developed for the Air Force made its maiden flight. The A-7D featured a TF41 engine producing 14,500 lbs of thrust and an M61 Vulcan 20-mm cannon with six rotating barrels (in place of four cannons of the same caliber). It also had more sophisticated navigation and strike systems and a rigid-probe, in-flight refueling capability. The A-7D entered service in 1970 and was also used in Vietnam for some months from October1972 until the withdrawal of the American forces.

In 1967 LTV used the A-7D as the basis for the A-7E model for the US Navy. The A-7E retained the A7-D's avionics but was powered by a TF41 engine uprated to produce 15,000 lbs of thrust. A total of 506 A-7Es were built, and the plane made its combat debut in 1970, flying from the carrier USS America. The A-7E was 45 feet 11 inches long, had a wingspan of 36 feet, a maximum take-off weight off of almost 21 tons and a top speed of almost 700 mph. It could carry a 15,000-lb weapons load. The Corsair II was an excellent aircraft, capable of carrying a notable variety and quantity of arms that it could release with precision at considerable distances. However, the workload for a one-man crew was sometimes excessive, and led to a number of accidents. The production total for the A-7 (including the models exported to Portugal and Greece and the two-seat TA-7C and TA-7K trainers) amounted to 1,526 planes.

The US Air Force was also widely involved in the Vietnam War with all types of aircraft. It used a number of new models during the conflict both for strategic reasons and also to verify their operational capabilities and gain useful experience.

231 first picture A Vought A-7A Corsair of the VA-147 series on the USS Ranger, before landing. This unit was the first to be used in Vietnam with the Corsair, in 1967.

231 second picture The North American A-5 Vigilante was designed in the 1950s as a high-performance bomber for the U.S. Navy. It remained in service until the 1980s. The version shown here has folding wings and rudder.

231 third picture The US Navy Grumman A-6A Intruder bomber was brought into the Vietnam War in 1965 and proved itself to be formidable in attacking enemy air defenses.

231 fourth picture An A-6A ready for take-off from an American aircraft carrier. The plane's thirty 500-lb bombs are distributed on the wing and body pylons. The A-6 could carry a load of up to 8 tons.

Along with the F-4 Phantoms and the A-7 Corsairs, the USAF employed other military aircraft with very different characteristics: these included the Northrop F-5 and the General Dynamics F-111 series. The first was a lightweight plane that General Dynamics developed privately, hoping it might interest the American government as a tactical fighter to be sold to allied countries. The company developed two planes: the N-156F and the two-seater N-156T (which eventually became the T-38). The N-156F completed its maiden flight on 30 July 1959. It was a compact, slim supersonic jet powered by two J85-GE-5 engines, each

Tigers were evaluated in tactical support missions, and acquitted themselves well. In 1967, the US began supplying them to the South Vietnamese air force. Over 1,100 of the F-5A/Bs were built; they were flown by the air forces of 20 countries. In 1969, on the basis of F-5A/B experience gained in the field, Northrop produced an improved version, the F-5E, which flew for the first time in production form on 11 August 1972. This model had a greater weapons load-carrying capacity and improved handling characteristics. Powered by J85-GE-21 engines producing 5,000 lbs of thrust, it had a top speed of Mach 1.64. About 1,500 F-4Es

232 left The Northrop F-5 light tactical fighter was designed for use by the air forces of the USA's allies. Shown here is a South Vietnamese air force F-5A dropping Mk. 117 bombs in 1966.

232-233 The General Dynamic F-111 was designed to give the USAF and US Navy a multi-role aircraft in common. The Navy, however, did not adopt it but the USAF's F-111A was always an effective precision bomber and was used in Vietnam. This F-111F is flying over a desert.

233 bottom left An F-111E landing. The plane had a variable-geometry wing and two large Pratt & Whitney TF30 engines able to provide 23,000 lbs of thrust and a top speed of 1,625 mph.

233 bottom right The US air forces used the F-5 in limited numbers, mainly as an aggressor airplane, i.e., to simulate enemy fighters during combat. This F-5E of the US Marine Corps' VMFT-401 is flying over Arizona.

producing around 3,850 lbs of thrust. In 1962, the US Defense Department chose the plane as the US contribution to the MAP (Military Assistance Program) and designated it the F-5A Freedom Fighter (the two-seater being the F-5B). The aircraft, which first flew on 31 July 1963, was powered by J85-GE-13 engines each producing around 4050 lbs of thrust with afterburn. It had seven mounting points for up to 6,000 lbs of external weaponry, two 20-mm cannons, a reinforced airframe, a maximum take-off weight of about 19,850 lbs, and a top speed of Mach 1.4. Even though it was primarily destined for export, the F-5A also went into service with the USAF, which sent a contingent of twelve to Vietnam within the ambit of the Skoshi Tiger evaluation program. These planes were fitted with in-flight refueling probes, new armor, and camouflage paint better suited to the Vietnam conflict theater.

Between 1965 and 1966, the Skoshi

were built; of these over 120 (single-seaters and F-5F two-seaters) were acquired by the USAF and the US Navy for use as trainers and aggressor planes in combat training.

The General Dynamics F-111 was the result of a very ambitious but never fully realized program. In 1960, the US Defense Department initiated the TFX program, aimed at equipping the USAF and the US Navy with a shared multi-role combat aircraft to replace the F-105, the F-8 and ultimately the F-4. In 1962, it announced that General Dynamics (together with Grumman) had been selected to develop its innovative project for a large, powerful airplane with variable-geometry wings and an ejectable capsule for the two-man crew. A contract was drawn up for the building of 18 F-111As for the USAF and 5 of the carrier-borne F-111Bs for the Navy. The first A-series prototype flew on 21 December 1964, but existing technology proved inadequate for

the development of an aircraft truly suited to the widely varying demands. In 1968, the US Congress halted development of the F-111B. In that same year, however, the F-111A entered service and was subsequently used in combat at the tail end of the Vietnam War. After early teething troubles, the F-111A proved itself to be an excellent bomber, above all at night and in critical bad weather conditions. In various versions, the F-111D, E and F, the aircraft demonstrated its capabilities as an air defense and all-weather, low-altitude strike aircraft.

The F model had a wingspan of between 62 feet 4 inches (minimum sweep) and 29 feet 6 inches (maximum sweep) and a length of 72 feet 2 inches. It was powered by two Pratt & Whitney TF30-P-100 engines producing 25,000 lbs of thrust with afterburn, and could attain a top speed of Mach 2.5 at high altitude. It could carry a total weapons load of up to 321,500 lbs.

The F model also formed the basis for the development of the EF-111A electronic warfare, the FB-111A nuclear strike, and the F-111C versions. This last version was built for export to Australia, which is now the only county still operating the aircraft in updated F-111G form. In all, General Dynamics built 562 of the F-111s.

Another Vietnam War protagonist was the Lockheed C-130 Hercules tactical transport plane, of which various versions were developed, with some used in combat roles. In a region such as Indochina, where the tropical vegetation, the lack of roads and guerrilla warfare made ordinary communications difficult and at times even impossible, transport planes performed a vital role, allowing combat units to be supplied and supported at great distances or when under siege by the enemy. When American involvement in Vietnam intensified, the Hercules had already been in service for a number of years in A, B and E forms.

The origins of the design dated back to the Korean War, when the USAF decided to equip itself with a turboprop-powered tactical

transport aircraft. The Lockheed design that was eventually chosen featured a high wing, a low undercarriage and a high tail, a configuration intended to favor loading and unloading operations from the large cargo door located beneath the tail. The first example, the YC-130, completed its maiden flight on 23 August 1954, and deliveries to the USAF of the first 216 C-130A models (powered by 3,800-hp Allison T56-1A engines) began in December 1956. While the aircraft was not a revolutionary machine, it brought together in one design highly advanced technologies and features that translated into great flexibility, the ability to use short, improvised runways, an excellent loading capacity, and notable flight characteristics. One of the versions developed from the C-130A was the AC-130A,

a flying gunship equipped with four 20-mm cannons and four 7.62-mm Gatling guns that continued the tradition of the AC-47 as a tactical support aircraft for ground troops. The AC-130A, which had a valuable night-flying capability, was tested in 1967 and used in Vietnam from 1968 on for saturation attacks on restricted areas of jungle identified as sheltering concentrations of enemy troops. The C-130B, introduced in 1957, had four-bladed propellers; the C-130E, which first flew in 1961, was equipped with new underwing fuel tanks to increase its range, a strengthened airframe to allow the maximum take-off weight to be increased, and 4,100 hp T56-7 engines. This version, with a maximum weight of over 67 tons, was the one most widely used in Vietnam.

ever, well suited to the most disparate applications and subject to the most disparate transformations. It has been exported throughout the world (to around 65 countries), even to nations not traditionally friendly to the United States, and to civilian operators. A total of over 2,200 have been produced to date, and the aircraft is currently offered in the C-130J Hercules II form that was introduced in 1995 and features all-new digital avionics, a modified airframe. and 4,600 hp Allison engines with six-bladed propellers.

The challenges of the Vietnam War highlighted the need to develop and expand certain specialist activities such as attacks on enemy anti-aircraft installations (Wild Weasel and Iron Hand missions). During the conflict, these had been were conducted with increasing determination, initially with the F-100F, EF-105F and A-6B and then with specialist planes such as the F-105G.

During the Vietnam War Lockheed developed other specialist versions of the C130. These included the EC-130 electronic warfare and flying command post aircraft, the AC-130E with improved weaponry and fire control systems, the KC-130 in-flight refueling tankers for the Marines, and the MC-130 for special nocturnal and clandestine operations. The definitive version of the Hercules was the C-130H, which was equipped with 4,560-hp T56-15 turboprop engines, new avionics and an increased maximum take-off weight of more than 87 tons. The C-130H had a wingspan of 131 feet 3 inches, a length of 95 feet 2 inches, and a top speed of just over 400 mph. Over the years the C-130 proved to be the most successful tactical transport aircraft

Another important type of mission was Combat Search and Rescue (SAR), undertaken to pluck downed pilots from enemy territory. Here HH-3E helicopters were used along with support and protection aircraft of various types, but primarily with the USAF's ancient propeller-powered A-1 Skyraiders.

Naturally, the Vietnam War also represented a turning point for army helicopter operations, with the chopper becoming one of the symbols of the conflict. The helicopter was irreplaceable for transportation, combat and medical-evacuation uses, and thousands of helicopters of all types were employed. In addition to the introduction of deadly defoliant chemicals intended to deprive the Vietcong of the cover of jungle vegetation, but which did terrible damage to the Vietnamese and the environment, the Vietnam War also saw the introduction of other new weapons. These included anti-radar missiles (AGM-78 Standards and AGM-45 Shrikes) and the first laser-guided bombs, the Paveway Is, which permitted a previously unthinkable degree of accuracy when used correctly.

Along with the US forces' numerous air-ground operations conducted, the Vietnam War also saw aerial duels between the large, advanced American fighters and the old, simple but agile Soviet planes flown by the North Vietnamese air force. From this point of view, the conflict provided a shock for the Americans who were completely unprepared for this type of engagement. In-depth analyses and the institution of new training techniques were required (resulting in the Top Gun and Red Flag courses for the Navy and the USAF respectively) before the F-4 pilots, late in the war, systematically began to get the better of the enemy's MiG-17s and MiG-19s.

The United States' military involvement in Vietnam effectively ended with the ceasefire of 27 January 1973. Between 1961 and 1972, America lost 3,792 aircraft and 4,922 helicopters in Vietnam, not to forget more than 45,000 men. Over seven million tons of bombs and other armaments were dropped and in practice every available weapon was used except those with nuclear warheads. And yet with the conquest of Saigon on 25 April 1975, it was clear to even the most stubborn observers that North Vietnam had won the war. The immovability, fanaticism and strength of those fighting on their own land, for themselves and for their own ideals eventually wore down the world's greatest military power. The Americans had never known or been able to adopt the more appropriate strategies and tactics that would have given them a chance of winning the war. America had lost on both the military and political planes a war that it never felt to be its own, the first war in history that had had been widely influenced by the media and public opinion.

236 left A squadron of multi-role UH-1 helicopters take South Vietnamese troops the 199th Light Brigade to the landing zone in 1967.

236 bottom right A transport helicopter transformed into an air-ambulance takes American wounded to a field hospital.

236-237 The Fairchild C-123 Provider, introduced in 1949, was the first tactical transport aircraft to adopt the "high tail, high wing, low undercarriage, rear loading ramp" arrangement still used today. This 1966 photograph shows a C-123 dropping defoliating liquid onto the jungle to prevent Vietcong ambushes.

237 bottom An F-8J Crusader armed with Mk.84 bombs flying over a zone under attack. The Marines used their own aircraft during troop support tasks.

Chapter 18

The Arab-Israeli Wars

Following the Second World War, the situation in Palestine became critical owing to a concomitance of diverse factors. These included the arrival of thousands of Jewish refugees from Europe, the end of the Great Britain's UN mandate regarding control over the territories (15 May 1948), and the refusal of the Arabs and the Jews to apply the international diplomatic plan approved by the UN. This plan had aimed to divide the area into two states, one Palestinian the other Jewish. In the spring of 1948, the skirmishing between the two parties peaked and led to the expulsion of the Palestinian people from many areas and the proclamation in Tel Aviv of the state of Israel. At this point the conflict took on international status as the Arab countries of Egypt, Syria and Iraq

of about 70 Spitfire, Mustang and Avia S.199 fighters; a number of B-17, Mosquito and Beaufighter bombers; and C-47, C-46 and Constellation transport planes. The most representative of these aircraft was the Avia S.199, a Czechoslovak fighter that combined the airframe of the Messerschmitt Bf-109G-14 (already built in Czechoslovakia by the Germans) and the 1,370-hp Jumo 211F engine. The Czechs disliked the Avia S.199 because of its unpredictability and tricky handling, but for the desperate state of Israel its two 30-mm cannons, four 13-mm machineguns and top speed of 366 mph were very welcome. Israel purchased 25 to equip the first fighter group, known as 101 Squadron. As the fighting proceeded, however, the Arab governments, with the exception of Egypt (which used Spitfires as its

front-line fighters), began to demonstrate their intention of withdrawing from the conflict. Left to fight on alone, Egypt also withdrew late in 1948. The Israeli war of Independence was over, but the state's struggle for survival had only just begun.

The second Arab-Israeli war broke out in 1956 on the occasion of the Suez Crisis. The Egyptian president, Gamal Abdel Nasser, who had seized power in 1952 through a coup d'état, decided to expel the British from the Middle East and to nationalize the Suez Canal. The French and the British reached an agreement regarding military intervention in order to regain control of the vital canal trade route. Operation Musketeer was expanded to include an Israeli airborne operation, and the tri-nation attack was set for 29 October 1956. The aerial forces wielded by the three allies enjoyed crushing superiority. The British had dispatched 28 squadrons equipped with Hunter and Meteor fighters, Venom fighter-bombers, Canberra and Valiant bombers and transport planes to Cyprus and Malta. Three aircraft carriers were at sea with a further 11 squadrons flying Sea Venoms and Sea Hawks. The French sent four groups to Israel equipped with Mystère and F-84 fighters and Noratlas transport planes, while two aircraft carriers were equipped with Corsair fighters. Lastly, the Israelis were equipped with over 110 Mystère, Meteor, Ouragan, P-51, and Mosquito fighters. For its part, Egypt had little with which to defend itself against these

238 top An Auster AOP.5 light reconnaissance aircraft with civilian markings used during Israel's War of Independence in May 1948. It was Israel's most numerically important aircraft (there were about 20) and was also used for transport and for dropping bombs by hand.

238 center A Vautour bomber flies over a column of Israeli Centurion tanks during the Six Day War in June 1967.

launched aerial and land-based military operations against the Israeli forces.

Subsequently, the Israelis did everything in their power to develop their military capabilities, above all in the field of aviation. The Israeli air force, the Chel Ha'Avir, was officially constituted on the 31 May 1948. In the second half of that year it was strengthened considerably with the acquisition from the most disparate sources forces: two squadrons of MiG-15s, one of Vampires, one of Meteors, and one of Il-28 bombers.

The operations began with an Israeli airborne assault in the Mitla Pass area in the Sinai, but the Egyptians (who thought that the Anglo-French leadership was bluffing) refused to be intimidated and responded with the full strength of its own air force. It was only on 5 November that the Anglo-French forces directly penetrated Egyptian territory, dropping paratroopers in the Canal Zone. Two days later, a ceasefire was declared, thanks in part to the international pressure exerted by the United States and the Soviet Union. Despite a numerical victory in military terms, the war proved to be a defeat for the West. Far from bringing commercial, political and diplomatic advantages, in fact, the crisis thrust Egypt and the other Arab countries into the arms of the Soviet Union, giving rise to a new Middle Eastern arms race. Air power had once again demonstrated its fundamental importance, and it was to be the Israelis who exploited its full potential in 1967, during the next conflict to devastate the area.

In May1967, the United Nations withdrew its peacekeeping forces from the Egyptian-Israeli border. That same month Egypt, Syria and Jordan signed a military alliance that involved the formation of a United Arab Republic air force. This was now a truly fearsome military unit, equipped with advanced Soviet aircraft such as MiG-17, Mig-19 and MiG-21 fighters, Su-7 fighter-bombers, and Il-28 and Tu-16 bombers. Israel had also increased its military strength, thanks to acquisitions from France, its principal supplier.

The Israeli air force was thus able to count on 72 Mirage IIICJs, 24 Super Mystères, and 18 Vautour fighters and bombers that reinforced Israel's existing front-line units operating Mystère IVAs and Ouragans.

The situation was extremely tense with both parties fearing a pre-emptive enemy assault. President Nasser of Egypt was confident that Israel would not attack and ordered his forces to stand down. Then, on the morning of 5 June, Israel staged a surprise attack on Egypt with three waves of 40 jets flying at very low altitude. The planes struck the Egyptian airfields with exceptional precision. The attackers returned to base, rearmed and refueled with great rapidity and proceeded to hit the targets again. In the space of just three hours the Egyptians lost about 300 aircraft, for the most part on the ground, against the loss of 19 Israeli fighters. The Israeli aircraft then headed east and attacked bases in Jordan, Iraq and Syria. Jordan's Hunter fighters were destroyed on the ground, as was most of the Syrian air force. Painstakingly planned and prepared, the Israeli aerial attack was perfectly executed; it has become the classic example of the application of air power in the initial phases of a conflict.

Over the following days, the Israeli air force concentrated largely on providing support for the army that was moving west to conquer the Sinai peninsula. With its surviving aircraft, the Egyptian air force was able to mount only limited counterattacks. On 9 June, an agreement was reached regarding a United Nations ceasefire on the western front only. At the same time, the

Syrians accepted the ceasefire, but the Israelis were determined to consolidate their positions in the east and to capture at least the Golan Heights. The fighting thus continued for another day until the guns were finally silenced at 6.30 on 10 June. The so-called Six-Day War thus concluded with a significant Israeli victory. From a political and diplomatic point of view, however, the situation was anything but straightforward. Peace between Israel and the Arabs was even more remote than ever and the two parties (above all the Arabs) immediately began yet another arms race to prepare themselves for the inevitable renewal of military conflict. Moreover, with its aggressive and ruthless conduct, Israel had outraged a number of previously friendly countries, above all France. The effect of this change in policy was evident in the Mirage 5 affair. Prior to Six-Day war, Israel had ordered 50 Mirage 5Js, a simplified multi-role aircraft developed from the Mirage III and intended for export. After the Six-Day War, the French government placed an embargo on these planes, even though they had largely been paid for in advance. They were eventually assigned to the French air force, with the Mirage 5J designated as the Mirage 5F. The Israeli government clearly had to rely as far as possible on its own arms production, while at the same time turning to a more powerful and reliable arms supplier, the United States.

The nascent Israeli aeronautical industry (IAI) was capable of partially satisfying the initial requirement thanks to the acquisition, apparently by way of its secret services, of the engineering drawings for the Mirage 5 and its SNECMA Atar 9C engine. The resulting aircraft was known as the Nesher; it was to all intents and purposes a copy of the French plane, and the first in a long line of aircraft derived from the delta-winged Dassault fighter.

The first American-built warplane Israel ordered was the Douglas A-4 Skyhawk, the robust fighter-bombers operated by the US Navy. The Israeli government had placed the order early as 1966, and 48 A-4Hs and two two-seat TA-4Hs were delivered from 1968 onward. At the same time, the Chel Ha'Avir was looking for a new multi-role, high performance fighter. The plane most closely matching the Israeli requirements was the McDonnell-Douglas F-4E Phantom II. This plane offered both fearsome air-to-air armament (with eight radar-guided Sparrow and infra-red Sidewinder missiles and the Vulcan cannon) and a large air-to-surface external weapons load amounting to almost 6 tons of bombs, rockets, and missiles, as well as fuel tanks and electronic warfare pods. The first 50 F-4Es (including six of the RF-4E reconnaissance version) reached Israel in 1969, equipping two squadrons that participated in the so-called War of Attrition, a low-intensity conflict waged against Israel between March 1969 and August 1970, with the aim of wearing down the Israeli air force.

Still smarting from defeat in the Six-Day war, the Arabs, first and foremost the Egyptians, were determined to be the first to strike next time. They spared no expense in acquiring Soviet armaments, including the new MiG-21 (along with numerous "volunteer" pilots from certain Warsaw Pact countries and the USSR), the Su-7 and Tu-16, Mi-8 helicopters. They also acquired a complex and powerful anti-aircraft missile system composed of SAM (surface-to-air) SA-3, SA-6, SA-7 and SA-9 missiles, as well as a vast quantity of armored vehicles. On the eve of the October 1973 conflict, the Arab forces could count on about 730 combat aircraft against Israel's 375.

The Arab attack was disguised by the

simple expedient of staging mass exercises. It came out of the blue at 14.00 hours on 6 October 1973, in the middle of the Yom Kippur celebrations, when the Israeli defenses were at their lowest level of alert. The only armed force anywhere near ready for the attack was actually the Chel Ha-Avir, whose commanders had suspected a probable enemy attack. The Arab assault used a pincer strategy, with the Syrians striking to the north on the Golan Heights and the Egyptians staging a mass invasion of the Sinai peninsula, crossing the Suez Canal in operations devised by its engineering corps.

The Israelis concentrated on the attack closest to home. Within two hours of the beginning of the attack, they dispatched as many F-4, Mirage and Nesher fighters as possible, primarily to attack the enemy's armored columns. Israeli losses were extremely high in terms of men, vehicles and aircraft, in the last case because of anti-aircraft fire. After three days of bitter fighting, the Syrians were obliged to retreat; they were now too weak to exploit possible gaps in the enemy defenses. On the western front too, the first few days of the fighting led to grave losses, above all for the Chel Ha'Avir, which in the first four days lost 81 aircraft. After its easy victories in the Six-Day War, the Israeli air force had in fact been taken by surprise by the new SAM missile systems used by the Arabs. In the meantime, the Arab coalition had been

reinforced by the intervention of aerial forces from Iraq, Libya and Algeria.

November 9 saw the initiation of Soviet and US airlifts supplying the Arabs and the Israelis respectively. The Soviets sent 100 new fighters to Egypt and to Syria, which alone received over 15,000 tons of supplies. The US sent Israel additional A-4N and F-4E fighters and 22,000 tons of equipment and munitions. These included CH-53 helicopters, Hawk anti-aircraft missiles, and new and more efficient arms such as Walleye and Hobo intelligent bombs and Rockeye fragmentation devices. Important in the aid were systems designed to combat Arab anti-

240 top Soviet ground-to-air SA-2 missiles provided effective anti-aircraft defense systems for Arab allies during the Yom Kippur War and offered an unwelcome surprise to the Israelis.

240 bottom The Sikorsky CH-53 is the heaviest helicopter used by the Israeli air force, and two squadrons are still in service in transportation, air ambulance work, search and rescue, and special operations.

240-241 A-4 Skyhawks were used in many Israeli attacks in the 1973 War, and they lost 53 aircraft. The two A-4Ns shown here bear the colors of the Hazerim flying school.

241 center An Israeli McDonnell Douglas F-4E from the Bat Squadron landing. The Phantom II was one of the most important aircraft for the Chel Ha'Avir, which bought about 230 from 1969 on. About 60 are still in service.

241 bottom A MiG-23 with Libyan insignia. During the 1982 war with Lebanon, the Israelis had to combat the Syrian air force's new MiG-23s.

aircraft defenses, namely AGM-45 missiles and electronic warfare pods to confuse the new Soviet SAM systems.

On 14 October, the Egyptians committed what was to be a costly error: their land forces advanced without cover from their anti-aircraft systems, becoming easy prey for Israeli fighter-bombers. The Israeli army then attacked in the Suez Canal area and succeeded in disabling a large part of the Egyptian anti-aircraft defenses. Having crossed the canal, Israeli tanks entered Egyptian territory. The situation was beginning to look bleak for the Arabs. On 20 October, Saudi Arabia played a political card by declaring the suspension of oil supplies to the west. The time had come for a ceasefire that received the backing of the superpowers. It came into force on the evening of 22 October, but the Israelis ignored it and continued with their military operations to encircle the Egyptian 3rd Army in the Sinai. It was only the intervention of the Americans that convinced Israel to accept the ceasefire on 24 October.

From an aeronautical point of view, in the 19 days of war, the Arabs lost 440 aircraft against more than 120 aircraft lost by the Israelis. Despite their advantage of surprise, the Egyptian and Syrian forces were unable to overcome their enemy and, after having lost the initiative in battle, were obliged to retreat.

The Yom Kippur War highlighted new aspects of aerial warfare that had in part already been seen in Vietnam. First, it became clear that the new Soviet anti-aircraft system's capabilities were far more efficient and dangerous than western analysts had predicted. Second, the importance of measures to counter anti-aircraft defenses became clear, especially the use of electronic warfare systems, dedicated weapons and new tactics; and third, in air-to-surface armaments the new precision bombs proved their worth. Further, the war saw the combat début of RPV pilotless aircraft used for reconnaissance, observation and deception purposes that were to become increasingly important in future conflicts. On a political level, the Yom Kippur War again failed to resolve any of the problems associated with the co-habitation of Arabs and Jews, although militarily it did underline the Israeli forces' superiority in terms of training, combat, and operational capabilities.

242 McDonnell Douglas (now Boeing) F-15s became the Israelis' leading fighter plane from December 1976, when the first four arrived. They quickly distinguished themselves in 1981 when they shot down a Mach 3 fighter, a Syrian MiG-25.

243 top A Kfir C2 flying over the Sinai. In building this multi-role fighter, which first flew in 1973, Israeli industry drew on experience gained from production of the Nesher fighter, derived from the Mirage.

243 bottom The cockpit of a Lockheed-Martin F-16D fighter-bomber, a sophisticated aircraft used mainly for precision attacks against enemy air defenses.

After the Yom Kippur War, the two combatants again continued to rearm; the Arabs drawing on the Soviet arsenal, in particular MiG-23 and MiG-25 fighters, while the Israelis continued to rely on America. At home, the Israeli aeronautical industry proceeded with the development of a national fighter based on the original Nesher. With the acquisition of the Phantom, Israel had also had access to the General Electric J79 engine, a far more modern and more powerful unit than the Atar 9C. The Israeli air force thus decided to create a new fighter with improved performance by combining the Nesher airframe and the new engine. Design work on the new fighter probably began in 1969, while the maiden flight of what was to be named the Kfir took place in the summer of 1973, preceded by a development program that also utilized a two-seater Mirage IIIB equipped with the J79 engine. The first Kfir C1s were officially introduced on 14 April 1975, and delivery of the first 40 began that year. Naturally, the Kfir also featured Israeli-produced specialist avionics including telemetric radar, a mission computer and electronic counter-measure equipment. The following year saw the introduction of the C2 model (along with the two-seater TC2), characterized by the appearance of two canard wings alongside the air-intakes; these considerably improved the aircraft's maneuverability. The Kfir C2 had a wingspan of 26 feet 3inches, a length of just over 49 feet, and a maximum take-off weight of more than 32,000 lbs. The J79-GE-17 engine delivered 17,900 lbs of thrust on afterburn and enabled the plane to achieve a top speed of Mach 2.3 (1,516 mph) without external loads. It was armed with two 30-mm cannons and up to 8,800 lbs of external weaponry. The Kfir C7 and TC7 were developed in 1983. The planes featured new avionics and an extra two underwing pylons that allowed the maximum external load to be brought up to 13,225 lbs. Israel has built about 240 Kfirs in various versions (some models were created by converting older planes). The total includes those reserved for export: Ecuador, Colombia and Sri Lanka have purchased about 40 Kfirs. The IAI currently offers the Kfir 2000 (purchased by Ecuador), equipped with advanced avionics and an in-flight refueling capability.

Used primarily as a fighter-bomber, the Kfir has been joined by two new aircraft, in 1976 by the F-15/B (and later the C/D), and in 1980 by the F-16 A/B (and later the C/D). Thanks to these acquisitions, in the 1980s the Chel Ha'Avir became the strongest air force in the Middle East, a predominant position confirmed by three separate military operations. The first was the bombing of the Iraqi nuclear reactor at Osirak, a pre-emptive strike in June 1981 aimed at preventing Iraq from building atomic bombs. The operation was difficult and complex as it involved flying for almost 700 miles beyond the Israeli borders over the territories of Jordan and possibly Saudi Arabia, striking the target and returning to base. The mission was made possible thanks to the recent acquisition of the F-16A. Four years later, in 1985, Israel provided further confirmation of its ability to strike distant targets by hitting the PLO

headquarters in Tunisia, about 12,000 miles from Tel Aviv. In this case the raid was carried out with eight F-15Ds that refueled in flight and, perhaps, used precision weapons.

The third mission that confirmed Chel Ha'Avir's capabilities was the "Peace in Galilee" operation, the invasion of southern Libya designed to counter the actions of Syria in the country and neutralize the PLO terrorists' bases. After Egypt had moved within the western sphere and the signing of the Camp David agreements in 1978, Syria had become Israel's principal adversary. Israel organized its aerial offensive after the assassination of its ambassador in London, and began it on 4 June 1982, followed two days later by a land-based assault. The main air battles developed over the Beka'a Valley where the Israeli F-4, A-4 and Kfir fighter-bombers struck the Syrian anti-aircraft defenses and troop positions, while the F-15s and F-16s flew support missions and engaged the enemy fighters. On 10 June a ceasefire agreement was reached that in effect brought the aerial operations to a close, although the land war along the Libyan coast and in Beirut continued for some months.

The result of the air battles was stunning: in just two days the Syrians had lost 85 MiG-21 and MiG-23 fighters while the Israeli forces remained completely intact. Syrian losses totaled 92 aircraft against a dozen aircraft and helicopters lost by the Chel Ha'Avir to anti-aircraft fire. The reasons for this crushing victory are once again to be found in the superior quality of the Israeli men and machines. They were able to employ highly efficient tactics in terms of identifying and attacking enemy anti-aircraft systems, thanks in part to the use of emote controlled RPVs, electronic warfare pods, and dedicated missile systems. Moreover, Israel's recently acquired Grumman E-2C Hawkeye radar planes (two of which were constantly in

flight), and the Boeing 707 electronic warfare and reconnaissance aircraft played a vital role. They provided Israeli fighter pilots with a global, precise and updated view of the situation, identifying Syrian fighters as soon as they took off from their home bases. These American planes also enabled the Israelis to neutralize the enemy's communication and identification systems.

Since 1982 the Chel Ha'Avir has had no further need to fight a true large-scale war. However, the persistence of the emotions underlying the Arab-Israeli conflict, which today primarily focus on jurisdiction over Jerusalem and the occupied territories, means that peace is no closer. Israeli aircraft continue to be used in anger, frequently for isolated pre-emptive or punitive raids against terrorist forces. In the light of other crisis situations such as the Gulf War of 1991 and the enduring hostility of countries such as Syria, Iran and Iraq, the Israeli air force has continued to maintain the level of its training programs and technology. It has updated some of its aircraft (such as the F-4Es, the F-16s and the F-15s), and has acquired new state-of-the-art aircraft and weaponry (such as the AH-64 Apache helicopters. With its F-15I multi-role fighters and the soon-to-be purchased F-16Is, as well as precision bombs and missiles, the Chel Ha'Avir continues to be one of the world's strongest and best prepared air forces.

Chapter 19

Great Airliners

In the 1950s the United States had achieved supremacy in the airliner sector with planes such as the Boeing 707 and the Douglas DC-8. During the following decade, this technological and economic predominance was reinforced by the introduction of excellent medium- and short-range aircraft and the world's largest commercial airliner, the Jumbo Jet. Europe was to reply with the Concorde, a technological marvel that was, however, never to enjoy commercial success.

Air transport was in continual expansion throughout the 1950s, and to satisfy the market demand, especially in the United States, the airlines needed jet aircraft suitable for use on medium- and short-range routes. While the first airliner of this type, the Caravelle, was actually designed and built in Europe, the most influential designs in the sector once again came from the U.S. giants, Boeing and Douglas.

Boeing took a long time to decide whether to produce a jet smaller than the 720, the shorter, lighter version of its 707. In 1957, it finally began work on such a plane.

This was no easy task given that the principal US carriers had differing requirements and could not agree on a preferred format. The aircraft would, however, have to be capable of operating from the short runways often found in the United States and around the world. Boeing eventually chose to produce a tri-engined design, with a layout identical to that of the de Havilland D.H121: three engines at the rear and a T-tail. The proposed purchase price that Boeing had set (a maximum of $3 million, the same price as the Caravelle) posed an additional design difficulty. The studies Boeing conducted led to the eventual creation of the 727, a plane that was to make its mark on the history of aviation. The 727 had three main features. Its wing was equipped with an innovative system of multiple-section flaps

that notably reduced the aircraft's stalling speed and thus allowed it to be operated from runways as short as 5,000 feet. It was powered by the brand-new Pratt & Whitney JT8F turbofans that were more economical and quieter than any other engine and also more powerful, providing over 13,200 lbs of thrust per engine. Last, the fuselage was the same width as that of the 707, which allowed 120 passengers to be accommodated. This last decision reduced production cost and thus the final sale price. Nonetheless, the 727 worked out at a good 30% more expensive than the threshold set previously. Boeing's president, Bill Allen, convinced of the design's validity, once again took a risk and authorized production of the 727 even though the firm had received orders and options for only 80 planes. The first 727, already in production form and finished in United Airlines' colors, took to the air on 9 February 1963. It proved to be an excellent aircraft, even better than the company had predicted, especially in terns of fuel consumption and payload. The 727, with a wingspan of almost 105 feet, a length of just over 150 feet, and a maximum take-off weight of about 210,000 lbs (the 727-200 Advanced model), was modified and improved on a number of occasions. It remained in production until the early 1980s. More than 1,800 727s have been built and sold in the US and throughout the world.

Douglas had also been working on a short-range aircraft. In the later 1950s, the Californian firm had cancelled its four-engined DC-9 project but had already begun work on a twin-engined design known as Model 2011. A few years later the company decided to go ahead with this more promising project, redesignating it with the unused DC-9 tag. A month after Douglas's announcement, Delta Airlines had already signed a purchase order

powerful engines and stretched fuselages), it was redesigned in 1977 and designated the Super-80. Then, from 1983 on, it became the MD-80, with various versions being developed (the MD-81, 82, 83, 87, 88, 90, 95) up until the present day. Including all versions, more than 2,200 planes have been built.

In the meantime, Boeing had also been working on a dedicated short-range airliner, a twin-engined plane that was designed to be more economical than the 727. Lufthansa, which had requested the plane and had insisted that it should be capable of carrying at least 100 passengers, provided considerable input during the design phase. The Model 737 was announced in February 1965. It benefited greatly from the experience gained with the earlier 707 (from which it borrowed the

tailplane design) and 727, with which it shared no fewer than 60% of components such as the airframe (the fuselage was almost identical), the avionics systems, and the wing characteristics. The 737 was powered by two Pratt & Whitney JT8D-7 engines producing 14,000 lbs of thrust. These units were the same as those fitted to the DC-9-30, but they were slung beneath the wings. The prototype 737-100 completed its maiden flight on 9 April 1967, and Lufthansa was able to begin operational service in February 1968. Owing to the rapid development of air transport in that period, Boeing announced that it would produce a new stretched version, the 737-200; this version was 6 feet longer and could carry up to 130 passengers. It entered service with United in April 1968. The Boeing 737 was not immediately successful, but the validity of the format was such that after a series of modifications, mainly concerning the engines and avionics, the aircraft is still in production, with over 3,000 having delivered to airlines throughout the world.

The spread of short- and medium-range jet airliners in the late 1960s changed the air transport scene, radically increasing number of people who were flying rather than taking trains. Constant streams of airliners were taking off and landing at major airports such as those of London, Paris, Chicago, Los Angeles and New York. Civil aviation was assuming the form that still distinguishes it today.

for DC-9s. The plane, about 101 feet 6 inches in length, was smaller than the 727; it could carry a maximum of 90 passengers, was powered by two rear-mounted Pratt & Whitney JT8D enginesproducing 12,250 lbs of thrust, and also had a T-tail. Its strengths were a flight crew reduced to just two pilots and reduced maintenance and fuel costs. The DC-9 series 10, the first of the line, went into operational service with Delta on 8 December 1965. The DC-9 soon proved to be the most popular aircraft for short-range flights and also one of the most versatile of all airliner designs: after having been developed through to the 50 series (with increasingly

244 top A Douglas DC-9-30 belonging to the Spanish airline Iberia. The DC-9 first flew in 1965; the basic design is still available as the Boeing 717, though with suitable modifications.

244 bottom The latest generation twin-jet Boeing 737 in a fine nose-on view. In order to reduce costs, the 737 was designed to share 60% of its components with the 727.

245 top A Cruzeiro Airlines Boeing 727 over the Rocky Mountains. More than 1,800 of these jets were built and almost two thirds of them are still in use around the world.

245 bottom A McDonnell Douglas MD.80 belonging to Aerolineas Argentinas taking off. Introduced in 1977 as the DC-9 Super 80, with new wings, tail unit and engines, this model could carry 170 passengers.

The early 1960s also saw the birth of two great aeronautical projects that were to produce contrasting planes. Both planes, however, were destined to achieve a place in history as exceptional aircraft of their time. Once again, economic and technological rivalry existed between Europe and America. France and Great Britain placed the emphasis on speed and decided to build a supersonic airliner; the United States instead placed faith in load-carrying capacity.

Back in 1962, the two European nations were working on similar projects for a high technology supersonic passenger jet that would be capable of breaking the American hegemony in the air transportation sector. It soon became evident that only with a joint

246-247 The Concorde, whose slim nose, extreme lines and extraordinary speed was a revolution in commercial air travel in 1969.

246 bottom left A British Airways Concorde taking off from Heathrow in June 2001. The Concorde made its maiden flight in 1969. To date, only 20 have been built.

venture in which expenses were shared would such an onerous project be possible and have any realistic chance of success.

The agreement (specifically, the Anglo-French Supersonic Aircraft Agreement) was signed by the two governments, which also committed themselves to financing the entire project. The participating manufacturing companies, Sud Aviation in France and BAC in the UK, would not be required to risk any capital. After the announcement was made, the American manufacturers began to worry. They

already knew, thanks to the feasibility studies they had conducted, that because of the costs involved, the design and construction of a supersonic airliner could not be carried out by a single company. The major firms had thus erased the concept from their future plans.

The new aircraft was given the name "Concorde," which was particularly appropriate, given the traditional rivalry between France and Britain. Work on the two prototypes, one for each company, began in 1963.

From a technical point of view, the Concorde was a major challenge. The chosen format featured a tapering, 223-foot long fuselage and a delta wing that optimized performance both in supersonic flight and at lower take-off and landing speeds. Nonetheless, the Concorde would still be landing at about 177 mph, roughly the speed of an F-104 fighter! In order to allow an optimum angle of attack, a tilting nosecone or "droop-snoot" was fitted to provide the pilots with forward vision when the plane was in a nose-up attitude. Among the Concorde's other notable characteristics was its top speed, which had to be restricted to within Mach 2.2 or 1,354 mph at a cruising altitude of about 51,000 feet. This allowed for the airframe to be built in aluminum rather than the far more expensive stainless steel or titanium that would have otherwise been necessary with higher speeds, owing to the heat generated by air friction. Concorde was to be powered by four afterburner-equipped turbojets mounted in pairs beneath the wing.

In the meantime, two interesting things had happened in the United States. First, the news that the Soviet Union was also working on a supersonic civil airliner (the Tupolev 144) rekindled American interest – and pride. Congress approved a resolution to finance 75% of the costs of an American SST (Supersonic Transport) project, and this was all it took for the US to enter the arena once again. Second, after responding to a USAF requirement for a new large transport aircraft (the C-5), Boeing, had lost out to Lockheed. Boeing then decided (under pressure from Pan Am) to derive some advantage from its proposed plane by transforming it into a huge commercial aircraft, an aircraft that would carry two and half times as many passengers as the 707.

247 bottom   The Tupolev Tu-144, extraordinarily similar to the Concorde, was the Soviet reply to its rival. Shown here is the presentation of the project in Moscow, May 1969. The second Tu-144 prototype flew at the Paris Air Show on 4 June 1973 but crashed shortly after, killing the six people on board. The Tu-144 was faster than Concorde but was never perfected.

The Rolls-Royce/SNECMA Olympus 593 Mk. 610 units were specially built; each produced an exceptional 38,000 lbs of thrust. The aircraft had a maximum take-off weight of just over 200 tons, and had a range of over 3,850 miles, thanks to the 34,000 gallons of fuel carried in its tanks.

While the development work continued, a number of shadows began to be cast over the project. The airlines felt that the aircraft was too small, but this was a relatively minor factor and the designer stretched the fuselage by 6 feet 6 inches to allow the total number of passengers to be increased to 136. There were two other significant problems, however. The first was the take-off noise and sonic boom that would accompany the Concorde's every flight, with the risk that many cities would refuse permission for the plane to land, citing reasons of public health. The second problem concerned sales. Initial projections had identified a market for between 160 and 400 examples to be sold over a period of about

20 years. By March 1967, however, only 74 options had been taken out by 16 airlines, including, of course, Air France and BOAC. The future appeared to be uncertain, but the Concorde was also a symbol of national pride for the two countries, and despite a degree of wavering (above all on the British side), the project went ahead. The French prototype successfully completed its subsonic maiden flight on 2 March 1969.

Boeing, Lockheed and North American committed themselves to the SST project and in December 1966 the government chose the Boeing design. However, the program soon ran into serious technical problems concerning the aircraft's excessive overall weight, while its exorbitant costs aroused public opposition. These problems led to the government's inevitable cancellation of the SST project on 20 May 1971.

Meanwhile, Boeing's giant airliner project, designated Model 747, had been having an easier ride. It was a vast machine, with a length of over 229 feet, a height of over 65 feet (the equivalent of a six-story building), a weight of well over 300 tons, and a surface area of over an acre. It was powered by four Pratt & Whitney JT9D engines; each developed 20,400 lbs of thrust. The 747 was not dissimilar in layout to an enlarged 707, but its distinguishing feature was its fuselage, which was over 19 feet 6 inches wide and over 180 feet long, unblocked from nose to tail because the pilots' cabin and the first-class section were located on an upper deck. The width of the fuselage led to the coining of the term "wide body," a format that since then has characterized all large commercial airliners because of its characteristics of greater comfort and capacity.

Having received sufficient orders from Pan Am, Lufthansa and Japan Air Lines, on 25 July 1966, Boeing announced that construction of the aircraft was about to begin. Here too, however, a number of problems had to be tackled. The further the project advanced, the heavier the plane became; moreover, Boeing lacked a sufficiently large factory in which to assemble the 747 and had to build one *ex novo* at Everett, in the state of Washington. These difficulties were overcome, however, and the new Boeing 747 advanced toward its maiden flight, an event that took place on 9 February 1969, a month earlier than the first Concorde flight. Pan Am inaugurated scheduled 747 service on the New York-London route on 22 January 1970.

The 747's design had been slightly modified before reaching definitive form, thanks in part to suggestions from Pan Am. The definitive version of the 747 had a greater wingspan, a different undercarriage configuration, and a maximum take-off weight that had been increased to almost 340 tons. The 747's physical dimensions led to its becoming known universally as the "Jumbo Jet." The plane was by no means free of teething troubles; first and foremost, the engines were not sufficiently powerful and pilots were frequently obliged to use excessive rpm, causing overheating which in turn translated into more frequent repairs and higher maintenance costs. The passengers were initially unenthusiastic about the 747 because the engine problems caused delays and the on-board services (primarily meals) and amenities (specifically toilets) were inadequate, given that almost 400 people could be carried. Finally, the world's airports were not yet equipped for such large aircraft, and the baggage handling services in particular were put under severe strain. The problems were gradually resolved, but those relating to the engines persisted for a couple of years until the introduction of the JT9D-3A. In the same period, Boeing was facing another predicament: in 1970 the firm had accepted 190 orders from 28 different companies, but these were insufficient to cover the plane's

248-249 *The "Jumbo Jet,"
with the pilots' cabin on the
upper deck, has an
unmistakable front profile.
The 747-400 model can
carry 568 passengers.*

*249 top With over 1,200
B747s already built, the
Jumbo Jet continues to be
brought out in increasingly
modern versions, like the 747-
400X Quiet Longer Range,
which should fly in 2004.*

*249 bottom A Virgin
Atlantic Boeing 747-400.
Nicknamed the Jumbo owing
to its enormous size, the 747
first flew in 1969 and is still
in production.*

development costs, while the onset of economic
depression and the oil crisis meant that all the
airlines were facing severe difficulties. It was not
until the end of the oil crisis and the renewed
expansion of the economy that orders for the
747 started coming in and Boeing could breath
a sigh of relief. By 1983, Boeing had delivered
588 of the 747s. The basic design was subjected
to continuous improvement, and Boeing had
introduced the 747-200B, powered by JT9D-
7FW engines producing 50,000 lbs of thrust,
with a maximum take-off weight of over 400
tons; the shortened 747SP version suitable for
extremely long-range flights; and the 747-300.
Then came the 747-400, currently in
production, and equipped with PW4056
engines producing 56,550 lbs of thrust (or
similar General Electric or Rolls-Royce units).
This version has a maximum take-off weight of
over 437 tons, a range of 8,370 miles, and a
maximum capacity of 568 passengers. To date,
over 1,200 Jumbo Jets have been built.

In Europe in the meantime, the cancellation of the SST program and in the Soviet Union the failure of the Tupolev 144 had lent new confidence to the Concorde executives: despite the difficulties still facing the program, they at least knew that they no longer had any competition. What they had to do, however, was to start to sell the airplane. In 1971, five confirmed orders came in from BOAC and four from Air France. This was better than nothing, but it has to be said that the state airlines of Great Britain and France were virtually obliged to purchase the supersonic jet. It was therefore necessary for one of the world's major airlines to order the plane so that others would be convinced of its potential. Concorde executives decided to concentrate on Pan Am, but the airline then withdrew. Despite the projections presented, Pan Am decided not to take the risk: the Concorde was too expensive (at $65 million, it was already three times the price of the already expensive 747), and tickets would be too expensive for the vast majority of passengers.

In order to publicize the Concorde's capabilities, demonstration tours were organized throughout the world and it was decided to start up scheduled service as soon as possible.

Regular service in fact began on 21 January 1976, with an Air France flight to Buenos Aires and a British Airways (the successor to BOAC) flight from London to Bahrain. Difficulties regarding landing permits for the United States were finally overcome and flights to New York and Washington began within a few months. Unfortunately, from the outset the two companies found it very difficult to fill their planes, and even the transatlantic service was running at a loss.

In the end, none of the companies who had taken options to purchase the Concorde actually took them up; only France and Britain, the two countries that had constructed the aircraft, operate it. Only 16 Concordes have been built, with each one eventually costing no less than $500 million. During the 1980s and 1990s the situation improved, but Concorde was doomed to remain little more than an exceptional symbol of prestige for the airlines and for the relatively few privileged passengers who have used it. A terrible accident involving an Air France Concorde in July 2000 led to the entire fleet being grounded until 2001, when service resumed.

In the meantime, the Jumbo Jet had opened the way for a new generation of wide-body jets. As result of the increase in air traffic, the airlines needed more capacious planes for their medium- and short-range services. At the behest of American Airlines, two new aircraft came into being. McDonnell-Douglas (formed by the St. Louis-based McDonnell's acquisition of Douglas) proposed the DC-10, which first flew on 29 August 1970. Work on the Lockheed L-1011 Tristar began in 1967, and the plane took to the air for the first time on 16 November 1970. Both were tri-engined airliners with a short landing capability and the possibility of carrying about 3090 passengers in a wide-body fuselage.

Despite initial sales successes, both planes then suffered a period of commercial stagnation, partly as a result of the mid-1970s' air transport crisis. A total of 250 Tristars were built, but this was insufficient to cover its development costs. The DC-10 was more successful, and in 1990 it was replaced by the MD-11, an improved version with new avionics, a stretched fuselage and new engines. Over 6000 MD-11s have been built.

In Europe, however, a new chapter in commercial aviation has opened. Airbus Industrie (a consortium France, Great Britain, and Germany set up in 1970 to meet European air transportation needs) has devoted itself to the creation of the A300, a wide-body jet for medium- and short-range routes. This aircraft has proved to the first of an exceptional range of airliners.

Chapter 20

The 1970s saw the appearance of a new generation of combat aircraft. They were the result of lessons learned and experience gained during the most recent wars (the Vietnam and Yom Kippur wars above all), and also the availability of new technologies and the advances made in the computing sciences. In the 1970s, Cold War strategies and the enormous numerical threat that the Warsaw Pact forces posed obliged the United States to concentrate on the quality of its defense forces. The US had to exploit the technological gap between the West and the USSR in order to guarantee that US military forces were capable of facing up to and defeating any attack from the East.

The United States, the world's leader in aviation, introduced a number of fighters during the 1970s that, after appropriate improvements, still represent the backbone of its own military air forces and those of many allied countries. The first to appear was the new air superiority fighter designed for the US Navy as the replacement for the F-4 Phantom II following the cancellation of the General Dynamics-Grumman F.111B. In 1969, the example of the aircraft, designated the F-14A Tomcat, took to the air on 21 December 1970. It was a two-seater with a tandem cockpit and was distinguished by a very wide fuselage with the two engines set well apart, twin rudders and fully mobile tailplanes. It was powered by two afterburner-equipped Pratt & Whitney turbofan engines each delivering about 20,900 lbs of thrust, sufficient to propel the plane to a top speed of Mach 2.34 (about 1,545 mph) at high altitude. It had a wingspan of between 62 feet 4 inches (minimum sweep) and 32 feet 9.5 inches (maximum sweep), a length of 62 feet 4 inches, and a maximum take-off weight of about 70,500 lbs. The weapons system comprised a Vulcan 20-mm cannon and eight AIM-9 Sidewinder, AIM-7 Sparrow or AIM-54 Sparrowhawk missiles. The principal combination was, however, the AWG-9 radar system with a range of over 180 miles and the Phoenix active guidance missile (fitted with its own radar), which had a range of over 80 miles. With this armament the Tomcat could provide the fleet with a degree of protection significantly greater than that offered by any other aircraft. In fact, the Tomcat took US Navy aviation to a new level of excellence.

During the development phase, three prototypes were lost, including the first prototype, which crashed nine days after its maiden flight. Nonetheless, the Tomcat demonstrated its worth, and deliveries to front-line units began in October 1972. The plane undertook its first operational cruise two years later, with VF-1 and VF-2s being embarked on the *USS Enterprise*. The only country to which the Tomcat was exported was Iran, which between 1976 and 1978 (when the Shah still governed) acquired 79 planes.

252 An F-14A Tomcat at low altitude over its aircraft carrier. In total, Grumman built 712 of these aircraft. The only ones exported were sold to Iran, which bought 80 in 1976-1978.

253 top A pair of Grumman F-14B Tomcats of the VF-103 squadron flying over the ocean. The fighter entered service in 1972 and is still considered an exceptional aircraft despite being close to retirement.

Grumman was declared the winner of a design competition. The Grumman design reprised a number of the F.111B's features including the variable-geometry wing, the engines, and the weapons system that hinged on the AWG-9 long-range radar and AIM-54 Phoenix missiles. The first

New versions of the aircraft were developed during the 1980s to resolve deficiencies in power output and to update its avionics.

The first F-14B (originally known as the F-14A Plus) flew in 1987; it was powered by new General Electric F110-GE-400 engines delivering almost 27,000 lbs of thrust and fitted with new avionics. In 1990 the F-14D was introduced, fitted with the same engines and digital avionics, along with a new APG-71 radar system. Planes in these two versions were built either from scratch or by converting older F-14A airframes.

From 1987 on, part of the Tomcat fleet could also be used for bombing missions, thanks to the development of LANTIRN (Low-Altitude Navigation and Targeting Infra-Red for Night) pods for navigation and attack and laser-guided weaponry; these planes were nicknamed Bombcats. In all, 712 Tomcats were produced, and the US Navy is still flying 150 of them. Since 2001, the old F-14As are in process of being replaced with the new F/A-18E/F Super Hornet, but the F-14D should continue to fly until 2010.

253 bottom 550-lb GBU-12 bombs being loaded under an F-14D of the VF-213 squadron in November 2001, during Operation Enduring Freedom.

In the mid-1960s, the USAF also turned its attention to a replacement for the F-4, and established the F-X program. McDonnell-Douglas was declared the winner of the competition in 1969, with an innovative design that was radically different from the F-4. Although the wing shape was similar to that of the Phantom, the new F-15A Eagle had a wide, flat fuselage with two straight rudders, square-cut, variable-geometry air intakes and a large nose section housing a large single-seat cockpit.

This cockpit offered great visibility, and was equipped with a head-up display (HUD) system and hands-on-throttle-and-stick (HOTAS) controls. The first of 20 pre-production F-15A Eagles flew on 27 July 1972; it immediately proved to be an exceptional aircraft that was easy to pilot and far more maneuverable than the Phantom. The first F-15As and two-seat TF-15As (later redesignated the F-15B) began to enter service at Luke Airforce Base in November 1974, while the first planes to be assigned to an operational squadron, the 1st TFW, arrived in 1977. The F-15A had a wingspan of 42 feet 7 inches, a length of 62 feet 4 inches, and a maximum take-off weight of 56,000 lbs. Its

two Pratt & Whitney turbofan engines each provided about 24,000 lbs of thrust on afterburn, good for a top speed of Mach 2.5 (about 1,650 mph). The principal armament consisted of four AIM-9 air-to-air missiles and a 20-mm Vulcan cannon. Up to 16,000 lbs of bombs or fuel tanks could also be attached externally. In air-to-air configuration, the F-15 was the first fighter to have an equal or positive thrust-weight ratio, which allowed it to climb with exceptional rapidity, even vertically if necessary.

Despite this performance, the replacement model, designated as the F-15C (the two-seater was the F-15D), was already flying by 1979 and featured larger internal fuel tanks, the possibility of using CFT tanks shaped to fit the flanks, new avionics, and a maximum take-off weight increased to 68,000 lbs. During the development of the aircraft, the new F100-PW-220 engines also appeared. The Multi-Stage Improvement Program (MSIP) was initiated in 1983, and first concerned the F-15 Cs and then the A models. The modifications comprised a new main computer, a new fire-control system that, among other advantages, allowed the use of new AIM-120 AMRAAM air-to-air missiles, improvements to the APG-63 radar, and new electronic defense and warfare systems. The F-15 has been exported to Israel, Saudi Arabia and Japan, where Mitsubishi built it under license.

With the F-15 2 Eagle, the USAF had a plane without rivals anywhere in the world. Its basic design, conceived above all for aerial combat, has also proved to be suitable for the development of a multi-role version, which Grumman developed in response to an air force for a dual-role fighter. The first F-15 Strike Eagle took to the air on 11 December 1986; in substance it represented a two-seater version of the F-15 equipped with CFT fuel tanks, new mission avionics including the APG-70 radar system, LANTRIN attack and navigation pods, and F100-PW-229 engines delivering about 29,000 lbs of thrust. Maximum take-off weight rose to

81,000 lbs, of which 24,500 lbs could be in the form of external loads. The Strike Eagle was crewed by a pilot and a systems operator, but the plane maintained the air-to-air combat capabilities of its predecessor. The aircraft entered service with the USAF in 1988, and since then about 220 have been delivered, along with derivative versions, the F-15I for Israel and the F-15S for Saudi Arabia, of which 25 and 72 have been produced respectively. To date, a total of around 1,500 F-15s have been produced, and many will continue to be used as front-line aircraft for many years to come.

254 top An F-15A of the Hawaiian National Guard in a vertical dive. The Eagle is able to carry up to eight air-to-air AIM-120, AIM-7 or AIM-9 missiles.

254 bottom right Two F-15E Strike Eagles from the USAF 3rd Flight Wing firing AIM-7M Sparrow air-to-air missiles. This model of the Eagle is a true multi-role airplane and operates happily on either attack or aerial combat missions.

255 top This F-15A Eagle clearly shows the aircraft's aerodynamic configuration, with a large wing, dual rudder and completely mobile tail surfaces behind the engines.

254-255 A multi-role Boeing F-15E belonging to the USAF 48th FW seen from the weapon system officer's seat in an identical aircraft. The F-15 offers its pilots exceptional visibility.

In 1971, the USAF launched another competition, this time for an aircraft designated the LWF (Light-Weight Fighter). As a partner for the F-15, the USAF wanted a smaller multi-role, single-seat, single-engine fighter that would also be less expensive and capable of replacing part of the F-4 and A-7 fleets still in service. The competition was narrowed down to the General Dynamics YF-16 project and the Northrop YF-17, and in January 1975 the former was declared the winner. The General Dynamics fighter had already flown on 20 January 1974 and, although small, it immediately appeared to be highly advanced and have great potential. The plane's aerodynamics were futuristic, with the oval air intake placed beneath the belly and the fuselage making a significant contribution to the lift provided by the wing.

For the first time fly-by-wire computerized controls were used, while the cockpit featured a lateral joystick, a seat inclined at 30° to counter G-force

and a fully glazed, high-visibility canopy. The thrust-weight ratio was again better than 1:1, and in flight the F-16 was extremely fast and maneuverable, to the extent that the first cases of pilots losing consciousness because of abrupt or extreme maneuvers were recorded.

The F-16A made its first flight in 1976, and the first operational unit received the aircraft in 1978, at Luke Air Force Base. In the meantime, in 1975, the F-16 had already earned a place in the history books thanks to the signing of the so-called "contract of the century" whereby four NATO countries, Belgium, Holland, Denmark and Norway, agreed to adopt the aircraft. In fact, 500 F-16s were, ordered to replace the old F-104Gs.

The F-16A had a wingspan of 29 feet 6 inches, a length of 45 feet 11 inches, and a maximum take-off weight of almost 35,400 lbs, with external loads accounting for up to 15,200 lbs. It was powered by the same engine as the F-15A, a single Pratt & Whitney F100-PW-100 unit delivering around 23,900 lbs of thrust that was good for a top speed of Mach 2. The F-15C version (D was the two-seater) was introduced in 1983 and featured a new APG-68 radar system, new avionics, and a reinforced airframe that allowed the maximum take-off weight to be increased to about 37,500 lbs. The F-15C Block 30 was the first version to introduce the possibility of selecting a General Electric F110-GE-110 engine (producing 28,000 lbs of thrust) or a Pratt & Whitney F100-PW22o unit (23,900 lbs), as well as improved avionics and weaponry such as the introduction of AIM-120 AMRAAM air-to-air missiles. In 1986 General Dynamics received a contract for the updating of the National Guard's 270 F-16As to the ADF specification that featured a new radio system, new APG-66 radar capabilities, and the ability to launch AIM-7 and Aim-120 missiles. The most recent model currently in production for the USAF is the Block 50, featuring advanced avionics, an F100-GE-129 engine delivering 29,000 lbs of thrust, a maximum take-off weight increased

256 top A pair of F-16CJs of the 35th FW display their main weaponry, an AGM-88 HARM antiradar missile. The F-16C Block 50 with HTS pod specializes in taking out enemy air defenses.

256 bottom The Lockheed-Martin F-16 Fighting Falcon is the most widely used modern fighter in the world. Shown here is the rear cockpit of an F-16D belonging to South Carolina's National Guard.

256-257 The F-16 is a superb multi-role fighter for both aerial combat and attack missions. This USAF F-16C is flying over the 'no-fly-zone' in Iraq; it is armed with laser-guided GBU-12 bombs and AIM-120 and AIM-9M air-to-air missiles.

257 bottom The Falcon is highly maneuverable. This F-16C from the USAF 52nd Wing has two smoke containers that underline the aircraft's dramatic handling during an air show.

to 42,295 lbs, and the possibility of using the most modern weapons and navigation and attack systems. The F-16, later named the Fighting Falcon, which since 1993 has been a Lockheed-Martin project, has been subject to continual improvements and has been exported to 20 countries around the world. Over 4,000 F-16s have now been produced, and it can safely be considered as the most successful and widely used jet fighter of all time.

Another American plane developed in the same period was the Fairchild-Republic A-10 Thunderbolt Ii, which made its maiden flight on 10 May 1972. This was a plane developed by the company in response to the USAF's A-X request for a new close air support plane designed primarily to neutralize the threat of Soviet armored forces in Europe.

Early in 1973, the YA-10 was declared the winner at the expense of Northrop's YA-9, and the first production A-10As entered service in 1976. This was an aerodynamically innovative plane that placed firepower and survival capabilities above traditional fighter characteristics. It featured a large straight wing, two engines paired above the fuselage and shielded by the wing and the dual-rudder tailplanes. The titanium cockpit was sufficiently armored to resist 23-mm shells, and its fixed weaponry consisted of an enormous Gatling GAU-8a cannon with seven 30-mm rotating barrels, capable of perforating tank armor. Powered by two General electric TF34-GE-100 turbofan engines, each producing around 9,000 lbs of thrust, the A-10 was a top speed of about 435 mph. The plane had a wingspan of 52 feet 6 inches, a length of 52 feet 6 inches, and a maximum take-off weight of 52,000 lbs; it could carry a weapons load of up to 16,600 lbs on eleven belly fittings. The A-

10A (with 713 planes built, all for the USAF) was considered to be virtually obsolete following the collapse of the threat posed by the Warsaw Pact and the Soviet Union. It was re-evaluated after its use in the Gulf War in 1991 and in NATO's aerial operations in the former Yugoslavia between 1993 and 1999. Even though many planes have been withdrawn, the A-10A (designated as the OA-10A for forward air control missions) should remain in service for many years, thanks to the establishment of modernization programs.

258-259 *Two A-10As launching heat flares designed to draw heat-seeking infra-red missiles off track. The A-10 can carry a varied payload of up to 16,000 lbs.*

259 top *The A-10A's design was based on tactical considerations: high engines shielded by the dual-rudder tailplanes, a raised cockpit and armor-plating on the nose.*

259 bottom *The Fairchild-Republic (today Northrop-Grumman) A-10A Thunderbolt II was introduced at the end of the 1960s as a tactical support craft for the USAF. Its main characteristic was its 30-mm Gatling anti-tank cannon with seven rotating barrels.*

Naturally, the Soviet Union was also proceeding with modernization of its aircraft in the1970s, introducing new planes that drew on the wartime experience and demands of the Soviet air force. The new planes had to match the operational capabilities of the United States and NATO. Even though the MiG-21 was an aircraft with excellent specifications, it lacked a weapons system capable of competing with those of the West's aircraft; moreover, the need to improve its maneuverability was recognized. Program 23 was thus launched, featuring a series of new components: Sapfir-23 radar, an AVM-23 analog computer, R-23 air-to-air missiles, and so on. Two prototypes were constructed, the

other minor modifications.

The first true MiG-23 was the M version, which flew for the first time in June 1972, and immediately entered large-scale serial production. It had a wing span of between 42 feet 8 inches (minimum sweep) and 22 feet 11 inches (maximum sweep), a length of 52 feet 6 inches, and was powered by a Soyuz/Khachaturov R29-300 engine producing about 27,550 lbs of thrust and good for a speed of Mach 2.35. The MiG-23M's maximum take-off weight was about 45,550 lbs, and it could carry weaponry weighing up to 4,400 lbs, principally composed of six R-23 and R-60 missiles. In 1973, the strike version was renamed the MiG-27 and in 1983, after 910 had been

260 top The Russian MiG-23 fighter first flew in June 1967; 5,000 of the interceptor version have been built since 1985. It is still in service today in many air forces in Europe, Africa and Asia.

260 bottom The MiG-25RBF, the electronic recognition version of the trisonic MiG-25P fighter, appeared in 1981. Shown here is one from the Soviet airbase at Finow, East Germany.

23-01 with a delta wing and the 23-11 with a variable- geometry wing, which (both) flew for the first time on 10 June 1967. The second version was chosen for serial production, and 28t May 1969 saw the maiden flight of the MiG-23S (known to NATO as the "Flogger-A") that was, however, still retained theMiG-21's avionics. This aircraft was powered by an R27F2M-300 engine delivering 21,825 lbs of thrust and was capable of a top speed of Mach 2.27. The airframe was particularly interesting as it broke with MiG traditions. The variable-geometry air intakes were located either side of the fuselage (like those of the Phantom) while beneath the tail was a stabilizing fin that folded away when the undercarriage was lowered. The variable-geometry wing (inspired by the F-111 design) improved take-off and landing characteristics while maintaining high-speed capabilities. The ground-attack version, designated the MiG-23B, flew for the first time on 20 August 1970; this model had a new nose section stripped of radar equipment, fixed air intakes, a Lyulka AL-21F3 engine, a reinforced airframe with larger tires, simplified avionics, and various

built, the production line was transferred to India. Various versions of the fighter model were developed, some for export to friendly countries. The series culminated in the MiG-23MLD (or "Flogger–K"), which had an R-35-300 engine producing 28,660 lbs of thrust, a radar system with close combat functions, a Shchel 3-U missile-guidance visor fitted to the pilot's helmet and R-73 missiles. By 1985, 5,047 MiG-23s had been produced, and it remained in service in the USSR/Russia until 1994. A total of 1,075 MiG-27s were built. The Mig23MLD and the Mig-27 were used by

the air forces of over 20 countries, and they saw combat in the Middle East, Afghanistan, Angola and India, where they were reasonably successful.

Development of the MiG-25, a project initiated in the early 1960s before that of the MiG-23, involved very different plane, designed to respond to the threat posed by the American's XB-70 intercontinental supersonic bomber then in development. Exceptional performance was required of the new super-interceptor: a maximum speed of 1,865 mph, a maximum ceiling of around 65,500 feet and a range of 2,5090 miles. In order to meet these criteria, the MiG design department came up with a large single-seat aircraft equipped with enormous turbofan engines, twin rudders at the rear and a high-mounted, moderately swept wing. The first prototype E-115R-1 (the reconnaissance model) completed its maiden flight on 6 March 1964, while the E-155P-1 interceptor took off six months later. Even though not all the performance requirements were achieved, the plane met the principal criteria and went into service on 13 June 1972 as the MiG-25P interceptor ("Foxbat-A" to NATO). This version was characterized by two Soyuz/Tumanski R-15B-300 engines, each producing almost 25,000 lbs of thrust on afterburn, sufficient to power it to a top speed of Mach 2.83 (about 1,865 mph). It had a wingspan of 42 feet 8 inches, a length of 68 feet 10 inches, and a maximum take-off weight of about 90,400 lbs. The weapons system was based on a Smerch-A radar and four R-40 missiles.

December 1972 saw the introduction of the MiG25-PD fitted with Sapfir-24 radar, R-40D missiles, and with further improvements to the avionics. The MiG-25BM version, dedicated to destroy enemy

anti-aircraft defenses, was also introduced that year. Its principal armaments were four Kh-58 air-to-surface missiles. Production of the MiG-25 ended with the 1,186th plane. Interceptor and reconnaissance versions were delivered to certain friendly countries: Algeria, Libya, Iraq, India and Syria. Only the reconnaissance and anti-radar strike versions remain in service today. The MiG-25 also formed the basis for a new two-seat interceptor designed to provide greater range and independent capability to engage multiple targets.

260-261 The MiG-23B attack model was derived from the MiG-23S interceptor and first flew in 1970. It was a simple aircraft without nose radar. In 1973 it was renamed the MiG-27 and in 1983 production was transferred to India. Shown here are two Indian Air Force MiG-27s.

261 bottom right When the MiG-25 appeared in 1964, it was the fastest interceptor fighter ever built. It was retired in the Soviet Union in 1994. This is a two-seat training MiG-25RU during landing.

263 bottom left A MiG-29A
fighter belonging to the
Slovak air force. More than
1,500 were built and used by
more than 25 countries
around the world.

263 bottom right A MiG-
31B being rolled in after
landing, with its parachute-
brake still attached. More
than 400 of these planes were
built; they can carry up to
10 missiles.

The first to be built, designated the MiG-25MP, completed its maiden flight on 16 September 1975, while December 1976 saw the first appearance of the pre-production MiG-31 ("Foxhound"). This was a heavier, more powerful fighter than the Foxbat. It featured a two-seat tandem cockpit, a reinforced undercarriage, a Zaslon radar system capable of tracking ten targets and attacking four simultaneously, and a weapons system composed of four-33 semi-active guidance missiles with a range of 75 miles, and two R-40TD missiles. It was powered by two Aviadvigatel/Solovyov D-30F-6 engines, each producing over 34,000 of lbs of thrust, and could attain a top speed of around 1,865 mph. The MiG-31 had a wingspan of 42 feet 7.5 inches, and a length of 72 feet 2 inches, and a maximum take-off weight of about 102,000 lbs. It went into service in December 1981, and since then over 400 have been built. The MiG-31M version was introduced in 1995, and features R-37 missiles, Zaslon-M radar, a maximum take-off weight increased to

more than 114,500 lbs, a greater internal fuel capacity, and more powerful engines. Only a few have been built because of the crisis the Russian aviation industry experienced in the 1990s.

The MiG-23's successor as the Soviet Union's principal air defense fighter was being discussed as early as 1969, when the government issued a request for a new fighter in the same class as the American F-15. Subsequently, the request was divided into two parts, and the MiG engineers concentrated on the creation of a lightweight fighter, the preliminary design for which was accepted in 1974. The plane was heavily influenced by the American designs, featuring twin rudders, a wing integrated with the fuselage, and square-cut belly air intakes. The first prototype, the 9-01, took to the air on 6 October 1977. Its official designation was the MiG-29, but NATO identified it as the Ram-L. The two-seat MiG-29UB flew in 1981, and serial production began the following year. Deliveries to operational squadrons began

in August 1983. The MiG-29, finally designated the "Fulcrum-A' by NATO, was powered by a pair of Klimov/Sakisov RD-33 engines each producing 18,300 lbs thrust on afterburn and good for a top speed of Mach 2.3 (close to 1,500 mph). The plane had a maximum take-off weight of 48,500 lbs, of which external armaments in the form of up to six R-27, R-73 and R-60 air-to-air missiles and a 30-mm cannon accounted for about 4,400 lbs. The MiG-29 could carry bombs and ground attack rockets if required. The plane's RLPK-29 radar system had a range of over 40 miles and was capable of tracking ten targets and attacking one.

The MiG-29 soon proved to be an excellent fighter, agile and capable of achieving extreme angles of attack. It was particularly deadly in dogfights, thanks in part to the capability of guiding missiles by means of a visor built into the pilot's helmet. In 1992, production concentrated on the MiG-29S, which was equipped with an improved radar system, and with a weapons load increased to 8,800 lbs. In all, more than 1,450 MiG-29s have been built, including such versions as the MiG-29M, the MiG-33 export variant, the naval MiG-29K (which never went into service), and the most recent MiG-29SMT, and the plane has been used by 25 countries around the world.

262 A heavy two-seat MiG-31 fighter climbing in Soviet skies. The fastest interceptor plane in the world, it can fly at 1,865 mph.

263 top A MiG-29UB fighter of the Soviet Union's air force during acrobatics in an air show. This is the two-seat training model of the modern Soviet aircraft.

During this period, another important combat aircraft was developed, but not by either of the two superpowers. Instead, Panavia, a European multinational corporation established by the principal aeronautical companies of Great Britain, Germany, and Italy on 26 March 1969, developed and built it. Panavia's Multi-Role Combat Aircraft (MRCA) project involved not only a new combat aircraft (to be constructed by BAC, MBB and Aeritalia), but also a new turbofan engine (entrusted to the tri-national Turbo Union corporation). The aircraft was essentially an all-weather, low-level fighter-bomber whose layout featured a two-seat tandem cockpit for pilot and navigator, a high-mounted variable-geometry wing, twin engines, large tailplanes with a single rudder, and sophisticated radar and avionics. Named the PA-200 Tornado, the German prototype P.01 completed its maiden flight on 14 August 1974. Pre-production planes began to fly in 1977, and in June 1979 the first of the interdiction-and-

strike (IDS) production planes was delivered to the Royal Air Force.

The Tornado had a wingspan of between 42 feet 7 inches (minimum sweep) and 26 feet 3inches (maximum sweep), a length of 52 feet 6 inches, and a maximum take-off weight of about 61,7000 lbs, of which external loads accounted for about 19,850 lbs. It was powered by two RB.199 Mk.101 turbofans, each producing 16,000 lbs of thrust on afterburn, and could attain a top speed of 920 mph at low altitude.

The basic IDS version was subsequently optimized for reconnaissance and anti-shipping strike missions through addition of pods and dedicated weaponry. In total, the RAF received 229 IDS planes, Germany 332, and Italy 100.

In order to satisfy British requirements for an interceptor, Panavia then developed the ADV (Air Defense Variant), which made its first flight on 27 October 1979. The main differences were sleeker aerodynamics resulting from lengthening the fuselage to 59 feet, addition of the Foxhunter long-range radar system and new avionics, removal of one of the two 27-mm cannons, adoption of RB.199 Mk.104 engines producing about 16,500 lbs of thrust.

The new version had a weapons system composed of four medium-range Sky Flash missiles and four AIM-9 short-range missiles. The RAF eventually acquired 173 Tornado ADVs, with which it replaced its F-4 Phantoms. Italy can also count on Tornado ADVs, having leased 24 from the RAF in 1995. The last version of the Tornado was the ECR (electronic combat reconnaissance) variant, dedicated primarily to suppression of anti-aircraft defenses. A total of 35 Tornado ECRs were built for the German Luftwaffe (entering service in 1990), and 16 for the Italian air force, which has used them since 1998.

The ECR is fitted with sophisticated electronic equipment for identification of enemy signals (ELS and RHWR), and dedicated anti-radar weapons such as AGM-88 HARM air-surface missiles; in addition, it is fitted with the latest version of the RB.199 engine, the Mk.105, producing 16,800 lbs of thrust. A total of 978 Tornados have been built in various versions, including 96 of the IDS and 24 of the ADV, which were exported to Saudi Arabia.

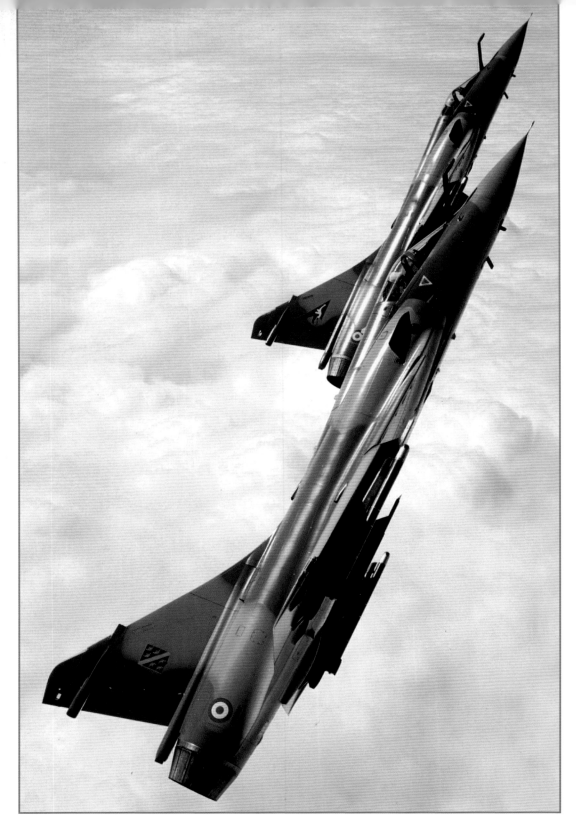

parity. In November 1982, following intensive development involving five prototypes, the French air force took delivery of the first production Mirage 2000Cs, optimized for interception and air superiority roles. The aircraft was 45 feet 11 inches long, with a wingspan of 29 feet 6 inches, and had a maximum take-off weight of about 24,000 lbs. Its SNECMA M53-5 engines produced 18,850 lbs of thrust and gave the aircraft a top speed of Mach 2.2 (about 1,430 mph). The weapons system was based on a mission computer, a Thomson-CSF RDM radar system, and up to four Matra Super 530D and 550 Magic 2 missiles, along with two 30-mm cannons. After the 38th plane had been built, all further ones were fitted with the RDI radar system and M53-P2 engine, which produced about 21,4000 lbs of thrust; both modifications added to the plane's performance.

The year 1983 saw the maiden flight of the 2000N. This version was designed for nuclear strike roles. It had a tandem cockpit with a second seat for a co-pilot dealing with the weapons and also radar and avionics systems optimized for low-level operations. The 2000N formed the basis for the 2000D version, which was designed for attacks using conventional weapons; it was fitted with new avionics and the capability for using sophisticated precision weaponry.

In 1984, the Mirage 2000E was introduced as the export version of the 2000C, but with multi-role capabilities. Next, in October 1990, the 2000-5 model completed its maiden flight. This version incorporated a redesigned cockpit with multifunction screens and digital instrumentation, a new RDY multi-mode radar system, up to six new Mica missiles and multi-role capabilities. The first 2000-5s were delivered in 1996; 37 went to the French air force and others to those of Qatar, Taiwan and Greece. To date, about 560 Mirage 2000s have been built, and 8 nations are using the plane.

The Dassault Mirage 2000 was last important fighter of the 1970s. The plane, approved by the French government in December 1975, was designed to provide the Armée de l'Air with a replacement for the Mirage F.1. The first prototype of the new fighter completed its maiden flight on 10 March 1978; it marked a return to the delta- wing layout that once again offered advantages, thanks to the introduction of fly-by-wire controls, new aerodynamic features, and a thrust-weight ratio close to

266 top A pair of French air force Dassault Mirage 2000Cs. The plane entered service in 1982 and began operations two years later. Over 550 have been constructed.

266 bottom The Mirage 2000N, the nuclear attack version of the Mirage 2000 family, now modified for conventional weapons missions. Shown here is a rocket-carrying Mirage of the French air force's 4th Wing.

267 top A Mirage 2000C interceptor of the French air force refueling in flight. The 2000-5 version in part resolved the problem created by the 2000C's short flight range.

267 bottom A two-seat French Mirage 2000B during a daring acrobatic maneuver at an air show. The fighter's delta wing and refined lines are clearly seen.

Chapter 21

The Third Level

The growth in commercial air traffic after the Second World War, and in particular its expansion during the 1950s, created a marked divide. The divide separated the major state or international airlines that served international capitals and major cities from the medium-to-small companies that concentrated on shorter routes, frequently within individual countries and geographical areas. This second type of business came to be defined as third level or regional air transport, and the aircraft used were grouped under the umbrella term "commuter planes." The first generation of this type of aircraft came into being during the second half of the 1960s.

From the outset, the principal characteristics of commuter aircraft have been their reduced dimensions, with restricted numbers of seats (usually between 10-20 and 30-40), propeller or turboprop propulsion, relatively short take-off and landing capabilities (STOL), and low operating costs. Regional transport aircraft

were used, and still are used, primarily to link secondary airfields with major airports (the so-called hubs) and vice versa. Passengers can reach the most important cities by air and then take advantage of connections to international and intercontinental flights departing from and arriving at the hubs. The United States was the first nation to distinguish and develop this sector. Its vast territory naturally demanded the creation of a dense network of air traffic routes linking the principal cities within a state to each

other and linking the various states to one another and to the major metropolises.

Oddly enough, however, despite recognition of the third level market, the American aviation industry remained focused on the production of jet airliners with over 100 seats and took relatively little interest in the third level's equipment needs. While Fairchild, Beechcraft and de Havilland Canada did produce some significant third-level aircraft in North America, many of the smaller airlines relied on planes built abroad.

The Swearingen Merlin IIA, an eight-seat turboprop designed in 1964, was the first of a successful range of American commuter planes. Five years later, the Merlin was used as the basis for the 226TC Metro; it was fitted with new engines and a stretched fuselage that could accommodate up to 20 passengers, the Metro first flew on 26 August 1969 and was immediately sold to Air Wisconsin and Mississippi Valley Airlines. Later Fairchild acquired the Swearingen project, and

268 top The de Havilland Canada DHC 8, known as the Dash 8, made its maiden flight in 1983. It was developed to provide a quiet, economical plane for regional flights.

introduced the structurally modified Metro II fitted with 950-shp engines. Then came the Metro III, with a greater wingspan, 1,100-shp engines, and a higher maximum take-off weight. The Metro 23, certified in June 1990, is the latest version; it has a wingspan of 55 feet 8 inches, a length of 59 feet, and is powered by two AlliedSignal TPE-12UHR engines, each delivering 1,100 shp. The plane has a maximum take-off weight of 16,500 lbs, and can reach a top speed of 348 mph. Staffed by a crew of two pilots and a flight assistant, the Metro 23 can carry up to 19 passengers. The cargo version, known as the Expediter, can carry a load of 5,500 lbs.

Beechcraft meanwhile developed its Model 99. It mated a fuselage capable of accommodating 15 passengers to a wing design based on the 65/80 Queen Air, and fitted it with two 557-shp turboprop engines. The prototype first flew in December 1965, and deliveries to clients began three years later. The C99 Commuter, the last model in the series, boasted two 774-shp turboprop engines and was produced until 1987. In the meantime, the Beechcraft 1900 had already appeared; it made its maiden flight on 3 September 1983. This was a larger aircraft a T-tail similar to that of the Super King Air, two Pratt & Whitney Canada PT6A turboprops delivering 1,110 shp and a cruising speed of 295 mph; maximum take-off weight was 16,600 lbs. The fuselage could accommodate up to 19 passengers or 4,500 lbs of cargo. The improved 1900D version appeared in March 1990, equipped with 1,280-shp engines and four-bladed propellers that provided a top cruising speed of about 330 mph. This version had a maximum take-off weight of 17,550 lbs. Over 680 1900Ds have been built.

In the mid-1960s de Havilland Canada (DHC) introduced an aircraft designed specifically for regional operations. It flew for the first time on 20 May 1965, and was named the DHC 6 Twin Otter. Designed with STOL capabilities, this rugged plane featured a fixed undercarriage, a high wing, a particularly robust airframe and twin turboprop engines. The Twin Otter had two PT6A engines that gave it a top speed of about 217 mph; the cabin accommodated 18 passengers, and the plane had a maximum take-off weight of 12,345 lbs. With its specifications and the possibility of fitting snow skis or floats to turn it into a snow surface or seaplane, the Twin Otter was particularly attractive to companies operating in difficult terrain such as the American Great North, and it was produced until the late 1980s. Given the Twin Otter's success, DHC decided to proceed with the design of a larger, more capacious aircraft with the same characteristics of robustness and economy as its predecessor.

The DHC 7 Dash-7 completed its maiden flight on 27 March 1975. It was an all-new plane with a fuselage capable of accommodating up to 54 passengers or 11,680 lbs of cargo. The Dash-7 had four 1,130-shp PT6A engines, a top speed of 280 mph, and a maximum take-off weight of 44,000 lbs. The Dash-7's STOL capabilities were enhanced by the use of large double-slot flaps; the plane could operate from runways less than 2,000 feet long. The success of this model was limited, however, and the similar but more modern Dash-8 replacement completed its maiden flight on 20 June 1983. This plane featured twin engines and an increased top speed, but had a lower loading capacity. The Dash-8 could plane could carry 39 passengers or about 7,825 lbs of cargo. Its two Pratt & Whitney turboprop engines each delivered 2,000 shp and a cruising speed of 310 mph. Responding to market demands for an even better plane, DHC then introduced the enlarged and uprated Dash-8 200, 300 and 400 versions. The latest variant, the 70-seat Q400 flew for the first time on 31 January 1998. To date, over 670 Dash-8 aircraft in all the various forms have been sold, a fact that places DHC's successor company, Canadair (now known as Bombardier), among the leaders in this manufacturing sector.

268 bottom The dual turboprop Beech 99 has a conventional design. It remained in production from 1968 till 1983.

269 top This de Havilland Canada DHC 6 Twin Otter is the hydroplane version. It was designed in 1964 to provide a regional aircraft capable of dealing with Canada's difficult terrain.

269 center left The Fairchild Metro II is one of the many light commuter planes derived from the Swearingen Merlin II, which first flew in 1965.

269 center right A four-engined de Havilland Canada DHC 7 (Dash 7) flown by the British Brymon company. It was designed to carry passengers and goods, and has the advantages of short take-off and landing capabilities.

269 bottom The Beechcraft 1900D, introduced in 1990, improved on the 1900 model with more powerful engines, a four-bladed propeller, and greater carrying capacity.

The South American manufacturer Brasiliana Embraer is another producer of successful commuter aircraft. This company, founded at the behest of the Brazilian government in the late 1960s, concentrated on the production of an original aircraft, a twin-engined light transport destined for the Brazilian air force. The aircraft was designed by the Frenchman Max Holste and was a fairly traditional, rather unsophisticated but robust design with a low wing, two PT6A turboprop engines and conventional tailplanes.

The prototype, designated YC-95, first flew on 26 October 1968, and the aircraft entered military service as the C-95 in transport, search-and-rescue, and maritime patrol roles. The civil version with a stretched fuselage was designated the EMB-110P Bandeirante, and was converted to seat up to 18 passengers. The EMB-110P had a maximum take-off weight of 12,500 lb, and was powered by two 750-shp engines providing a top speed of 286 mph. By 1994, 469 Bandeirantes had been built. The EMB-120 Brasilia model followed the 120, making its maiden flight on 27 June 1983, with the first production deliveries made in 1985 to the America Atlantic Southeast company. The new Brasilia represents a considerable all-round improvement over the earlier plane, and is equipped with a T-tail and two Pratt & Whitney Canada PW118 engines producing 1,800 shp. It is capable of a cruising speed of 342 mph and can carry up to 30 passengers or just over 7,700 lbs of cargo. In all, seven different versions of the Bandeirante have been developed to respond to diverse requirements and in all more than 350 planes have been sold. A military version is also offered.

The greatest proliferation of third-level transport aircraft occurred in Europe, where the aeronautical industries of Great Britain, Holland, Germany, France, Spain, Italy and Sweden have produced a number of designs. The first was the Fokker F27 Friendship, a design conceived as early as 1950 and developed two years later, thanks to the backing of the Dutch government. The prototype first flew on 24 November 1955, and presented features that were to become familiar characteristics of commuter planes in general: a high wing, turboprop engines, traditional tailplanes, a retractable undercarriage and a

pressurized fuselage with a maximum capacity of 48 seats. The initial Mk.100 series was equipped with Rolls-Royce Dart 514 engines, but they were replaced in the Mk.200 by more powerful Dart 532-7R engines that developed 2,285 shp. The Mk.200 had a maximum take-off weight of 45,000 lbs, and a cruising speed of about 300 mph. Production got under way in 1958 in both the Netherlands and the United States, where Fairchild had acquired a license to manufacture it. The Fokker 27 finally went out of production in 1987, with about 785 planes having been built

Prior to this, the Dutch company had launched the Fokker F50 in 1983. In effect, the F50 was a complete revision of the earlier model, with 80 percent of the components being replaced. The first F50 flew on 28 December 1985, and deliveries began in 1987, with Lufthansa Cityline being the first purchaser. The plane was equipped with two 2,500-shp

Pratt & Whitney Canada PW125B turboprop engines driving six-bladed propellers and providing a top cruising speed of 330 mph. A maximum of 58 passengers could be carried. A total of 319 F50s were built prior to 1996, when Fokker declared bankruptcy and production ceased. Despite the company's problems, the F27 and the F50 were sold throughout the world, and the former in particular was a true leader in its market sector.

The British Britten-Norman BN 2 Islander was another of the earliest true European commuter planes, and was specially designed for short-haul flights. The aircraft completed its maiden flight on 13 June 1965 and went into service two years later with Aurigny and Loganair. The Islander was a small plane with twin piston engines, a high wing, a fixed undercarriage, a square-section fuselage, STOL capabilities, and room for nine passengers. The improved BN 2A version went into production in 1969, while 1970 saw the

introduction of a tri-motor variant designated the BN 2A Mk.III Trislander. This version had a longer fuselage that accommodated more passengers and a third engine installed on the rudder. It never enjoyed significant sales success, and went out of production in 1984. However, the original Islander is still in production, in both piston-engined form and in a version equipped with turboprop engines. Over 1,200 have been built. The Swiss firm

270 top left The Britten Norman BN2 Islander is a successful commuter plane also used for search and rescue operations. More than 1,200 have been built.

270 center The Brazilian Embraer company was also busy at the end of the 1960s producing commuter planes. The EMB-110 Bandeirante shown here entered production in 1972.

270 bottom The Fokker F-27 Friendship was one of the first regional turboprop planes. The development project, which was launched in 1950, benefited from grants from the Dutch government.

engine, and had a maximum take-off weight of 23,000 lbs and a cruising speed of about 217 mph. The 330 formed the basis for the Sherpa cargo plane and, above all, the model 360 that flew for the first time on 1 June 1981. The 360 was a larger aircraft, with 36 seats, new traditional tailplanes and 1,440-shp PT6A engines. The maximum weight at take-off was increased to 26,450 lbs and the cruising speed to about 245 mph. Modified versions of the Shorts 360 were subsequently developed and featured new six-bladed propellers.

On 28 March 1981 the British Aerospace Jetstream 31 made its maiden flight. It was a slim twin-turboprop plane with a low wing and a retractable undercarriage derived from the Handley Page HP.137 Jetstream, an aircraft developed in the late 1960s. While the first Jetstream had not been particularly successful, the Jetstream 31 enjoyed far better fortunes. It introduced new Garret TPR331 engines producing 950 shp and equipped with four-bladed propellers. These power units brought a considerable increase in performance, the top speed rising to 298 mph and the maximum take-off weight to about 15,325 lbs, with a payload of up to 19 passengers or about 3,950 lbs of cargo. In the 1980s, this aircraft was virtually the market leader, winning, for example, 60 percent of the difficult American market's commuter segment. In 1988, the Super 31 flew for the first time; it was equipped with 1,100-shp AlliedSignal TPE331-12UAR engines, which provided a top speed of 304 mph and permitted a maximum take-off weight of 16,200 lbs. In 1991, the Jetstream 41 appeared, fitted with more powerful engines and with room for up to 29 passengers.

270-271 The Embraer EMB-120RT Brasilia, introduced in 1983, was a natural successor to the Bandeirante. The slender twin turboprop is shown here displaying Flight West Airlines' colors.

271 center The British Aerospace Jetstream 31 of 1980 derived from the same-name aircraft built by Handley Page at the end of the 1960s. The Jetstream Super has been in service since 1988.

271 bottom The Shorts 360 made its first flight in 1974 as the SD3-30. It is used to carry passengers, cargo and for military use.

Pilatus now owns the company. The BN 2T model is powered by two 320-shp Allison 250-B17C turboprop engines and can maintain a top cruising speed of about 195 mph. It has a maximum take-off weight of 7,000 lbs, and can take-off from runways just 835 feet long.

The Northern Irish Shorts company also entered the sector, first in 1963 with the Skyvan, a rustic twin-turboprop aircraft with a large square-section fuselage, suitable for both civil and military purposes, and then with the 330, which flew for the first time on 22 August 1974. This aircraft, which also had STOL capabilities, was developed from the earlier plane, but had a greater wingspan and a new stretched fuselage equipped with a retractable undercarriage. It could seat up to 30 passengers. The 330-200 version was powered by the ubiquitous 1,215-shp PT6A

In Sweden, Saab created a family of highly successful regional air transport planes originally born out of a joint venture with Fairchild in America. On 25 January 1983, the Saab-Fairchild SF.340A, which became the Metro II's successor, completed its maiden flight. It was a fairly large plane, with a low wing, a retractable undercarriage and sleek lines, and was powered by two General Electric CT7-5A2 engines producing 1,750 shp, good for a cruising speed of 320 mph and a maximum take-off weight of 27,270 lbs. The 340A could carry 35 passengers or up to 7,580 lbs of cargo. Fairchild withdrew from

perhaps owing to cost. It went out of production in 1999 after 64 planes had been built. Production of the 340 also ceased that year after the 461st plane had been delivered. A military version of the 340, the S110B Argus, was also produced and used by the Swedish air force as radar plane.

Spain was also active in the commuter sector, initially with an aircraft derived from a military design. The CAA C-212 Aviocar was designed in the early 1970s as a transport plane for the Spanish armed forces. It was a rugged STOL design characterized by a square-section fuselage with a high wing and

the series 1985, but Saab went on to introduce the Saab 340B in 1989. This version had a higher maximum take-off weight of 29,200 lbs, allowing for more passengers or cargo. The Swiss airline Crossair was the 340's first purchaser, as it would be for its successor, the Saab 2000.

The Saab 2000 completed its maiden flight on 26 March 1992, earning the nickname "Concordette" because at the time it was the world's fastest turboprop. The 2000 represented a redesign of the 340 and shared numerous components with it. However, the 2000 had a greater wingspan, a longer fuselage capable of seating up to 58 passengers, 4,150-shp Allison GMA2001 engines, a maximum take-off weigh of 48,500 lbs, and a top speed of 422 mph. Despite predictions to the contrary, the 2000 never achieved the hoped-for commercial success,

traditional tailplanes over the rear cargo door. The C-212 completed its maiden flight on 26 March 1971, and enjoyed reasonable sales in both military and civilian versions, the latter optimized for passenger- and cargo-carrying duties. The most recent model in the series is the 212-300, capable of seating 26 passengers or carrying about 6,170 lbs of cargo, with a maximum take-off weight of 16,975 lbs. This version is powered by two 900-shp AlliedSignal TPE331 turboprops, and has a cruising speed of 220 mph. The 212M military version is certified for slightly higher take-off weight and can perform various duties such as parachute-drops, air-ambulance, reconnaissance and observation.

In 1979, CASA signed an agreement with the Indonesian company Nurtanio for the design and construction of a new, second-generation civilian transport plane for the

third level market, with possible military applications. Designated as the CN-235 and built by the Airtech consortium, the plane had a similar layout to the previous model, but was larger and sleeker. The prototype flew for the first time on 11 November 1983. The initial series 10 version was followed by the 100/110 series equipped with two 1,750-shp General Electric CT7-9C turboprops driving four-bladed propellers and guaranteeing a top speed of 298 mph and a maximum take-off weight of 33,289 lbs (34,833 lbs for the 200 series). Planes in the 100/110 series could carry a payload of up to 44 passengers or 8,800 lbs of cargo (9,480 lbs for the 200 series). Over 220 CN-235s were built, with the majority sold to military operators. The plane also formed the basis for the CN-295, an enlarged version that is currently under development.

The early 1980s saw the proliferation of new projects for regional air transport, a sector then in rapid expansion. The development of a new aircraft for this sector led to the establishment in 1982 of the ATR (Avions de Transport Régional) consortium, founded by the French firm Aérospatiale and the Italian firm Alenia. The result was the ATR-42, which completed its maiden flight on 16 August 1984. The first production plane was delivered to the French Air Littoral company in December 1983. The aircraft reflected fairly traditional design, with a high wing, a T-tail, and two 2,000-shp Pratt & Whitney Canada PW120 turboprop engines driving four-bladed propellers. These engines were used throughout the ATR-42-300 series. Later, the more powerful PW121 engines were adopted, and finally the PW127Es, which were used in the ATR-42-500 series. The ATR-42-500 has a power output of 2750-shp per engine (restricted to 2,160-shp), offering a cruising speed of 348 mph and a maximum take-off weight of 41,000 lbs. ATR-42-500 aircraft could carry up to 50 passengers, the equivalent of a payload of 1,190 lbs.

In 1985, ATR announced the introduction of a stretched 72-seater version of the plane, appropriately designated the ATR-72, to satisfy operators' demands for greater capacity. The first prototype took to the air on 27 October 1988, and in 1989 the first aircraft were already being delivered to the Finnish carrier, KarAir. The most powerful version currently in production is the ATR-72-500, launched in 1998 and equipped with 2,475-shp PW127 engines that permit a cruising speed of over 370 mph and a maximum take-off weight of 47,400 lbs. To date, over 580 ATR series aircraft have been sold, and the planes have won a leading position in the third level sector, with deliveries to commercial operators throughout the world.

273 center right The CASA 212 resulted from the Spanish air force's need in the early 1970s to replace some of its transport planes. The military model was followed by several civilian passenger and cargo versions.

273 bottom The ATR-72 of 1988 was developed from the basic ATR-42. It has more powerful engines and a lengthened fuselage to take more passengers.

Following the airline deregulation of the 1990s, European regional air transportation boomed. The new frontier in commuter planes became represented by jet aircraft, better suited to satisfying the demands of operators on the numbers of passengers carried and the reduction of flight times.

The Hawker Siddeley HS.146 was first aircraft of this new generation. It was actually designed and developed back in 1973, and completed its maiden flight on 3 September 1981, named the British Aerospace 146. The 146 had a high wing and a fairly traditional T-tail, but was characterized by its four particularly quiet turbofan engines that made it suitable for operation from inner-city airports. The BAe 146 100 was fitted with Avco Lycoming ALF502R-5 engines producing 7,000 lbs of thrust; it had a top cruising speed of 441 mph, a maximum take-off weight of about 93,000 lbs, and could carry up to 93

passengers. The first customer was the British DanAir company, which began operating the 146 in 1983. Subsequent development led to the introduction of the 200 and 300 series with stretched fuselages seating up to 109 passengers. In 1993 the series passed into the hands of Avro International, a BAe subsidiary. In 1994, after the construction of the 222nd series 146 plane, production concentrated on the improved Avro RJ70, 85, 100 and 115 versions, the names of which indicate the number of passengers carried. The most successful model in the series, fitted with electronically governed AlliedSignal engines and digital avionics, is the RJ85, of which over 80 have been sold. This model flew for the first time on 23 March 1992 and is equipped with four LF507-1F turbofans producing 7,000 lbs of thrust, providing with a top speed of 497 mph, and a maximum take-off weight of 97,000 lbs.

In 1989, Canadair (now Bombardier) developed its Regional Jet in Canada, basing

design on the Challenger business jet. The new Regional Jet completed its maiden flight on 10 May 1991. The plane is powered by two jet engines mounted at the tail; it features a T-tail, a low wing and seats for 50 passengers. The first deliveries were made to Lufthansa CityLine in October 1992. In 1995 Bombardier introduced the RJ200 series, powered by General Electric CF34B1 engines producing 9,225 lbs of thrust, good for a cruising speed of 534 mph and a maximum take-off weight of 47,443 lbs. The RJ200 could seat up to 54 passengers, the equivalent of 12,000 lbs of cargo. In 1997 Bombardier announced the RJ700 model, characterized by a fuselage stretched by just over 13 feet to bring the passenger capacity up to 70, and fitted with CF34-8C1 engines producing 12,675 lbs of thrust, and maximum take-off weight of 72,500 lbs. The Bombardier RJ series has enjoyed notable success, and has received orders for more than 450 planes.

In the late 1980s, following its success with turboprops, the Brazilian firm Embraer launched a regional jet project. The firm's internal problems and redesign needs delayed the project, but the first EMB-145 prototype, a plane with clean, conventional lines, took to the air on 11 August 1995. Continental Express, which had been involved in launching the project, was taking the its first deliveries in 1996. In October 1997, the EMB-145 was redesignated the ERJ-145 (Embraer Regional Jet 145) in order to emphasize its precise market position. The first version was 50-seat ERJ-145ER, which was equipped with two Allison AE3007A turbofans, each producing 70,54 lbs of thrust and ensuring a cruising speed of 516 mph and a maximum take-off weight of 45,415 lbs. Next came the 70-seat ERJ-170 and the ERJ-135, introduced in 1997. The latter had a shortened fuselage and a reduced seating capacity of 37 passengers. Over 400 ERJ series planes have been sold, and the aircraft is still in production since it appears that the regional air transport market is likely to expand still further in the future.

274-275 *The BAe 146 boasts short take-off and landing requirements and low noise levels.*

275 top *The BAe 146 version featuring four jet engines dated back conceptually to Hawker Siddeley's 1973 project launch. During the 1970s world crisis the project was put on hold, but later British Aerospace took it up, and the aircraft first flew in 1981.*

275 center *The BAe 146 project was transferred in 1993 to the company's Avro International subsidiary, which produced the RJ series with different load capacities. This Lufthansa RJ85 is shown landing.*

275 bottom *The 1995 Embraer RJ-145, seating 50 passengers, reflected a regional transport shift to jet planes that began at the start of the 1990s.*

Chapter 22

The Gulf, Kosovo and Afghanistan: the Last Wars

I n the last years of the 20th century, just when the world appeared to be heading toward a period of enduring peace supported by ongoing East-West dialog, an explosion of tension and conflict occurred. Paradoxically, it was the ending of the Cold War and superpower confrontations that triggered the new hostilities.

On one hand, the political collapse and disintegration of the Soviet Union and the Warsaw Pact military alliance reduced

world, the Gulf War in 1991, the Kosovo conflict in 1999, and the war in Afghanistan in 2001-2002 have been the most important and have attracted the most widespread public attention. In each of these cases, the air force contributions – the most technological and advanced of the military forces – were the most effective and decisive.

On 2 August 1990, at 2.00 o'clock in the morning, the armed forces of Iraq under the leadership of the president-dictator Saddam Hussein, crossed the borders of the tiny state

and Saudi Arabia soon managed to assemble a powerful coalition with the aim of protecting the Arabian peninsula from further Iraqi attacks and eventually liberating Kuwait by force and neutralizing Iraq's armed forces.

The Arab nations that responded to the appeal were Bahrain, Qatar, the United Arab Emirates, Egypt, Morocco, Oman, Syria and, naturally, Kuwait and Saudi Arabia. Further coalition forces were provided by Great Britain, France, Italy, The

tension in Europe and North America, on the other, it appears to have stimulated nationalistic ambitions for independence in many countries and ethnic groups around the world.

In the early 1990s, many leaders recognized that the surveillance and control the United States and the Soviet Union had exercised in many areas in the past was weakening. These leaders now saw opportunities for the conquest of new territories and new spheres of influence. Of the many conflicts that have broken out or flamed back into life in many parts of the

of Kuwait and overran the country in a matter of hours. For some time Saddam Hussein had been claiming that Kuwaiti territory was in fact the 16th province of Iraq. Above all, Kuwait's vast oil reserves attracted Iraq.

The dictator's strategy was simple: no other Arab country would dare attack him (at that time Iraq had the world's fourth largest army, with 1,200,000 men, 5,500 tanks and 9,500 armored vehicles) and at all would refuse permission for western military intervention in the area. His calculations proved to be short sighted. Thanks to a United Nations resolution, the United States

277 center A Lockheed-Martin F-117A Nighthawk was the first allied aircraft to enter in action in Operation Desert Storm. It is shown here en route to attack the Baghdad command centers.

276 AH-64 attack helicopters and OH-58 reconnaissance planes at a US Army Aviation advance base in Kuwait during Operation Desert Storm in 1991.

277 top An F/A-18C and an F-14A prepare to take off on an attack mission, while another F/A-18C is pulled into its parking slot. These flight operations on the USS Theodore Roosevelt occurred during the Kosovo conflict in 1999.

Netherlands, Belgium, Portugal, Spain, Greece, Poland, the Czech Republic, Canada, Australia, New Zealand, Senegal, Pakistan, Bangladesh, South Korea, Canada, Australia, and New Zealand, as well as the United States.

It was not long before Operation Desert Shield got under way, with the Allied nations dispatching contingents to the Persian Gulf in readiness for war, should it prove inevitable. The United States sustained the greater part of the war effort.

To meet anticipated needs, the Pentagon mobilized about 2,000 aircraft (1,200 from the USAF and 800 from the US Navy and the Marines), six aircraft carriers and five helicopter carriers, together with the cream of the armed forces, especially in the fields of combat aviation, surveillance and electronic warfare.

277 bottom A formation of F-15Cs, F-15Es and F-16Cs flying over burning oil wells at the end of the Gulf War. The image symbolized American air power during Operation Desert Storm.

Spearheading the American air combat force was the Lockheed F-117A Nighthawk fighter-bomber, the famous yet top secret "stealth" fighter, around which many rumors and legends had grown. The origins of this remarkable aircraft date back to 1974, the year in which the United States government issued a requirement for a revolutionary new fighter with a very low radar footprint. In 1976, the government selected the design proposed by Lockheed's secret "Skunk Works" group and authorized the Have Blue research program calling for the construction of two prototypes. The first of these completed its maiden flight in December 1977, and production of the definitive F-117 commenced the following year, with a batch of 20 aircraft.

The F-117 was highly revolutionary; its shape was almost exclusively the result of research into the refraction of electromagnetic waves. The skin was faceted like a cut diamond, with the plane's fuselage almost integral with the V-shaped wing. The two butterfly tailplanes were fully mobile. The F-117's handling left much to be desired, and it was largely controllable in flight thanks to the application of computerized flight controls. The single-seat aircraft was powered by two General electric F404-GE-F1D2 turbofans producing

10,800 lbs of thrust with no afterburners. Its top speed was no higher than 646 mph, and maximum take-off weight was about 52,470 lbs. The weapons load (a maximum of 5,000 lbs) was carried in two internal bays and was typically composed of two laser-guided 2,000-lb Paveway bombs. In practice the F-117 was a night bomber which, thanks to sophisticated navigation and strike avionics, was capable of carrying out surprise attacks without being picked up by enemy radar. The first F-117s went into service in 1982, but only in 1988 was the plane's existence officially acknowledged, and it made no public appearances until 1990. A total of 64 expensive and sophisticated F-117s have been built, and 42 of them were employed in the Gulf War.

The F-117 Nighthawks were the first Allied planes to see active combat, attacking command centers in Baghdad during the night of 17 January 1991. This date marked the commencement of Operation Desert Storm and the beginning of the aerial offensive against Iraqi forces that followed the United Nations' the vain formal requests for Iraq's withdrawal from Kuwait.

278 top A Lockheed-Martin F-117A Nighthawk refueling in flight.

278 bottom and 279 top The F-117A's aggressive lines in close-up. The aircraft's square and triangular shapes were dictated by research into radar invisibility and by experimentation during the 1970s.

279 bottom Two Nighthawks over the New Mexico desert. From 1982 to 1988, the unit at Tonopah AFB, Nevada, that flew these planes was kept completely secret.

280 top Two F/A-18Cs carrying Mk.82 Snakeye controlled bombs. The Hornet made its first flight in 1978; since then over 1,500 have been constructed.

Switzerland and Malaysia.

The early 1990s saw the introduction of the F/A-18D Night Attack, a multi-role two-seater version developed for the Marines to replace the A-6E as an all-weather bomber. The F/A-18E/F super Hornet project was launched in 1992, aimed at developing the Hornet into an aircraft capable of replacing both the F-14 as the navy's defense fighter and also the earliest F/A-18s. The Super Hornet is a far larger and more versatile machine. Its wingspan was extended to 42 feet 7.5 inches and its length to 59 feet; maximum take-off weight was increased to 66,000 lbs, and the internal fuel tanks'

The aerial assault was carried out primarily with F-117, F-16, F-15E, F-4G, F-111, A-10, Tornado IDA, Buccaneer Mirage F.1 and Jaguar fighter-bombers, along with F-15, Tornado ADV and Mirage 2000 air-superiority fighters, backed up by imposing support services for in-flight refueling, surveillance and electronic warfare. The carrier-borne forces were composed of F-14, A-6 and A-7 fighters, but primarily by F/A-18s and AV-8Bs, two new planes that represented the backbone of the US Navy and Marines' strike force. The McDonnell-Douglas F/A-18 Hornet could trace its origins back to the Northrop YF-17 project, the plane that together with the YF-16 had participated in the USAF's Light-Weight Fighter (LWF) competition in 1971. With the aim of optimizing resources, in 1974 the American government had decided that the new fighter produced by the US Navy's VFAX program (a replacement for the Navy and the Marines' A-7s and F-4s in strike and aerial combat roles) should also be chosen from the LWF contenders. McDonnell-Douglas proposed an alliance with Northrop in order to exploit its experience with carrier-borne aircraft, and in 1976 the Navy chose the project jointly presented by the two companies. This project involved the construction of two almost identical planes, the F-18 air combat fighter and the A-18 strike version. Subsequently, thanks to technological advances and the Navy's logistical requirements, a single multi-role model was defined, the F/A-18, which completed its maiden flight on 18 November 1978.

The F/A-18 was a twin-engined plane with a high wing and dual rudders that benefited from the recent aerodynamic research into flight at high angles of attack. The plane was highly maneuverable, especially at low speeds. Thanks to its mission computer and radar systems' capabilities the F/A-18 could carry air-to-air and air-to-surface weapons, taking on the role required by the various phases and demands of its mission. Deliveries of the F/A-18A (and the two-seater B) to operational units began in May 1980. By June 1982 exports had begun, first to Canada and then to Australia and Spain. In 1987, the F/A-18C/D model appeared, featuring new avionics that supported the possibility of using new weapons (such as the ATM-20 missiles), night-fighter capabilities, and subsequently improved engines and radar. The F/A-18C had a wingspan of 36 feet and a length of 55 feet 9 inches, and was powered by two General Electric F404-GE-402 turbofans, each producing about 17,700 lbs of thrust and guaranteeing a top speed of about 1,180 mph (Mach 1.8). The plane had a maximum take-off weight of 56,000 lbs; its weapons system comprised a 20-mm Vulcan cannon and up to 18,000 lbs of external load. About 1,400 F/A-18s were built, and the aircraft was exported to Kuwait, Finland,

capacity was increased by 3,600 lbs in order to extend the plane's range. Two extra underwing pylons were added to carry weapons, and F414-GE-400 engines delivering 22,000 lbs of thrust were adopted. The first F/A-18E flew on 29 November 1995, and the plane went into service with the first training unit in 2000. The US Navy plans to acquire aout 1,000 examples of the Super Hornet by 2015.

In the Gulf War Hornets carried out a large percentage of the missions assigned to the Navy, including ground attacks, air defense attacks, and air superiority sorties.

280 center *An F/A-18C launching air-to-ground rockets into the polygon in China Lake in California. The Hornet is a true multi-role fighter with equal capacity for air-to-air and air-to-ground combat.*

280 bottom *A F/A Super Hornet on a carrier deck. This multi-role fighter was developed from the F/A-18C/D but is practically a new aircraft: it is more powerful and has greater capabilities. It was designed to replace the US Navy's F-14s and older F/A-18s.*

281 top *A pair of F/A-18Cs above the* USS Kitty Hawk *in the Pacific Ocean. The model C Hornet, incorporating improvements over the model A, first flew in 1987.*

281 bottom *A formation of McDonnell Douglas (today Boeing) F/A-18D Hornets belonging to the Marines during in-flight refueling. This plane is not a trainer but a multi-role fighter in which the second crew member is the weapons' system operator.*

The Marines also made good use of the Hornets during the conflict, using it together with four squadrons of V/STOL McDonnell-Douglas AV-8B Harrier II fighter-bombers. This plane was born in 1976 out of the collaboration between British Aerospace and McDonnell-Douglas, which had resulted from a program designed to produce an improved version of the Harrier fighter then in use with the Marines in its AV-8A version. The YAV-8B, the prototype of the new plane, first flew on 9 November 1978. In practical terms, the YAV-8B was an all-new aircraft, even though it reflected the general layout of its predecessor. It had a new, larger wing offering greater lift and more weapon-mounting points; the engine was new, and the weapons load and range had been increased.

New avionics were fitted and the airframe, largely composed of composite materials, had a new cockpit. The AV-8B (and the TAV-8B two-seater) entered service with the Marines in January 1984, and it was delivered to the RAF (as the Harrier GR.Mk.5) in July 1987. The AV-8B had a wingspan of 29 feet 6 inches and a length of 45 feet 11 inches; its Rolls-Royce Pegasus F402-RR-408A engine provided 23,800 lbs of thrust, good for a top speed of 652 mph. Its maximum take-off weight was 31,000 lbs, and the plane could carry a weapons load of up to 13,225 lbs. Subsequently, in its AV-8B Night Attack and Harrier GR.Mk.7 versions, the plane was equipped with night-strike capabilities. In 1987 the Harrier II Plus program was launched to transform the fighter into a multi-role plane also suitable for aerial combat.

The Plus version is in fact equipped with an APG-65 radar system (the same as that fitted to the early F/A-18s) and air-to-air weaponry such as AIM-9 and AIM-120 missiles. In 1993, the Plus version went into service with the U.S. Marines and the Italian and Spanish navies. More than 450 Harrier IIs have been built.

282 top An AV-8B Harrier II fighter-bomber lands on the USS Essex' flight deck during Operation Enduring Freedom, Afghanistan, October 2001.

282-283 A Harrier II armed with laser-guided GBU-12 bombs weighing 500 lbs each taking off from the helicopter-carrier USS Bataan in January 2002 during Operation Enduring Freedom.

283 top F-14D and F/A-18C fighters, an E-2C radar plane, an EA-6B electronic warplane, an S-3B anti-submarine plane and an A-6E bomber flying over the USS Carl Vinson. The photograph was taken in 1996 during Operation Southern Watch in the Persian Gulf.

As mentioned earlier, electronic warfare aircraft played a key role in the Gulf War. Although not strictly belonging to this category, the Boeing E-3 AWACS radar plane was one of the Allies' crucial aircraft in the their complex aerial operations. Development of the E-3A began in 1970. The design derived from the civilian 707-320B model, and drew on the experience gained in Vietnam by the

USAF's first C-121 radar planes. The new aircraft (then designated as the EC-137D) made its maiden flight on 9 February 1972, and deliveries of the production version began on 24 March 1977. In essence, the E-3A Sentry was a flying container for the Westinghouse AN/APY-1 radar system characterized by the enormous antenna located in a rotating disc above the fuselage, inside which were the radar

operators' work stations. The system could be used not only as a flying radar station (to track other aircraft at distances of up to 250 miles), but also as a true airborne command post. The E-3s were subsequently updated to B and C specifications through installation of the APY-2 radar system, new tactical evaluation command and control computers, new electronic support systems (ESM), and new secure communications and data exchange equipment. A total of 68 E-33s have been built, and are currently in service with the United States, Great Britain, France, Saudi Arabia and a NATO unit.

Other electronic warfare aircraft employed in the Gulf included the EF-111A and the EA-6B for the electronic neutralization of anti-aircraft defenses; the EC-130E/H for tactical command-post operations, electronic spying and psychological warfare; and the RC-

284 bottom The Boeing E-6A Mercury is based on model E-3. The US Navy uses to the plane maintain contact with its fleet of nuclear submarines. The plane has been in service since 1989.

285 top A Grumman EA-6B Prowler on the USS Theodore Roosevelt's flight deck during Operation Enduring Freedom, December 2001.

135U/V/W for the interception of communications and electronic signals. During Gulf War operations, the RF-4C, Mirage F.1CR and U-2R reconnaissance planes gave these electronic warfare planes invaluable support.

The war against Iraq was virtually one-way, especially in the air. Apart from a few dogfights (in which Coalition fighters shot down 41 enemy aircraft without loss) the greatest threat to Coalition aircraft came from the anti-aircraft missile and artillery systems. These, however, managed to shoot down only 43 Allied aircraft in 110,000 combat missions. Much of the Allies' success in the air was due to the work of the

284-285 The Grumman EF-111A Raven, developed from the F-111 fighter-bomber, was the USAF's equivalent of the US Navy's Prowler. It remained in service from 1981 until 1998.

SEAD (Suppression of Enemy Air Defences) planes that attacked the enemy anti-aircraft defenses. The F-4G, F-16, EA-6B, A-7, F/A-18 and Tornado aircraft, armed with HARMs (High-speed Anti-Radiation Missile) and employing increasingly sophisticated tactics, were able to pinpoint the Iraqi positions; they frequently managed to silence them either by force or by their mere presence, obliging the Iraqis to shut down their radar systems. After almost 40 days of air attacks, the Coalition's land forces (540,000 men and 3,700 tanks) finally attacked on 24 February, and in just 100 hours overran the relatively untrained and demoralized Iraqi troops. The Gulf War ended on 28 February 1991.

285 center The Boeing E-3 Sentry is the AWACS version of the Boeing 707-320 airliner. The main system (with the antenna installed in the large rotating disk) is the Westinghouse AN/APY-2 radar.

285 bottom The Prowler is a ship-based electronic warplane used to blind enemy air defenses electronically. It first flew in 1968, and has a four-man crew.

At much the same time, however, another major center of tension and subsequently war was developing in the Balkans as Slovenia and Croatia decided to abandon the Yugoslav federation and proclaim their status as independent nations. The war between Yugoslavia (Serbia) and Croatia expanded into Bosnia, provoking reaction from the United Nations and NATO. These organizations decided upon the formation of a military and aerial force that would re-establish and maintain peace. Airborne operation began in summer 1992, with the airlift that brought relief to Sarajevo and in spring 1993, with Operation Deny Flight that was intended to impose control over the region's airspace and prevent military actions. These activities gradually intensified until winter 1998-99 when Serbian troops began a series of criminal "ethnic cleansing" operations against people of Albanian origin in the province of Kosovo. This led to a new UN and

and the frequency of the missions that were carried out night and day. About 75 percent of the aircraft were supplied by the United States (operating from bases in Italy, France, Germany, Spain and Great Britain), with the remaining 25 percent supplied by eleven NATO countries including Italy, which provided abut 50 aircraft and offered the use of some 20 airfields. The Yugoslav air force was able to sustain opposition only in the conflict's very earliest phases, when five of its MiG-29s were shot down. Thereafter, Serbia's coordinated and constantly mobile and anti-aircraft defenses posed the main threat to NATO – one that was greater than that faced in the Gulf War.

The Balkan conflict saw three very different types of aircraft in action for the first time. One was the AMX fighter-bomber, an aircraft developed in Italy in the early 1980s by a consortium formed by Aeritalia, Aermacchi and the Brazilian company Embraer. The AMX designed to

286 *The Russian MiG-29, shown here in 1998, before the Kosovo conflict began, is the Yugoslav air force's most important fighter.*

286-287 *The AMX resulted from a 1980 Italian-Brazilian project to build a light tactical fighter-bomber; 192 were built. The Italian air force used the AMX with success during the 1999 war in Kosovo.*

NATO initiative that, given the failure of negotiations, took the form of military intervention begun during the night of 24 March 1999.

Operation Allied Force saw the onset of aerial attacks on Serbian military and strategic targets. The aerial offensive against Yugoslavia (the first war NATO had fought in its fifty-year existence), was initially conducted with a limited number of aircraft (about 500 combat and support planes). However, given the opposition's strength and tenacity, the Coalition intensified its effort both in terms of numbers (over 1,000 aircraft, including those embarked on five aircraft carriers)

replace the Italian air force's G.91s and F-104Gs. The first prototype flew on 15 May 1984, and the first production planes went into service in 1989. The AMX is a single-seat, single-engined plane with traditional lines but a moderately swept high wing, developed from the profile of the Tornado's wing. It has a wingspan of 26 feet 3 inches and a length of 32 feet 7.5 inches. Powered by a Rolls-Royce (FIAT Avio) Spey RB-168-807 engine delivering 11,000 lbs of thrust with no afterburner, it has a top speed of Mach 0.86. (The RB-168-107 is an old engine with an unexceptional power output but moderate fuel consumption; it was to cause

considerable problems in terms of reliability.) The AMX has a maximum take-off weight of 28,660 lbs, and can carry an external weapons load of up to 8,377 lbs, together with a 20-mm Vulcan cannon. The two-seater AMX-T version appeared in 1990. Over the years the plane matured into an effective fighter-bomber and tactical reconnaissance plane of consistent reliability (diurnal capabilities), equipped with generally advanced avionics and precision weaponry such as laser and infra-red guided bombs. During operations over Kosovo, the Italian AMXs were continuously employed for support missions, and performed admirably.

287 bottom left Puma helicopters take French paratroopers to Kosovka Mitrovica during NATO peace force operations in Kosovo, September 1999.

287 bottom right A Puma helicopter transports French commando paratroopers over Macedonia during Kosovo war operations in April 1999.

The second plane that made its operational début in the Balkans was the American strategic bomber, the Rockwell B-1B Lancer, which operated from Great Britain. For various reasons, the United States did not used the B-1B Lancer in the Gulf War. It is a large, four-engined aircraft with a variable-geometry wing and intercontinental range. It dates back to 1970, to the development project launched to find a replacement for the Boeing B-52. The first prototype of the supersonic B-1A completed its maiden flight on 23 December 1974, but then in 1977 President Carter canceled the project. Four years later, President Reagan authorized the revival of the project in BI-B form, for a slightly simplified and subsonic version of the original design but one featuring improved avionics and structural technology. Plans called for building 100 BI-Bs rather than 244 B-1As. The BI-B has a wingspan of between 75 feet 6 inches (maximum sweep) and 134 feet 6 inches (minimum sweep) and a length of 144 feet 4 inches. It is powered by four General Electric FI01-GE-102 engines, each delivering 30,800 lbs of thrust on afterburn, good for a top speed of 746 mph. Maximum take-off weight is 238 tons, of which the weapons load accounts for up to 61.5 tons. The plane has a crew of four and is capable of dropping both nuclear and conventional weapons. Deliveries of the B-1B began in 1985.

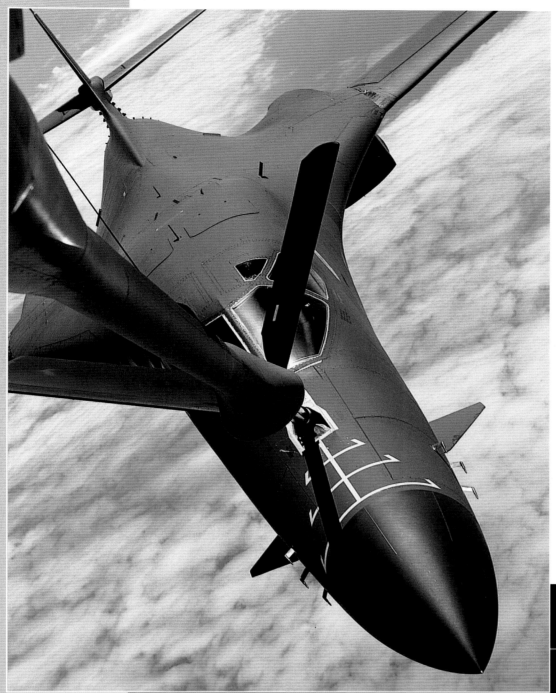

288 top A B-1B Rockwell Lancer creating aerodynamic compression visible in the humid air as it flies at high speed. It has a top speed of 750 mph.

288 bottom The B-1B lancer can carry up to 56 tons of bombs in its ventral holds. The plane has been in service since 1985 and about 100 have been built.

289 top A B-1B Lancer refueling. This aircraft first flew in 1974 as the B-1A but the project was put on hold; President Reagan revitalized it in 1981.

289 bottom A Lancer in a maneuver, with two of its four afterburners alight. The four General Electric F101 engines each produce a thrust of almost 14 tons.

The Northrop-Grumman B-2A Spirit was the third plane to receive baptism of fire during the Kosovo war. This was the first "invisible" strategic bomber in the history of aviation. The origins of the project date back to the second half of the 1970s, following the launch of the Have Blue program and the F-117. The development program for the B-2 was signed off in 1981.

The plane revived Jack Northrop's original ideas from the 1940s for a flying-wing bomber, but was adapted and improved to benefit from the technological advances available in the 1980s. An aircraft with highly futuristic lines, the B-2A has no aerodynamic line-breaking appendages whatsoever; its only protuberances are the cockpit and the four engines on the top of the airframe, all very carefully faired. The first B-2 completed its maiden flight on 17 July 1989 and the first production version

was delivered to the USAF in 1993. The plane has a wingspan of 170 feet 7 inches and a length of 68 feet 11, and is powered by four General Electric F118-GE-100 engines, each providing 19,000 lbs thrust, for a top speed of 528 mph. Maximum take-off weight is over 167 tons, and a weapons load of 40,000 lbs can be carried. The flight crew numbers two persons.

Thanks to the combined use of sophisticated materials, coatings and shapes, the B-2A is practically invisible to enemy radar and can strike targets of great strategic importance on a global scale, with either nuclear or conventional weapons. Its performance in the Kosovo War confirmed the plane's potential; taking advantage of in-flight refueling, the B-2As flew a number of missions against targets in Serbia, with the planes taking off and landing from their home base of Whiteman, Missouri.

290 top A Northrop-Grumman B-2A Spirit stealth bomber taking off. The Spirit's performance is not exceptional, its effectiveness is due to its range and invisibility to radar systems.

290-291 The B-2A's two-man cockpit in close up. Also visible are the air intakes of the four jet engines housed inside the wings.

290-291 bottom The B-2A Spirit's unconventional and science-fiction forms show to advantage in this ground-based photograph.

291 bottom right The Spirit bomber's radar-absorbent paint accounts in part for its invisibility to radar.

292 top, 292-293 and 293 bottom The B-2's purity of line is captured in these three photographs. This is one aircraft that cannot be confused with any other.

292 center This B-2A in flight clearly shows the engine vents typical of a stealth aircraft.

Operation Allied Force officially concluded with the ceasefire of 20 June 1999. The objectives set by the political leaders of the NATO countries had been achieved, in particular the withdrawal of Serbian troops from Kosovo.

Of notable importance in this conflict was the fact that, despite the immense military and economic expenditure, the Allies attained a successful result with the loss of only two combat aircraft and without having to make recourse to land forces.

Given the particular political and ethnic scenario in the Balkan theater, land-based operations could have resulted only in expansion of the conflict and new international tensions, as well as the indefinite prolongation of the war with further suffering for the civilian population and significant casualty numbers on both sides.

292 bottom The B-2's ventral surfaces are perfectly smooth and slightly convex. This shot of a Spirit makes it easy to understand why some people thought the plane was a flying saucer from outer space!

At the dawn of our civilization's third millennium, a new and potentially very dangerous war broke out, the one against terrorism.

The 11 September 2001 attacks made against the United States by the terrorist organization, Al Qaeda, led by Saudi sheikh Osama bin Laden, caused a division to open between the Western and Moslem worlds, and led to international military action against those responsible, with the aim of destroying their organization.

Roughly a month after the attacks on the World Trade Center in New York and the Pentagon in Washington, which caused thousands of deaths, President Bush, authorized Operation Enduring Freedom, initially aimed against Afghanistan, bin Laden's terrorist stronghold.

This operation, still in progress at the time of writing, involves many US air units, including the US Navy's ship-borne aircraft, the USAF's tactical and strategic aircraft, and the special helicopter-based forces of the US Army and USAF. Forces of other allied countries have also contributed to the war effort. The 21st century has, unfortunately, begun in the same way the 20th century ended.

Chapter 23

Airbus and Boeing

In the 1960s, the global market for large airliners was in effect an American prerogative, with Boeing, Douglas and Lockheed sharing the vast majority of orders. However, during that period a new wind began to blow through Europe. Thanks to the intervention of national governments, the foundations were laid for the rebirth of the European aeronautical industry. A number of international projects, such as the Anglo-French Concorde and Jaguar and the tri-national Tornado, came into being. But the initiative that most influenced the global industrial scene was the Airbus project, which began in 1965 as the result of collaboration by France, Germany and Great Britain's governments and aviation industries.

The need for a twin-engined, wide-body, 300-passenger jet for medium-range operations was identified. The agreement that initiated the development of the aircraft, designated the Airbus A300, was signed on 26 September 1967. According to its terms, France and Great Britain were each to contribute 37.5% of the cost of the development and construction of the airframe, while Germany would provide the remaining 25%. With regard to the engines, Great Britain was to contribute 75% of the cost of developing the Rolls-Royce RB207 turbofan, while France and Germany were each to contribute 12.5%. The primary contractor for the airframe was to be Sud Aviation (later Aérospatiale). Airbus Industrie was officially constituted on 18 December 1970, to oversee the development, production and marketing of the A300. The Spanish firm CASA subsequently joined the consortium. Rolls-Royce announced that it would be unable to develop the RB207 engine in time, and this unit was replaced by the proven General Electric CF6-50 delivering 49,000 lbs of thrust. Another significant modification involved the reduction of seats from 300 to 250, as requested by the principal potential clients.

Construction of the prototype A300B1 began in September 1969, and its maiden flight took place on 28 October 1972 at Toulouse. In 1971, the consortium received its first order, with Air France requesting six planes plus options for a further ten. Two years later, in 1973, Lufthansa ordered three planes and placed options on a further four. After the third plane had been built, design modifications were made; the plane's fuselage was lengthened by 6 feet 6 inches and the more powerful CF6-50C engine, providing 51,000 lbs of thrust, was adopted. This modified model, designated the A300B2, could carry a greater payload and had a greater range .In March 1974, the European and American authorities certified the aircraft, and the fifth plane flew for the first time that year. It was the first to be delivered to a client, going to Air France on 11 May and entering service on 23 May on the Paris-London route.

The A300 had yet to win the confidence of the market, however, and sales were slow; in fact in 1976 the consortium failed to win a single order for the A300. It received a massive boost in May 1977, when the

296 top The four-jet A340 that first flew in 1991 is the largest plane in the Airbus family. This one belongs to Virgin Atlantic.

296 bottom The nose of an American Airlines' Airbus A300-600 in close-up. This model can seat 360 and was designed for medium- and long-range flights.

American company Eastern Airlines agreed to lease four A300B4s: this was the first contract to be won in the United States, and in breaking the monopoly American manufacturers enjoyed on their home turf, Airbus had taken a fundamental step forward. Nonetheless, by the end of 1978, the production total had almost reached 50 planes, and the break-even point appeared to be little closer. Airlines and their pilots considered the A300 to be an excellent aircraft and in 1979 and thereafter, thanks in part to the publicity provided by the Eastern Airlines deal, Airbus's stock began to rise. In the meantime, new versions of the original design were in mind that would eventually materialize as new projects. In 1983 the A300-600, which was to become the principal production variant, made its maiden flight. The A300-600 a wingspan of 144 feet 4 inches, a length of 177 feet 2 inches and a maximum take-off weight of about 189 tons. It could be ordered with two Pratt & Whitney PW4156 engines (delivering 56,000 lbs of thrust) or two PW4158s (58,000 lbs thrust) or alternatively with General Electric CF6-80C2A1/A3/A5 units delivering similar outputs. The plane had a top cruising speed of Mach 0.82 and in standard configuration could carry 266 passengers, with up to 361 in high-density configuration. The A310 model, with a shorter fuselage seating 210-234 passengers (255 at high density), a new wing and smaller tailplanes, had gone into development in 1978. The prototype flew for the first time on 3 April 1982 and the first delivery (to Lufthansa) took place in March 1984. The early 1980s saw development of the A320 model, an aircraft for medium- and short-haul work that could seat up to 179 passengers; it incorporated a

number of innovative features such as fly-by-wire controls and offered reduced operating costs. Air France was the first airline to order the 320, signing as early as 1981 for 25 planes. The prototype made its maiden flight on 22 February 1987. This base model was followed by a further two variants, the stretched A321 and the shortened A319. The A321 first flew on 11 March 1993 and was delivered to Lufthansa the following year. The A319 first flew on 29 August 1995, with the first delivery being made to Swissair the following year.

In the late 1980s Airbus was working on completion of its range with a large aircraft for medium- and long-haul flights. The A330/340 project was launched in 1987 and resulted in an average-capacity wide-body plane with a four-engine configuration (A340) or a-two-engine configuration (A330). The A340-300 prototype flew for the first time on 25 October 1991, followed by the short-fuselage

A340-200 version. The base model had a wingspan of 196 feet 10 inches and a length of 206 feet 8 inches, with a maximum take-off weight of about 283 tons. It was powered by four CFM International CFM-56-5C engines, each delivering 31,000 lbs of thrust, and was capable of a top speed of Mach 0.83 and had an operational range of about 6,800 miles. The standard configuration provided between 250 and 350 seats, but 440 could be squeezed in a maximum density format. The A330, which flew for the first time on 2 November 1991, retained the same dimensions, but was powered by two General Electric, Pratt & Whitney or Rolls-Royce engines (as specified by the client), with power outputs ranging from 64,000 to 67,000 lbs of thrust. It had a maximum take-off weight of about 233 tons and passenger capacities similar to those of its four-engined sister plane. The first A340 was delivered to Lufthansa in January 1993.

297 top The A320 developed by the Airbus consortium for short- and medium-range distances, seen here in Air Jamaica colors. The A320 first flew in 1987; it can seat 180 passengers.

296-297 An Alitalia Airbus A300 landing. The A300 was the first Airbus produced; it made its maiden flight in 1972.

299 bottom Boeing announced the 767 at the same time as the 757. The two are similar in shape. The 767 has much greater capabilities than its smaller brother and can carry up to 350 passengers, even on intercontinental flights. Shown here is the fuselage of a Boeing 767 being built in Boeing's Seattle, Oregon factory.

The American aircraft manufacturing industry was by no means idle in the face of the Airbus' growing technological and commercial importance. Boeing, now the sole remaining major company active in the civil airliner sector, began developing two new planes in the late 1970s that became operational in the 1980s. These planes marked the opening of a new era for Boeing and were intended to maintain the firm's advantage over its European rival.

The first of the two new Boeing planes was the 767, which flew for the first time on 26 September 1981.

In appearance the 767 was similar in appearance to the Airbus A300, with a wide-body fuselage, two engines slung beneath the wing and traditional tailplanes. It had a wingspan of 154 feet 3 inches, a length of 157 feet 6 inches and a maximum take-off weight of 345,000 lbs. It was powered by two turbofan engines, which could be chosen by the client from a list of twenty units built by General Electric, Pratt & Whitney and Rolls-Royce that ranged in power outputfrom 52,000 to 62,000 lbs of thrust. The standard configuration provided between 180 and 224 seats (285 at maximum density) and the 767-200 could maintain a cruising speed of Mach 0.8. The first production 767-200 was delivered to

United Airlines in 1982.

In 1986 Boeing introduced the 767-300 with a fuselage stretched to just over 180 feet and a standard configuration offering 218 seats, which could be increased to 350 in a maximum density format. The 767-300ER is the long-haul version; it has a maximum take-off weight of 204 tons and a range of more than 7,000 miles. The latest version is the 767-400ER, an aircraft capable of carrying about 290 passengers, and the first 400-ER was delivered to Delta Airlines on 29 August 2000.

The heir to the Boeing 727, this aircraft was designed for use on medium-range routes as a direct competitor to the A300. While it retained the same fuselage section as the 727, the 757 was an all-new plane that resembled a scaled-down version of the 767. The first 757 went into service with

Eastern Air Lines in January 1983. It had a wingspan of 124 feet 8 inches and a length of 154 feet 2 inches. Two Rolls-Royce RB211 or Pratt & Whitney PW2037 engines (delivering 40,000 and 38,000 lbs of thrust respectively) provided the 757 with a cruising speed of Mach 0.86 and a maximum take-off weight of 254,850 lbs. The 757 could carry between 150 and 178 passengers in standard configuration and 239 in a high-density format.

Naturally, the existing 747 "Jumbo Jet" series was exploited to the full, and in 1988 the 747-400 was introduced, featuring updated aerodynamics, engines and avionics. The typical configuration seated 420 passengers, but a high-density format for short-haul domestic flights allowed a maximum of 568 to be squeezed in.

In order to meet its clients' demands,

Boeing also introduced the 777 version, which completed its maiden flight on 12 June 1994. Externally, the new aircraft is very similar to the smaller 767, but is in fact an all-new design incorporating the most advanced technology. The launch customer for the 777 was United Airlines, which acquired the first one in May 1995. The 777 is a truly impressive aircraft, despite the fact the twin-engine layout makes it appear smaller than it really is: it has a wingspan of 196 feet 10 inches, a length of 206 feet 7 inches, and a maximum take-off weight of over 534,800

lbs. The engines (chosen by the client from units produced by the usual big three of General Electric, Pratt & Whitney and Rolls-Royce) have power outputs ranging from 74,000 lbs to 86,500 lbs of thrust. Passenger capacity ranges from 320 in a standard seating format to 440 in a high-density format. The basic 777 was followed in 1995 by the stretched 777-300. This variant has a length of 239 feet 6 inches (it is, in fact, the world's longest airplane) and with its increased maximum weight can carry between 350 and 550 passengers, depending on the seating format and the flight range required by the operating airline.

In the 1990s, McDonnell-Douglas decided to exploit the positive trends dominating the air transport markets by modernizing its MD-80 series. The first plane of the MD-90 series made its maiden flight on 22 February 1993. The plane featured electronically controlled engines, improved avionics and structural features, and a stretched fuselage that allowed for ten additional seats. The introduction of the MD-95 followed in 1995; this was an airliner in the 100-passenger class that, following Boeing's acquisition of McDonnell-Douglas in 1997, was redesignated the Boeing 717, joining the smallest 737 models at the lower end of the market.

Airbus has also continued to expand its aircraft range in the lower end of the sector, launching the A318 on 26 April 1999. This is a slightly smaller version of the 319, equipped with two Pratt & Whitney PW6000 engines and carrying about 100 passengers. The maiden flight of the new aircraft was scheduled for the end of 2001, but orders for over 120 planes have already been accepted.

In order to compete with Airbus's diversified range in the medium- and short-haul sector (where the 3 existing Airbus models had been joined by the A218), Boeing decided to revitalize its best-seller in this sector, the now antiquated 737. In the 1990s Boeing launched the 737 Next-Generation, once it could spare enough energy from its 767, 757 and 777 projects. The new project aimed to get the best out of the 737 design by equipping it with the most advanced technology available (engines, aerodynamics, avionics), in order to keep it competitive with the Airbus A319/320/321 in the important 100-200 seat sector.

The first 737 Next-Generation to fly was the 737-700, on 9 February 1997. This plane, which was positioned in the 128/149-seat segment, had a maximum take-off weight of about 77 tons and two engines producing

between 20,000-22,000 lbs of thrust. Other versions followed the 737-700. First was the 737-800, which flew for the first time on 31 July 1997. It was a 160/189-seat plane with a maximum take-off weight of 88 tons. Next came the 737-600 (maiden flight on 22 January 1998), 108-132 seats, maximum take-off weight of about 71 tons), and last, the 737-900 (the largest of the 737 family, maiden flight on 3 August 2000), with 177-189 seats and a similar specification to the 800 model.

These Boeing aircraft are dividing a significant portion of the commercial market with Airbus models. In January 1998, Airbus (with four models in the A318-A321 series) had a portfolio of 2,565 confirmed orders; Boeing had 1,360 orders for the 737 Next-Generation series. In fact, in June 2000 Boeing received a major order for 290 of the 737-700s from the Southwest Airlines, the American airline that in 1998 had been the launch customer for the model and which was already operating a fleet of 323 of the 737s in various guises.

With the world market in expansion and now divided between Boeing and Airbus, the two industrial colossi have recently launched themselves into the latest sector for new aircraft, that of the long-range super-giants. Their approaches to this market are quite

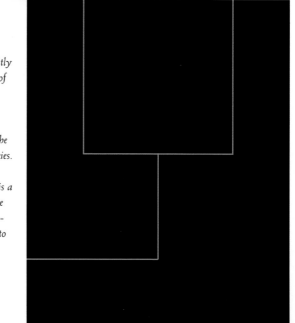

300-301 The Boeing Sonic Cruiser is the most advanced and innovative project currently being developed in the world of commercial aviation. Unlike Airbus, which has opted for large capacity, Boeing is focusing on greater speed in the battle for dominance of the skies.

300 center The Boeing 717 is a 100-seater jet derived from the McDonnell-Douglas MD80-90 family. It was brought into service in 1998.

300 bottom *The new 717 pilots' cabin, with advanced "glass-cockpit" instrumentation dominated by six multi-function color screens.*

301 center *An Airbus A380 in the colors of Emirates Airlines, one of the first to place an order for the new gigantic Airbus, capable of carrying 555 passengers in its standard version.*

301 bottom *A proposed interior for the large A380, the new generation Airbus for the third millennium.*

are the following versions: the 50R (with a shorter fuselage and maximum capacity of 481 seats), the 100R (longer flying distance) and the 200 (maximum weight of 590 tons and seats for 656 passengers). The A380's maiden flight should take place around the end of 2004.

different. After careful evaluation and research, Airbus has opted for the construction of the largest airplane ever built, while Boeing has chosen to go for the fastest (apart from Concorde).

The Airbus aircraft – the A380 – was officially launched on 19 December 2000 when an order from Virgin Airlines brought the order book to a total of 50, which had been fixed as the minimum number for Airbus to begin the program. The basic A380-100 will have a wingspan of 259 feet 4 inches, a length of 237 feet 3 inches and a maximum take-off weight of 540 tons. The standard layout will have an upper and lower deck capable of seating 555 passengers. The motors will be Rolls-Royce Trent 900s or General Electric GP7000s, both of which can produce 68,200 lbs of thrust. The plane's range should be 8,875 miles. Also planned

Boeing, on the other hand, is following a different path: that of building a smaller but faster long-range plane, the Sonic Cruiser. The project was announced in March 2001, and revolves around an airplane with canard twin-jets with a dual delta-wing, able to cruise at an altitude of between 39,000 and 48,750 feet at a speed of Mach 0.98 so as to reduce current flying times by 15 to 20%

(two or more hours on Atlantic routes). It should be able to seat around 300 passengers. Boeing estimates that the Sonic Cruiser will come into production between 2006 and 2008. At the same time, the American company is continuing development of the 747 with plans for the 747-400X Quiet Longer Range that will meet the strictest limits on noise pollution.

The struggle between Boeing and Airbus has only just begun; significant developments are likely to occur in the 21st century, reflecting trends in the air transport market and the ability of the world's skies to absorb increased airline traffic.

They have, however, many plans for the future, and innovation seems more drawn toward aerodynamic efficiency and cutting down on noise pollution than toward speed. Lockheed-Martin and Airbus are separately studying models fitted with a "box wing" (or "joined wng"), i.e., a single wing in the shape of a rhomboid. The European Commission is financing a project (directed by Airbus and Daimler-Chrysler) to develop a new aircraft with hydrogen-powered engines (the Cryoplane), whose emissions would be simply harmless water and nitrogen oxide.

Chapter 24

Today and Tomorrow

The twenty-first century future of aviation has already begun, and the trends and problems likely to affect this avant-garde aspect of modern technology and the global industrial economy can already be seen. In the field of air transport, the research programs initiated by the industrial giants Boeing and Airbus have identified a market in dramatic expansion. Passenger transport ought to grow by an average of 4.8% per year, reaching 1.5 billion passengers by 2015, against the 600 million currently carried. It appears, therefore, that between 2000 and 2020 the world's airlines will require more than 22,000 new passenger planes, and the global airliner fleet is likely to increase from a current total of 13,670 aircraft to over 31,000. These are stunning figures that, should they prove to be accurate, will not only inflate the profits and market values of the manufacturing companies and airlines, but will also create

severe problems for the air-traffic control systems and airport structures and facilities.

Boeing, however, does not foresee a great demand for enormous aircraft, but rather the expansion of the 70-seat class of regional airliners. Moreover, the company is convinced that on long-haul flights, passengers prefer medium-sized planes for the greater comfort they offer and the convenience of being able to catch direct flights from airports that are less congested than the great international hubs such as London, Los Angeles, and New York. Airbus has a contrasting view of future trends and, has now given the go-ahead for its A380 project for a vast new aircraft.

The military sector is not in such good health as the civil aviation industry, even though the forecasts for the period 1999-2003 indicate the possible sale of 2,600 aircraft, the equivalent of 38% of the entire global production. Naturally, the end of the Cold War is largely responsible for the

contraction of the sector, along with increases in purchase and operational costs, and the reduction of military budgets around the world.

Nonetheless, the need to modernize many air forces (albeit with the acquisition of ever smaller numbers of aircraft) will ensure that the fighter sector in particular will remain active and interesting over the coming years.

The fighter aircraft field is dominated by a

302 top A pair of JAS39 Gripen multi-role fighters with air-to-surface missiles. The Gripen is a small and relatively low-cost aircraft built to meet Swedish defense requirements.

302-303 The Lockheed-Boeing F-22A Raptor is the new superfighter selcted by the USAF. It is an exceptional aircraft in a class apart from other nations' new entries.

new generation of combat planes about to enter active service. One of these, the JAS 39 Gripen, is already in service with the Swedish air force. Produced by Industrigruppen JAS (led by Saab), the Gripen was conceived in Sweden in the early 1980s as a multi-role successor to the Viggen and the Draken. Characterized by sophisticated fly-by-wire flight controls, simplified maintenance, advanced avionics, and true multi-role capabilities, the JAS 39 flew for the first time on 9t December 1988. However, owing to delays in the development of the control software (which caused two crashes), deliveries to the air force began only in 1993, with the first military pilots being able to fly the plane two years later.

The Gripen is a small airplane, with a wingspan of 26 feet 3 inches, a length of 45 feet 11 inches, and a maximum take-off weight of about 27,500 lbs. Its Volvo RM12 turbofan delivers just over 18,000 lbs of thrust on afterburn and can power the Gripen to a top speed of about 1,243 mph. A two-seat combat training version has also been developed. Sweden has ordered 204 Gripens, with deliveries due to be completed

very advanced multi-role fighter's entrance into service has been postponed more than once for reasons of cost. The Rafale was developed as the successor to the French air force's Jaguars and Mirage 2000 series and the French navy's F-8s and Super É/Etendard's, and the first Rafale prototype flew on 4 July 1986, with the plane due to enter service in the mid-1990s. The Rafale is a twin-engined design that to ensure maximum maneuverability features canard aerodynamic surfaces and a delta wing. It has a wingspan of 32 feet 9.5 inches, a length of 49 feet 2.5 inches and a maximum take-off weight of 43,000 lbs. Its weapons system comprises up to 17,630 lbs of external armament along with a 30-mm cannon. Three versions of the aircraft have been developed: the C and B (two-seater) for the air force and the carrier-borne M version and the two-seater MB) for the navy. The M version was actually the first to enter service, in the December of 2000, at the Llandivisiau base, while the first planes for the air force will not enter service before 2005-2006, a delay caused by budget problems that have also had a negative effect on exports. The Rafale (of which 350 are due

demonstrator built by Lockheed-Martin and Boeing to compete with the Northrop-McDonnell-Douglas YF-23 in the USAF's ATF competition, designed to produce a successor to the F-15 Eagle. In April 1991, the YF-22 was officially declared the winner, and six years passed before the maiden flight of the first pre-production F-22A Raptor on 7 September 1997. In the meantime, a number of modifications that were made and the project was revised for budgetary reasons, leading to a delay in production start-up and a reduction from 750 to 442 — and then to 339 — in the number of planes to be built. The testing program was due to be completed by the end of 2002, and the first F-22As should reach the selected air force units in 2003 but will not be operational until 2005. By any criterion, the Raptor is an exceptional aircraft, a generation in advance of other new fighters: it boasts a supersonic cruising speed (apparently Mach 1.5), highly advanced avionics and sensors, fantastic maneuverability combined with stealth technology, and armaments contained in three internal bays. These comprise up to eight air-to-air missiles or about 2,200 lbs of

303 right A Dassault Rafale B two-seater in flight. This French multi-role fighter first flew in 1986 but economic difficulties delayed its entry into service with the French navy until December 2000. The French air force will begin using the Rafale in 2005-2006.

in 2007. This model could also enjoy significant export success as Saab has joined up with British Aerospace in the marketing field. Large contracts have already been signed with the air forces of South Africa, Hungary and the Czech Republic, and others are expected for nations that require a new modern fighter at a relatively limited cost.

The Dassault Rafale anticipated the Gripen's maiden flight by two years, but this

to be produced for the two French armed forces) is certainly an expensive as well as sophisticated aircraft, but it represents a valid alternative for those countries unwilling to over-commit themselves to products from the United States or Russia.

In the United States, on 29 September 1990, the first prototype for the USAF's future air-superiority fighter made its maiden flight. The plane is the YF-22, a technological

bombs, plus a further 19,850 lbs carried on four underwing pylons. The Raptor has a wingspan of 42 feet 7.5 inches, a length of 59 feet, and a maximum take-off weight of over 59,500 lbs. It is powered by two Pratt & Whitney F119-PW-100 turbofans delivering about 34,830 lbs of thrust on afterburn and thrust-vectoring nozzles, and providing a thrust-weight ration of 1.4 and a top speed of over 1,245 mph.

Another European contender among the new generation of fighters for the 21st century is the multinational Eurofighter 2000, built by a consortium formed by Great Britain, Germany, Italy and Spain. The origins of the project date back to 1983, and in 1986 British Aerospace flew a technology demonstrator (the EAP) in order to gather data for its new fighter designated the EFA (European Fighter Aircraft) that was due to enter service in the mid-1990s. The EJ200 engines were also all new and built by a four-nation consortium. The aircraft features a delta wing with canard aerodynamic surfaces, a square-section belly air intake, twin engines and single vertical stabilizer. However, the project development encountered a series of political, economic and technical nature, and early in the 1990s it was revised and the plane redesignated the EF.2000. The first of seven prototypes flew for the first time on 27 March 1994, and deliveries of the first pre-production planes already took place in 2002; in 2003 should then see the first deliveries of the production version. The EF.2000 will replace various aircraft operated by the armed forces of the four nations involved, including the F-104, F-4, Jaguar, Tornado ADV and Mirage F.1. It will have multi-role capabilities and be equipped with advanced radar systems, sensors, avionics and armaments and it will be highly maneuverable. The EF 2000 has a wingspan of 32 feet 9.5 inches, a length of 49 feet 2.5 inches and a

The very latest super-fighters are two planes developed in the United States by Lockheed-Martin and Boeing in response to the competition the U.S. Department of Defense launched in 1996 for a the Joint Strike Fighter (JSF), a new fighter-bomber for the USAF, the US Navy and the Marines. The new plane would replace numerous aircraft currently in use, such as the F-16, A-10, F/A-18 and AV-8B. The British Royal Air Force and the Royal Navy are also looking at this plane as a replacement for their Harrier fleets. The program is on a vast scale and should eventually involve a total of about 3,000 aircraft, business worth some $200-400 billion over a period of thirty-plus years. The plane will be developed in three different forms with a high percentage of common components: a land version (CTOL), a carrier-borne version (CV) and a short take-off and vertical landing variant (STOVL).

Boeing has introduced the X-32, which completed its maiden flight on 18 September 2000. The X-32 is a single-engine, single-seat plane with a curved trapezoidal wing, dual vertical stabilizers and a large chin intake. The definitive version of the aircraft

304 top A Eurofighter EF.2000 during a maneuver at a high attack angle, as shown by its wingtip trails. The Typhoon is highly maneuverable and powerful; it is rated second only to the F-22 as the most advanced Western fighter.

304 center An EF.2000 with German colors. The four nations in the consortium have already ordered 593 of these aircraft.

304 bottom A prototype of the X-35C, a vertical take-off and landing plane built by Lockheed-Martin for the Joint Strike Fighter competition. It is the tactical fighter of the future for the USAF, US Navy and Marines.

maximum take-off weight of more than 49,500 lbs. It is powered by two Eurojet EJ200 turbofans, each delivering about 19,850 lbs of thrust on afterburn, and should be capable of a top speed of about 1,300 mph. Named the Typhoon, the EF.2000 should enjoy reasonable success on the export markets. Greece has already signed an initial contract for 60 planes.

should have had a swept wing with horizontal tailplanes and modifications to the air intake and stabilizers. With regard to the STOVL version, Boeing had chosen the "direct lift" system, similar to that already employed in the Harriers and using a Pratt & Whitney 119-614 engine delivering about 42,000 lbs of thrust with afterburn.

Lockheed-Martin proposed its X-35 design, with a prototype that flew for the first time on 24 October 2000. The prototype seemed to be more conventional, with a wing and tailplanes similar to those of the F-22, dual vertical stabilizers and air intakes either side of the fuselage. The plane is powered by a &W 119 engine in 611 form, with a power output of about 36,800 lbs of thrust. The STOVL utilizes the "lift fan" system in which part of the thrust is provided by the engine (with a nozzle that can be directed downward through 110°), while the remainder comes from a fan located in the forward part of the fuselage. Both aircraft are equipped with internal bomb bays, stealth technology, and highly particularly advanced avionics.

The winner of the JSF competition was announced by the US. Department of Defense on 26 October 2001: it was the Lockheed-Martin project that will be designated the F-35. The versions will be referred to as the F-35A for the conventional model, the F-35B for the ship-borne model, and the F-35C for the STOVL version. The first deliveries to the American forces are expected to be begin in 2010, with the first planes being delivered to the Marines.

The program also involves the participation of a number of other countries, NATO states and otherwise, whose aerospace industries will probably be involved in the serial production of the aircraft, making it possibly the most important military project of the first half of the 21st century.

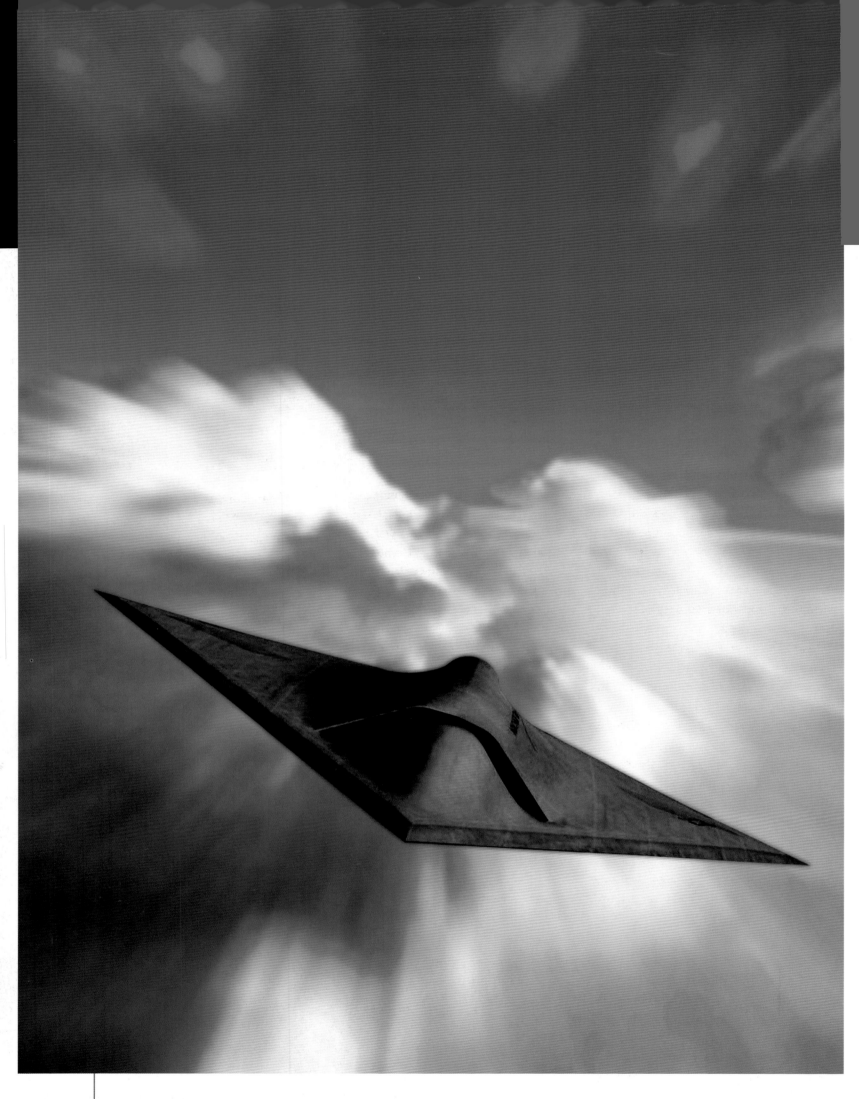

306 The X-47 Pegasus, a UCAV (Unmanned Combat Air Vehicles which fly without a pilot) project that Northrop-Grumman presented to the US Navy in 2001. UCAVs will probably be the combat aircraft of the future.

307 top left The HyperSoar is one of the projects that may affect the future: it is a hyperfast (roughly Mach 10) aircraft, 77 feet long, able to fly at an altitude of 195,000 feet. This US government study could have repercussions in both the military and civilian fields.

307 top right The Lockheed-Martin Dark Star, a UCAV for 21st-century wars, is one of the many projects currently under development.

307 bottom left The Northrop-Grumman Global Hawk, a UAV (unmanned air vehicle) that the USAF used for strategic reconnaissance in the war in Afghanistan. UAVs will become increasingly common in reconnaissance roles.

307 bottom right A General Atomics RQ-1A Predator, used by the USAF's 57th Flight Wing. This UAV was used in combat for reconnaissance during the war in Kosovo and, more recently, has been armed with Hellfire missiles.

Quite apart from development that will focus individual technological components and systems such as materials, engines and avionics (hardware and software), anther developmental thrust is evident. An entire category of aircraft appears to be destined to establish itself, and perhaps dominate the new century. Designated Unmanned Air Vehicles (UAVs), these planes are the heirs to the reconnaissance and observation craft that began to be used in the military sphere from about the 1970s. UAVs came to general attention during the Kosovo War in 1999, when they were widely used for perilous reconnaissance missions over enemy territory. The most advanced UAV technology is currently in the hands of the United States and Israel, who produce a vast range of machines with diverse characteristics, especially in terms of range, dimensions and the size of their payloads. UAVs are small, lightweight aircraft, often relatively inexpensive and propeller-driven. They are generally used for surveillance and target-identification roles. Among the UAVs currently in service are the USAF's General Atomics RQ-1A Predator (used by the USAF), the Bombardier CL-289, and Israel's IAI Hunter and Pioneer. Other models, such as the Teledyne Ryan Global Hawk and the Lockheed-Martin Dark Star, are under development. Research is continuing on increasing the size and complexity of UAVs so that they can execute increasingly sophisticated missions. The future will, in fact, see the introduction of UCAVs, SUAVs and URAVs. The UCAVs (Unmanned Combat Air Vehicles) will be pilotless planes capable of undertaking combat missions such as the suppression of enemy anti-aircraft defenses or attacks on well-protected targets, both of which tasks are highly dangerous for conventional piloted airplanes. Two projects in particular that are current under way, the Lockheed-Martin/US Navy and the Boeing DARPA/Air Force UCAV, could also be developed for use in air defense roles.

SUAVs (Support UAVs) and URAVs (Unmanned Reconnaissance Air Vehicles) will be developed for specialized tasks such as maintenance of satellite communications, monitoring of meteorological conditions, airborne-radar control and reconnaissance in various forms (electro-optical, radar and infra-red) in order to overcome the deficiencies of satellite systems. The introduction of UCAVS will probably be very gradual, first alongside and under the control of piloted aircraft, but eventually undertaking independent missions, guided by pilots safely seated in front of control consoles in air-conditioned bunkers.

It is, of course, very difficult to predict the technological developments that may be introduced in 20 or 30 years time, especially given the incredible and rapid progress made in information technology and wireless communications at the end of the 20th century. Spaceports, passenger vehicles capable of cruising in space, hydrogen engines and so on are already being discussed.

What is certain, however, is that the aerospace sector, ever the cutting edge of the industrialized world, will remain one of the most significant areas of research and development in the future, and the one capable of providing mankind with the most remarkable surprises.

Chapter 25

The Space Shuttle

The Apollo 11 mission launched by NASA (National Aeronautical and Space Agency) in 1969, which culminated in man's first steps on the moon, also crowned the famous "space race." This is the technological battle the United States and the Soviet Union fought throughout the 1950s and 1960s for what was unrealistically termed the "conquest of space." In fact, Apollo-type missions revealed all too evident limitations: enormous costs for what were effectively throwaway space systems with restricted payloads. By the 1960s it was clear that NASA would have to establish an alternative space program that would permit an enduring and productive presence in space and thus a greater return on the necessary investment. NASA then opted for the Space Transport System (STS), a reusable shuttle capable of carrying large loads into orbit and performing both civil and military duties.

Historically, the idea of the space shuttle dated as far back as the 1940s, as confirmed by the studies Saenger and von Braun conducted in Germany. In the 1950s, German scientists working in the United States revived the concept when NACA

(later reorganized as NASA) focused on various research projects that culminated in the design of a piloted space glider for the USAF. While this vehicle had to be launched aboard a missile, it could return to earth and land as an aircraft. The program was named the X-20 Dyna Soar in 1959 and was to have used a Titan III missile as a carrier. In 1963, owing to the high costs and restricted payload, as well as the channeling of resources toward the Apollo program, the X-20 was abandoned. NASA nonetheless continued to support research into "lifting bodies," i.e., gliding aircraft with load-bearing fuselages. Late in 1969, NASA's Integrated Space Program called for a permanent space station with 50 occupants, space shuttles linking it to the earth, and possibly a moon colony and another on Mars, to be operational by 1985. Central to this program was the concept of the reusable spacecraft. On 3 January 1972 President Nixon gave the Space Shuttle Program the go-ahead, by and by year-end NASA and North American Rockwell completed their initial examination of the new vehicle's required technical specifications. The first shuttle launch was planned for March 1979.

The program's underlying concept was

the creation of two complementary piloted units: one being a carrier, the other to be used for operational missions. However, the costs involved in this approach proved to be unacceptable, and NASA decided to go ahead with a single piloted mission craft (the Orbiter), with two boosters used to lift it into orbit that would be detachable but still reusable. With regard to the boosters, the choice of a liquid or solid propellant was still problematical. Painstaking research eventually came down in favor of a solid propellant as this made the recovery and reuse of the booster units easier.

The shuttle's final configuration featured a forward section containing the crew module, with the cockpit and all the flight and control avionics; a central bay destined to house the payload; and a rear section containing the engines and their shielding. To this was added the wing and undercarriage and the vertical stabilizer. The airframe was constructed in aluminum or aluminum alloys. The shuttle's nervous system was composed of five IBM AP101 computers. Of these, four were dedicated to flight, navigation, and reciprocal control functions; the fifth governed the on-board systems during orbital operations and was available

308 top John W. Young and Robert L. Crippen, the crew in the first Space Shuttle mission (STS-1). They lifted off on 12 April 1981.

308 bottom The NASA control room for Shuttle missions.

fuel supply is contained in a detachable external tank 154 feet long and just over 26 feet wide, holding 665 tons of liquid oxygen and 111 tons of liquid hydrogen. The external tank is the only non-reusable part of the space shuttle. Two large solid rocket boosters (SRB) 147 feet 8" long provide an extra 3,300 tons of take-off thrust from a solid propellant. With this propulsive system, the shuttle is capable of accelerating from standstill at ground level to Mach 25 (around 15,500 mph) at an altitude of around 77.5 miles in 8.5 minutes.

as an emergency backup during the approach and landing phases. The principal features of the Space Shuttle Program concerned the propulsion system and the thermal shield; both were sources of significant problems and made notable contributions to the delays suffered by the project.

The shuttle engines have different functions and uses. Three main engines make up the SSME (Space Shuttle Main Engines) system, their principal characteristic is that they have been designed for repeated use, the equivalent of around 7.5 hours or 55 shuttle missions; each unit provides around 200 tons of thrust. The main engines can be ignited or shut down a number of times during a mission, thrust delivery can be adjusted (within a range of 65-105% of full power), and they have vectoring nozzles. The shuttle is also equipped with two smaller engines, each providing about 6,150 lbs of thrust. These are used to achieve orbit once the main engines have been shut down and to provide thrust for maneuvering and re-entry. Lastly, 42 small rockets developing between 22 and 880 lbs of thrust provide fine maneuvering control in space. The main

The shuttle's second crucial feature is its thermal protection system (TPS). This is the skin designed to protect the shuttle from the enormous temperatures it generates as it re-enters the earth's atmosphere. The most critical surface areas (which add up to about 400 square feet) record about 1,650°C, while

the entire underside records about 1,260°C. To protect these surfaces, NASA and Rockwell developed 8"x 8" heat-resistant tiles, designed to last up to 100 missions before needing replacement. Some 32,000 of these tiles cover the shuttle's key areas. Tiles made of carbon fiber impregnated and coated with silicon protect the shuttle's most critical areas; tiles made of fiberglass impregnated with boron silicate and covered with black silicon carbon cover all other areas of the shuttle that are affected by the heat build-up. Unfortunately, the shuttle's test-flight program has revealed that mechanical stresses cause a number of tiles to detach, and that they are not as durable as had been expected. The problem has been resolved by impregnating the undersurface of the tiles with a silicon-based bonding concentrate. The tiles were also reinforced with boron fibers.

The first shuttle to be completed was OV-101 *Enterprise,* used for flight-testing the aerodynamics and the electronics, above all in the landing phase. These tests were

conducted at NASA's Dryden Center at Edwards Air Base in California.

Assembly work on *Enterprise* began on 4 June 1974 at Palmdale, California and the finished vehicle was presented on 17 September 1976. Initial testing was conducted between 18 February and 2 March 1977, with five flights undertaken with the shuttle installed piggyback on a NASA Boeing 747, with no astronauts aboard. In the second phase, conducted between June and July, *Enterprise* remained attached to the 747, but carried its own pilots who were able to check that all systems were functioning correctly. Finally, between August and October 1977, five glides from an altitude of 24,000 feet were completed, with the shuttle landing on Edwards Air Base's salt-lake facilities. Subsequently, *Enterprise* was subjected to further tests, while the second vehicle, OV-102 *Columbia,* was prepared for the first true mission, STS-1. The space shuttle's maiden flight in fact took place on 12 April 1981, at 12.00.04 GMT, with a take-off from the Kennedy Space Center, Florida. Aboard were astronauts John Young (commander) and Robert Crippen (pilot); the mission lasted 54 hours, 20 minutes and 32 seconds, with *Columbia* landing at Edwards Air Base runway 23 on 14 April. Seven months later, on 12 November 1981, *Columbia* also undertook mission STS-2, thus demonstrating the perfect re-usability of the space shuttle system.

In total, two test-bench vehicles, MPTA-098 and STA-099, and two orbiters, OV-101 *Enterprise* and OV-102 *Columbia* were constructed. While *Enterprise* was never used for space flight, one of the experimental vehicles, STA-099, was subsequently modified to orbiter specification and redesignated the OV-099. NASA thus had four flying shuttles, OV-102 *Columbia*, OV-099 *Challenger* (first flight, 4 April1983), OV-103 *Discovery* (30 August 1984) and OV-104 *Atlantis* (3 October 1985).

On 28 January 1986, a terrible accident rocked the program. A leak in the *Challenger*'s fuel system caused a fire and explosion that completed destroyed the shuttle as it took off for the 26th mission; all seven crew were killed. Shuttle OV-105 *Endeavor,* ordered in 1987 and delivered on 25 April 1991, made its first orbital flight on 7 May 1992. *Endeavor* featured numerous improvements resulting from almost a decade of operational experience. The new space shuttle boasted uprated avionics, engines, tiles (lighter and stronger), fuel system, APU and on-board systems that enabled it to stay in space for up to 28 days. Moreover, the new shuttle introduced a braking parachute capable of reducing its landing run by about 1,650 feet. These modifications were subsequently introduced into the other three shuttles during routine maintenance operations.

The Space Shuttle Program has been

widely used to transport and release into orbit telecommunications and observation satellites, to repair the Hubble space telescope, to conduct scientific experiments in a zero-gravity environment and to install instrumentation for further experiments. Recently, the suttles have been working primarily on the construction of the International Space Station, a project involving 16 nations, countries a structure

that has been in orbit since 1998 and permanently inhabited since 2000. The ISS will be completed in 2005. Shuttle mission STS-111 (the next as this book goes to press), was due to take-off on 30 May 2002. The Space Shuttle Program itself is due to continue for another 15-20 years, but there is considerable pressure for the entire fleet and the related infrastructure to be radically modernized to ensure that operations can proceed safely until the shuttle's successor is introduced.

Currently, the shuttle program is incredibly expensive. Each launch is estimated to cost more than $450 million, and the annual number of missions has recently been reduced from six to four. NASA employs about 30,000 people just to maintain keep its shuttle fleet. Unfortunately, the X-33 and X-34 programs launched in the late 1990s to develop the re-usable vehicle of the future were cancelled on 1 March 2001, owing to an unacceptable rise in costs. As a result, the future of American orbital space flights is uncertain.

310 top Astronauts Hoffman and Musgrave install the Hubble space telescope in the hold of the shuttle Endeavor in December 1993.

310 bottom The shuttle Challenger in orbit with its hold open and the mechanical arm ready for use.

311 left Atlantis is shown docking with the Mir space station in June 1995 during a joint US-Soviet mission.

311 right Astronaut Tamara Jernigan was a member of the STS-96 mission; here she is busy with a component of the Russian Strela crane, part of the mission's load. The Earth's surface can be seen behind her.

312-313 What the future holds in store: the International Space Station is nearly complete and a Shuttle is attached to the docking point.

BIBLIOGRAPHY

BOOKS

AA.VV., *Ali italiane,* vols.1-4, Milan, 1978.

AA.VV., *Guerre in tempo di pace,* dal 1945, Novara, 1983.

AA.VV., *Ali sul mondo,* Florence, 1990.

AA.VV., *Russia's Top Guns,* New York, 1990.a

AA.VV., *Gulf Air War Debrief,* London, 1991.

AA.VV., *Warplanes of the Luftwaffe,* London, 1994.

AA.VV., *Brassey's World Aircraft & Systems Directory,* London, 1996.

AA.VV., *Aerei di tutto il mondo, militari e civili,* Novara, 1997.

AA.VV., *The Aerospace Encyclopedia of Air Warfare,* vols.1-2, London, 1997.

AA.VV., *Aerospace Encyclopedia of World Air Forces,* London, 1999.

Angelucci, E. & Matricardi, P., *Atlante enciclopedico degli aerei militari del mondo,* Milan, 1990.

Chant, C., *Aviation Record Breaker,* London, 1988.

Cohen, E., *Israel's Best Defence,* Shrewsbury, 1994.

D'Avanzo, G., *Evoluzione del caccia NATO,* Florence, 1987.

Dorr, R. F. & Bishop, C., *Vietnam Air War Debrief,* London, 1996.

Francillon, R. J., *The United States Air National Guard,* London, 1993.

Jarrett, P., *Ultimate Aircraft,* London, 2000.

Kaminski, T. & Williams, M., *The United States Military Aviation Directory,* Norwalk, 2000.

Licheri S., *Storia del volo e delle operazioni aeree e spaziali da Icaro ai nostri giorni,* Rome, 1997.

Luttwak E. & Koehl S. L., *La Guerra Moderna,* Milan, 1992.

Niccoli R., *American Eagles,* Novara, 1997.

Niccoli R., *Aerei,* Istituto Geografico DeAgostini, Novara, 1998.

Niccoli R., *Ali Tricolori,* Novara, 1998.

Salvadori M. L., *Storia dell'età contemporanea,* vol. 3, Loescher Editore, 1986.

Steijger C., *A History of the United States Air Force Europe,* Shrewsbury, 1991.

Taylor M. J. H., *Jane's American*

Fighting Aircraft of the 20th Century, New York, 1991.

Willmott N. & Pimlott J., *Strategy & Tactics of War,* London, 1983.

Yenne B., *The History of the US Air Force,* London, 1990.

Zetner C., *La guerra del dopoguerra,* Milan, 1970.

ENCYCLOPAEDIAS

The Epic of Flight, AA.VV., 23 volumes, 1981.

L'Aviazione, grande enciclopedia illustrata, AA.VV, 12 volumes, Novara, 1982.

MAGAZINES

Rivista Aeronautica, Stato Maggiore Aeronautica, Italy.

Volare, Editoriale Domus, Italy.

JP-4, mensile di aeronautica, ED.A.I., Italy.

Rivista Italiana Difesa, Giornalistica Riviera Coop., Italy.

Air International, Key Publishing, Great Britain.

Air Forces Monthly, Key Publishing, Great Britain.

Wings of Fame, Aerospace Publishing, Great Britain.

International Air Power Review, AIRtime Publishing, USA-Great Britain.

Combat Aircraft, AIRtime Publishing, USA.

INDEX

PHOTOGRAPHIC CREDITS

PREFACE
Page 1 Il Dagherrotipo
Pages 2-3 John M. Dibbs/The Plane Picture Company
Pages 4-5 Corbis/Grazia Neri
Page 5 bottom right Mary Evans Picture Library
Pages 6-7 Contrasto
Pages 8-9 Corbis/Grazia Neri

CHAPTER 1
Page 11 right Index
Pages 12-13 Il Dagherrotipo
Page 12 bottom left Il Dagherrotipo
Page 13 top Il Dagherrotipo
Page 13 bottom Il Dagherrotipo
Page 14 top Photos12
Pages 14-15 Mary Evans Picture Library
Page 15 left Mary Evans Picture Library
Page 15 top Mary Evans Picture Library
Page 15 right Mary Evans Picture Library
Page 15 bottom left Photos12
Page 15 bottom right Photos12
Page 16 top Double's
Page 16 bottom Photos12
Pages 16-17 Photos12
Page 17 bottom Photos12
Page 18 top left Science Photo Library/ Grazia Neri
Page 18 center Otto Lilienthal Museum
Page 18 top right Otto Lilienthal Museum
Page 18 center top right Otto Lilienthal Museum
Page 18 center bottom right Otto Lilienthal Museum
Page 18 bottom right Hulton Achive/Laura Ronchi
Page 19 top Otto Lilienthal Museum
Page 19 left center left Otto Lilienthal Museum
Page 19 center right Otto Lilienthal Museum
Page 19 bottom right Mary Evans Picture Library
Page 19 bottom center Archivio Privato
Page 20 top right Hulton Archive/ Laura Ronchi
Page 20 bottom Roger Viollet/Contrasto
Page 21 top Hulton Archive/Laura Ronchi
Pages 20-21 Photos12
Pages 22-23 Photos12
Page 22 left Mary Evans Picture Library
Page 22 right Mary Evans Picture Library
Page 23 top Photos12
Page 23 bottom Il Dagherrotipo

CHAPTER 2
Page 24 Photos12
Pages 24-25 top Roger Viollett/Contrasto
Pages 24-25 bottom Il Dagherrotipo
Page 26 left Archiv Luftshiffbau Zeppelin
Pages 26-27 bottom Hulton Archive/ Laura Ronchi
Page 27 top Archiv Luftshiffbau Zeppelin
Page 27 center right Archiv Luftshiffbau Zeppelin
Page 27 bottom Archiv Luftshiffbau Zeppelin
Pages 28-29 Archiv Luftshiffbau Zeppelin
Page 28 bottom right Archiv Luftshiffbau Zeppelin
Page 28 bottom left Archiv Luftshiffbau Zeppelin
Page 29 top Archiv Luftshiffbau Zeppelin
Page 29 bottom left Archiv Luftshiffbau Zeppelin
Page 29 bottom right Archiv Luftshiffbau Zeppelin
Pages 30-31 Hulton Archive/Laura Ronchi
Page 30 bottom left Archiv Luftshiffbau Zeppelin
Page 30 bottom right Archiv Luftshiffbau Zeppelin
Page 31 top Hulton Archive/Laura Ronchi
Page 31 center right Hulton Archive/ Laura Ronchi
Page 31 bottom Hulton Archive/Laura Ronchi
Page 32 top Publifoto Olimpia
Page 32 center Archivio G. Apostolo
Page 32 bottom left Il Dagherrotipo
Page 32 bottom right Il Dagherrotipo
Page 33 top Il Dagherrotipo
Pages 32-33 Hulton Archive/Laura Ronchi
Page 34 top Archivio Privato
Page 34 bottom Il Dagherrotipo
Pages 34-35 Archivio G. Apostolo
Page 35 center right Archivio Privato
Page 35 bottom Il Dagherrotipo
Page 36 top Moffet Field Historical Society

Page 36 bottom Moffet Field Historical Society
Page 37 top left Corbis/Grazia Neri
Page 37 top right Moffet Field Historical Society
Page 37 bottom Moffet Field Historical Society

CHAPTER 3
Pages 38-39 Hulton Archive/Laura Ronchi
Page 38 bottom left Roger Viollet/Contrasto
Page 39 top left Hulton Archive/ Laura Ronchi
Page 39 top right Hulton Archive/ Laura Ronchi
Page 39 bottom left Popper Foto/Vision
Page 39 bottom right Popper Foto/Vision
Page 40 top Roger Viollet/Contrasto
Pages 40-41 Il Dagherrotipo
Page 40 bottom Corbis/Grazia Neri
Page 41 bottom Hulton Archive/Laura Ronchi
Page 42 top left Roger Viollet/ Contrasto
Page 42 top right Musee De L'Air
Page 42 center right Roger Viollet/ Contrasto
Page 42 bottom left Roger Viollet/ Contrasto
Page 43 top left Archivio A. Colombo
Page 43 top right Photos12
Page 43 bottom right Hulton Archive/ Laura Ronchi
Page 44 top Musee De L'Air
Page 44 bottom Roger Viollet/Contrasto
Page 45 top left Photos12
Page 45 top right Hulton Archive/ Laura Ronchi
Page 45 bottom Publifoto Olimpia
Page 46 Hulton Archive/Laura Ronchi
Page 47 top Musee De L'Air
Page 47 center Popper Foto/Vision
Page 47 bottom Archivio G. Apostolo
Page 48 Popper Foto/Vision
Pages 48/49 Archivio G. Apostolo
Page 49 top Publifoto Olimpia

CHAPTER 4
Page 50 left Il Dagherrotipo
Page 50 right Il Dagherrotipo
Page 50 bottom Il Dagherrotipo
Page 51 top left Denver Public Library
Page 51 center Il Dagherrotipo
Page 51 bottom left Il Dagherrotipo
Page 51 bottom right Il Dagherrotipo
Page 52 top Publifoto Olimpia
Page 52 bottom Il Dagherrotipo
Pages 52-53 Il Dagherrotipo
Page 53 bottom left Il Dagherrotipo
Page 53 bottom right Il Dagherrotipo
Page 54 top Hulton Archive/Laura Ronchi
Page 54 bottom Photos12
Page 55 top left Photos12
Page 55 top right The Bridgeman Art Library
Page 55 bottom Roger Viollet/Contrasto
Page 56 top Roger Viollet/Contrasto
Page 56 top left TRH Pictures
Page 56 center left TRH Pictures
Page 56 bottom Archivio R. Niccoli
Page 56 bottom right Archivio R. Niccoli
Page 57 top Aviation Picture Library
Page 57 bottom left TRH Pictures
Page 57 bottom right Musee De L'Air
Pages 58-59 John M. Dibbs/The Plane Picture Company
Page 59 top right Peter March/R. Cooper
Page 59 center right Philip Makanna / Ghosts
Page 59 bottom right Peter March/R. Cooper
Page 59 bottom TRH Pictures
Page 60 A. J. Jackson Collection
Page 61 top Archivio G. Apostolo
Page 61 center Archivio R. Niccoli
Page 61 bottom Archivio G. Apostolo
Page 62 La Presse
Page 63 top left Hulton Archive/ Laura Ronchi
Page 63 top right Il Dagherrotipo
Page 63 center Il Dagherrotipo
Page 63 bottom right Il Dagherrotipo
Pages 62-63 Il Dagherrotipo

CHAPTER 5
Page 64 top left TRH Pictures
Page 64 bottom left Popper Foto/Vision
Page 64 top right Double's
Page 64 bottom right Double's
Page 65 Aviation Picture Library
Page 65 bottom left Roger Viollet/ Contrasto

Page 65 bottom right TRH Pictures
Page 66 top TRH Pictures
Page 66 bottom left Aviation Picture Library
Page 66 bottom right TRH Pictures
Page 67 top left TRH Pictures
Page 67 center left TRH Pictures
Page 67 center right TRH Pictures
Page 67 bottom left TRH Pictures
Page 68 top Aviation Pictures Library
Page 68 bottom Aviation Pictures Library
Page 69 top left Photos12
Page 69 center left Photos12
Page 69 bottom left Photos12
Page 69 bottom right Aviation Pictures Library
Pages 70-71 Aviation Picture Library
Page 70 bottom Aviation Picture Library
Page 71 top Hulton Archive/Laura Ronchi
Page 71 center A.J. Jackson Collection
Page 71 bottom Aviation Picture Library
Page 72 top Popper Foto/Vision
Pages 72 center left Corbis/ Grazia Neri
Pages 72 center right TRH Pictures
Page 72 bottom Hulton Archive/ Laura Ronchi
Page 73 top left TRH Pictures
Page 73 top right Library Of Congress
Page 73 bottom TRH Pictures
Page 74 top A.J. Jackson Collection
Page 74 left Corbis/Grazia Neri
Page 74 bottom AP Photo
Page 75 top Denver Public Library
Page 75 bottom Aviation Picture Library
Pages 76/77 TRH Pictures
Page 76 center Archivio R. Niccoli
Page 77 top Hulton Archive/Laura Ronchi
Page 77 center Aviation Picture Library
Page 77 bottom left Aviation Picture Library
Page 78 top TRH Pictures
Page 78 bottom left A.J. Jackson Collection
Page 78 bottom right A.J. Jackson Collection
Page 79 top left TRH Pictures
Page 79 top right Corbis/Grazia Neri
Page 79 bottom Hulton Archive/Laura Ronchi

CHAPTER 6
Page 80 bottom Il Dagherrotipo
Pages 80-81 Photos12
Page 81 top right Roger Viollet/ Contrasto
Page 81 bottom left Aviation Picture Library
Page 81 bottom right Photos12
Pages 82-83 top Roger Viollet/Contrasto
Pages 82-83 bottom Archivio R. Niccoli
Page 83 top Aviation Picture Library
Page 83 center TRH Pictures
Page 83 bottom F. Selinger Collection/ Aviation Picture Library
Page 84 top left Hulton Archive/Laura Ronchi
Page 84 top right Gentile concessione del Museo Gianni Caproni
Pages 84-85 Boeing Co. Archives
Page 85 right TRH Pictures
Page 85 bottom left Musee De L'Air
Page 86 center Il Dagherrotipo
Page 86 bottom left Archivio R. Niccoli
Page 86 bottom right Il Dagherrotipo
Pages 86-87 Musee Municipal Historique de l'Hydraviation
Page 87 top right Il Dagherrotipo
Page 87 center left Aviation Picture Library
Page 88 top TRH Pictures
Page 88 center Photos12
Page 88 bottom Musee Municipal Historique de l'Hydraviation
Page 89 top Photos 12
Page 89 top right Musee Municipal Historique de l'Hydraviation
Page 89 bottom TRH Pictures
Page 90 top A. J. Jackson Collection
Page 90 center TRH Pictures
Page 90 bottom Aviation Picture Library
Pages 90-91 Musee Municipal Historique de l'Hydraviation
Page 92 top Aviation Picture Library
Page 92 center Musee Municipal Historique de l'Hydraviation
Page 93 top A. J. Jackson Collection
Page 93 bottom Archivio G. Apostolo
Page 94 top Archivio G. Apostolo
Page 94 bottom TRH Pictures
Page 95 top TRH Pictures
Page 95 bottom Aviation Picture Library

Page 96 top Photos12
Page 96 bottom right Thopam/ICP/Double's
Page 97 top right Aviation Picture Library
Page 97 top right Photos12
Page 97 bottom left Mary Evans Picture Library
Page 97 bottom right Publifoto Olimpia
Page 98 top TRH Pictures
Page 98 bottom TRH Pictures
Page 99 top left Mary Evans Picture Library
Page 99 top right TRH Pictures

CHAPTER 7
Pages 100-101 Musee De L'Air
Page 100 Popper Foto/Vision
Page 101 top Publifoto Olimpia
Page 101 center top Musee De L'Air
Page 101 center bottom Archivio G. Apostolo
Page 101 bottom Aviation Picture Library
Page 102 left Roger Viollet/Contrasto
Page 102 right Archivio R. Niccoli
Page 102 bottom Corbis/Grazia Neri
Page 103 top Hulton Archive/Laura Ronchi
Page 103 bottom AP Photo
Page 104 Archivio G. Apostolo
Pages 104-105 The Flight Collection/Quadrant Pictures Library
Page 105 top left Peter March/R. Cooper
Page 105 bottom right Archivio R. Niccoli
Page 105 bottom Archivio G. Apostolo
Page 106 top Richard Cooper
Page 106 center Peter March/R. Cooper
Pages 106-107 AP Photo
Page 107 Hulton Archive/Laura Ronchi
Page 108 top left Roger Viollet/ Contrasto
Page 108 top Archivio G. Apostolo
Page 108 bottom left Archivio G. Apostolo
Page 109 top left The Flight Collection/ Quadrant Pictures Library
Page 109 top right Archivio G. Apostolo
Page 109 bottom The Flight Collection/ Quadrant Pictures Library
Page 110 Philip Makanna/Ghosts
Page 110 top right Philip Makanna/Ghosts
Page 111 top Hulton Archive/Laura Ronchi
Page 111 left Peter March/R. Cooper
Page 112 top Hulton Archive/Laura Ronchi
Page 112 center left Philip Makanna/Ghosts
Page 112 bottom right Mark Wagner
Page 113 left Mark Wagner
Page 113 right Philip Makanna/Ghosts
Page 114 top right Archivio G. Apostolo
Page 114 center left Aviation Picture Library
Page 114 bottom Aviation Picture Library
Pages 114-115 Roger Viollet/Contrasto
Page 115 bottom Aviation Picture Library
Pages 116/117 Hulton Archive/Laura Ronchi
Page 117 top left NARA (National Archives & Records Administration)
Page 117 top right Magnum/Contrasto
Page 117 bottom left Magnum/Contrasto
Page 117 bottom right Corbis/Grazia Neri
Page 118 Hulton Archive/Laura Ronchi
Page 118 center Roger Viollet/Contrasto
Page 119 top Imperial War Museum, London
Page 119 center left Roger Viollet/ Contrasto
Page 119 center right Roger Viollet/ Contrasto
Page 119 bottom Hulton Archive/Laura Ronchi
Page 120 top Photos12
Page 120 center Roger Viollet/Contrasto
Page 120 bottom Archivio R. Niccoli
Page 121 top Aviation Picture Library
Page 121 center Aviation Picture Library
Page 121 bottom Hulton Archive/Laura Ronchi
Page 122 top Aviation Picture Library
Page 122 center La Presse
Page 122 bottom left TRH Pictures
Page 122 bottom right Archivio R. Niccoli
Page 123 top Archivio G. Apostolo
Page 123 center Archivio G. Apostolo
Page 123 bottom Musee De l'Air

CHAPTER 8
Pages 124-125 Hulton Archive/Laura Ronchi
Page 125 top left Hulton Archive/ Laura Ronchi
Page 125 bottom right Aisa
Page 126 top left Roger Viollett/ Contrasto

Page 126 top right Roger Viollet/ Contrasto
Page 126 bottom Roger Viollet/Contrasto
Page 127 top left Archivio G. Apostolo
Page 127 top right Musee De l'Air
Page 127 bottom left Roger Viollet/ Contrasto
Page 127 bottom right AP Photo
Page 128 top Corbis/Grazia Neri
Page 128 center left Roger Viollet/ Contrasto
Page 129 top left Roger Viollet/ Contrasto
Page 129 top right Il Dagherrotipo
Page 129 center Il Dagherrotipo
Page 129 bottom Il Dagherrotipo
Page 130 top Aviation Picture Library
Page 130 center Archivio R. Niccoli
Pages 130-131 basso Aviation Picture Library
Page 131 center Archivio G. Apostolo
Page 131 bottom TRH Pictures
Page 132 top Il Dagherrotipo
Page 132 bottom left La Presse
Page 132 bottom right Musee De l'Air
Page 133 top La Presse
Page 133 center left Musee De l'Air
Page 133 center right Il Dagherrotipo
Page 133 bottom Musee De l'Air
Page 134 left La Presse
Page 134 bottom Publifoto Olimpia
Page 135 top Musee De l'Air
Page 135 bottom Musee De l'Air
Page 136 top Roger Viollet/Contrasto
Page 136 center Archivio G. Apostolo
Page 136 bottom Aviation Picture Library
Page 137 top AP Photo
Page 137 center Aviation Picture Library
Page 137 bottom AP Photo

CHAPTER 9
Page 138 top TRH Pictures
Pages 138-139 A. Toresani/Photoskynet
Page 139 top Il Dagherrotipo
Page 139 bottom Hulton Archive/Laura Ronchi
Page 140 top John M. Dibbs/The Plane Picture Company
Page 140 center John M. Dibbs/The Plane Picture Company
Page 141 top left Aviation Picture Library
Page 141 top right TRH Pictures
Page 141 center TRH Pictures
Pages 140-141 TRH Pictures
Page 141 bottom right TRH Pictures
Page 142 top AP Photo
Page 142 center right Aviation Picture Library
Page 142 bottom Corbis/Grazia Neri
Page 143 top TRH Pictures
Page 143 bottom TRH Pictures
Page 144 top Peter March/R. Cooper
Page 144 bottom Archivio G. Apostolo
Page 145 top Archivio R. Niccoli
Page 145 bottom John M. Dibbs/The Plane Picture Company

CHAPTER 10
Page 146 top Aviation Picture Library
Page 146 bottom Aviation Picture Library
Page 147 top TRH Pictures
Page 147 center Roger Viollet/Contrasto
Page 147 bottom A. J. Jackson Collection
Page 148 top Archivio G. Apostolo
Page 148 center Archivio R. Niccoli
Page 149 top left A. J. Jackson Collection
Page 149 top right Boeing Co. Archives
Page 149 bottom Corbis/Grazia Neri
Page 150 top Peter March/R. Cooper
Page 150 bottom Archivio R. Niccoli
Page 151 top Boeing Co. Archives
Page 151 center right Archivio R. Niccoli

CHAPTER 11
Page 152 top The Flight Collection/ Quadrant Pictures Library
Page 153 top Archivio G. Apostolo
Page 153 center Archivio G. Apostolo
Page 153 bottom John M. Dibbs/The Plane Picture Company
Page 154 top The Flight Collection/ Quadrant Pictures Library
Page 154 bottom TRH Pictures
Pages 154-155 Archivio R. Niccoli
Page 155 bottom Corbis/Grazia Neri
Page 156 top Corbis/Grazia Neri
Page 156 center Corbis/Grazia Neri
Page 157 top TRH Pictures
Page 157 bottom K. Tokunaga/Dact Inc.
Page 158 top Corbis/Grazia Neri
Page 158 center Corbis/Grazia Neri

319

Page 158 bottom Peter March/R. Cooper
Page 159 top Peter March/R. Cooper
Page 159 bottom Luigino Caliaro/Aerophoto

CHAPTER 12
Page 160 center Archivio G. Apostolo
Page 161 top TRH Pictures
Page 161 bottom Corbis/Grazia Neri
Page 162 top Aviation Picture Library
Page 162 bottom Rick Llinares/Dash2
Aviation Photography
Page 163 top Archivio G. Apostolo
Page 163 bottom Archivio G. Apostolo
Page 164 John M. Dibbs/The Plane Picture
Company
Pages 164-165 TRH Pictures
Page 165 bottom Archivio R. Niccoli
Page 166 top Archivio G. Apostolo
Page 166 center Corbis/Grazia Neri
Page 166 bottom Corbis/Grazia Neri
Page 167 top Richard Cooper
Page 167 bottom Richard Cooper
Pages 168-169 John M. Dibbs/The Plane
Picture Company
Page 169 top Corbis/Grazia Neri
Page 169 center right Gamma/Contrasto
Page 169 bottom Photos12

CHAPTER 13
Page 170 top Il Dagherrotipo
Pages 170-171 Hulton Archive/Laura
Ronchi
Page 170 bottom Photos12
Page 171 top Hulton Archive/Laura Ronchi
Page 171 bottom Hulton Archive/Laura
Ronchi
Page 172 top left Il Dagherrotipo
Page 172 center Royal Aeronautical Society
Page 172 bottom right Il Dagherrotipo
Page 173 alto Archivio A. Colombo
Page 173 bottom TRH Pictures
Page 174 top TRH Pictures
Page 174 center Anodos Foundation
Page 174 bottom Anodos Foundation
Page 175 center Aviation Picture Library
Page 175 bottom Hulton Archive/Laura Ronchi
Page 176 top Archivio G. Apostolo
Page 176 center left TRH Pictures
Page 176 bottom TRH Pictures
Page 177 top Igor Sikorsky Historical Archives
Page 177 center TRH Pictures
Page 177 bottom AP Photo
Page 178 top P. Steinemann/Skyline APA
Page 178 bottom Peter March/R. Cooper
Page 179 top Photos12
Page 179 center John M. Dibbs/The Plane
Picture Company
Page 179 bottom left Contrasto
Page 179 bottom right P. Steinemann/
Skyline APA
Pages 180-181 TRH Pictures
Page 180 bottom John M. Dibbs/The Plane
Picture Company
Page 181 top Igor Sikorsky Historical
Archives
Page 181 bottom Stephen Jaffe/AFP
Photo/De Bellis
Pages 182-183 AP Photo
Page 182 bottom Photos12
Page 183 top Archivio R. Niccoli
Page 183 center AP Photo
Page 183 bottom TRH Pictures
Page 184 Richard Cooper
Page 185 top AP Photo
Page 185 center Corbis Stock Market/
Contrasto
Page 185 bottom Corbis/Grazia Neri
Page 186 top AP Photo
Pages 186-187 A. Toresani/Photoskynet
Page 187 top left Photos12
Page 187 center right Mark Wagner
Page 187 bottom right K. Tokunaga/
Dact Inc.
Page 188 top Photos12
Page 188 center left TRH Pictures
Page 189 top TRH Pictures
Page 189 center left Archivio Agusta spa
Page 189 center right Archivio R. Niccoli

Page 189 bottom right Photos12

CHAPTER 14
Page 190 top Denver Public Library
Page 190 bottom left Hulton Archive/
Laura Ronchi
Page 190 bottom right Hulton Archive/
Laura Ronchi
Page 191 top Hulton Archive/Laura Ronchi
Page 191 center Hulton Archive/Laura Ronchi
Page 191 bottom The Flight Collection/
Quadrant Pictures Library
Pages 192/193 John M. Dibbs/The Plane
Picture Company
Page 192 top Archivio R. Niccoli
Page 192 center Archivio G. Apostolo
Page 192 bottom The Flight Collection/
Quadrant Pictures Library
Page 193 center right Archivio R. Niccoli
Page 193 bottom Philip Makanna/Ghosts
Page 194 top K. Tokunaga/Dact Inc.
Page 194 bottom John M. Dibbs/The Plane
Picture Company
Page 195 top Peter March/R. Cooper
Page 195 center left Peter March/
R. Cooper
Page 195 center right R. Lorenzon
Page 195 bottom P. Steinemann/Skyline
APA
Page 196 top left Peter March/
R. Cooper
Page 196 top right P. Steinemann/ Skyline
APA
Page 196 center Peter March/R. Cooper
Page 197 P. Steinemann/Skyline APA
Page 198 top left Luigino Caliaro/
Aerophoto
Page 198 center left Boeing Co. Archives
Pages 198-199 P. Steinemann/Skyline APA
Page 199 top John M. Dibbs/The Plane
Picture Company
Page 199 center right Archivio R. Niccoli
Page 199 bottom right Aviation Picture
Library
Pages 200-201 K. Tokunaga/Dact Inc.
Page 201 top A. Pozza
Page 201 center Richard Cooper
Page 201 bottom Richard Cooper
Pages 202-203 John M. Dibbs/The Plane
Picture Company
Page 202 bottom Philip Makanna/Ghosts
Page 203 bottom Aviation Picture Library
Pages 204-205 P. Steinemann/Skyline APA
Page 205 top P. Steinemann/Skyline APA
Page 205 center John M. Dibbs/The Plane
Picture Company
Page 205 bottom Archivio R. Niccoli

CHAPTER 15
Page 206 Corbis/Grazia Neri
Page 207 top Corbis/Grazia Neri
Page 207 top left Mark Wagner
Page 207 bottom left Aviation Picture
Library
Page 207 bottom right Aviation Picture
Library
Page 208 top Aviation Picture Library
Page 208 center Aviation Picture Library
Page 208 bottom Corbis/Grazia Neri
Page 209 center Aviation Picture Library
Page 209 bottom Aviation Picture Library
Pages 210-211 Aviation Picture Library
Page 210 center Aviation Picture Library
Page 211 top Aviation Picture Library
Page 211 bottom Aviation Picture Library
Page 212 top Archivio R. Niccoli
Pages 212-213 Archivio R. Niccoli
Page 213 top Aviation Picture Library
Page 213 center Aviation Picture Library
Page 213 bottom Aviation Picture Library
Page 214 top Joe Pries
Page 214 center A. Pozza
Page 215 top Aviation Picture Library
Page 215 center Aviation Picture Library
Page 215 bottom Aviation Picture Library
Page 216 top Archivio R. Niccoli
Pages 216-217 John M. Dibbs/The Plane
Picture Company

Page 216 bottom Aviation Picture Library
Page 217 top Aviation Picture Library
Page 217 bottom Aviation Picture Library

CHAPTER 16
Page 218 top Archivio G. Apostolo
Pages 218-219 Luigino Caliaro/Aerophoto
Page 219 top Archivio G. Apostolo
Page 220 K. Tokunaga/Dact Inc.
Page 221 John M. Dibbs/The Plane Picture
Company
Page 222 top Archivio R. Niccoli
Page 222 bottom John M. Dibbs/The Plane
Picture Company
Page 223 top John M. Dibbs/The Plane
Picture Company
Page 223 center left The Artarchive
Page 224 top left Richard Cooper
Page 224 top right Lassi Tolvanen/Fly High
Page 224 center Archivio R. Niccoli
Page 224 bottom K. Tokunaga/Dact Inc.
Pages 224-225 Archivio R. Niccoli

CHAPTER 17
Pages 226-227 Horst Faas/AP Photo
Page 226 center left Henri Huet/
AP Photo
Page 226 bottom Corbis/Grazia Neri
Page 227 bottom Corbis/Grazia Neri
Pages 228-229 Hulton Archive/
Laura Ronchi
Page 228 bottom Corbis/Grazia Neri
Page 229 top Boeing Co. Archives
Page 229 center Mark Wagner
Page 229 bottom left Archivio R. Niccoli
Page 230 top Archivio R. Niccoli
Pages 230-231 Corbis/Grazia Neri
Page 231 top Aviation Picture Library
Page 231 center top Aviation Picture
Library
Page 231 center bottom The Flight
Collection/Quadrant Picture Library
Page 231 bottom Archivio R. Niccoli
Page 232 Corbis/Grazia Neri
Pages 232-233 Rick Llinares/Dash2 Aviation
Photography
Page 233 center right Rick Llinares/ Dash2
Aviation Photography
Page 233 bottom left Aviation Picture
Library
Pages 234-235 John M. Dibbs/The Plane
Picture Company
Page 235 bottom AP Photo
Pages 236-237 AP Photo
Page 236 center right AP Photo
Page 236 bottom Corbis/Grazia Neri
Page 237 bottom Photos12

CHAPTER 18
Page 238 top Israeli Air Force
Page 238 center Israeli Air Force
Page 238 bottom Archivio R. Niccoli
Page 239 center right Israeli Air Force
Page 239 bottom Israeli Air Force
Page 240 top Archivio R. Niccoli
Page 240 bottom Israeli Air Force
Pages 240-241 Israeli Air Force
Page 241 center left Archivio R. Niccoli
Page 241 center right AP Photo
Page 242 TRH Pictures
Page 243 top Archivio R. Niccoli
Page 243 bottom Israeli Air Force

CHAPTER 19
Page 244 top Stefano Pagiola
Page 244 bottom John M. Dibbs/
The Plane Picture Company
Page 245 center Corbis/Grazia Neri
Page 245 bottom Mark Wagner
Pages 246-247 Grover Paul/FSP/
Gamma/Contrasto
Page 246 center Daher/Gamma/Contrasto
Page 247 bottom Keystone/Grazia Neri
Pages 248-249 De Malglaive
Etienne/Gamma/Contrasto
Page 249 top John M. Dibbs/
The Plane Picture Company
Page 249 center John M. Dibbs/

The Plane Picture Company
Pages 250-251 Stefano Pagiola
Page 251 center Peter March/R. Cooper
Page 252 bottom Aviation Picture Library

CHAPTER 20
Page 252 Rick Llinares/Dash2 Aviation
Photography
Page 253 top K. Tokunaga/Dact Inc.
Page 253 bottom Gamma/Contrasto
Page 254 top left John M. Dibbs/The Plane
Picture Company
Page 255 Mark Wagner
Page 255 Jamie Hunter/R.Cooper
Page 256 center K. Tokunaga/Dact Inc.
Page 256 bottom G. Agostinelli
Pages 256-257 Gamma/Contrasto
Page 257 bottom Mark Wagner
Pages 258-259 John M. Dibbs/The Plane
Picture Company
Page 259 center Rick Llinares/Dash2
Aviation Photography
Page 259 bottom Richard Cooper
Page 260 center Archivio R. Niccoli
Page 260 bottom Archivio R. Niccoli
Pages 260-261 P. Steinemann/Skyline APA
Page 261 center K. Tokunaga/Dact Inc.
Page 262 K. Tokunaga/Dact Inc.
Page 263 top Mark Wagner
Page 263 bottom left Archivio R. Niccoli
Page 263 bottom right K. Tokunaga/
Dact Inc.
Pages 264-265 John M. Dibbs/The Plane
Picture Company
Page 264 center Luigino Caliaro/Aerophoto
Page 264 bottom Aeronautica Militare
Italiana
Page 265 top Aeronautica Militare Italiana
Page 265 center Richard Cooper
Page 265 bottom Richard Cooper
Page 266 top K. Tokunaga/Dact Inc.
Page 266 bottom Archivio R. Niccoli
Page 267 Luigino Caliaro/Aerophoto
Page 267 bottom Mark Wagner

CHAPTER 21
Page 268 top Aviation Picture Library
Page 268 bottom P. Steinemann/Skyline
APA
Page 269 top Aviation Picture Library
Page 269 center left Aviation Picture
Library
Page 269 center right Peter March/
R. Cooper
Page 269 bottom Aviation Picture Library
Page 270 top Peter March/R. Cooper
Page 270 center Aviation Picture Library
Page 270 bottom Aviation Picture Library
Page 270-271 Aviation Picture Library
Page 271 center Jamie Hunter/R. Cooper
Page 271 bottom Aviation Picture Library
Page 272 top Aviation Picture Library
Page 272 center left Peter March/
R. Cooper
Page 272 center right Peter March/
R. Cooper
Page 273 top Jamie Hunter/R. Cooper
Page 273 center Archivio R. Niccoli
Page 273 bottom Aviation Picture Library
Pages 274-275 John M. Dibbs/The Plane
Picture Company
Page 275 top Aviation Picture Library
Page 275 center Aviation Picture Library
Page 275 center Aviation Picture Library

CHAPTER 22
Page 276 Magnum/Contrasto
Pages 276-277 Hulton Archive/Laura
Ronchi
Page 277 top Archivio R. Niccoli
Page 277 center Gamma/Contrasto
Page 278 top Contrasto
Page 278 bottom Mark Wagner
Pages 278-279 Corbis/Contrasto
Page 279 bottom Rick Llinares/Dash2
Aviation Photography
Page 280 top Boeing Co. Archives
Page 280 center Corbis/Grazia Neri

Page 280 bottom Archivio R. Niccoli
Page 281 bottom P. Steinemann/Skyline
APA
Page 282 top Gamma/Contrasto
Pages 282-283 Gamma/Contrasto
Page 283 top AP Photo
Pages 284-285 Corbis/Grazia Neri
Page 284 bottom Archivio R. Niccoli
Page 285 top Gamma/Contrasto
Page 285 center John M. Dibbs/The Plane
Picture Company
Page 285 bottom K. Tokunaga/Dact Inc.
Pages 286-287 Luigino Caliaro/Aerophoto
Page 286 bottom AP Photo
Page 287 bottom left Georges
Merillon/Gamma/Contrasto
Page 287 bottom right Jean Luc
Moreau/Gamma/Contrasto
Pages 288-289 Richard Cooper
Page 288 Corbis/Grazia Neri
Page 289 top John M. Dibbs/The Plane
Picture Company
Page 289 bottom Gamma/Contrasto
Page 290 top Mark Wagner
Pages 290-291 top Corbis/Grazia Neri
Pages 290-291 bottom Angelo
Toresani/Photoskynet
Page 291 bottom right Mark Wagner
Page 292 top Mark Wagner
Page 292 center Rick Llinares/Dash2
Aviation Photography
Page 292 bottom Rick Llinares/Dash2
Aviation Photography
Pages 292-293 Mark Wagner
Page 293 bottom Mark Wagner
Page 294 Johnny Bivera/US Navy/Getty
Images/ La Presse
Page 295 top Courtesy Of British
Forces/Getty Images/La Presse
Page 295 center US Navy/Getty Images/ La
Presse
Page 295 bottom Howard La Tunya/US
Navy/Getty Images/La Presse

CHAPTER 23
Page 296 top Peter March/R. Cooper
Page 296 bottom De Malglaive Etienne/
Gamma/Contrasto
Pages 296-297 Peter March/R. Cooper
Page 297 center Peter March/R. Cooper
Page 298 top Corbis/Grazia Neri
Pages 298-299 Boeing Co. Archives
Page 299 center right John M. Dibbs/The
Plane Picture Company
Page 299 bottom Boeing Co. Archives
Pages 300-301 Boeing Co. Archives
Page 300 center Boeing Co. Archives
Page 300 bottom Boeing Co. Archives
Page 301 center Gamma/Contrasto
Page 301 bottom Gamma/Contrasto

CHAPTER 24
Page 302 top Aviation Picture Library
Pages 302-303 Archivio R. Niccoli
Page 303 Archivio R. Niccoli
Page 304 top Archivio R. Niccoli
Page 304 center Aviation Picture Library
Page 304 bottom Aviation Picture Library
Pages 304-305 top Paolo Franzini
Pages 304-305 bottom Archivio R. Niccoli
Page 306 Gamma/Contrasto
Page 307 top left Contrasto
Page 307 top right Aviation Picture Library
Page 307 bottom left Mark Wagner
Page 307 bottom right Archivio R. Niccoli

CHAPTER 25
Page 308 top NASA Archives
Page 308 bottom NASA Archives
Page 309 top Gamma/Contrasto
Page 309 center Corbis/Grazia Neri
Page 309 bottom Gamma/Contrasto
Page 310 top Contrasto
Page 310 bottom NASA Archives
Page 311 center left NASA/AP Photo
Page 311 center right Gamma/Contrasto
Pages 312-313 Hulton Archive/Laura Ronchi

The Publisher would like to thank:

Italian Airforce

Agusta spa

Arthur Block, Joan Schleicher (Anodos Foundation)

Barbara Waibel (Zeppelin Museum)

Bernd Lukasch (Otto Lilienthal Museum)

Carol Henderson, Jim Lyons, Dave Black (Moffet Field Historical Society)

Cauntess Maria Fede Caproni

Igor Sikorsky Historical Archives

Israeli Air Force Magazine

NASA Johnson Space Center - Media Resource Center

Paolo Franzini